EXPLORE AUSTRALIA'S

Outback

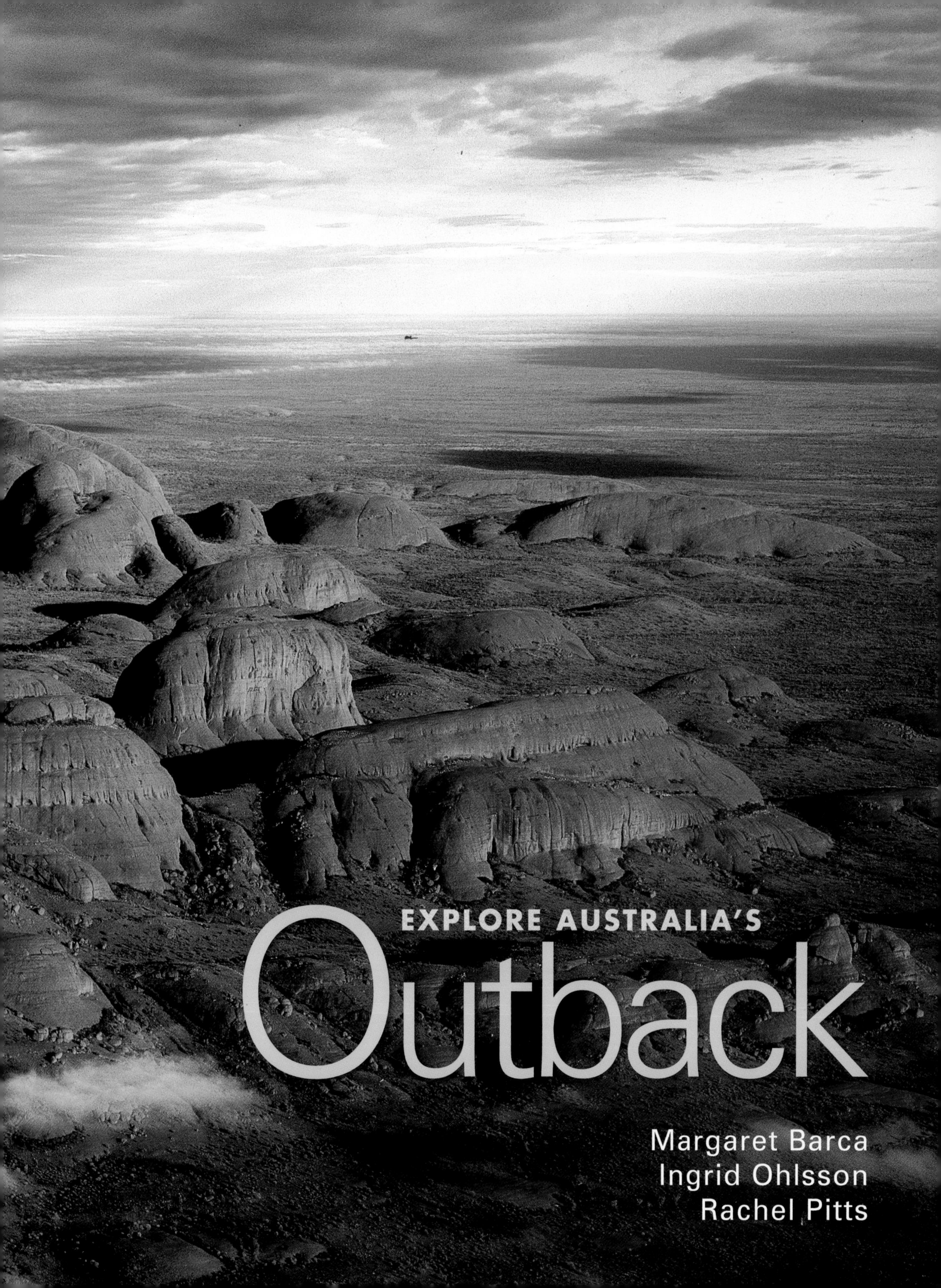

EXPLORE AUSTRALIA'S

Outback

Margaret Barca
Ingrid Ohlsson
Rachel Pitts

King's
TOURS

contents

How to Use this Book

Explore Australia's Outback features eight regions across Australia's outback – from the arid regions of the south-east to the lush tropical landscapes of northern Australia.

Explore Australia's Outback is divided into eight main regions. The regions are shown on the map of Australia, on page xii.

Each of the main regions has an overview map, and a short, general introduction to the background, history and special features of that region. The *Travel Tips* file contains general information regarding the best time to go, climate charts, national park guidelines within the region and so on.

Each of these regions is divided into sub-regions, with their own more-detailed maps, descriptive text, and specific contact details.

MAP SYMBOLS

A1 1 Highway with route marker
36 B83 Secondary road with route marker
Minor road
4WD track
Walking track
Railway
23 Distance in kilometres

DARWIN Major city
Katherine Major town
Noonamah Small town
Bulla Community Aboriginal community
Kings Creek Station Homestead
Nganalam Art Site Place of interest
Endeavour Hill 210 Mountain or hill with height in metres

State border
River
Lake, perennial
Lake, dry or intermittent

National park
Other reserves
Aboriginal land
Prohibited area

Information
4WD area
Remote fuel supplies
Camping
Water
Fires prohibited
RH Roadhouse
Ranger-patrolled park
Aboriginal rock art

Bushwalking
Lookout
Canoeing/kayaking
Fishing
No swimming
Crocodiles
Marine stingers
Wildlife
Birdlife

BEST OF THE OUTBACK

Map shows location of highlights.

A list of specific highlights, with page references.

OUTBACK REGIONS

Main Region

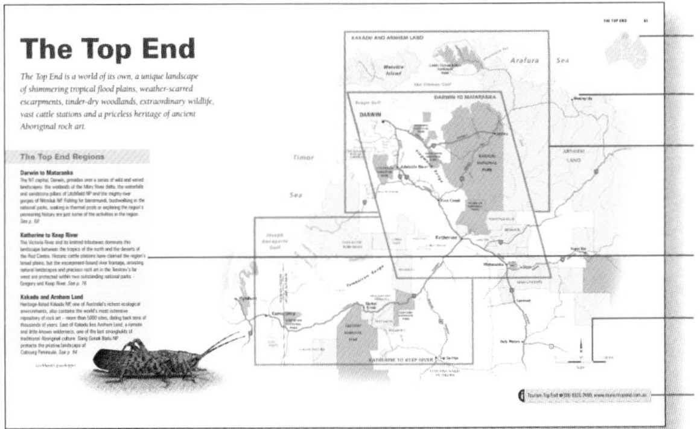

Australia locator map.

Overview map.

Boxes indicate the boundaries of subregions.

Summary of subregions with page references.

Scale bar – note that maps vary in scale.

Visitor information details for the region.

Travel Tips contains:
Best time to go
National parks
General information
Warnings
Climate charts.

Subregion

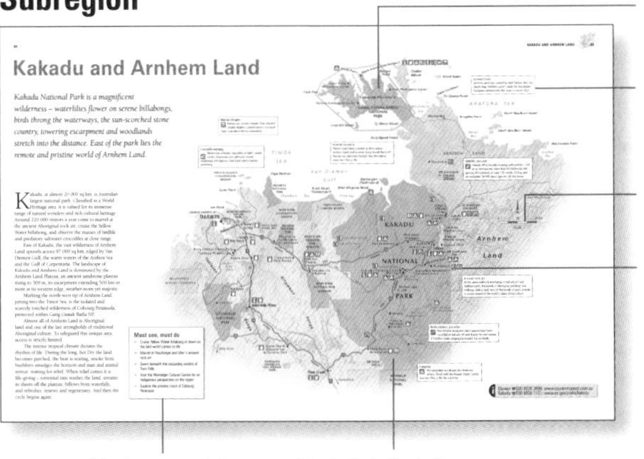

Detailed map.

Text panels feature specific regional information.

Scale bar – note that maps vary in scale.

Fact File contains top outback events, specific information on national parks and reserves, information on road closures and more.

Must see, must do special highlights.

Symbols indicate key visitor information locations, outback fuel supplies, bushwalking areas (see *Map symbols* opposite, for full list).

Contacts contains phone numbers and websites for visitor information centres, station stays, key information on activities and more.

ON THE ROAD

A 20-page section on how to make the most of your trip. It contains information on planning, preparing and advice for when you are on the road. It includes safety guidelines and a detailed list of phone numbers and websites of useful contacts for outback regions.

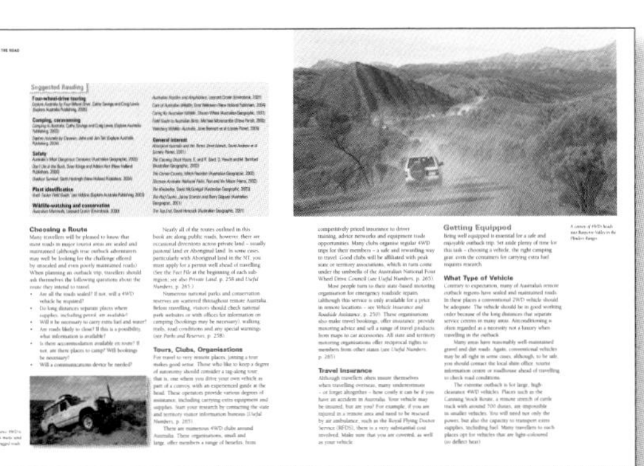

The Land Beyond
a timeless, ancient country

The outback starts somewhere beyond – back o'Bourke, beyond the black stump, or at any rate, always just a little bit beyond reach. It's at once real and legendary, yet the sights, the sounds, the history and the myths seem deeply embedded in the national psyche. We may cling to the coast, we may be essentially an urban, beach-going culture, but somewhere in our hearts there is a special place for the country and the landscape that stretches endlessly beyond the reach of the cities, whether it is the arid Red Centre, or Australia's remote tropical north.

The outback is big – larger than life – and so is everything out there. Australia is the world's largest island, and the sixth largest country in the world. It covers more than seven and half million square kilometres, but only six percent is arable and – on average – there are only 2.5 people per square kilometre (compare that to the UK's 224 people per square kilometre). Once you get into the outback, there really is plenty of open space. And there's a reason the outback is renowned for its 'big skies': this is the lowest, flattest and (apart from Antarctica) the driest continent in the world. In total, 70 percent of the mainland is arid and semi-arid.

The first explorers and first settlers saw Australia with a jaded vision. Perhaps they had hoped for something so entirely different that they could not reconcile themselves to what they found. Early reports are almost always resolutely negative, or so far from reality as to guarantee future disappointment. There were exceptions, of course, Captain James Cook and the dedicated botanist Joseph Banks being notable enthusiasts for the great southern land. But on the whole it was seen as a wild and forbidding country, where the seasons were reversed, where the trees towered dry and straggly instead of lush and green, losing their bark instead of their leaves; where animals defied description, and birds were awkward and offensively noisy.

One of the most enduring early obsessions was the determination that there were inland rivers or perhaps a great inland sea, and many exploring parties pushed doggedly on in pursuit of the water that would ensure riches. But no such sea existed. Riverbeds were sometimes there, but bone dry – frustratingly, killingly dry. Others occasionally swelled and flooded the land after torrential rains, then petered out into dry salt lakes, or shrivelled to small pools and billabongs.

Aboriginal people knew a different outback – or at least they looked at it with different eyes. They knew that water lay hidden in rock pools, or could be tapped from within certain trees, or reached by digging far enough below the sandy bed of a river. In the north, where monsoonal rains drench the country for months, they knew that the seasons would change, and waited patiently, at one with the land.

It seems, as time goes by, more people are looking at the outback with a different vision and

Opposite *A towering palm and two walkers are silhouetted against a red rock gorge in the Kimberley.*

understanding it just a little more. They're setting off to explore a country that is ancient and timeless, where the landforms are millions of years old, and where the history of Aboriginal occupation dates back 50 or 60 thousand years. The scenery is spectacular and remarkably diverse. It's not all long, lonely roads across endless desert or spinifex plains – though there's plenty of that. There are remote and pristine beaches, magnificent gorges, palm-filled valleys, unique landforms, and mighty rivers shaded by river red gums. The wildlife is extraordinary, and there are literally hundreds of bird species. Along the outback coastline whales, rare marine turtles, dugong and giant manta rays swim. From the Red Centre to the far northern corners of the Kimberley and Cape York, a legacy of ancient rock art recalls Australia's rich Indigenous heritage. And signs of more recent history – from trees blazed by explorers to old mining towns, sprawling pastoral properties and water wells – all have a story to tell.

A trip to the outback can be many things – staying on a remote station, testing your mettle on a rugged 4WD stock route, hauling in a barra, sharing a yarn over a campfire or a beer in an outback pub, kayaking along a silent gorge, flying over the wilderness of Kakadu NP or the ravaged folds of the time-worn Flinders Ranges. Most of all, a trip to the outback is the chance to understand a little more about some of the places and people that make Australia so special.

Australia's Outback

key to the maps

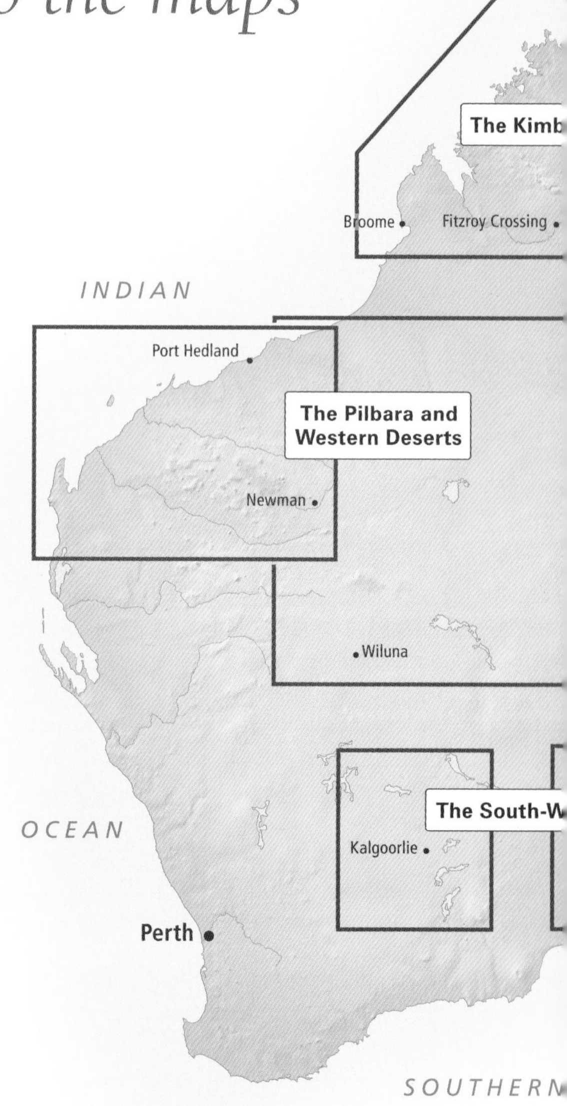

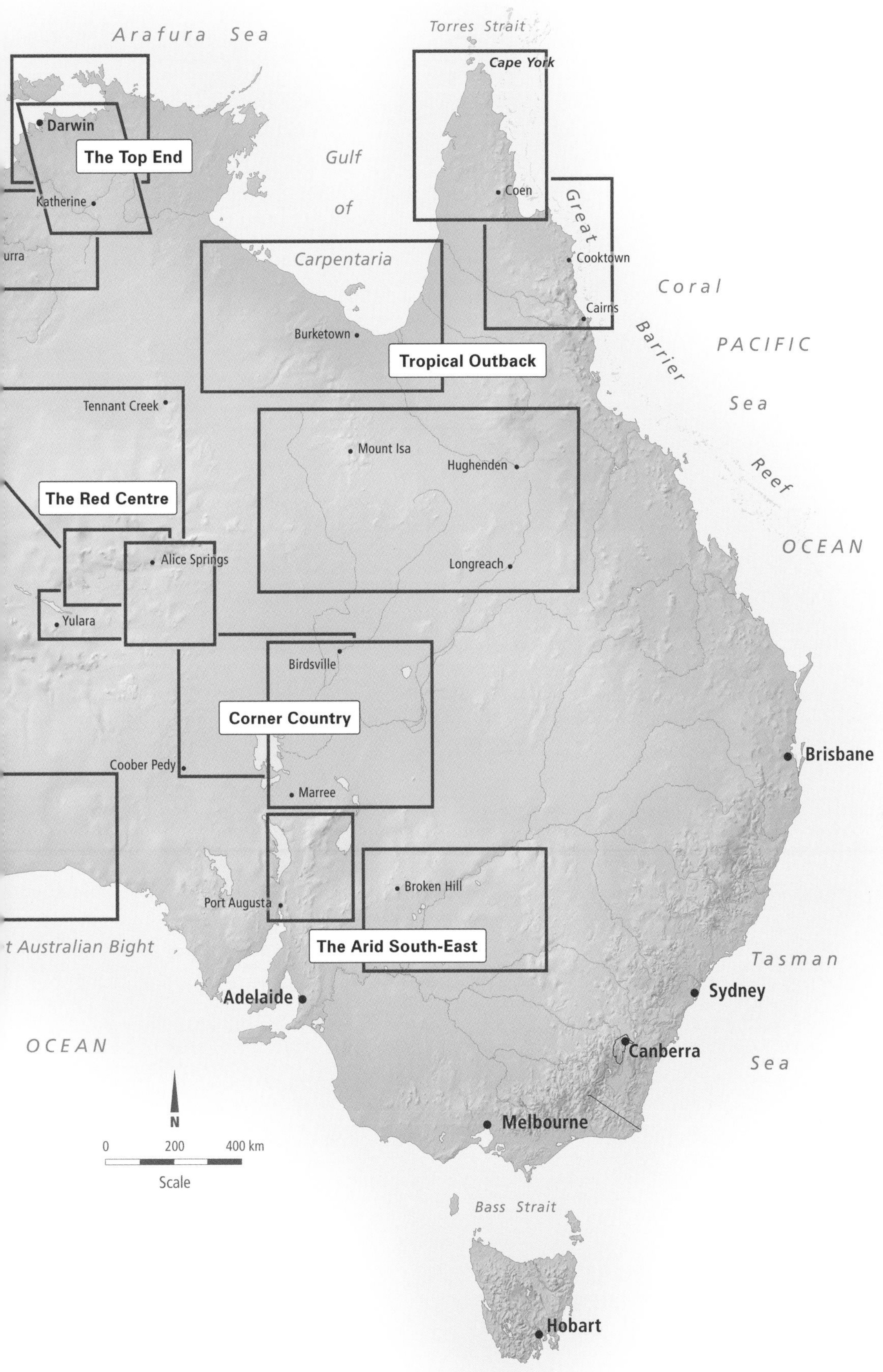

Arafura Sea
Torres Strait
Cape York
Darwin
The Top End
Katherine
urra
Gulf
of
Carpentaria
Coen
Great
Cooktown
Coral
Cairns
Barrier
PACIFIC
Burketown
Tropical Outback
Sea
Tennant Creek
Mount Isa
Hughenden
Reef
The Red Centre
OCEAN
Alice Springs
Longreach
Yulara
Birdsville
Corner Country
Brisbane
Coober Pedy
Marree
Broken Hill
Port Augusta
t Australian Bight
The Arid South-East
Tasman
Sydney
Adelaide
OCEAN
Canberra
Sea
N
0
200
400 km
Scale
Melbourne
Bass Strait
Hobart

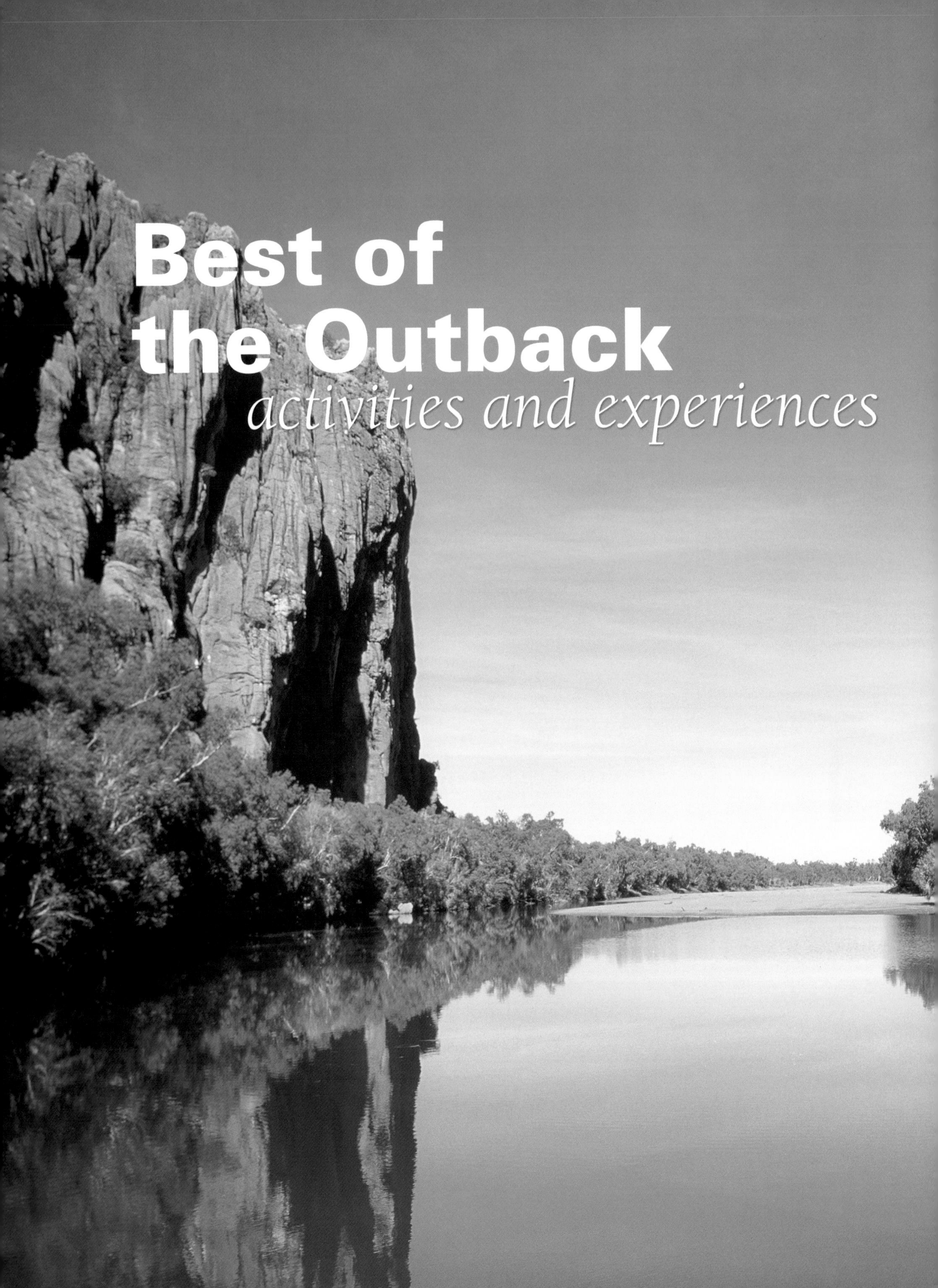

Best of the Outback

activities and experiences

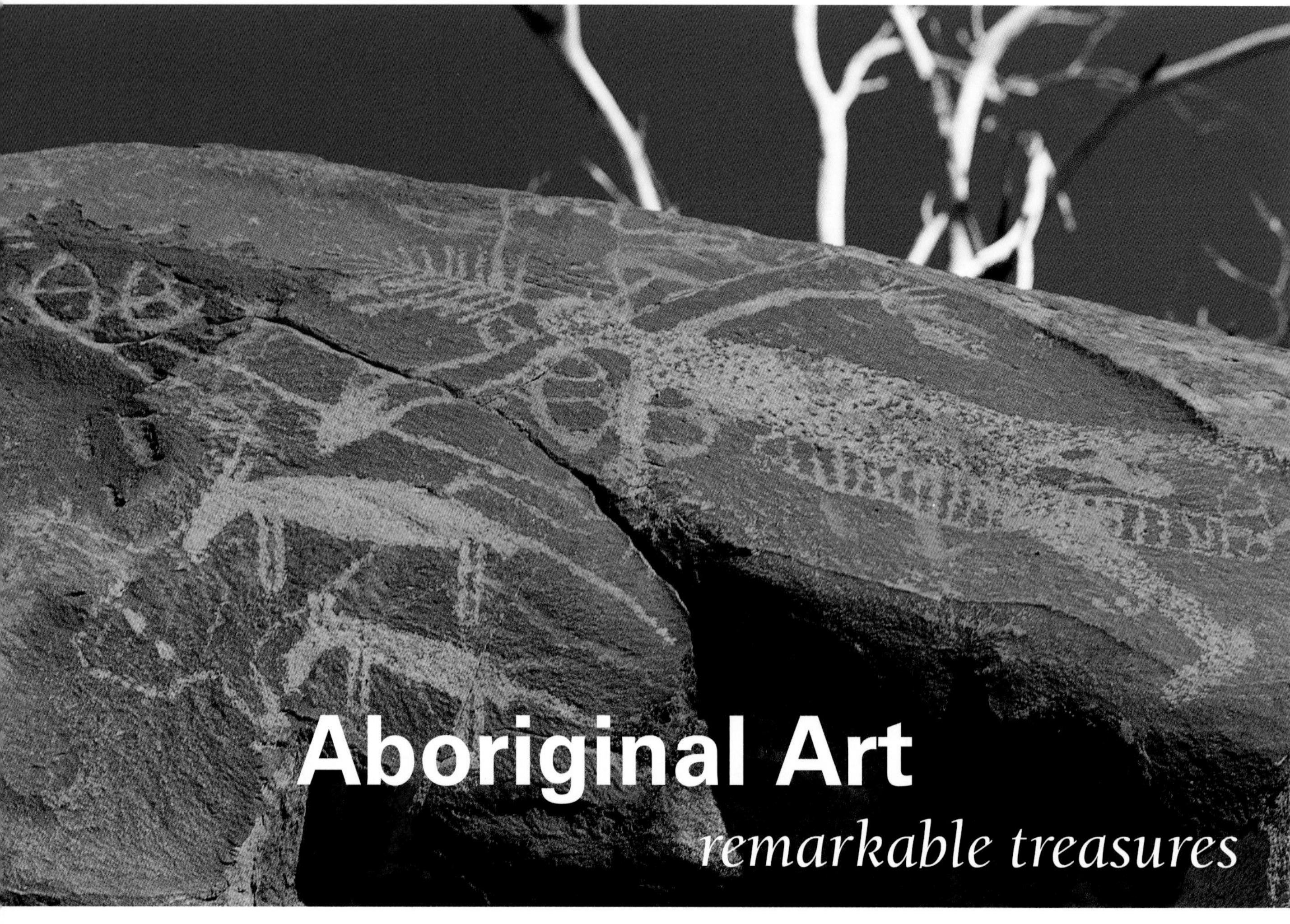

Aboriginal Art

remarkable treasures

The rock art in Australia is extraordinary – an unrivalled collection in terms of size, diversity of styles, standard of preservation and sheer aesthetic delight.

Art is the most tangible and enduring symbol of the long settlement of Australia by an estimated 600 Indigenous groups. Traditionally, Aboriginal art has served to document the spiritual beliefs, tribal law and environmental practices of particular groups, as well as to describe their daily activities, such as hunting. Thousands of art sites fan out across the continent, marking a wonderful legacy of cultural endeavour.

From region to region there are enormous variations in style and technique. In the remote Kimberley, for example, there are two distinct styles: the spindly Dreamtime figures known as the Bradshaws, or Gwion Gwion, and the strangely haloed spirit representations known as the Wandjinas. Kakadu, which is the site of one of the world's richest rock-art collections, features a wide range of styles but is most famous for what is known as the X-ray style, in which the skeleton is a graphic part of the image.

Although there are sacred sites that are off-limits, a number of sites are open to the public. In some places, such as Aboriginal-owned Arnhem Land, it is usually necessary to travel as part of a tour.

Visitors with an interest in contemporary art should consider visiting one of the art centres located in remote communities in Queensland, the NT and WA. Aboriginal art sites are protected by state and federal heritage legislation making it illegal to disturb or damage a site in any way.

Above *Petroglyphs on the Burrup Peninsula, in the Pilbara region.*

Opposite *Ancient rock art at Angbanbang Gallery, in Kakadu NP.*

Where to look

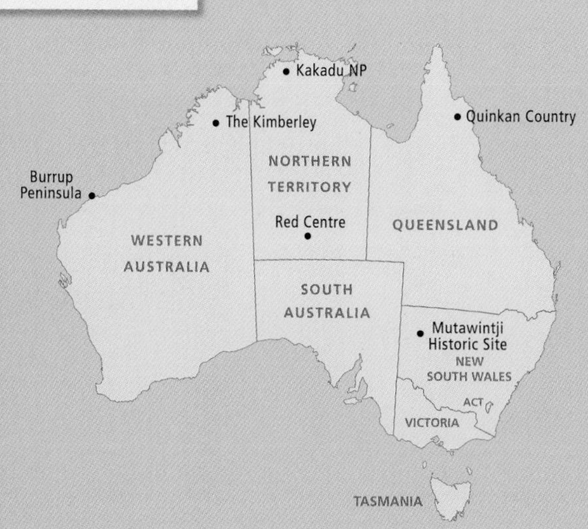

The Red Centre
The art of the Red Centre may be less prolific than the riches found in the tropical north, but its storytelling adds shades of meaning to one of the country's most famous landscapes. Key sites include Uluru and the East MacDonnell Ranges. To see contemporary work, head for the galleries of Alice Springs. See *The Red Centre*, p. 28

Kakadu NP, The Top End
The rock galleries of Kakadu are one of the world's great cultural treasures. The main sites, at Ubirr and Nourlangie, demonstrate a vast range of styles and subject matter – even the sighting of European ships is depicted – and show how the various styles developed over the ages. See *Kakadu and Arnhem Land*, p. 84

Burrup Peninsula, The Pilbara and Western Deserts
The wonders of the Burrup Peninsula, near Dampier, have yet to be fully exposed. This landscape, the site of huge regional industrial enterprises, is said to contain 10 000 ancient petroglyphs – rock engravings – which are among the oldest, most varied, and most densely concentrated in the world. See *The Pilbara and Outback Coast*, p. 204

Quinkan Country, Tropical Outback
Near the outback town of Laura in Far North Queensland, the sandstone rock shelters are elaborately decorated with a series of large, human-like spirit figures known as Quinkans. The spirits themselves are believed to be hiding in the rock crevices. See *Mossman to Lakefield NP*, p. 100

Mutawintji Historic Site, The Arid South-East
Located within Mutawintji NP, this site contains the most extensive collection of rock art in NSW. The work dates back 8000 years and includes stencils, engravings, paintings and drawings. Traditionally, this was a meeting point for several tribes and the site of various ceremonies. Access is by tour only. See *Broken Hill and Beyond*, p. 156

The Kimberley
The art of the Kimberley is superlative and diverse, scattered through the region in rock overhangs, shelters and gorges. Some examples can be seen on stations, such as Mt Elizabeth Station and El Questro, where guided tours explain some of the intricacies of the styles and their meanings. See *The Kimberley*, p. 220

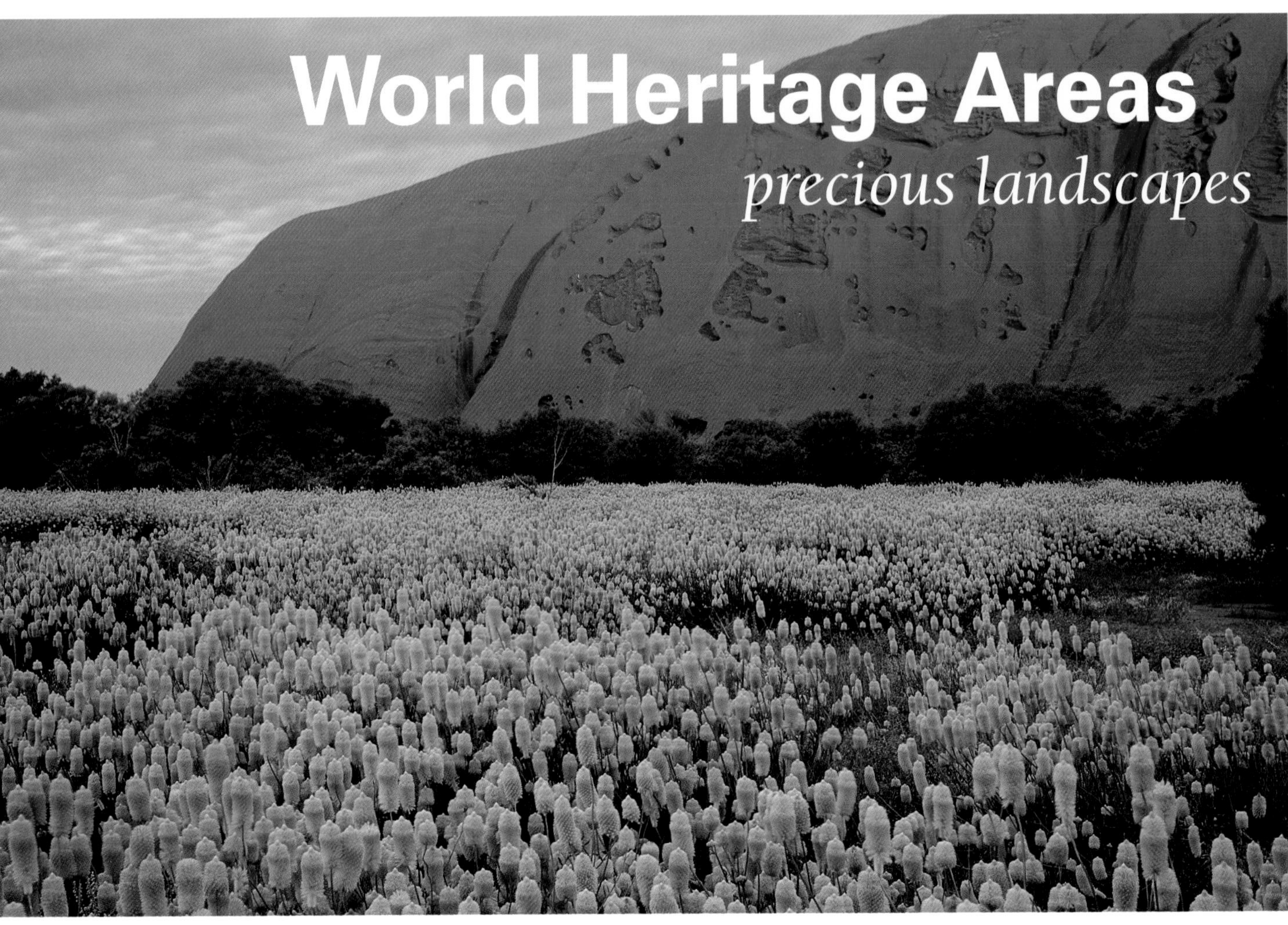

World Heritage Areas
precious landscapes

Australia's World Heritage areas preserve some of the most famous sights of outback Australia, as well as a few surprises.

From the fossils of Riversleigh to the Gondwana-era vegetation of the Wet Tropics and the reddened monoliths of the desert heart, Australia's World Heritage properties preserve some of the monumental beauty, environmental wonder and cultural richness of outback Australia. The country claims 15 World Heritage areas, approximately half of which might be considered 'outback' in character.

World Heritage sites are selected by the United Nations Educational, Scientific and Cultural Organisation (UNESCO) for their outstanding universal value, and are considered the ultimate heritage listing. Some sites are included for their natural values, some for their cultural values, and a very small number – 23 out of nearly 800 – are listed for both. In this last – and exclusive – category, there are four Australian sites: Kakadu NP, Uluṟu–Kata Tjuṯa NP, the Willandra Lakes Region and the Tasmanian Wilderness.

Many of Australia's World Heritage sites are internationally famous places – most notably, Uluṟu and the Great Barrier Reef – attracting hundreds of thousands of visitors each year. Others, such as the incomparable Purnululu NP, are so remote that their fame, while substantial, does not translate into big tourist numbers. And then there are those places acclaimed by scientists and environmentalists, but visited only by a small number of travellers; they are still waiting to be 'discovered' by the broader public. These include Willandra Lakes, one of the world's most important archeological sites, and Riversleigh, a fossil site that has redirected the course of paleontology in recent years.

Above *Pussytails bloom in front of Uluṟu, one of Australia's most famous World Heritage sites.*

Opposite *The Magela wetlands in Kakadu NP are a major wildlife habitat.*

Not-to-be-missed sites

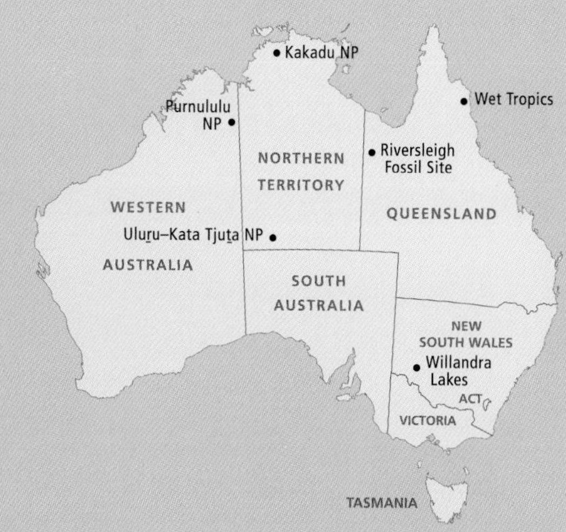

Uluṟu–Kata Tjuṯa NP, The Red Centre
The icon of outback Australia, Uluṟu, along with the less famous but equally spectacular Kata Tjuṯa, was inscribed in 1987 for its geology, extraordinary scenic beauty and tangible evidence of the traditional Aboriginal way of life. See *Uluṟu and Kata Tjuṯa*, p. 50

Kakadu NP, The Top End
As well as spectacular Top End scenery, Kakadu has one of the largest and most significant collections of rock art in the world, a quarter of all Australian bird species, and all the major habitats of northern Australia. See *Kakadu and Arnhem Land*, p. 84

Wet Tropics, Tropical Outback
The tropical jungle of eastern Cape York contains a near-complete record of the major stages of plant evolution. Running alongside the Great Barrier Reef, this is the only place on earth where two World Heritage sites meet. See *Mossman to Lakefield NP*, p. 100

Riversleigh Fossil Site, Tropical Outback
This is one of two sites that form the Australian Fossil Mammal Sites – the other is Naracoorte Caves in south-east SA. Inscribed in 1994, these sites represent the major stages in evolutionary history. Join a tour and see mammal remains that date back 20 million years. See *Gulf Country*, p. 114

Willandra Lakes, The Arid South-East
One of the first sites to be inscribed (1981), this arid landscape features ancient sand dunes – lunettes – and lakes that have not seen water for 15 000 years. The dunes bear evidence of Aboriginal occupation dating back as far as 50 000 years. See *Broken Hill and Beyond*, p. 156

Purnululu NP, The Kimberley
This park protects the distinctive beehive formations of the Bungle Bungle Range. Its World Heritage listing recognises its remarkable geology – the patterns reveal the forces that formed them over hundreds of millions of years. See *The East Kimberley*, p. 236

A Look at the Past

history and heritage

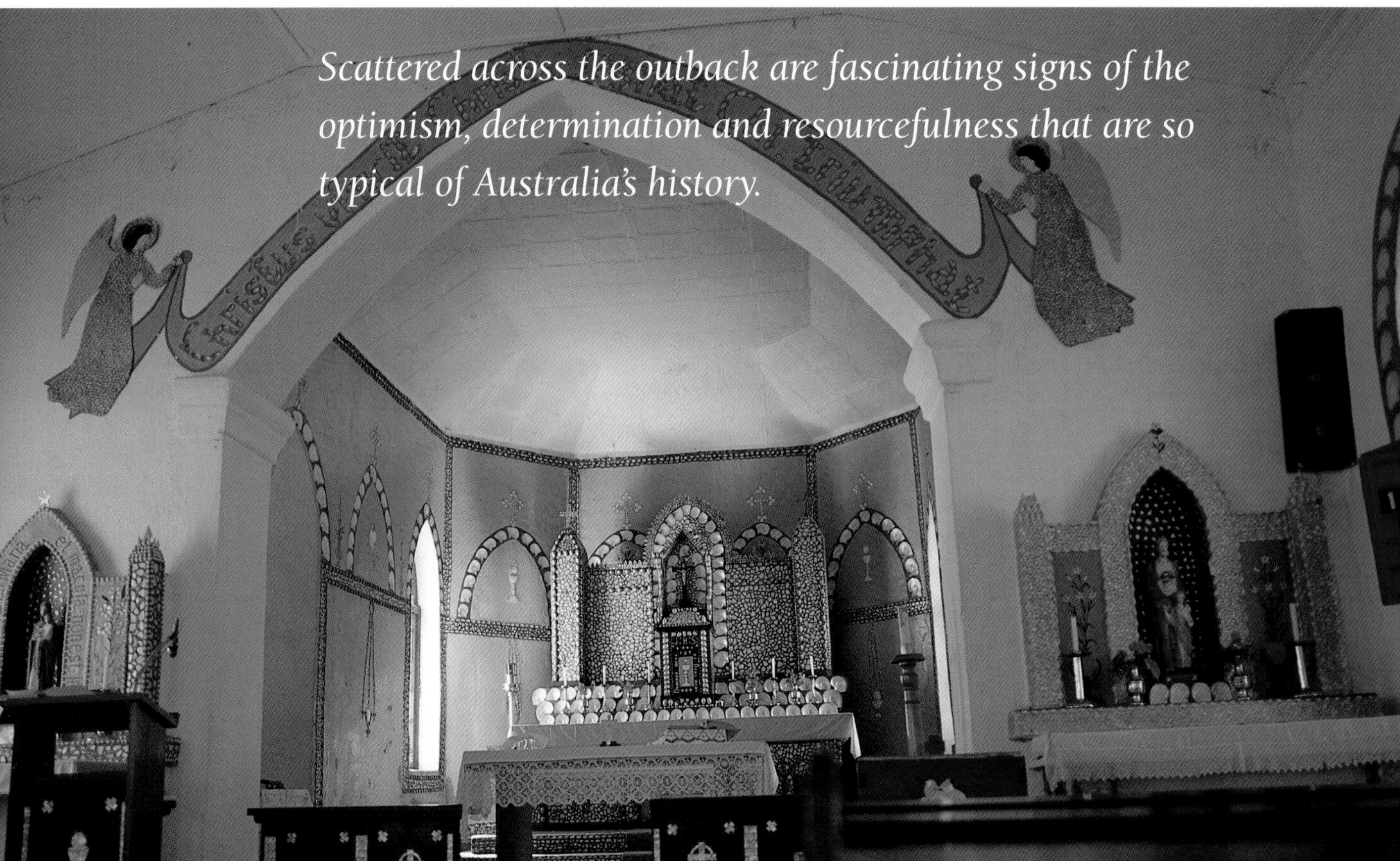

Scattered across the outback are fascinating signs of the optimism, determination and resourcefulness that are so typical of Australia's history.

Above *The pearl-shell embellished Sacred Heart Church at Beagle Bay, near Broome.*

Opposite *The remains of the once-thriving sheep station, Kanyaka, in SA.*

Australia has two pasts – the rich and multi-layered history of the Indigenous people who have occupied this ancient land for as much as 60 000 years, and the short, sometimes poignant story of those who have settled and made a mark in the last 200 years.

The first explorers trudged relentlessly across arid, difficult terrain, determined to find an inland sea, green pastures or mighty rivers. Pastoralists soon followed in their steps, and so too did gold-seekers and ambitious miners. Drovers moved their stock along forbidding routes that cut trails across the land. For those exploring the outback today there are tangible signs of this more recent past, from trees blazed by explorers to collapsing water wells and ghost towns.

In some areas, buoyed by optimism – and perhaps greed – settlers pushed beyond the reasonable boundaries for farming. It didn't take long for nature to regain the upper hand. Crumbling stone buildings bear testimony to failed farms. Woolsheds, weathered to a pale grey hue, their floor timbers soaked in lanolin, recall immense outback stations that prospered briefly, then foundered.

Repeater stations (some of them restored) along the route of the Overland Telegraph Line are reminders of this outback engineering feat – more than 3000 km across some of the world's harshest desert.

In every state, the gold-rush era has left its mark – grand hotels, magnificent public buildings, humble miners' cottages, and an often deeply scarred landscape.

Museums in outback towns recount the history and acknowledge that past.

Some historic highlights

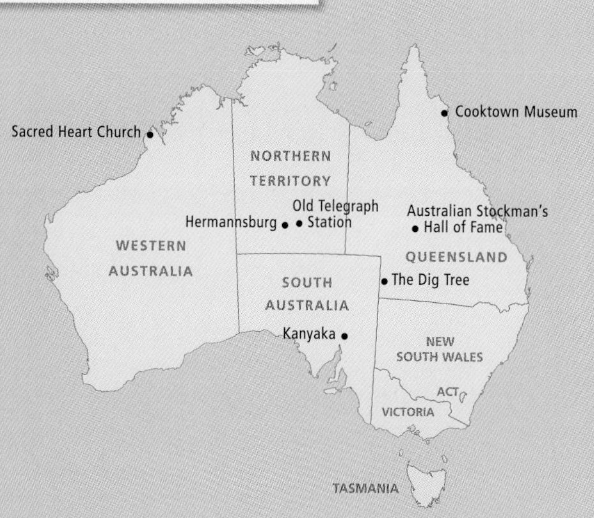

Old Telegraph Station, The Red Centre
A complex of restored buildings, the station is near the original 'Alice Springs', a waterhole on the telegraph line. Historic photos and interesting artefacts explain some of the station's fascinating history. See *Alice Springs and Beyond*, p. 32

Hermannsburg, The Red Centre
This small cluster of whitewashed stone buildings was built by German missionaries, who settled here in the 1870s, with the help of the Arrernte people. The buildings and the land are again owned by the Arrernte. See *West MacDonnell Ranges and Watarrka*, p. 40

James Cook Museum, Tropical Outback
This excellent museum is in an 1880s former convent in the former 'Queen of the North', Cooktown. One of Captain Cook's cannons, from the *Endeavour*, is a prized exhibit, there are displays relating to the Chinese on the goldfields, as well as Indigenous artefacts. There's also a fine view from the upstairs balcony. See *Mossman to Lakefield NP*, p. 100

Australian Stockman's Hall of Fame, Tropical Outback
A fascinating and wide-ranging collection highlights the pioneers, pastoralists, stockmen and others who settled Australia's remote outback regions. See *Outback Queensland*, p. 122

The Dig Tree, Corner Country
The Dig Tree, near Innamincka, is a poignant memorial to Burke and Wills, whose 1860s expedition across the continent ended in tragedy. See *Desert Tracks*, p. 142

Kanyaka, The Arid South-East
Tumbledown fences and crumbling farm buildings scattered across the wind-scoured paddocks are all that remains of a vast wool station, that once carried 40 000 sheep. See *Flinders Ranges*, p. 166

Sacred Heart Church, The Kimberley
This white stone church, at Beagle Bay on the remote Dampier Peninsula, was constructed 1914–17 by Pallottine monks who once lived here, with the help of Aboriginal people. The altar is richly embellished with pearl shell. See *Broome and Beyond*, p. 226

Outback Towns

the heart of the country

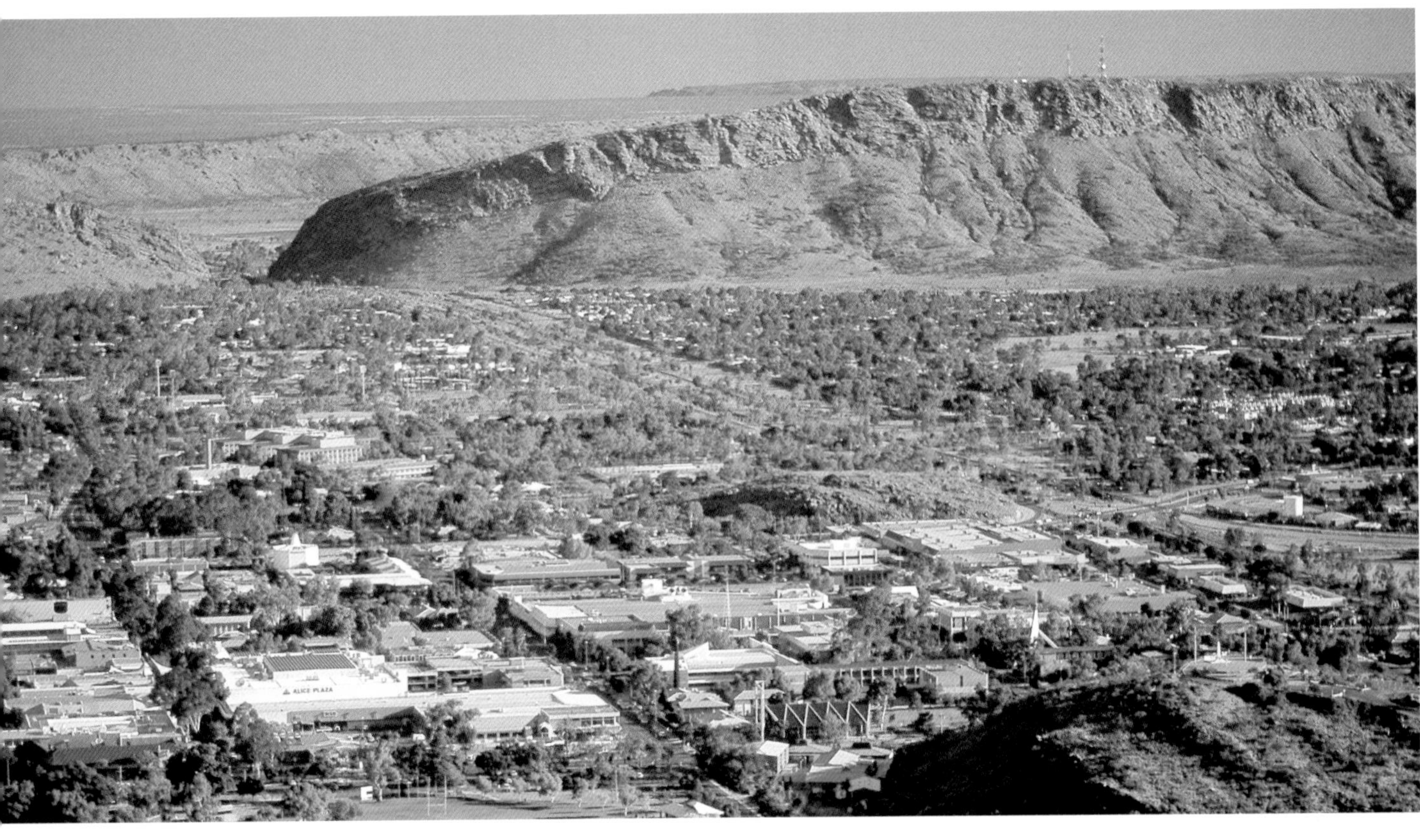

Often hot, dusty and remote, but rich in heritage and character, Australia's outback towns enjoy reputations that far exceed their size.

Above *Alice Springs, considered by many to be the unofficial capital of the outback.*

Opposite *Grand buildings in Cooktown's peaceful Charlotte Street.*

Over the years places such as Alice Springs, Birdsville and Kalgoorlie have acquired fame via a rich repository of tales – tall and true. Interwoven with these are the themes that have come to define the Australian character: mateship, egalitarianism, enterprise and hardiness. The less savoury aspects of the pioneering spirit only add to the sense of local drama and colour in Australia's outback towns.

Most of the better known centres started as single-industry settlements: Kalgoorlie was fired by a gold rush, Coober Pedy by the discovery of opals. Often it was a simple accident of geography that meant some towns survived while others floundered. The patch of land that was to become Alice Springs was just another point in the path of the Overland Telegraph Line until surveyor William Whitfield Mills discovered a permanent waterhole there in 1871. A repeater station was built, and the rest, as they say, is history.

Regardless of their past reputations, most of Australia's more famous outback towns are now well-ordered places with good resources. Many rely heavily on tourism: Broome, once one of Australia's more boisterous outposts, is now a resort with an international reputation; Broken Hill, site of a massive mining operation, is replete with art galleries, cafes and other markers of urban life. Nevertheless, much of the wit, energy and spirit needed to establish communities in remote landscapes still survives. If in doubt, pay a visit to the local pub in any town, on any Friday afternoon.

A few of the finest

Alice Springs, The Red Centre
The Alice, framed by the arid swell of the MacDonnell Ranges, is packed with cultural institutions that celebrate the town's status as the unofficial capital of the outback. Galleries with Aboriginal art showcase the rich past and present of the area's Indigenous inhabitants – the Arrernte and the Anangu. See *Alice Springs and Beyond*, p. 32

Cooktown, Tropical Outback
On the fringe of a near-trackless wilderness on Cape York, this is a small, surprisingly well-organised pocket of wide streets, statues and Victorian-era architecture, a legacy of its booming gold days in the 19th century. See *Mossman to Lakefield NP*, p. 100

Birdsville, Corner Country
This tiny desert town is home to two legendary institutions: the Birdsville Pub and the Birdsville Races. Perched on the edge of the vast Simpson Desert, it is as much an oasis for today's 4WD adventurers as it was for drovers of the late 19th century. See *Birdsville and Beyond*, p. 134

Coober Pedy, Corner Country
Coober Pedy services the world's largest opal field, while most of its residents live in underground structures known as dugouts. The surrounding lunar-like landscape only adds to its sense of otherworldliness. See *Desert Tracks*, p. 142

Broken Hill, The Arid South-East
The landscape that so excited prospectors with its infinite store of mining riches, now attracts artists and filmmakers with its sparse, iconic beauty. The town sits comfortably in its surrounds – a prosperous community with an extensive 19th-century heritage on proud display. See *Broken Hill and Beyond*, p. 156

Kalgoorlie, The South-West
Of all Australia's outback towns, Kalgoorlie seems the least inclined to shrug off all its wild and unruly ways, with the pubs still a prominent attraction. Alongside, however, are fascinating historic sites, mining sites, museums and galleries. See *Goldfields Country*, p. 182

Broome, The Kimberley
Broome was a major pearling centre in the early 1900s, attracting divers and brokers from around the world; now international tourists flock here, drawn by the beautiful beaches, wilderness surrounds, unique history and laidback ambience. See *Broome and Beyond*, p. 226

Wildlife-watching

life in the bush

Australia's distinctive fauna and the diversity of habitats across the outback ensure some fantastic wildlife-watching opportunities.

Australia's vast distances and often extreme climate have made settlement a challenge, but the size of the continent and the range of habitats have ensured a rich and diverse wildlife. Kakadu NP, for example, is one of the most species-rich parks in the world. More than 64 species of mammals, 128 reptile, 25 frog and 59 fish species (not to mention birds) provide some brilliant wildlife-watching opportunities. Kakadu is the world's most important breeding ground for saltwater crocodiles and there are regular tours to watch for these primeval creatures, but as you cruise the waters you might also see turtles, water snakes and water monitors. The park also contains myriad insect species, including fascinating stick insects.

On Cape York, the mosaic of habitats – jungle-like rainforest, sparse woodlands and swampy mangroves – accommodate an impressive array of animals from rare species, such as Bennett's tree kangaroo at renowned Daintree NP, to tropical butterflies.

Arid areas in particular are the domain of lizards, from the perentie, Australia's largest lizard, to the small thorny devil, on average just 15 cm long, and brilliantly adapted to the desert environment.

The coast also offers wildlife-watching. In northern Australia dugong, manta rays and marine turtles cruise the tropical waters. Whale sharks – the largest fish in the world – are a special feature of the Pilbara coast, while whales swim off the Kimberley and Nullarbor coasts.

Kangaroos and wallabies, Australia's best known marsupials, can be seen from the arid south-east to the woodlands and rocky ramparts of the Kimberley and Kakadu, but many of Australia's native species are shy, or nocturnal, and patience is required for the best wildlife-watching.

Above *A shingleback, or sleepy lizard, in the Flinders Ranges.*

Opposite *The best time to see kangaroos is usually early morning or at dusk.*

Where to watch

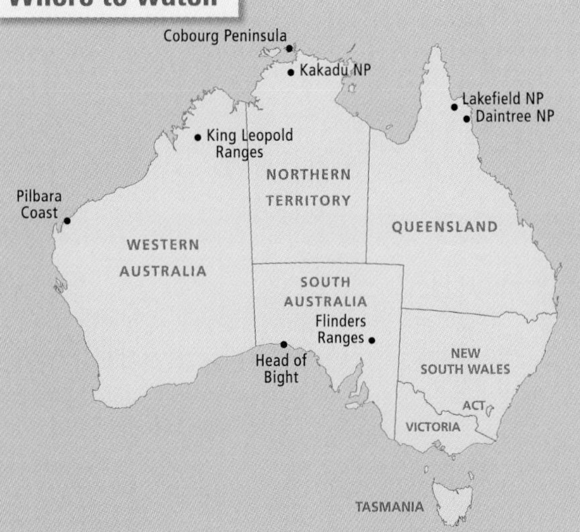

Mossman to Lakefield NP, Tropical Outback
The World Heritage-listed Daintree rainforest is dense with species – from butterflies and bats to rare marsupials and reptiles. Further north, 18 mammal and 38 reptile species, including saltwater crocodiles, inhabit Lakefield NP's open woodlands and wetlands. See *Mossman to Lakefield NP*, p. 100

Kakadu NP, The Top End
Kakadu boasts a bewildering array of species, including both rare and endemic varieties inhabit the park. There are 28 bat species, wallaroos, echidnas, possums, and reptiles including the distinctive frilled lizard and a range of snakes. See *Kakadu and Arnhem Land*, p. 84

Cobourg Peninsula, The Top End
Bandicoots, wallabies, grey kangaroos and a host of reptiles are among the abundant wildlife. Feral animals include banteng cattle and wild boar. Offshore, dugong, manta rays and marine turtles swim in the balmy waters. See *Kakadu and Arnhem Land*, p. 84

Pilbara Coast, The Pilbara and Western Deserts
Highlights along this coast are humpback whales in autumn, and whale sharks that congregate offshore from April to June. See *The Pilbara and Outback Coast*, p. 204

Head of Bight, The South-West
Groups of calving southern right whales make an annual migratory trip to the waters off the Bight, providing an impressive spectacle. See *The Nullarbor*, p. 192

Flinders Ranges, The Arid South-East
Watch for red kangaroos on the plains, and wallabies – especially the lovely yellow-footed rock wallabies – around rocky gorges. See *The Flinders Ranges*, p. 166

King Leopold Ranges, The Kimberley
Look for lizards, water monitors and other reptiles sunning themselves by day; in the evening nocturnal marsupials, such as the small fierce quoll and bandicoots, emerge in search of food. See *Broome and Beyond*, p. 226

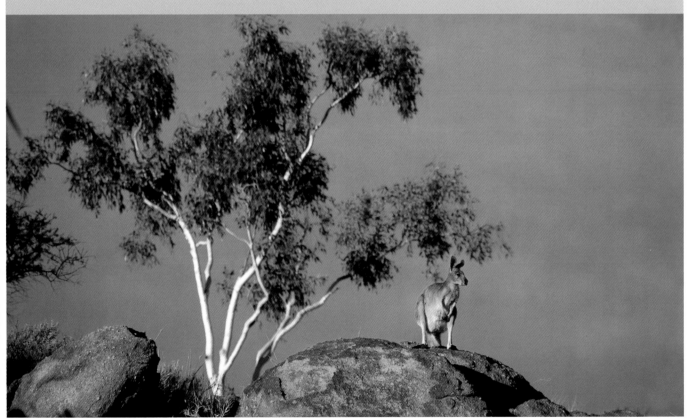

Birdwatching
on the wing

Across the immense reaches of outback Australia diverse habitats ensure some outstanding birdwatching – take your binoculars and a field guide on your travels.

Above *Corellas take off in the Flinders Ranges.*

Opposite *A falcon at Newhaven Reserve, in the Red Centre.*

In northern Australia's lush and tropical wetland region birds are an intrinsic part of the web of life. In extensive parts of Kakadu NP and the wetlands of the north-east Kimberley, they enjoy a constant supply of food and their numbers flourish. Jabirus, egrets, stately brolgas, throngs of whistling ducks, magpie geese and other species – more than 60 in all – congregate in astonishing numbers around billabongs, rivers and waterholes, creating wonderful birdwatching opportunities. These areas are also strategic stopovers on the migratory paths of Northern Hemisphere species, including curlews from Siberia.

In the North's drier areas, such as the southern part of Kakadu NP, parrots and black cockatoos feed on seeds, honeyeaters devour the sweet nectar of woodland flowers, grass wrens and bowerbirds nest, and falcons, kites and other raptors soar above in search of prey.

Iron Range NP, an isolated outpost on Cape York's eastern coast, guards a precious pocket of pristine rainforest and woodland, edged by mangrove forest. The diverse habitats are a haven for rare and endemic species, such as the vivid eclectus parrot, and birds of paradise.

Central Australia's harsh and usually dry landscapes, with poor-quality plant life and meagre water supply, cannot sustain birdlife in large numbers. But come the rains, nomadic and migratory birds flock to the region. In Innamincka Regional Reserve, after good summer and autumn rains further north fill the lakes, thousands of fish-hungry pelicans, waders, ducks and migratory birds descend, clustering in and around Coongie Lakes.

Along the outback coast, majestic species such as the white-breasted sea eagle ride the wind currents, while shorebirds and waders prowl the shallows in search of a seafood feast.

Where to look

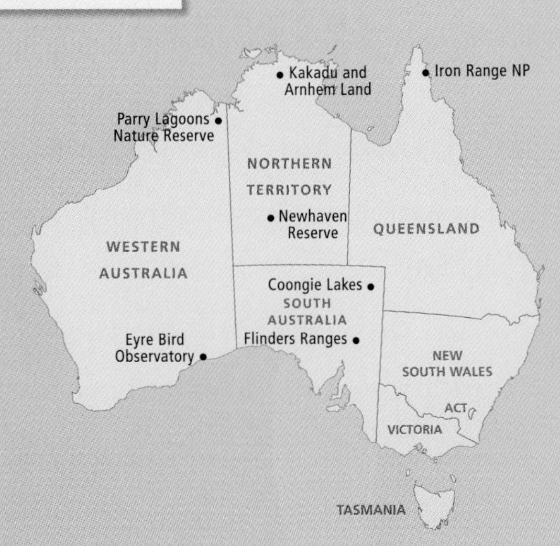

Newhaven Reserve, The Red Centre
At least 138 species, including nine threatened species, have been sighted in this arid-zone reserve managed by Birds Australia and the traditional custodians. See *The Tanami and Tennant Creek*, p. 56

Kakadu and Arnhem Land, The Top End
A birdwatcher's paradise – one-third of Australian species have been recorded in Kakadu, from prolific waterbirds to the rarely seen Gouldian finch. See *Kakadu and Arnhem Land*, p. 84

Iron Range NP, Tropical Outback
The vividly coloured eclectus parrot, the green-backed honeyeater, the fawn-breasted bowerbird and the red-bellied pita are highlights in this isolated park. See *Coen to the Cape*, p. 106

Coongie Lakes, Corner Country
After good rains in Queensland the Cooper River overflows, spilling into the Coongie Lakes and welcoming myriad bird species. See *Birdsville and Beyond*, p. 134

Flinders Ranges, The Arid South-East
Vividly plumed parrots, pigeons, noisy cockatoos and corellas in vast numbers enjoy the varied habitats as you head further north into the Flinders Ranges. See *The Flinders Ranges*, p. 166

Eyre Bird Observatory, The South-West
Within the Nuytsland Nature Reserve, this observatory is a birdwatching haven – Major Mitchell cockatoos, honeyeaters and Naretha bluebonnets are regularly sighted. See *The Nullarbor*, p. 192

Parry Lagoons Nature Reserve, The Kimberley
The wetlands near Wyndham are well known as feeding and breeding grounds for migratory shorebirds. See *The East Kimberley*, p. 236

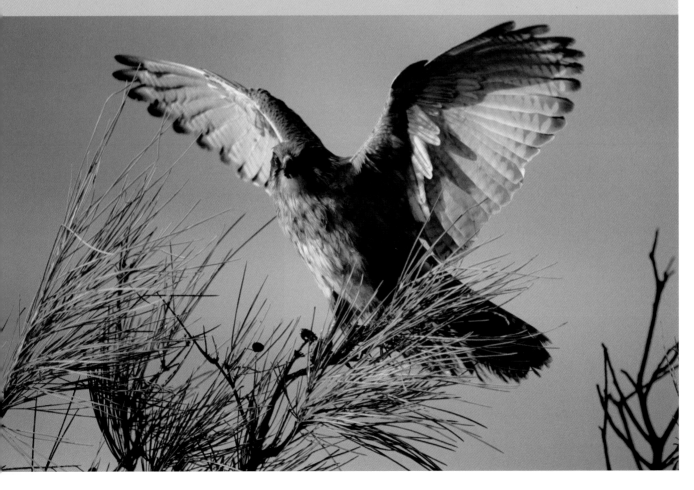

Walking and Camping
the country up close

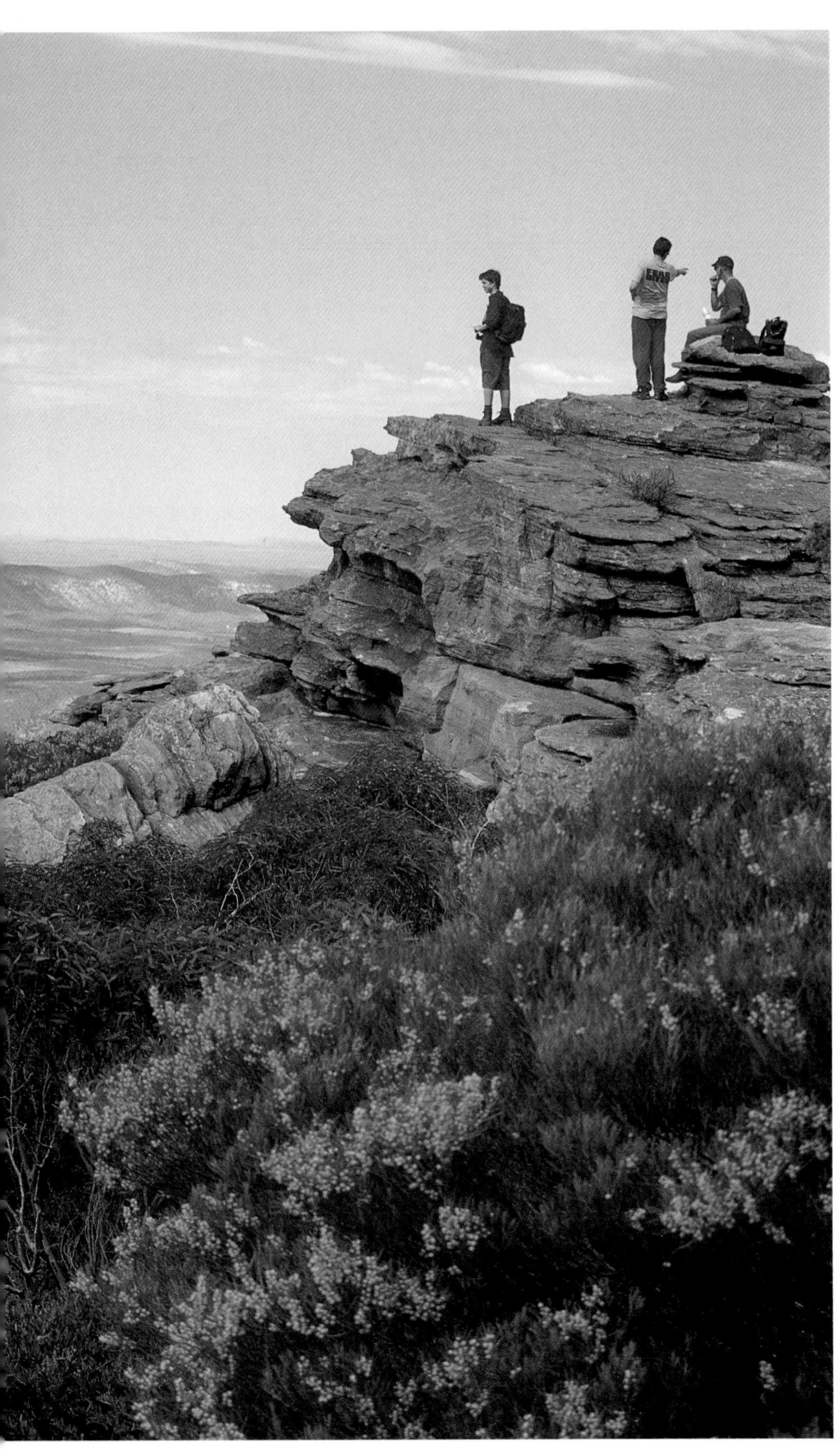

Pitching a tent beneath a sweep of hills or on a coolibah-fringed riverbank can be the best way to soak up the atmosphere of the outback, while heading off on foot can lead you to magnificent, little-visited destinations.

Camping is known as the cheapest way to travel, but it is also an unparalleled opportunity to visit and linger in some of the country's most superb landscapes. For a miniscule fee, and sometimes for nothing, you can find yourself camped in a palm-filled valley deep within the Red Centre, or on the savannah-like plains of the Gulf of Carpentaria.

With camping comes walking, especially in the country's vast network of parks and reserves. From short walks to multi-day treks complete with walk-in campsites, walking is an up-close introduction to the drama and nuances of a landscape. Most of the popular parks, such as Kakadu NP in the NT, have clearly marked trails and campsites with facilities; in more remote places, such as Iron Range NP in Queensland's Cape York, visitors are left to their own devices.

Along the tracks that connect the vast central deserts, there's nothing better than unrolling your swag amid the dunes, and then settling in to watch the stars.

In other places, walking is without doubt the iconic activity. The Flinders Ranges are targeted by adventure walkers from around the world. Striding out across this long roll of ancient hills lets you experience the region's extraordinary wildlife, dramatic rock formations and rich collection of rock art up close.

Left *A panoramic view rewards walkers in the Flinders Ranges.*
Opposite *Camping near Chambers Pillar in the Red Centre.*

Some top spots

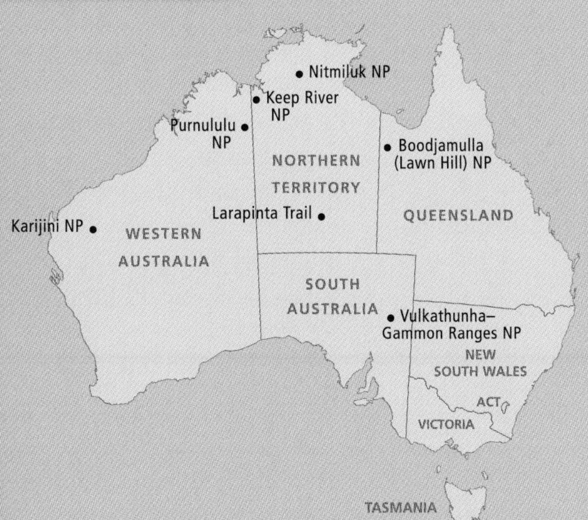

Larapinta Walking Trail, The Red Centre
One of Australia's great walks, this 220 km trail leads into the heart of the magnificent West MacDonnell Ranges, on the western flank of Alice Springs. The trail can be walked in sections and has various vehicle-access points. See *West MacDonnell Ranges and Watarrka*, p. 40

Nitmiluk NP, The Top End
Ten well-marked walking trails fan out alongside the red-hued gorges of this scenic NT park. The ultimate is a five-day, 66 km trek north-west to Leliyn (Edith Falls). Park campsites provide excellent facilities. See *Darwin to Mataranka*, p. 68

Keep River NP, The Top End
One of the NT's best-kept secrets, Keep River, on the WA border, attracts just 10 000 visitors a year. Walks lead to Aboriginal rock-art sites, gorge scenery and rock formations that echo the distinctive shapes of the Bungle Bungle Range. See *Katherine to Keep River*, p. 76

Boodjamulla (Lawn Hill) NP, Tropical Outback
In the dry season it's probably harder to get a campsite here than it is to get a room at the London Ritz. Book at least six weeks ahead particularly for the Easter period. When you arrive, enjoy the wildlife and lush vegetation and canoe through the gorges. See *Gulf Country*, p.114

Vulkathunha–Gammon Ranges NP, The Arid South-East
At the northern end of the Flinders Ranges, the Gammons offer a genuine off-the-beaten-track experience. A couple of historic huts provide accommodation, or visitors can camp. Walks lead across the rock-clad landscapes to Italowie and Weetootla gorges. See *The Flinders Ranges*, p. 166

Karijini NP, The Pilbara and Western Deserts
This remote walking and camping destination explores the gorge-riddled hills of the Hamersley Range – scenery that many say rivals that of the Red Centre for sheer spectacle. See *The Pilbara and Outback Coast*, p. 204

Purnululu NP, The Kimberley
Serious walkers in this park set out for Piccaninny Creek and Gorge, a trek that will take a couple of days. Look out for palm-fringed waterholes, pebbled creek beds, seasonal wildflowers and some of the park's 130 or so bird species. See *The East Kimberley*, p. 236

Fishing
angling for a catch

Australia's remote regions offer superb opportunities for the adventurous angler, from barramundi fishing in big tropical rivers to game-fishing off the northern coast.

Australians are keen anglers, and thousands of holidays to the outback have fishing as their focus. In Queensland's remote Gulf region, for example, it is estimated that four out of five visitors come to fish. Across the northern half of the continent, from the tip of Cape York to Garig Gunak Barlu NP in the NT, there are lodges and resorts dedicated to the holidaying angler, as well as experts offering charter services, hiring equipment and offering hard-won advice. The quality of the fishing in these remote areas is sensational, but more than that, anglers come for the chance to test themselves in the sometimes extreme conditions, and to pursue their passion in superb natural, scarcely touched environments.

Barramundi fishing has a large and devoted following, not least because barra can be found in some magnificent locations. The species inhabits the northern rivers and coastal areas and is prized for its sweet taste along with its fighting spirit. Top barra spots include the Mary River in the NT and the Gulf rivers in Queensland. Equally rewarding is the offshore fishing across the entire northern coastline. Anglers can team up with an operator and head towards the horizon looking for some of the legendary ocean fish that cruise Australian tropical waters: black marlin, tuna, sailfish and mackerel. As well, there are myriad islands, many unpopulated, scattered off the coast, and long stretches of reefs, including the Great Barrier and Ningaloo, teeming with tropical fish.

Left *A spot of peaceful fishing at Borroloola, in the Gulf Country.*
Opposite *Fishing from a tinnie in Kakadu NP.*

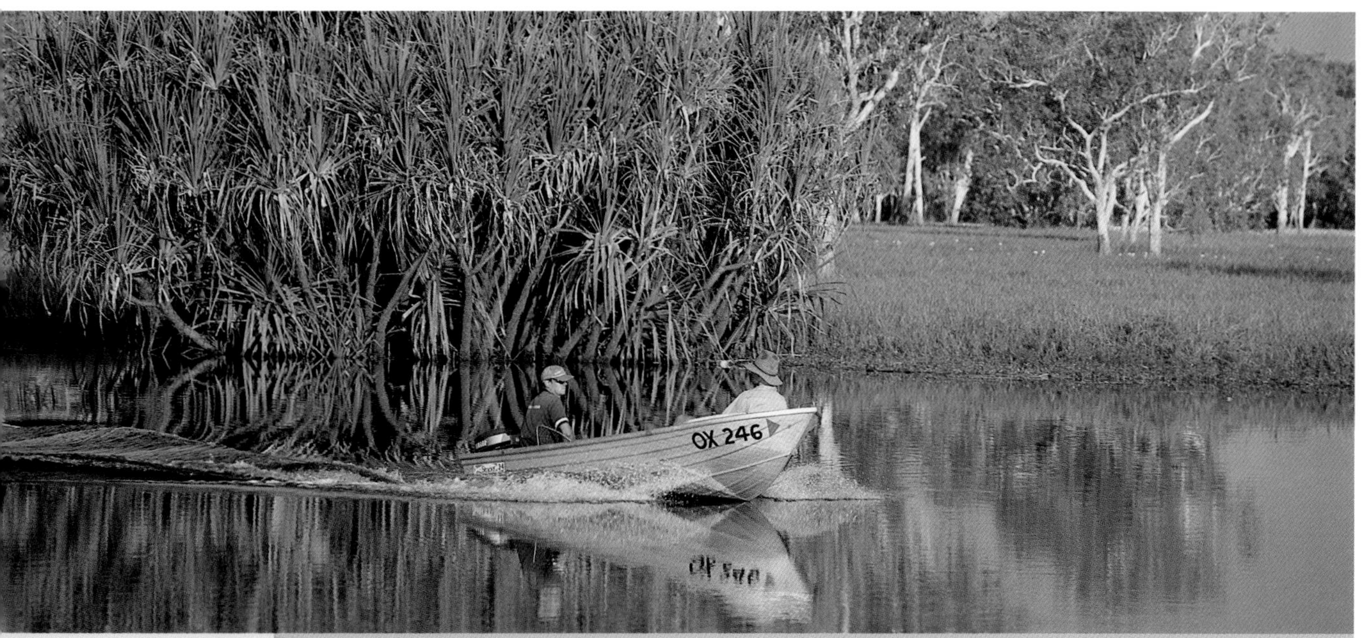

Where to toss a line

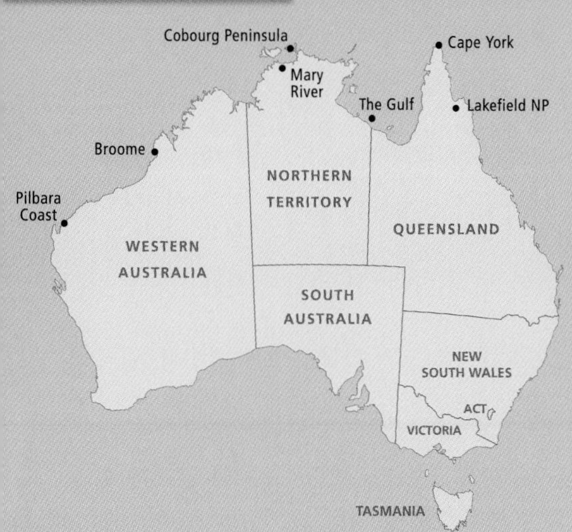

Mary River delta, The Top End
Hot, steamy, tangled, remote and snapping with saltwater crocs, the Mary River delta off the NT's Van Diemen Gulf is just how barramundi anglers like it. Camping and lodge-style accommodation is available. See *Darwin to Mataranka*, p. 68

Cobourg Peninsula, The Top End
With strict limits on visitor numbers, this NT peninsula, protected within Garig Gunak Barlu NP, is a true fishing frontier, with barramundi in the creeks and myriad reef fish and pelagics in the warm, pristine waters of the Arafura Sea. A marine park protects the surrounding waters. See *Kakadu and Arnhem Land*, p. 84

Lakefield NP, Tropical Outback
This remote park in northern Queensland is a mecca for anglers. Barramundi is the target. There are boat ramps for launching a tinnie and campsites with varying facilities – as elsewhere in the tropics, watch for crocs. See *Mossman to Lakefield NP*, p. 100

Cape York, Tropical Outback
There are numerous options for the angler around mainland Australia's most northerly point. Seisia is renowned for its pier fishing and offshore charters are available; book into the fishing lodge at Punsand Bay and fish from the rocky platforms and beaches that form the tip of the cape. See *Coen to the Cape*, p. 106

The Gulf, Tropical Outback
The Gulf's calm coastal waters, islands, overflowing rivers and tangled vegetation are a boon for anglers: the rivers are well stocked with barramundi, the offshore waters team with queenfish, mackerel, tuna and trevally. See *Gulf Country*, p. 114

Pilbara Coast, The Pilbara and Western Deserts
The Pilbara offers extraordinary fishing particularly around the Dampier Archipelago. Ningaloo Reef forms part of the Outback Coast – again, fantastic fishing, particularly for reef species, but observe regulations. See *The Pilbara and Outback Coast*, p. 204

Around Broome, The Kimberley
Broome is perfect for both land-based and offshore angling, while the coastline to the north is nothing short of awesome. Charter boats cruise the coast, enabling anglers to enjoy spectacular scenery while fishing for big pelagic species such as tuna and sailfish. See *Broome and Beyond*, p. 226

Four-wheel-drive Tours

on-road adventure

By virtue of its sheer size, Australia has some of the world's longest and most challenging 4WD routes, from dusty cattle tracks to outback 'highways'.

True enthusiasts know that outback travel in Australia is as much about the journey as it is about the destination. How could it be otherwise in a country where huge distances separate the smallest of towns and where the feats of early explorers are always there as a spur and a challenge?

For the Indigenous inhabitants, the outback was negotiated via an intricate network of what are known as songlines – the routes first laid down by the Dreamtime beings during the creation period. These pathways served thousands of generations of travellers and proved reliable, even in the featureless expanses of the harshest deserts.

European explorers, oblivious to the idea of songlines, set out to establish their own routes. Some perished, but their example inspired others to journey towards what Ludwig Leichhardt called 'the heart of the dark continent'. Remarkably, in many places modern roadways follow the original routes taken by these adventurers. For example, the road that traces the wide scoop of the Gulf of Carpentaria, from Queensland into the NT, mirrors the course taken by Leichhardt when he crossed the top of the continent in 1844–45.

Until the 1970s, the outback regions were the preserve of Indigenous groups, surveyors, miners, the military and pastoralists. But with improvements in vehicle and communication technology, travel along some of the country's roughest, longest and loneliest tracks is now relatively commonplace. A word of warning: those intending to follow some of the more difficult routes described in this book need to be extremely well prepared. See *On the Road*, p. 246, for details.

Above *Heading along a red dirt road in the Red Centre.*

Opposite *Outback tracks provide a challenge to 4WD enthusiasts.*

Some great tracks

Tanami Track, The Red Centre
The Tanami Track is a 1000 km journey between Alice Springs and the far-flung Kimberley. Traversing some of the country's most arid regions, it provides an awe-inspiring introduction to Australia's desert heartland. See *The Tanami and Tennant Creek*, p. 56

Cape York, Tropical Outback
Forging through the dark tangle of Cape York's tropical jungles to gaze at the northern horizon is the dream of many 4WD enthusiasts. Travellers can still expect a high degree of difficulty despite the small increase in facilities and the slowly improving road conditions. Many of the roads are closed during the wet season. See *Coen to the Cape*, p. 106

Birdsville Track, Corner Country
Stretching 517 km across the deserts of SA and Queensland, this route may not be Australia's harshest or longest outback track, but its fascinating droving history makes it one of the most famous. See *Birdsville and Beyond*, p. 134

French Line, Corner Country
The French Line, at 438 km, is the most direct route across the formidable 170 000 sq km Simpson Desert, but adventurers seek it out for its constant dune crossings, including the 90 m high Big Red, and extreme conditions, including temperatures of up to 50 degrees Celsius. See *Desert Tracks*, p. 142

Canning Stock Route, The Pilbara and Western Deserts
The world's longest stock route stretches 1700 km from Wiluna in the south to Halls Creek in the Kimberley. The only signs of civilisation along the route are the historic wells built for drovers in the early 1900s, some now servicing modern-day travellers. See *The Western Deserts*, p. 214

Gibb River Road, The Kimberley
This iconic 700 km former cattle route plunges into the heart of the Kimberley, providing access to a landscape of spectacular gorges and rugged ranges, intersected by the vast spread of cattle stations. See *Broome and Beyond*, p. 226

Station Stays

the real outback

Some of Australia's pastoral stations are opening their gates and welcoming visitors for the quintessential outback experience.

Australia may no longer ride on the sheep's back, but sprawling sheep and cattle properties still occupy vast tracts of land and exert an undeniable pull on the imagination of outback travellers. Increasingly, station owners are realising that there is value in more than just their livestock. Stations that have been in families for generations provide a fascinating glimpse of Australian history and a reminder of the challenges pioneers faced. Farming on this scale, in such remote places, is not for the faint-hearted.

Out here, everything is big – the landforms, the properties, the size of the herds, the length of the droughts, and the warmth of the welcome. In the Kimberley the average property spreads across 2000 sq km. In the Top End, your nearest neighbour could be a day's drive away. These stations fan out across grassy plains, with mountain ranges, unique landforms and natural spring pools. They embrace mighty rivers, ragged gorges, and ancient rock art.

For most stations, the day-to-day business of running a property the size of small kingdom continues, with tourists something of a sideline. For others, tourists are the very heart of their business. Some stations are low-key, with fishing and bushwalking, while others have a raft of activities. In season there might be mustering by helicopter or motorbike, horse riding or flights across the property, crocodile-spotting, swimming in tranquil gorges, wildlife-watching or tours to explore the country's unparalleled legacy of rock art. At night, visitors might settle into a swag, bunk down in the old shearers' quarters, or retreat to a historic homestead. Whichever they choose, they will wake to an outback dawn, and the promise of more uniquely Australian experiences.

Above *Curtin Springs Station in the Red Centre.*

Opposite *El Questro, in the Kimberley, offers camping and homestead stays.*

Some top stopovers

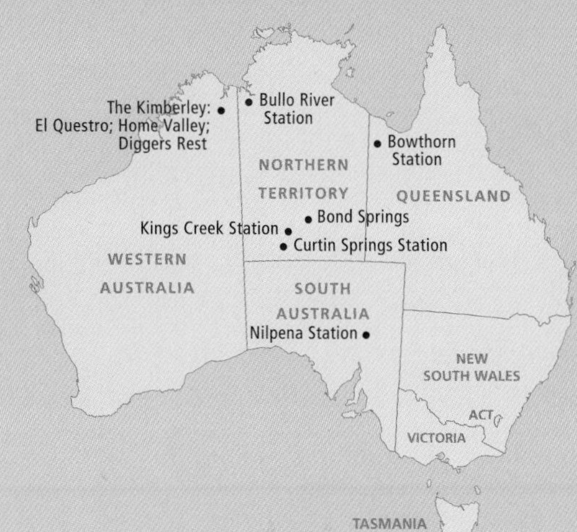

Bond Springs Outback Retreat, The Red Centre
In the MacDonnell Ranges, historic Bond Springs Outback Retreat offers cottage and homestead accommodation on its 1515 sq km Hereford beef-grazing property. Country cooking served in the traditional homestead kitchen is a highlight. See *Alice Springs and Beyond*, p. 32

Kings Creek Station, The Red Centre
Near dramatic Watarrka NP, Kings Creek Station farms both cattle and camels. The camping grounds have a small swimming pool, and a general store where you can book for camel rides, quad bike tours or helicopter flights. See *West MacDonnell Ranges and Watarrka*, p. 40

Curtin Springs Station, The Red Centre
Although only offering camping and basic accommodation at its roadhouse, there are 4WD and tag-along tours where you can see the historic property (in the Severin family for three generations) and marvel at monumental Mount Conner up close. See *Uluṟu and Kata Tjuṯa*, p. 50

Bullo River Station, The Top End
This cattle property covers 2000 sq km, a wild domain of grassy plains, hidden gorges, river frontages, and masses of birds and animal life. Exceptional fishing, mustering in season and tours of the station's Aboriginal rock art are highlights of a stay here. There is homestead accommodation, but no camping. See *Katherine to Keep River*, p. 78

Bowthorn Station, Tropical Outback
In the isolated Gulf Country, Bowthorn is a working cattle property where Brahman crossbreeds are mustered by helicopter and motorbike. Peaceful (and bountiful) fishing is the big lure here. There's homestead accommodation, or you can camp at Kingfisher Camp. See *Gulf Country*, p. 115

Nilpena Station, The Arid South-East
Tucked deep in the Flinders Ranges, on a plain near Lake Torrens, this working cattle station enables visitors to experience the arid country at its best – plenty of wildlife, freshwater springs, clear desert skies and starry nights. See *The Flinders Ranges*, p. 166

The Kimberley
Quite a few Kimberley stations welcome visitors. The world-renowned El Questro caters to all tastes: its luxurious homestead is dramatically perched on a river frontage, but there are also safari cabins and camping, and a multitude of activities. Home Valley Station has great fishing; at Diggers Rest, on the banks of the King River, you can ride a horse or fish for barra. See *The East Kimberley*, p. 236

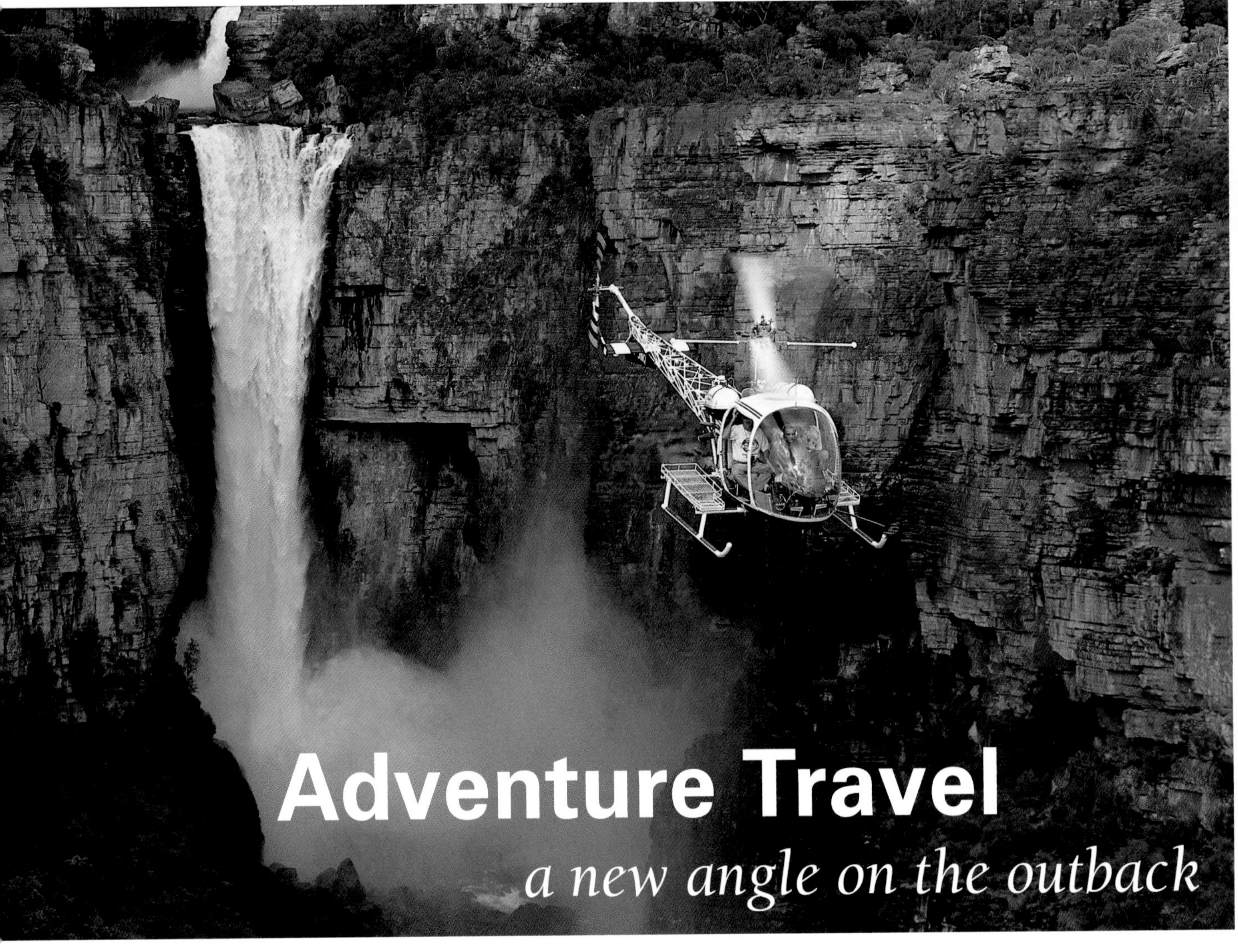

Adventure Travel

a new angle on the outback

For the adventurous, there seems to be no end of ways to explore the outback, to see it at a different angle, or just at a different pace.

No longer content to simply drive the rugged roads, or pile off a bus to inspect the sights, many travellers are seeking to experience the outback in different ways – from paddling a canoe or lurching along on a camel to soaring above the landscape in a hot-air balloon.

Camel treks recall tougher times, harking back to the country's pioneering history. Well suited to the arid outback, these hard-working animals played an integral role in opening up the countryside, carrying months of supplies for explorers such as Burke and Wills, carting goods for the Overland Telegraph Line and to remote goldfields. These days camels sway along Broome's Cable Beach at sunset, or carry visitors on short forays across the desert sands.

The peaceful rhythm of canoeing or kayaking enables travellers to enjoy the stillness of the bush, the myriad colours of gorge walls, and the sight of birds swooping for a drink or fish skimming just beneath the water's surface.

Helicopters, light planes and, perhaps most exceptional of all, hot-air balloons, afford bird's-eye views of some of the outback's most spectacular sights. Elsewhere, planes and boats provide a unique perspective of largely inaccessible regions – the ragged, island-strewn Kimberley coast, secluded gorges and waterfalls, or the salt lakes of the interior.

More traditional are some of Australia's exceptional rail journeys. In the Gulf Country visitors can rattle across the landscape in a quirky motor rail, or take the grand 4352 km transcontinental journey from Sydney to Perth on the *Indian Pacific*, a mesmerising trip that traverses the seemingly limitless expanse of the Nullarbor.

Above *A helicopter zooms in for a close-up of Jim Jim Falls in Kakadu NP.*

Opposite *Sailing over the MacDonnell Ranges in a hot-air balloon.*

Some top touring options

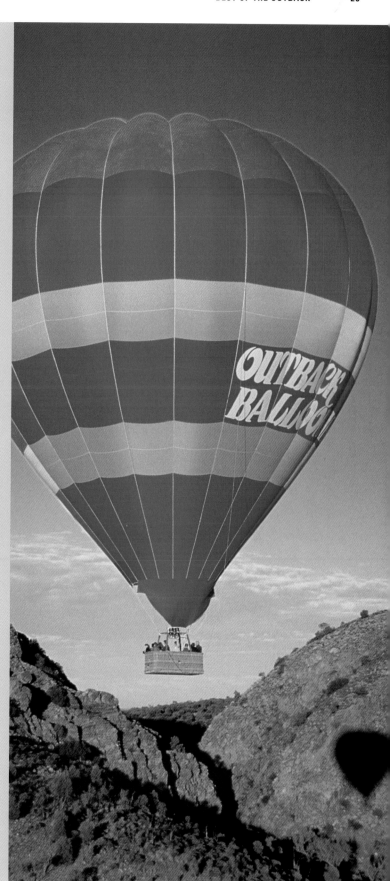

Camel treks, The Red Centre
Take a short, bumpy ride at a Red Centre camel farm, or test your mettle on a longer jaunt across desert sands. See *Alice Springs and Beyond*, p. 32

Hot-air balloon flights, The Red Centre
Hot-air balloons drift above the rugged folds of the MacDonnell Ranges and flights from Ayers Rock Resort at Yulara soar above the central deserts. These flights are a fascinating way to experience the monumental grandeur of the Red Centre's landscape. See *Alice Springs and Beyond*, p. 32, and *Uluṟu and Kata Tjuṯa*, p. 50

On track, The Top End, The South-West
Join the *Ghan* for the 3000 km journey that sweeps across the country's arid heart, from Adelaide to Darwin. See *Darwin to Mataranka*, p. 68. Or board the *Indian Pacific* that links Sydney with Perth. See *The Nullarbor*, p. 192

Helicopter flights, The Top End
The only way to enjoy the majesty of Jim Jim Falls at the height of the Wet is by air – an exhilarating ride over Kakadu NP. There are some wonderful helicopter rides in other inaccessible areas, such as the Kimberley. See *Kakadu and Arnhem Land*, p. 84

Canoeing, Tropical Outback
The cool, clear waters of Lawn Hill Gorge in remote Boodjamulla (Lawn Hill) NP are the perfect place for canoeing and kayaking. Watch for birdlife as you paddle past the pandanus trees. See *The Gulf Country*, p. 114

Light plane flights, Corner Country
Australia's largest lake, the salty expanse of Lake Eyre, can best be appreciated by flying over it. Under its usual crystalline crust, or in flood, it is an awesome sight. See *Desert Tracks*, p. 142

Outback Pubs

icons of the bush

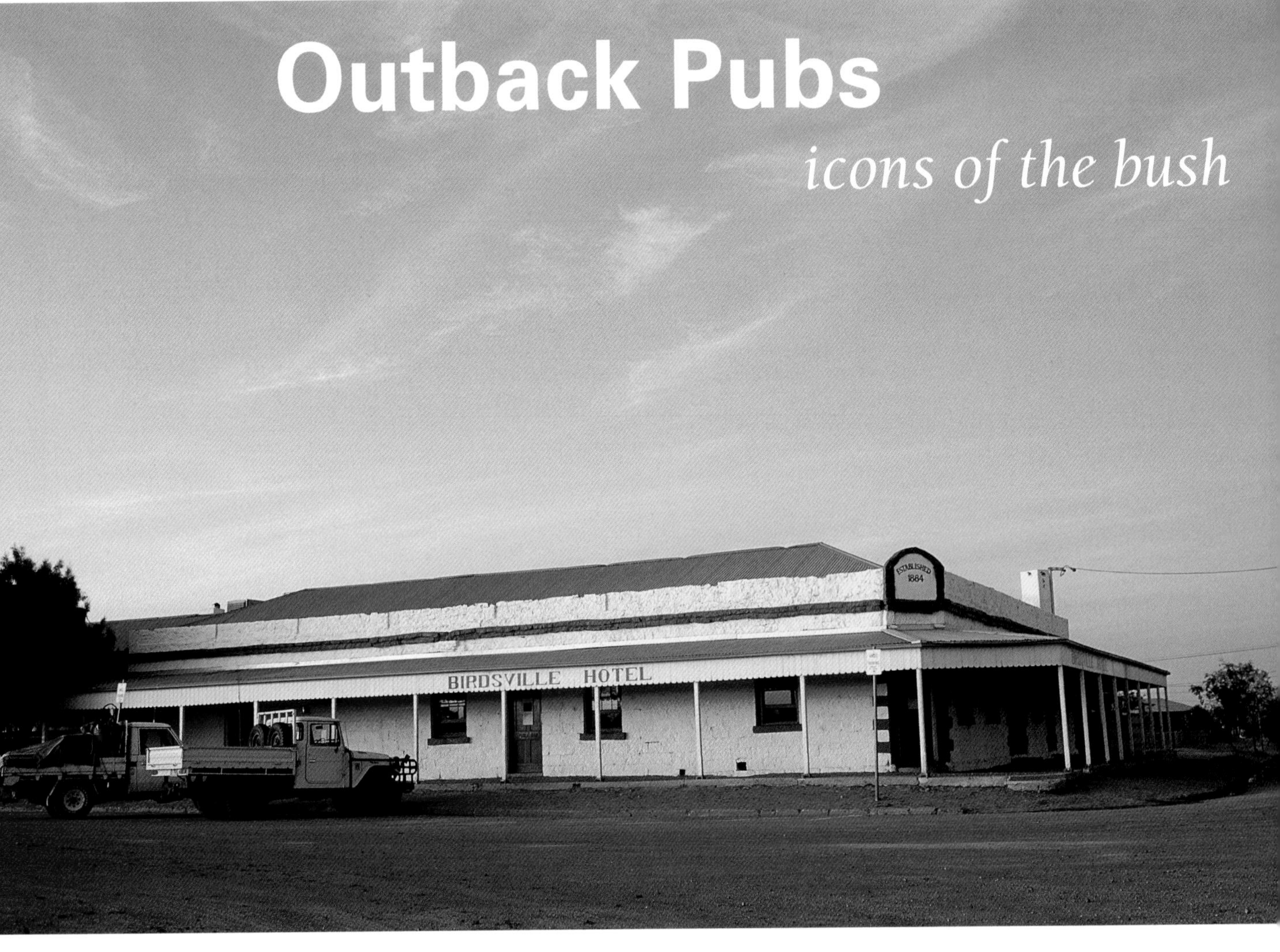

Buy yourself a beer, pull up a pew, and learn a little more about the outback from the locals who know it best.

Australia's outback pubs are legendary. Scattered across the countryside – from ramshackle lean-tos to grand, verandahed hotels – they epitomise the spirit of adventure, optimism and dogged determination that led pioneers, pastoralists and fortune-seekers to the farthest reaches of the continent. They symbolise the rough and ready, the makeshift and the make-do, as well as the good times, the heady days of the gold-rush era, of booming river ports and mining towns.

When Burke and Wills trudged north on their ill-fated expedition to the Gulf, they stayed overnight at the Menindee (now Maidens) Hotel. You may be in a 4WD instead of heading a camel train, but you can still call in here for a drink before heading further north.

On the edge of the Simpson Desert, the famed Birdsville Hotel dates back to 1884, a sturdy stone structure that is embedded in Australia's folklore. In the days when customs duties were payable on goods crossing state borders, Birdsville was a busy town. Things are a little more sedate now, but at the annual Birdsville Races the population swells from 100 to around 6000, and a good proportion of those stop at the pub for a cold one.

Outback pubs aren't just watering holes, though. If you need information, a bed, a meal, or advice on road conditions or where the fish are biting, this is the place to go. A pub is often the first building in a town, and it may well be the last one standing. You haven't really experienced the outback until you've had a beer with the locals in a true-blue pub.

Above *The renowned Birdsville pub offers a true taste of the outback.*

Opposite *The Prairie Hotel in the Flinders Ranges.*

Where to look

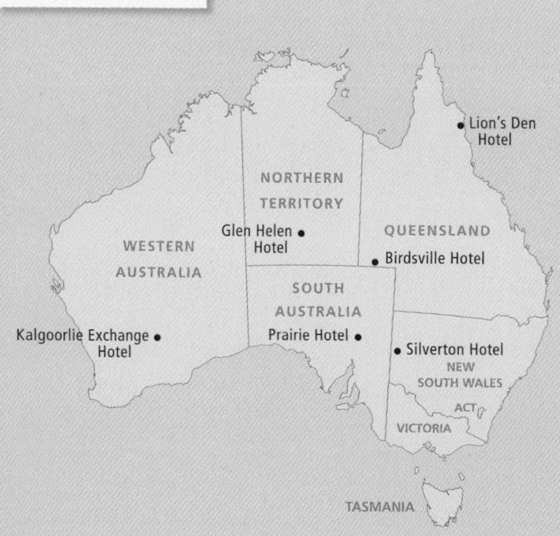

Glen Helen Hotel, The Red Centre
Buy a beer and pull up a chair on the verandah overlooking the sheer wall of Glen Helen Gorge for a truly Aussie experience. See *West MacDonnell Ranges and Watarrka*, p. 40

Lion's Den Hotel, Tropical Outback
A wooden slab building at Helenvale, the Lion's Den is said to be the oldest pub in Queensland, and an essential stop on the long haul to the tip of Cape York. The small, rustic pub, on the edge of the rainforest, is surrounded by shade trees. See *Mossman to Lakefield NP*, p. 100

Birdsville Hotel, Corner Country
The legendary Birdsville Hotel, built in 1884, is perhaps the country's best known pub – and justifiably so. A pub with history, character and about as far outback as you can go. See *Birdsville and Beyond*, p. 134

Silverton Hotel, The Arid South-East
The Silverton Hotel is another outback icon, standing isolated but proud in the remnants of a goldmining town. The pub has starred in a swag of movies, including *Mad Max*. Photos inside recall some of the characters who've leant against the bar. See *Broken Hill and Beyond*, p. 156

Prairie Hotel, The Arid South-East
Tucked away at Parachilna, on the plains of the Flinders Ranges, this pub prides itself on its 'feral food', such as emu and kangaroo, and its almost unbeatable view. The skies out here seem to go on forever. See *The Flinders Ranges*, p. 166

Kalgoorlie Exchange Hotel, The South-West
In a town renowned for its pubs, The Exchange's credentials include a proud history, impressive architecture and classic corner site. It's also handsomely restored. See *Goldfields Country*, p. 182

The Red Centre
heart of a continent

The Red Centre

The heart of the country, the Red Centre, is an ancient, timeless land. Extraordinary rock outcrops and crumbling ranges, eroded gorges and hidden pockets of greenery, enormous skies and red sand dunes create one of the world's most striking landscapes.

The Red Centre Regions

Alice Springs and Beyond

Alice Springs offers a range of galleries, museums, historic buildings and an outstanding nature park, which help introduce visitors to the extraordinary diversity of the Red Centre. Within easy driving distance are the East MacDonnell Ranges, with gorges, old goldmines and ancient rock art. This region also extends south-east, taking in some unique landscape and the edge of the formidable Simpson Desert. *See p. 32*

West MacDonnell Ranges and Watarrka

The journey west from Alice Springs reveals ghost gums silhouetted against weathered gorges, ancient cycads, the historic former mission of Hermannsburg, a comet crater and the remarkable Kings Canyon at Watarrka NP. There are some wonderful walking trails. *See p. 40*

Uluṟu and Kata Tjuṯa

No trip to the Centre would be complete without seeing Uluṟu (Ayers Rock) and Kata Tjuṯa (The Olgas). These remarkable geological forms are of profound spiritual importance to the Aboriginal people of Central Australia, yet also evoke a powerful response from all who see them. *See p. 50*

The Tanami and Tennant Creek

The infamous Tanami Track (officially the Tanami Road), a red-dirt road for much of its 1000 km, stretches across the spinifex plains of the Tanami Desert, linking Alice Springs with Halls Creek in WA. Five hundred km north of Alice along the Stuart Hwy is Tennant Creek, the largest town between the Centre and Darwin. *See p. 56*

Spinifex hopping mouse

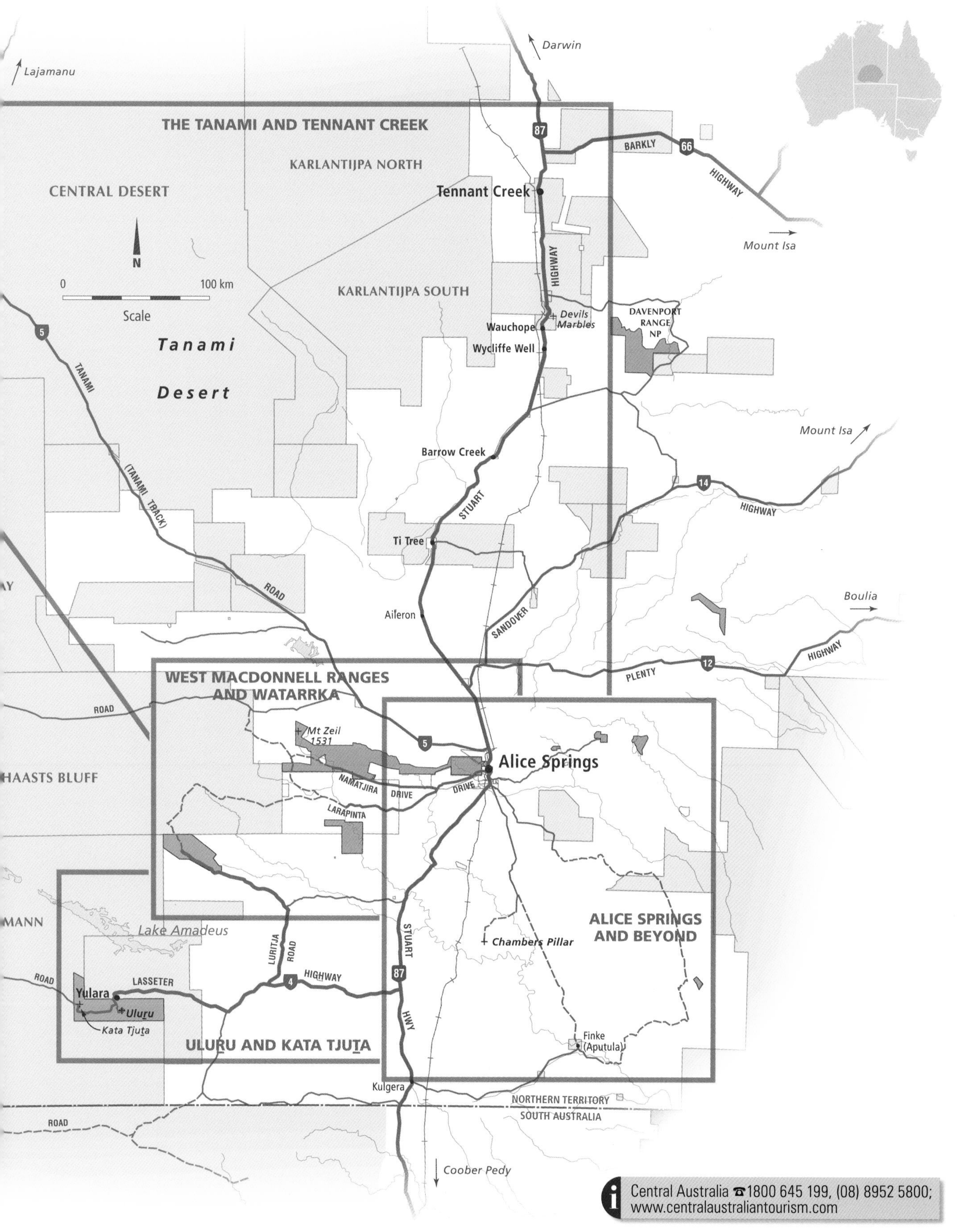

Central Australia ☎1800 645 199, (08) 8952 5800; www.centralaustraliantourism.com

Travel Tips

When to go

Autumn and spring (April–May and Sept–Oct) are the ideal times to visit – clear and sunny by day and not too cold at night. In the middle of winter (June–July) the daytimes can be cool (around 12°C), and the temperature can plunge to freezing at night. This is also when most tourists come to the region. In summer, temperatures climb above 40°C, and it is too hot to be out in the middle of the day. Rainfall is irregular, but any heavy falls usually occur Dec–Mar.

Aboriginal land

Large areas in Central Australia are Aboriginal land and there are also many areas of special significance to Aboriginal people. In most cases public roads crossing this land are open to general use. If you wish to deviate more than 50 m from the main road, or to camp on Aboriginal land, a permit is required, unless otherwise stated. Some Aboriginal communities have shops selling fuel and supplies, and these may be open to the public. Some communities are closed communities and access is strictly controlled. If you do enter communities, respect people's privacy. Some Aboriginal communities are 'dry' and no alcohol is permitted at all.

For all queries relating to Aboriginal land in Central Australia, contact the Central Land Council: 27 Stuart Hwy, PO Box 3321, Alice Springs, 0871; (08) 8951 6211; www.clc.org.au

Parks and reserves

The Parks and Wildlife Service of the NT (PWSNT) administers all but two of the NT parks. Uluru-Kata Tjuta NP is jointly administered by the Anangu people and the federal government's Parks Australia and has its own regulations (see *Fact File*, p. 52).

A permit is not required for camping at designated campgrounds in NT national parks (except for Garig Gunak Barlu NP in the Top End). A permit is required if you plan to camp outside a designated camping area. A small fee is payable at some sites. For further information contact the Parks and Wildlife Service of the NT (PWSNT), South Stuart Hwy, Alice Springs: (08) 8951 8250; www.nt.gov.au/nreta/parks

Walkers Registration Scheme Travellers undertaking overnight walks in parks should register with the PWSNT's Registration Scheme: 1300 650 730. A refundable deposit (payable by credit card or cash) is required in case help is needed. Not all parks are covered by the scheme.

CLIMATE												ALICE SPRINGS
	J	F	M	A	M	J	J	A	S	O	N	D
Max °C	36	35	33	28	23	20	20	23	27	31	34	35
Min °C	21	21	17	13	8	5	4	6	10	15	18	20
Rain mm	38	44	33	18	19	15	14	10	9	22	28	38
Raindays	5	5	3	2	3	3	3	2	2	5	6	6

CLIMATE												RABBIT FLAT ROADHOUSE
	J	F	M	A	M	J	J	A	S	O	N	D
Max C°	39	37	36	33	30	26	26	29	33	37	39	39
Min C°	24	23	21	16	12	8	7	9	14	18	22	23
Rain mm	100	110	43	21	14	11	9	3	10	17	32	58
Raindays	10	9	5	2	2	1	1	1	2	3	6	7

Warnings

Road conditions Avoid driving at dawn, dusk and at night when wildlife and stock may wander onto roads. Many roads in the Centre are 4WD only; others are suitable for 2WD but conditions can deteriorate quickly. Even on main roads there can be long distances without fuel stops. Drivers should be well prepared and carry adequate water and other supplies and advise a reliable person of travel plans, departure time and arrival. Keep to existing tracks – to preserve vegetation and avoid erosion. For NT road conditions contact NT Dept of Planning and Infrastructure (DPI): 1800 246 199; www.ntlis.nt.gov.au/roadreport

Maps Maps in this book are guidelines only – carry detailed maps.

Walking Carry adequate drinking water at all times. Wear sensible shoes and clothes, a shady hat, sunscreen and insect repellent. Observe all safety signs. (See also *Walkers Registration Scheme*, above.)

See also *On the Road*, p. 246.

Opposite *A stark white ghost gum at the foothills of the MacDonnell Ranges.*

Below *A knob-tailed gecko, one of the many small creatures that survive in the arid zone.*

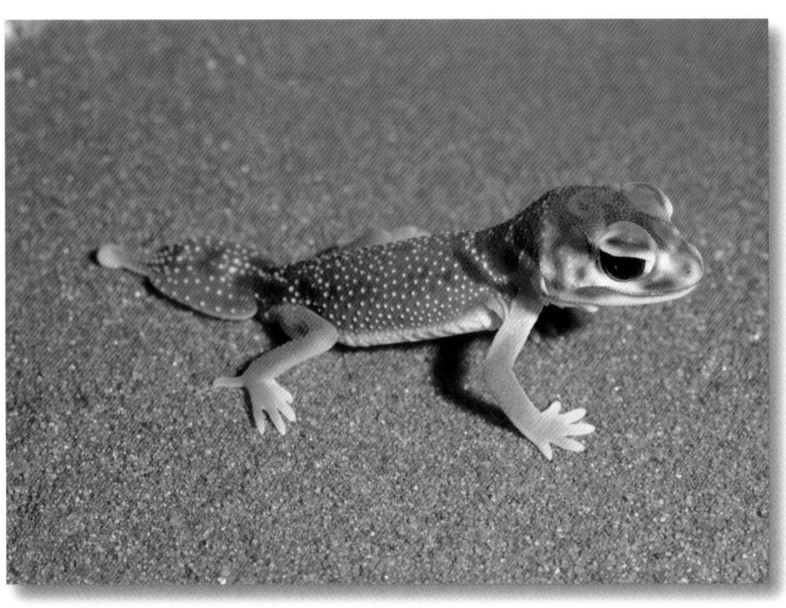

The Red Centre is just that – the heart of the country, stained an incredible russet red, from rugged gorge walls, sand dunes and gibber plains to the monolithic Uluru. Yet looking across from a highpoint, the landscape is a tapestry of tones and textures: the dusky green of desert oaks, red dunes, the gold or sage green of sharp spinifex, the stark white of arching ghost gums, the purple haze that hangs over the distant ranges.

Much of the Red Centre is desert, but not Sahara-like as you might imagine. The country is dry – most of the time – but it is not always barren. In fact, it is surprisingly rich in plants and wildlife – there are 11 species of fish, more bird species than are found in the whole of Britain, and just one square kilometre of sand plain may be home to 40 different types of lizard. Secreted within hidden gorges and damp crevices are delicate ferns, palms

.nd cycads from an ancient era when rainforest pread over the continent.

Most vegetation in this region is drought-olerant – hardy plants that have learnt to survive he rigours of the desert. The ubiquitous spinifex urls its leaves into long spikes to conserve noisture. Bushes are shaped to funnel precious lrops of water to their parched roots. Desert oaks end their taproot to the water table before they start o spread their limbs.

In this arid region there are riverbeds, but they re often bone dry. The Todd River and the ancient inke are broad, sandy and empty for much of the ear. After heavy rains, however, they fill, swell and lood, and all around a flush of new growth and ields of flowers emerge.

Still, there is no denying that this is harsh ountry. Summer temperatures can soar to 50°C, or plummet to freezing in winter. This makes it even more remarkable that Aboriginal people have survived in this environment for 30 000 years or more. The Centre's rich Indigenous history is evident in the many rock paintings and carvings. It is also evident in the knowledge Aboriginal people have of the landscape, of bush foods and medicines and the rich lore of their Dreamtime stories. They know this country intimately.

For visitors, there is so much to see and to learn. You can walk through the ranges and sleep in a swag beneath a galaxy of stars; join a 4WD tour and camp beside remote riverbeds; try a camel trek; soar over the countryside in a hot-air balloon; swoop in a helicopter; or stay in a five-star lodge. However you experience it, it is hard not to be moved by the drama of the landscape and its ancient culture.

Alice Springs and Beyond

Alice Springs is the quintessential outback town – small scale, easygoing, friendly. It's also the perfect base for exploring the East MacDonnell Ranges with their quiet gorges and Aboriginal art. South-east of Alice lie the vast, red-rippled sands of the arid Simpson Desert.

Alice Springs, at the heart of the Red Centre, sprawls around the wide, silvery-sand bed of the usually bone-dry Todd River in a break in the rugged MacDonnell Ranges. It's a city of only 28 000 or so, but services a vast area of the outback and a passing throng of national and international travellers. More than a quarter of a million people make the trip here each year.

Most visitors to Alice are on their way somewhere else – to Uluru, to the West Macs, north to Darwin, or just 'outback' in their 4WDs. But the town has its own attractions. You could easily spend a couple of days soaking up the atmosphere, learning a little about the Red Centre's pioneering history, its ancient Aboriginal culture and its unique landscape, flora and fauna. It's also a practical base for exploring the surrounding countryside.

East of Alice, the crumpled East MacDonnell Ranges are less visited and less dramatic than the West Macs, but still offer shaded gorges, Aboriginal rock art, the goldmining ghost town of Arltunga and tranquil camping.

South-east of Alice lie rust-red sand and gibber plains and an unbelievably vast expanse of sand dunes cascading off into the distance. This is the edge of the Simpson Desert, inhospitable to people, yet home to 92 reptile and 44 mammal species.

This region, with its strange landforms and intense colours, offers yet another aspect of Australia's always surprising outback.

Must see, must do

- Listen to the 'singing wire' at Alice Springs Overland Telegraph Station
- See Aboriginal rock carvings at Ewaninga
- Photograph dramatic Chambers Pillar at sunset
- Enjoy the tranquillity at Ruby Gap Nature Park
- Visit Old Andado Station on the fringe of the Simpson Desert

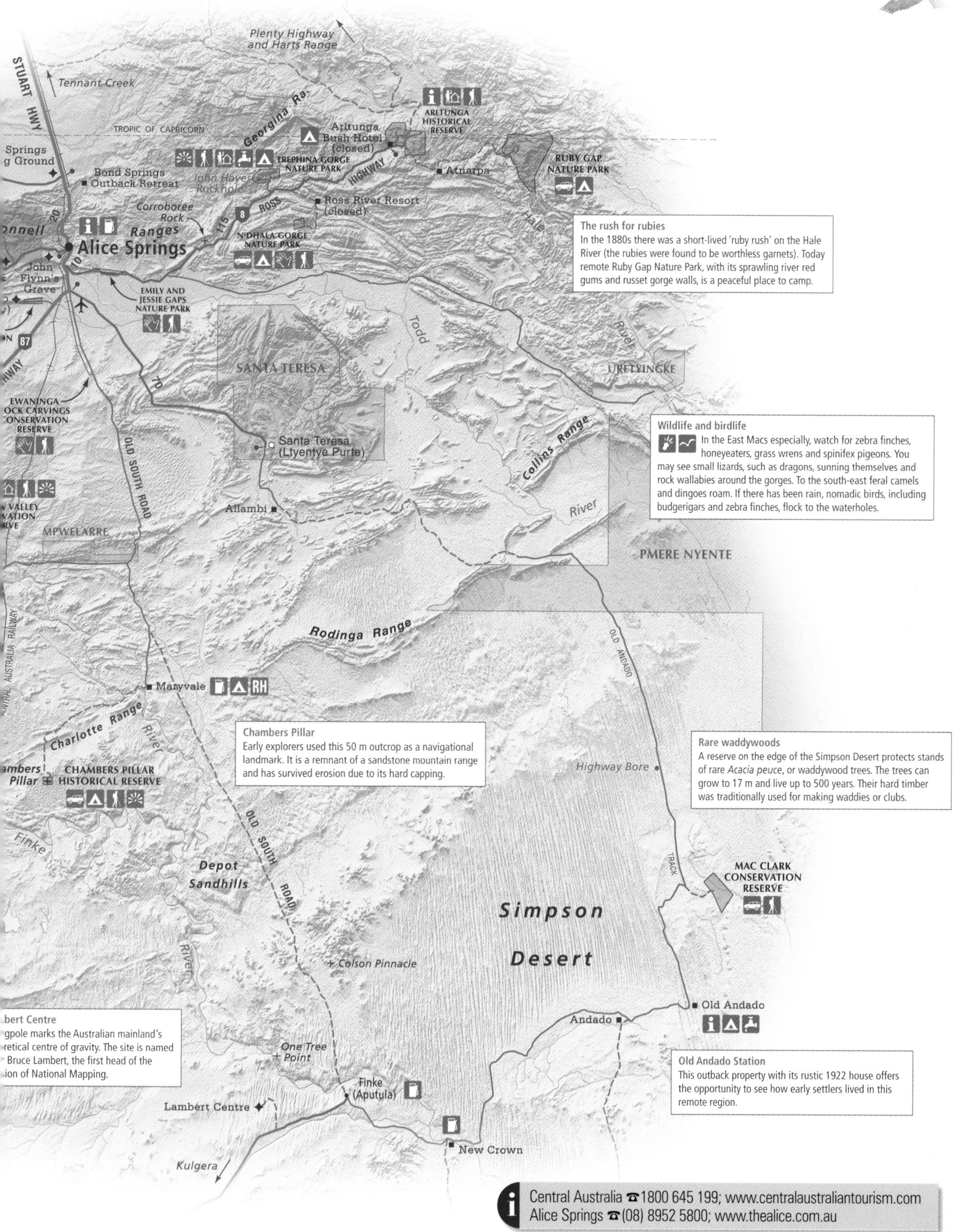

The rush for rubies
In the 1880s there was a short-lived 'ruby rush' on the Hale River (the rubies were found to be worthless garnets). Today remote Ruby Gap Nature Park, with its sprawling river red gums and russet gorge walls, is a peaceful place to camp.

Wildlife and birdlife
In the East Macs especially, watch for zebra finches, honeyeaters, grass wrens and spinifex pigeons. You may see small lizards, such as dragons, sunning themselves and rock wallabies around the gorges. To the south-east feral camels and dingoes roam. If there has been rain, nomadic birds, including budgerigars and zebra finches, flock to the waterholes.

Chambers Pillar
Early explorers used this 50 m outcrop as a navigational landmark. It is a remnant of a sandstone mountain range and has survived erosion due to its hard capping.

Rare waddywoods
A reserve on the edge of the Simpson Desert protects stands of rare *Acacia peuce*, or waddywood trees. The trees can grow to 17 m and live up to 500 years. Their hard timber was traditionally used for making waddies or clubs.

…bert Centre
…gpole marks the Australian mainland's …retical centre of gravity. The site is named … Bruce Lambert, the first head of the …ion of National Mapping.

Old Andado Station
This outback property with its rustic 1922 house offers the opportunity to see how early settlers lived in this remote region.

Central Australia ☎1800 645 199; www.centralaustraliantourism.com
Alice Springs ☎(08) 8952 5800; www.thealice.com.au

Fact File

Top events

April/ May *Alice Springs Cup Carnival (horse racing)*
May *Bangtail Muster Parade (Alice Springs)*
June *Alice Springs Show*
July *Camel Cup Festival (Alice Springs)*
Aug *Alice Springs Rodeo*
Desert Mob (exhibition of Central Desert Aboriginal art, Alice Springs)
Sept *Alice Springs Festival (art and culture)*
Henley-on-Todd Regatta (bottomless boats on the dry riverbed, Alice Springs)
Nov *Corkwood Festival (art, craft and music, Alice Springs)*

Permits and regulations

Aboriginal land Those wishing to visit Santa Teresa (Ltyentye Purte) community require a permit (no permit is required to just drive through). Check with the Central Land Council, 27 Stuart Hwy, PO Box 3321, Alice Springs, 0871; (08) 8951 6211; www.clc.org.au Note that Finke (Aputula) is a dry community (see *Travel Tips*, p. 30).

Parks and reserves

For general information regarding parks in this region contact visitor information in Alice Springs (see *Contacts*, opposite) or Parks and Wildlife Service of the NT (PWSNT) in Alice Springs: (08) 8951 8250.

Arltunga Historical Reserve No camping; no fossicking in the reserve. For information contact the ranger: (08) 8956 9770.

Chambers Pillar Historical Reserve The drive to the pillar is 4WD only. Camp sites, but BYO water and firewood.

Corroboree Rock; Emily and Jessie Gaps Nature Parks No camping permitted.

Ewaninga Rock Carvings Conservation Reserve No camping permitted.

Mac Clark Conservation Reserve Access by 4WD only. Camping is not recommended.

N'Dhala Gorge Nature Park Bush camping but no drinking water. For information contact ranger at Trephina Gorge.

Rainbow Valley Conservation Reserve Access by 4WD only. Camp sites but BYO water and firewood.

Ruby Gap Nature Park A high-clearance 4WD is needed for this park. Bush camping only; no drinking water. This park is isolated. Travellers should advise park rangers at Arltunga of their plans before and after visiting, or register with the PWSNT's Walkers Registration Scheme: 1300 650 730 (see *Travel Tips*, p. 30).

Trephina Gorge Nature Park Several campsites. The camp at John Hayes Gorge is best accessed by 4WD; no drinking water at this campsite. BYO firewood. For information contact the ranger: (08) 8956 9765.

Warnings

Fuel and supplies Particularly south-east of Alice Springs, headed towards the Simpson Desert, fuel, food and accommodation are limited; travellers need to plan ahead.

Road access and closures Many of the roads in this region are 4WD only, including the roads into N'Dhala Gorge and Ruby Gap nature parks. A 4WD vehicle is advised for the Old Andado Track. Heavy rains may close the roads. For road reports contact: 1800 246 199; www.ntlis.nt.gov.au/roadreport or seek local advice.

Walking Carry plenty of drinking water. Wear sensible shoes and clothes, a hat, sunblock and insect repellent. Walkers undertaking extended walks are strongly advised to advise local rangers, or register with the PWSNT's Walkers Registration Scheme. (See *Travel Tips*, p. 30.)

See also *On the Road*, p. 246.

Bond Springs Outback Retreat

Historic Bond Springs Station offers an 'Outback Retreat' just 25 km from Alice Springs. The accommodation has a touch of luxury about it, but it's also a chance to see a working station up close. Bond Springs, covering 1515 sq km, is a cattle-grazing property. Bookings are essential (see *Contacts*, opposite).

Alice Springs

Alice Springs may have a smattering of smart restaurants and even a casino, but it's really a down-to-earth place that caters well for locals and its endless stream of visitors. It's a town that makes the best of what it has – witness the Henley-on-Todd Regatta, where crews run their bottomless boats down the dry Todd riverbed. It's outback irony at its laconic best.

Opposite *Alice Springs' original telegraph station, opened in 1872, has been restored.*

Below *The broad sandy bed of the Todd River is most often dry.*

Europeans settled here in 1872, when a repeater station for the Overland Telegraph Line (see *The singing wire*, p. 36) was set up near a spring (named Alice after the wife of Charles Todd, Postmaster General of SA). Todd supervised the telegraph line's construction. A 'ruby rush', followed by a short-lived gold rush in the 1880s, saw a brief flurry of activity, but the population didn't start to grow until 1929 when the railhead was extended from Oodnadatta and the original *Ghan* steam train pulled into town. Tourism began in a modest way in the 1950s (Ayers Rock NP was declared in 1957) but the discovery of oil and gas at Mereenie Basin near Lake Amadeus in the 1970s, more regular flights into Alice and the growth of international tourism have seen the town expand.

At the original Overland Telegraph Station 2 km from town a cluster of buildings, from the 1870s homestead to a smithy shop, have been handsomely restored and stand peacefully shaded by peppercorn trees. Not all the history is positive – for some years children of the 'stolen generation' were accommodated here. Original equipment and photos capture the station's varied history, including the pioneering days when all supplies arrived by horse or camel.

For an outstanding introduction to the various habitats of the Red Centre and its fascinating wildlife visit the extensive Desert Park, also on the edge of town. Try to time your visit to catch the amazing raptor display.

A stroll around town reveals other aspects of the Centre's culture and heritage. Adelaide House, designed by the Reverend John Flynn (see p. 125), was the region's only medical centre until 1939. The National Pioneer Women's Hall of Fame is in the Old Alice Springs Gaol. Opposite is the Residency, built in 1927 for the region's first government administrator. The tiny Stuart Town Gaol (the town was called Stuart for some years) dates from 1908. The Royal Flying Doctor Service building, opened in 1939, is still functioning and open for daily tours. Walk up to Anzac Hill to see the sun's last rays bathe the ragged walls of the Heavitree Range in golden light.

The Araluen Cultural Precinct includes the Strehlow Research Centre, where photos and diaries reveal the Strehlow family's long association with nearby Hermannsburg (see p. 44); many priceless cultural artefacts and customs belonging to the Arrernte people were preserved by the Strehlows. (Most are too sacred to be displayed.) The excellent Museum of Central Australia features fine natural history exhibits.

The Aboriginal Art and Culture Centre has displays and can arrange tours with Indigenous guides to many sites, and there are a number of Aboriginal art galleries. Ask at the visitor information centre – staff are extremely helpful.

The East MacDonnell Ranges

The West MacDonnell Ranges are spectacular – and you wouldn't want to miss them – but if you prefer to escape the crowds, you should head east. The East MacDonnell Ranges, or East Macs, have their own character and their own riches. To the Arrernte people they are the Dreamtime birthplace of the mountain range, and Aboriginal rock paintings and carvings are scattered through the region.

The East Macs are reached via the Ross Hwy, which turns east from Stuart Hwy just south of Alice Springs. About 10 km east along the road, sacred sites and galleries of rock art at Emily and Jessie Gaps are protected within a small nature park. Emily Gap, a registered sacred site, is especially significant, a dreaming trail where caterpillar beings of Mparntwe (Alice Springs) originated. There is no camping, but pleasant walks, picnic areas and the semi-permanent waterholes attract birds such as plump spinifex pigeons.

Further east, Corroboree Rock, protected within its own conservation reserve, is a deeply spiritual site, thought to have been a keeping place for ceremonial objects. The rough outcrop of tan dolomite rises in front of the ranges, flanked by needle-sharp spinifex, red mallee and scrawny native fig trees.

Another 85 km along the Ross Hwy, to the end of the sealed road, lies Trephina Gorge Nature Park, a favourite with locals and visitors alike. After turning off the highway, there is a 9 km drive, 5 km of this on a gravel road. At Trephina Gorge the sun strikes the sheer quartzite cliffs of the ranges, shady river red gums edge the creeks, and pale beach-like sand lines creek beds and waterholes. John Hayes Rockhole is an ideal swimming spot during the warmer months, though the drive to it is best tackled in a 4WD. There are several camping spots. For seasoned bushwalkers Trephina Ridge Top

Contacts

Visitor information

Alice Springs
Gregory Tce
08) 8952 5800 or 1800 645 199
www.centralaustralian
tourism.com

Parks and reserves

See *Fact File*, opposite

Station stays, hotels

Old Ambalindum
(08) 8956 9993
www.oldambalindum
homestead.com.au

Bond Springs Station
(08) 8952 9888
www.outbackretreat.com.au

Old Andado Station
(08) 8956 0812

Other

Aboriginal Art and Culture Centre
(08) 8952 3408

Araluen Cultural Precinct
(08) 8951 1120
www.nt.gov.au/nreta/arts/ascp

Alice Springs Desert Park
(08) 8951 8788
www.alicespringsdesertpark
.com.au

Alice Springs Telegraph Station
(08) 8952 3993

National Pioneer Women's Hall of Fame
(08) 8952 9006
www.pioneerwomen.com.au

Royal Flying Doctor Service (RFDS)
(08) 8952 1129

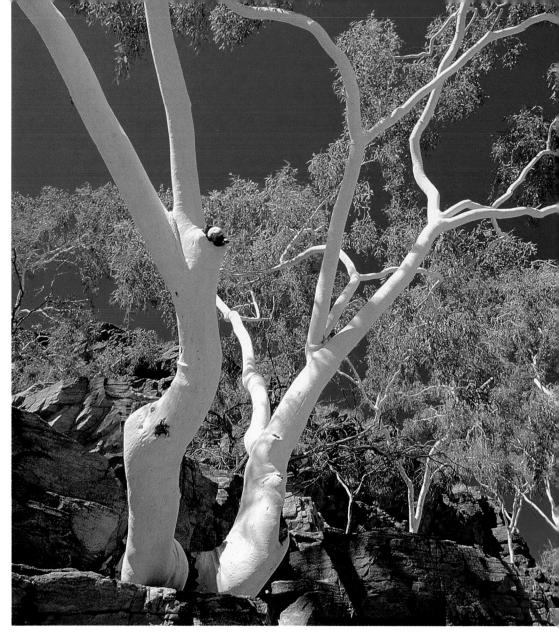

A ghost gum emerges from the fractured red rock at Trephina Gorge.

The singing wire

The Overland Telegraph Line played a huge role in Australia's development. When it began operation in 1872 it linked Australia with the rest of the world, dramatically reducing communication time from months to just hours. The line, completed in only two years, covered 3000 km, from Darwin to Port Augusta, traversing some of the world's most remote and harsh desert. Repeater stations were built along the way, at what are now well-known places such as Alice Springs and Tennant Creek. The purpose of the stations was to boost the morse code signals so the sound would carry over the long distance of the telegraph wire. As the sound was transmitted, the wires hummed – an eerie 'singing' in the remote desert country.

Gorge (6.5 hours return) offers wonderful views and typically Red Centre colours – brilliant blue sky, craggy red ranges and the green and white of ghost and river red gums. Shorter walking tracks, swimming holes (often extremely cold even in summer) and some fine lookouts are other attractions.

N'Dhala Gorge

For those equipped with a 4WD, a track winding through the Ross River Valley leads to N'Dhala Gorge Nature Park, with its stark ghost gums. Aboriginal people have been coming to this deep, narrow gorge for thousands of years, and there is a wealth of ancient rock engravings, as well as shelter sites. Thousands of faint images, often of animal tracks and geometric symbols, are etched into the rock. Check road conditions before travelling if it has been raining, as the road may be impassable.

Arltunga and Ruby Gap

Past Trephina Gorge the unsealed road winds 33 km to Arltunga Historical Reserve. The lure of gold was strong here in the 1880s and the thought of sudden riches had eager prospectors trundling their possessions in wheelbarrows from the Oodnadatta railhead, 600 km south. The gold rush at Arltunga – or Paddy's Rockhole as it was known – lasted long enough for a small town to spring up, but it was soon abandoned. A legacy of rusting mining machinery and stone buildings, crumbling in the scrubby outback, recalls those days. The police station and gaol have been restored, and displays at the visitor centre convey the isolation and hardship of life in this dry and dusty outpost. Take a torch if you want to inspect one of the old mines. On Arltunga Tourist Road (Binns Track) past Arltunga Historical Reserve, Old Ambalindum has homestead, bunkhouse and camping accommodation on a working cattle station.

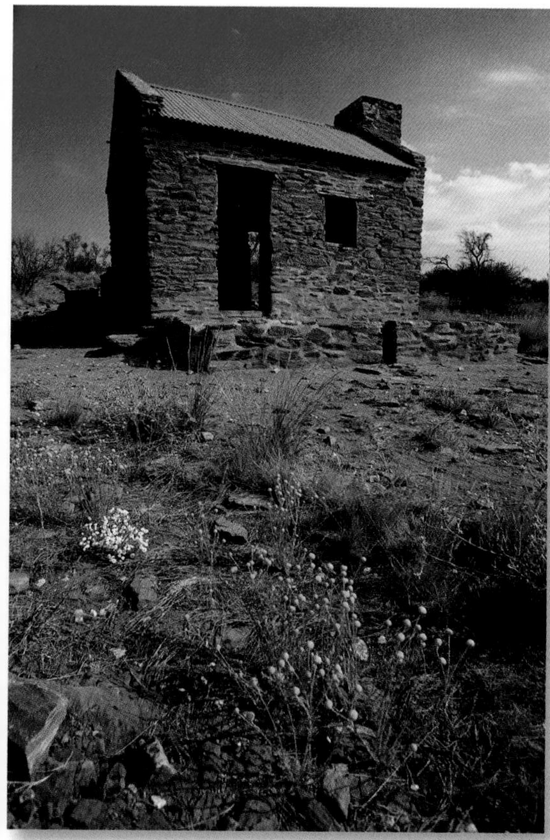

Beyond Arltunga lies one of the Centre's lesser known attractions, Ruby Gap Nature Park. A high-clearance 4WD is needed to negotiate the route, about 40 km along the Atnarpa Road, leading to this rugged but tranquil site on the Hale River. In 1886 the discovery of 'rubies' sparked a rush of diggers, but the rubies proved to be garnets and the prospectors soon moved on. Today, the area makes for a quiet camp (BYO everything, including water) and if you look closely, you may well spot some tiny garnets glittering red in the riverbed.

This park is remote, there are no facilities and the river is subject to flash floods, so be prepared and advise someone of your travel plans.

Those interested in gems and fossicking might well head north from Arltunga to Harts Range, where zircon, quartz and other semi-precious stones keep fossickers occupied.

South to Old Andado and the Simpson Desert

South and east of Alice Springs is cattle-station country – low and scrubby with scattered rocky hills – leading to the Aboriginal community of Santa Teresa, or Ltyentye Purte. Those interested in Indigenous culture might arrange a tour to learn about bush tucker and medicine, and the spiritual connection Aboriginal people make with the land. Ask at the visitor information centre in Alice Springs about tours (see *Contacts*, p. 35). Individual travellers will need to arrange a permit to visit (see *Fact File*, p. 34).

Ironwoods and wattles line the track from Santa Teresa to Allambi Station. Past that the road deteriorates, with sections of deep bulldust, as low, pale sand dunes herald the western fringes of the Simpson Desert.

The Simpson is one of the world's great sand-ridge deserts, covering 170 000 sq km – an area twice the size of Tasmania – with parallel, red sand ridges up to 500 km long and 35 m high. Low, knotty gidgee trees, perennial grasses and saltbush hold the sand together. How barren the dunes are depends on how much rain there has been in preceding seasons. Rains might bring a dense blanket of wildflowers in spring or, as can happen suddenly in the Australian outback, enough rain to flood the countryside.

In an arid, windswept pocket of the Simpson, on a barren stretch of gibber plains, the Mac Clark (Acacia peuce) Conservation Reserve protects stands of rare waddywood trees, or *Acacia peuce*. These trees, which look similar to desert oaks, can grow up to 17 m in height, are known for their incredibly hard timbers and their ability to survive – and thrive – in harsh conditions. Aboriginal people used them to make waddies or clubs, and the wood became part of their mythology. Early settlers cut them down for building, but found them too tough to even drive a nail into.

Above left *Abandoned buildings and mining relics dot the landscape at Arltunga.*

Below *Wildflowers add colour to the red desert sands.*

Right *Molly Clark lived on the edge of the Simpson Desert for more than 50 years.*

Below *Camels played an integral role in opening up the Red Centre for settlement.*

Camel trek

Most travellers cross the Simpson, or at least part of it, in a 4WD, ideally in a convoy or tag-along tour for safety. For the more adventurous, or more leisurely trip, and for a taste of how the early explorers may have covered the countryside, there are camel treks (contact Visitor information, see *Contacts*, p. 35).

Old Andado

Past the reserve, another 38 km of bone-jarring 4WD track leads to Old Andado, where Molly Clark's ramshackle corrugated iron and coolibah-timbered homestead is a unique tourist attraction. Molly, who lived out here for more than 50 years, epitomises the enterprise and indomitable spirit that pioneered the outback. Though no longer living at Old Andado, Molly is something of a legend and a reminder that the outback is not just about the landscape but the people who know and understand this country. Visitors can go inside the homestead or camp. Make sure you book ahead (see *Contacts*, p. 35).

There is no fuel for sale at Old Andado but there is at New Crown Station, 75 km south-west, en route to Finke (Aputula).

Chambers Pillar

From Old Andado it's possible to head further into the Simpson, or to loop back towards Alice Springs. It is 120 km west to Finke, an Aboriginal community of about 200, also known as Aputula, and a former supply stop for the old *Ghan*. You don't need a permit to refuel or buy supplies here.

After Aputula it's a serious 165 km, 4WD trek along the soft sandy bed of the Finke River. This is a long slow drive, so make sure you are prepared. You'll have ample time to look out at the red sand with clumping spinifex, spindly desert oaks and occasional remnants of the old Overseas Telegraph Line or the heavy sleepers of the former *Ghan* railway tracks.

The turn-off to Chambers Pillar is at Maryvale Station, where the roadhouse sells fuel and basic

provisions including food. The nearby Titjikala community supply arts and crafts for sale here.

After the rhythm of flat land and sand hills, sometimes broken by a flat-topped mesa, the shaft of the 50 m Chambers Pillar comes as a surprise. This and other weathered formations, remains of a sandstone mountain range, create yet another of the Red Centre's haunting, slightly surreal landscapes. In 1860 the first European to sight the pillar, John McDouall Stuart, described the pillar as a 'locomotive engine with its funnel', comparing it and other outcrops here to 'old castles in ruins'. To the Arrernte, the pillar is Itirkawara, a mythical gecko ancestor, punished and turned to stone for his misdeeds.

Early explorers used the pillar as a landmark and many carved their names on the distinctive outcrop; visitors these days are asked to respect the history that is already there (a hefty fine applies for those who don't), and to sign a visitor's book instead.

The track into Chambers Pillar Historical Reserve is 4WD only. Camp beneath the whistling desert oaks and wait for sunrise or sunset, the best time to view the pillar, when the golden hues accentuate its red- and yellow-streaked stone.

Rainbow Valley

The sandstone ridge of Rainbow Valley rises above a vast claypan, in an almost treeless valley with pillows of spinifex. The sun's early morning or late-day rays highlight the stone's iron-rich red, ochres, yellow, orange and white. If there has been enough rain, the claypans will fill with water, attracting flocks of nomadic birds. There is a small camping ground, but the reserve is fairly barren and can be searingly hot in summer, so take precautions. Note that there is no drinking water.

Rainbow Valley Conservation Reserve is only accessible off the Stuart Hwy, 77 km south of Alice Springs and then 24 km east along an unsealed road (4WD is recommended) to the park. Visitors will need to take the Hugh River stock route across to the Stuart Hwy and then retrace their steps if they also want to see the rock carvings at Ewaninga.

Ewaninga Rock Carvings

Just south of the old Ewaninga rail siding, within the small Ewaninga Rock Carvings Conservation Reserve, is more evidence of the ancient occupation of the country by Aboriginal people. Circles and animal tracks have been etched into the soft sandstone, in carvings dating back thousands of years. A marked walking trail with interpretive signs provides viewing points. According to Aboriginal custodians, many of the markings are sacred and their meanings cannot be divulged; the custodians advise Arrernte women not to enter the site.

From the reserve, it is 39 km north to Alice Springs along the Old South Road.

Chambers Pillar, a distinctive outcrop south of Alice Springs.

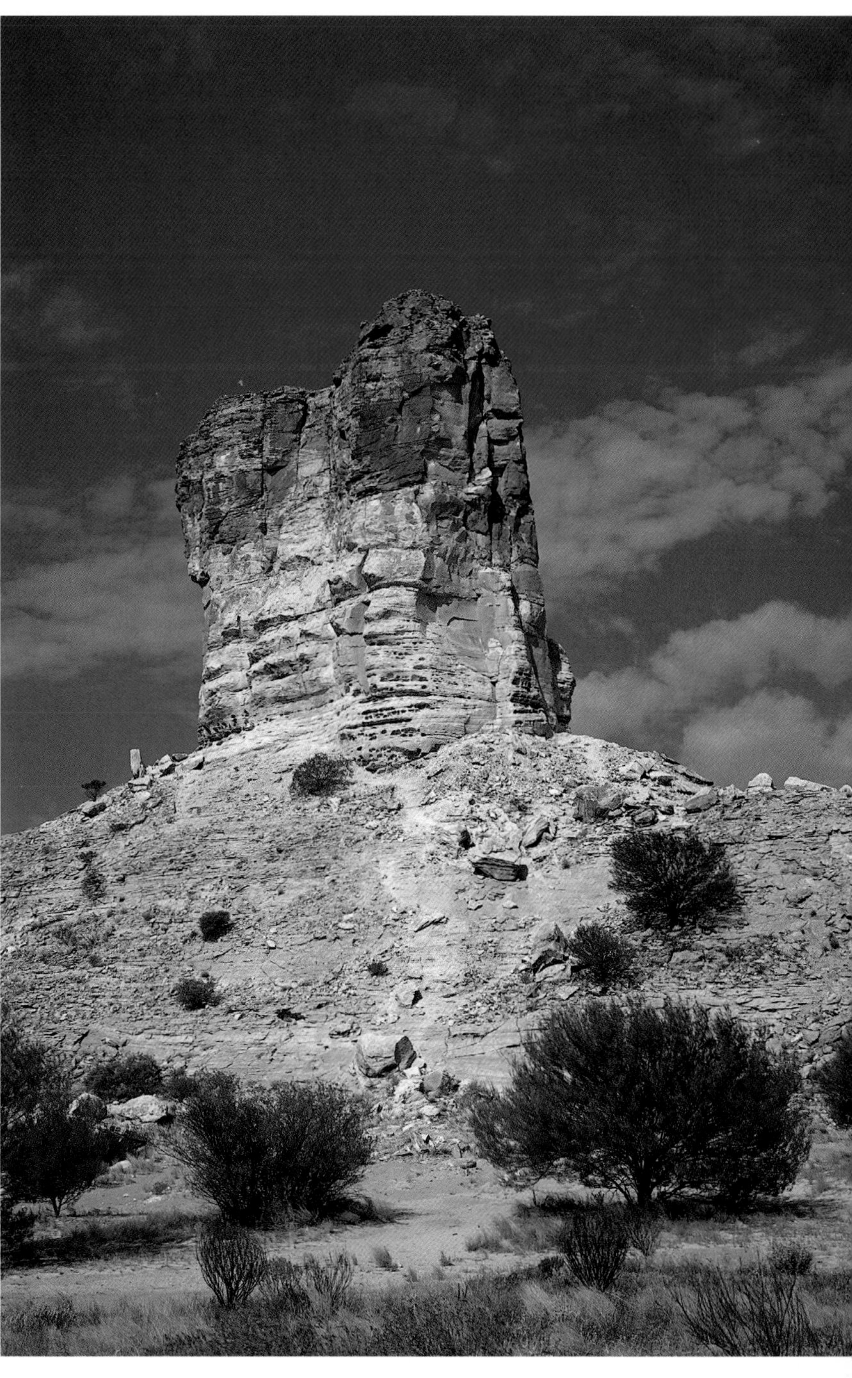

West MacDonnell Ranges and Watarrka

The folded ridges, craggy red rock gorges and cool waterholes of the 'West Macs' and the awe-inspiring Kings Canyon at Watarrka epitomise the timeless grandeur of the Red Centre.

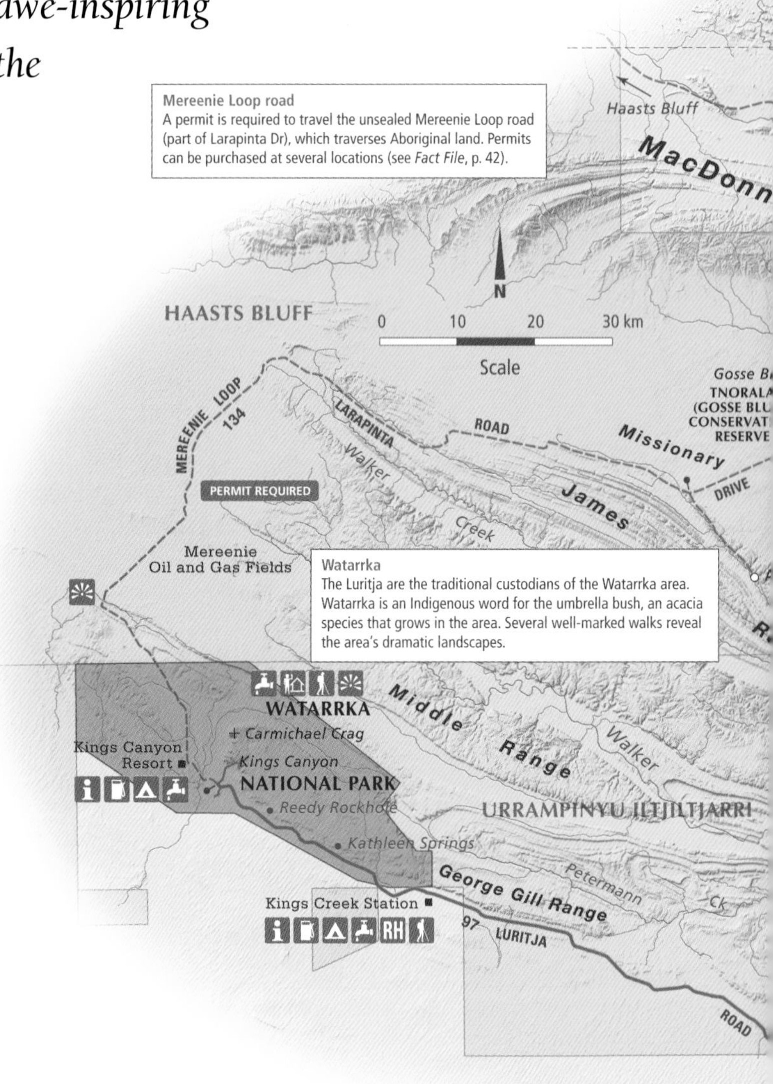
Mereenie Loop road
A permit is required to travel the unsealed Mereenie Loop road (part of Larapinta Dr), which traverses Aboriginal land. Permits can be purchased at several locations (see *Fact File*, p. 42).
Haasts Bluff
HAASTS BLUFF
N
0
10
20
30 km
Scale
MEREENIE LOOP
134
LARAPINTA
ROAD
Missionary
DRIVE
Walker
James
Creek
PERMIT REQUIRED
Mereenie Oil and Gas Fields
Watarrka
The Luritja are the traditional custodians of the Watarrka area. Watarrka is an Indigenous word for the umbrella bush, an acacia species that grows in the area. Several well-marked walks reveal the area's dramatic landscapes.
WATARRKA
Carmichael Crag
Kings Canyon
NATIONAL PARK
Kings Canyon Resort
Reedy Rockhole
Kathleen Springs
Middle Range
Walker
URRAMPINYU ILTJILTJARRI
George Gill Range
Petermann
Ck
Kings Creek Station
RH
97
LURITJA
ROAD

The MacDonnell Ranges stretch 400 km east–west across Central Australia, a rugged spine of low mountains known to the Arrernte people as 'yeperenye', or caterpillar. Flying in over Alice Springs or seen from a distance as the light caresses the ranges' many folds, that description seems apt. The parallel ridges, worn down over 300 million years, rise around 1000 m from the flat plains, rippling off into the distance, cloaked in tough spinifex and hardy drought-tolerant shrubs. Hidden within these ranges are fascinating gorges and cool, shady waterholes.

Much of the area is protected within the 2100 sq km West MacDonnell NP, which extends west from Alice Springs to Mount Zeil, at 1531 m the highest point in the ranges. The park contains around 40 rare and relict plants, a tangible reminder of the ancient times when tropical forests thrived here. It also shelters native wildlife and is a refuge for about 160 bird, 23 mammal, 85 reptile, 5 frog and 10 fish species. To the Western Arrernte people the area is of great cultural significance, a place of Dreaming trails and sacred sites.

South of the ranges is Finke Gorge NP, a surprising find with its hidden treasure of rare and flourishing livistona palms. The often-dry Finke River meanders through the park, its sandy bed and rocky patches used as a track by experienced 4WD enthusiasts. The river, the oldest watercourse in the world, covers about 400 km before petering out in the Simpson Desert. South-west of Finke Gorge, in Watarrka NP, the soaring gorge walls of Kings Canyon are another of the Red Centre's highlights.

Must see, must do

- Watch for wildlife as you cycle to Simpsons Gap
- Have a beer on the shady verandah at the Glen Helen pub
- See a shaft of sunlight illuminate Standley Chasm
- Visit the historic mission buildings at Hermannsburg
- See rare livistona palms at oasis-like Finke Gorge

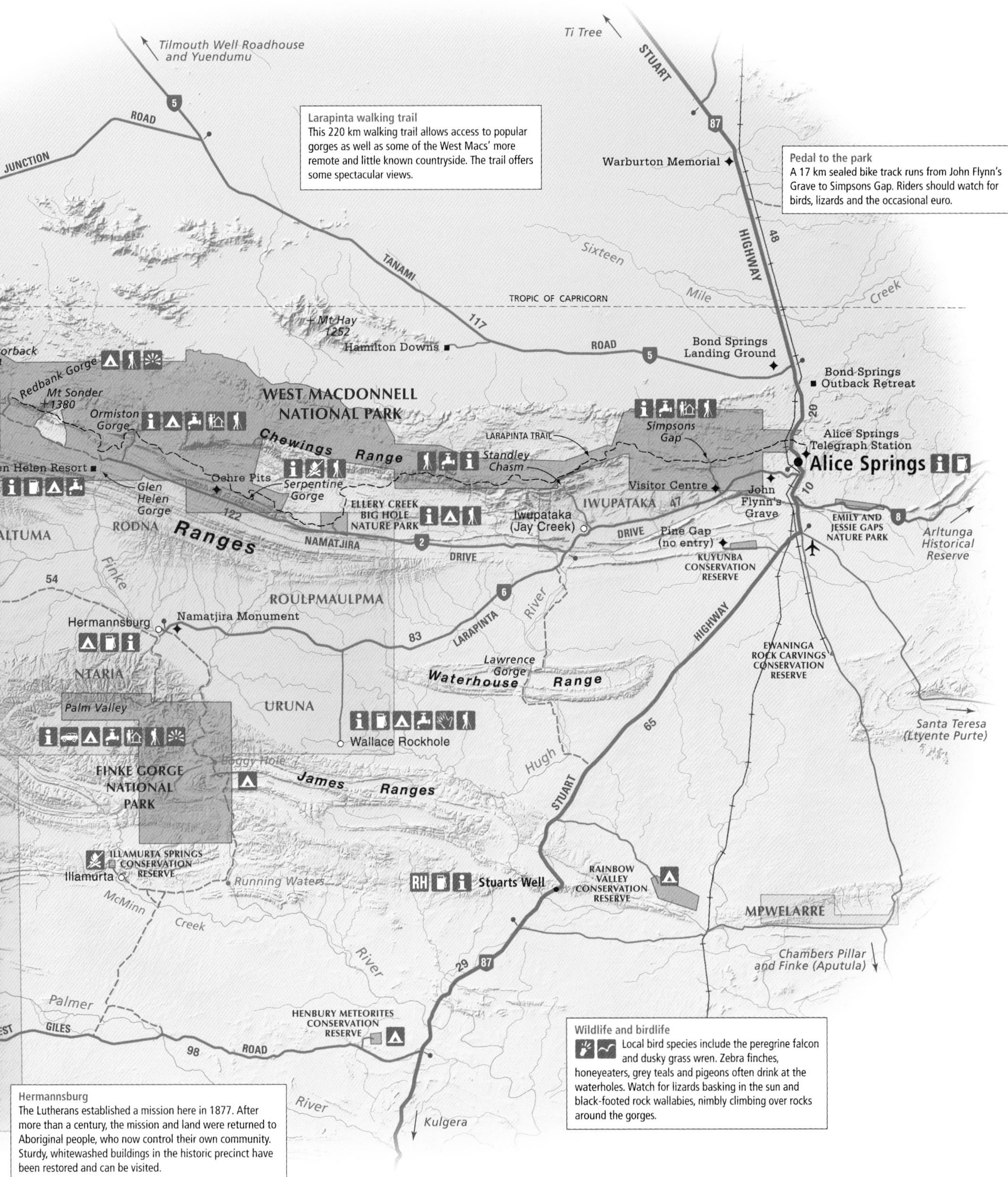

Larapinta walking trail
This 220 km walking trail allows access to popular gorges as well as some of the West Macs' more remote and little known countryside. The trail offers some spectacular views.

Pedal to the park
A 17 km sealed bike track runs from John Flynn's Grave to Simpsons Gap. Riders should watch for birds, lizards and the occasional euro.

Wildlife and birdlife
Local bird species include the peregrine falcon and dusky grass wren. Zebra finches, honeyeaters, grey teals and pigeons often drink at the waterholes. Watch for lizards basking in the sun and black-footed rock wallabies, nimbly climbing over rocks around the gorges.

Hermannsburg
The Lutherans established a mission here in 1877. After more than a century, the mission and land were returned to Aboriginal people, who now control their own community. Sturdy, whitewashed buildings in the historic precinct have been restored and can be visited.

Central Australia ☎ 1800 645 199, (08) 8952 5800; www.centralaustraliantourism.com

Fact File

Permits and regulations

Aboriginal land A permit is needed to travel the unsealed Mereenie Loop road (part of Larapinta Dr). Purchase in person from Visitor Information, Gregory Tce, Alice Springs, open daily: (08) 8952 5800; Glen Helen Resort: (08) 8956 7489; Hermannsburg Petrol Station: (08) 8956 7480; Kings Canyon Resort: (08) 8956 7442.

Parks and reserves

For general information regarding parks in this region conact visitor information in Alice Springs (see *Contacts*, opposite) or Parks and Wildlife Service of the NT (PWSNT) in Alice Springs: (08) 8951 8250.

Finke Gorge NP Camping is available at designated sites only; take in firewood. Most of the park is accessible to 4WD (parts are high-clearance 4WD only); roads may be closed after rainfall. Stay on the route wherever possible to minimise disturbance to the plant life. For further information contact the ranger: (08) 8956 7401.

Illamurta Springs Conservation Reserve No camping; fires prohibited.

Watarrka NP No camping in the park, but accommodation is available at Kings Canyon Resort, or at Kings Creek Station (see *Contacts*, opposite). There are emergency radios in the park; check the information sign in the carpark for locations. For further information contact the ranger: (08) 8956 7460.

West MacDonnell NP Basic and bush camping are available at a number of places; commercial accommodation is available at Glen Helen Gorge. There are no entry fees to the park, but fees for camping and overnight walkers apply. There are ranger stations at Simpsons Gap and Ormiston Gorge. There are ranger-guided tours over the winter months. For information about the park or Larapinta Trail contact visitor information in Alice Springs (see *Contacts*, opposite).

Warnings

Roads Avoid driving at dawn, dusk and at night when wildlife and stock may wander onto roads. The Mereenie Loop road is an unsealed road, usually graded every few months, but conditions can vary due to weather and traffic. Although not strictly a 4WD route, it is not recommended for conventional vehicles, caravans or trailers. A permit is required (see *Aboriginal land*, above).

Swimming Most swimming holes in the gorges are extremely cold. Avoid prolonged exposure, even in summer.

Walking Carry plenty of drinking water. When walking, wear sensible shoes and clothes, a hat, sunblock and insect repellent. Walkers undertaking extended walks are advised to notify local rangers, or register with the PWSNT's Walkers Registration Scheme: 1300 650 730 (see *Travel Tips*, p. 30). If camping in winter, be prepared for extremely cold weather.

See also *On the Road*, p. 246.

West MacDonnell Ranges

Simpsons Gap

From Alice Springs it is an easy trip along Larapinta and Namatjira drives to the impressive gorge at Simpsons Gap. Located only 18 km from town, this part of the West MacDonnell NP can be busy during the peak season. Still, the jagged cleft has a permanent waterhole and some lovely walks, and the nimble, black-footed rock wallabies that make their homes around the boulder-strewn gorge can often be glimpsed. There is a visitors centre; the small campsite is only for those walking the Larapinta Trail (see p. 44).

Opposite *The sun lights the folds of the MacDonnell Ranges.*

Below *River gums shade the water at Serpentine Gorge.*

Cyclists might consider pedalling to Simpsons Gap. From John Flynn's Grave (see *The Royal Flying Doctor Service*, p. 125) 7 km from Alice along Larapinta Drive, a sealed bike track meanders 17 km cross-country to the Gap, past woodland and shady river red gums. Ride early morning or late afternoon for the best chance to see birds or other wildlife (mainly small lizards), and remember to take plenty of water.

Standley Chasm to Ellery Creek Big Hole

Further on, 50 km from town, is the much-photographed Standley Chasm, one of the best known – and busiest – of the gorges. A short walk along the rocky, usually dry bed of Angkerle Creek, past ancient cycads and delicate ferns, leads to the striking chasm, where for about an hour in the middle of the day the sun casts a shaft of light, illuminating the golden red walls. A kiosk, barbecues and picnic tables are near the carpark.

The pragmatically named Ellery Creek Big Hole offers a permanent waterhole (cold at any time of the year, but a popular swimming spot when summer temperatures soar). If you want to swim across to the small sandy 'beach', take an inflatable mattress – for safety, and so that you can float back on the still, deep water, marvelling at the blueness of the sky.

Serpentine Gorge and the Ochre Pits

To reach narrow Serpentine Gorge it's a 45-minute walk across rocky terrain to the deep – and chilly – waterhole. The water attracts birdlife, including

Contacts

Visitor information

Alice Springs
Gregory Tce
(08) 8952 5800 or 1800 645 199
www.centralaustraliantourism.com

Parks and reserves

See *Fact File*, opposite

Resorts, station stays

Glen Helen Resort
(08) 8956 7489
www.glenhelen.com.au

Kings Canyon Resort
(08) 8956 7442
www.kingscanyonresort.com.au

Kings Creek Station
(08) 8956 7474
www.kingscreekstation.com.au

Other

Larapinta Walking Trail
Parks and Wildlife Service of the NT (PWSNT)
South Stuart Hwy
Alice Springs
(08) 8951 8250
www.treklarapinta.com.au

Wallace Rockhole
Larapinta Dr
(08) 8956 7993
(bookings essential)
www.wallacerockholetours.com.au

tiny fairy martins, and insects such as dragonflies skim across the water's surface.

Close by are the Ochre Pits, where a steep ravine and 700 million-year-old cliffs reveal the source of colourful ochres taken over the years by the Arrernte people. These ochres were used as bush medicine, for traditional body painting and ceremonies, for artwork, and to coat hunting implements for good luck.

Back on the main road heading west, the soft contours and subtle mauve shades of Mount Sonder (1380 m) bring to life the vibrant paintings of famed Hermannsburg artist Albert Namatjira.

Ormiston Gorge to Redbank Gorge

At spectacular Ormiston Gorge, 128 km west of Alice, the rugged flanks of the gorge walls, carved over aeons by the Finke River, change colour in the sunlight, and the near-permanent waterhole (icy-cold most of the year) and variety of vegetation support diverse wildlife. There are a number of walks, but highly recommended is the Pound Walk, a 7 km, two to three hour trek. It is moderately hard, with little shade most of the way, so start early, especially in warm weather, and carry plenty of water. The rewards are plentiful – views are spellbinding, you might spot euros and rock wallabies and ample birdlife including zebra finches and rust-coloured spinifex pigeons.

At Glen Helen Gorge an old homestead building with solid mudbrick walls is now a pub, with a surprisingly good restaurant. A wide back verandah looks out onto a towering cliff of crumpled sandstone. At night the cliff is dramatically floodlit, while at dawn the sunlight pans across the time-worn rock, streaking it with colour until it glows. A short walk leads along the usually dry, pebble-lined Finke riverbed, with its beach-white sand and native grasses, to the waterhole. The water is heart-stoppingly cold in midwinter, but refreshing in summer when the heat shimmers off the red rock. Although called a resort, the cabins and campsites at Glen Helen are fairly basic; you can also refuel here.

Beyond Glen Helen, 20 km along an unsealed, often rough road, 5 km to the carpark and then a short hike up a stony creek bed, lies Redbank Gorge.

Black-footed rock wallabies clamber over the rocks in the cool gorges of the MacDonnell Ranges.

Larapinta walking trail

One of the great Australian walks, this 220 km trail makes the superb countryside of the West Macs accessible. The trail extends from Alice Springs to Mount Sonder and can be done in sections – in fact, that's the way most people, locals and visitors alike, undertake the walk. Walkers are rewarded by breathtaking scenery and a close-up view of the rugged landscape, and plant and animal life that make this region unique. There are sections suitable for walkers of various capabilities and fitness levels. The trail, divided into 12 sections, has vehicle access points and water supplies at approximately two-day intervals. Parks and Wildlife and visitor information in Alice Springs have brochures and full details of amenities. Visitors should register before undertaking overnight walks (see *Travel Tips*, p. 30 and *Contacts*, p. 43).

The high, narrow gorge walls block the sun, leaving the waterhole cold all year. You are a little off the beaten track here, and it's usually possible to enjoy the scenery in solitude. The last section of the Larapinta Trail winds from here to the summit of Mount Sonder.

Tnorala (Gosse Bluff)

From the road, Gosse Bluff looks like a small range of hills, but it is actually one of the world's largest comet craters, 5 km across. Around it, in a 20 km circle, the rolling hills were possibly created by the shock waves of the comet's impact 140 million years ago. The hills appear soft and pale green, but are thickly crusted with spiky spinifex. A drive up to Tylers Pass lets you take in an eagle's-eye view. A rough 4WD track leads 8 km into the crater itself, but Tnorala is a registered sacred site, within a conservation reserve, and access is limited. From Tnorala you can take the Mereenie Loop to Watarrka NP (see p. 46) or drive east towards Hermannsburg.

Hermannsburg

One of the Red Centre's best known locations, Hermannsburg was established as a Lutheran community by German missionaries in 1877. After a tough beginning the mission developed, at one time having at least 500 residents, a cattle station, school, tannery and more. In 1982, the Lutherans transferred the mission and land to the traditional Arrernte owners.

The restored, white-washed original buildings, of locally quarried stone, flattened kerosene tins and corrugated iron, stand behind picket fences, shaded by gums and date palms. The buildings, including a small church, are a fascinating glimpse into the determination of the missionaries to create a small pocket of the world they knew, in this remote outpost. Well-known Aboriginal artist Albert Namatjira was born here in 1902 and two of his watercolours are displayed in the gallery, along with work by other local Indigenous artists. An entry fee is payable at the tea room (open daily) and there are artefacts and paintings for sale.

Hermannsburg is on Aboriginal land, but a permit is not required to visit the historic precinct, or the well-stocked supermarket. You can also refuel at the service station and purchase a pass for the Mereenie Loop road, and there is a camping site. Visitors are asked to respect the privacy of the local community.

Wallace Rockhole

Further east, in the James Ranges, is Wallace Rockhole, a small Western Arrernte community. A basic store offers drinks, ice-cream and a few local crafts. Limited tours by a member of the community guide visitors to the waterhole, past the red-rimmed hand stencils on a rock overhang, or on bush tucker walks. A surprisingly lush garden has orange trees and other plants emerging from the vivid red soil. There are campsites, cabins and clean if basic facilities. Make sure to ring ahead to book (see *Contacts*, p. 43).

Finke Gorge National Park

About two hours' drive (138 km) west of Alice Springs, and some 20 km south of Hermannsburg, lies one of the Red Centre's highlights, the wonderful Finke Gorge NP, covering 460 sq km.

A 4WD route in along the rocky river bed of the 250 million-year-old Finke River, believed to be the oldest watercourse in the world, leads to Finke Gorge and Palm Valley. The riverbed is usually no more than a string of waterholes, although there are soaks below the pale sand, and occasionally the river floods dramatically. The Western Arrernte people traditionally used the riverbed as part of a trading route and its waterholes were a rich source of game for hunting.

This is a true oasis – a walking trail winds beside dense clusters of towering red cabbage palms, *Livistona mariae*, up to 300 years old, relicts of the era millions of years ago when this region was tropical rainforest. This is the only place in the world where this particular species of palm grows, with the nearest similar palms around 1000 km north. River red gums, bulrushes and palm-like cycads contrast with the rusty gorge walls. There are over 400 plant species in this precious gorge. In the red rock you can sometimes detect fossilised shells, a reminder that this was once beneath the ocean. A walking trail winds up to a plateau and panoramic views of the natural amphitheatre. One of the Red Centre's prettiest campsites is on the way into Palm Valley, on a curve of Palm Creek.

A challenging 4WD route, about seven or eight hours' drive, runs south from Hermannsburg through the national park, past sandy riverbeds, cycads, elegant river red gums and whispering desert oaks to the peaceful Illamurta Springs Conservation Reserve. (Check with rangers before undertaking this route.) There's camping – and even fishing – at Boggy Hole, a permanent waterhole where explorer Ernest Giles camped in 1872. The track finally comes out onto Ernest Giles Road, where you can turn west for Watarrka NP and Kings Canyon, or east to the Stuart Hwy.

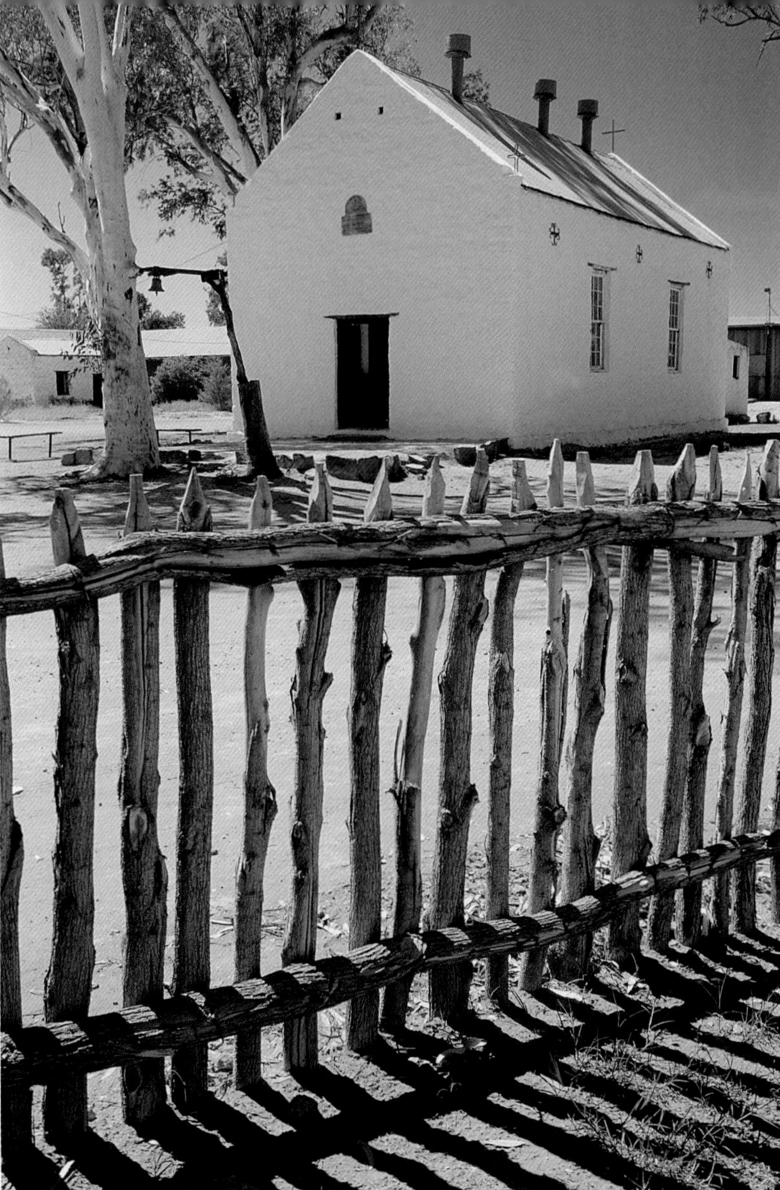

White-washed stone buildings at Hermannsburg recall the German missionaries who first settled there.

If you are headed back to the Stuart (64km) you will see a sign for Henbury Meteorite Craters Conservation Reserve, which is 11 km off the road. The arid country in the reserve is pockmarked with 12 craters, gouged out by fragments from a huge meteor break-up 4700 years ago. There is camping, but conditions here are often windy, dusty and hot.

The Mereenie Loop

The unsealed Mereenie Loop – a wide, red, corrugated road of around 177 km – provides a tantalising glimpse of isolation and wilderness within easy reach of Alice Springs. The Loop is part of Larapinta Drive. Depending on how recently it's been graded – usually every three months but there can be wash-outs after heavy weather – it can

Right *Hidden within Finke Gorge is a rare stand of towering red palms.*

Below *A majestic wedge-tailed eagle nesting.*

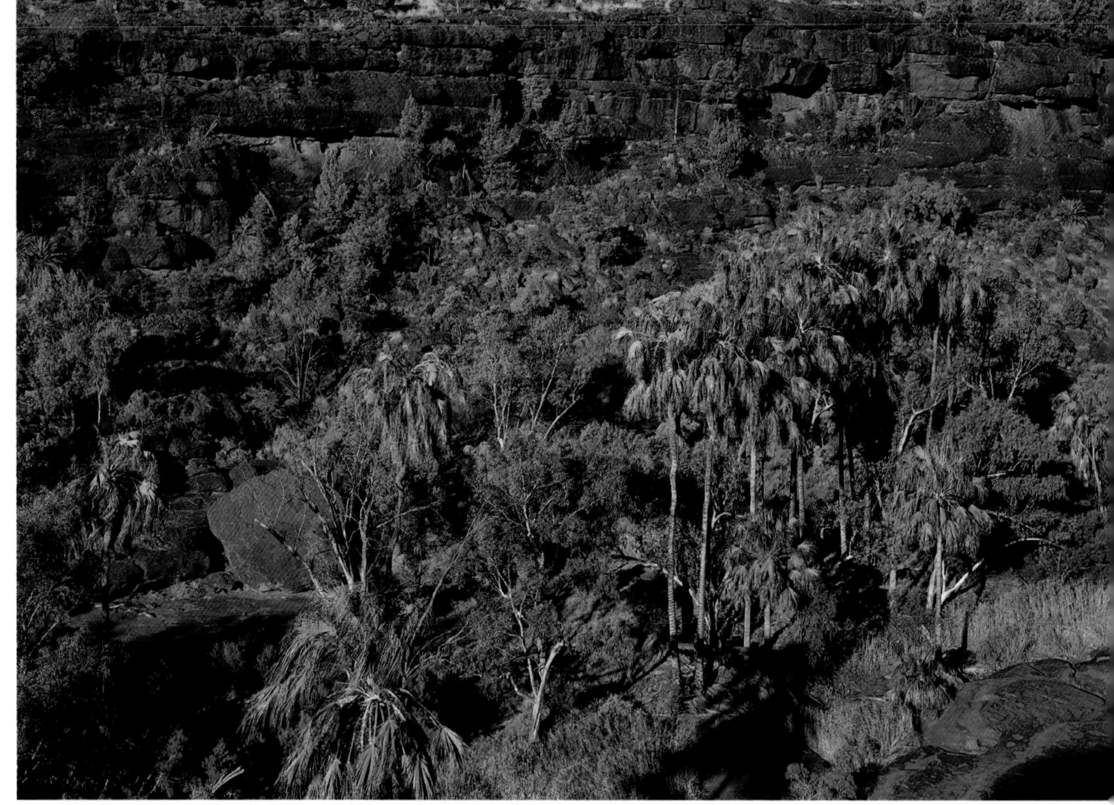

Wedge-tailed eagle – magnificent hunter

Soaring effortlessly on the thermals, the wedge-tailed eagle (*Aquila audax*) appears majestic. Australia's largest bird of prey, the eagle is brilliantly equipped for hunting. It has a wingspan of 2 m, it can swoop at up to 95 km an hour, its eyesight is three times as acute as a human's in daylight, and its claws can clamp with formidable force. Its hooded beak and lethal talons can easily rip shreds from a carcass. 'Wedgies', easily recognisable by their distinctive wedge-shaped tail, usually hunt early in the morning or late afternoon, and can often be seen beside the highway, feasting on road kill. After being ruthlessly culled in the 1960s, the birds are now a protected species.

be a *very* bumpy trip. But it is a memorable drive: desert oak forests, twisted mulgas and the rippling, rich red sand stretch to the blue horizon. Brumbies, feral camels, goats and donkeys run wild, grazing on the tough vegetation.

The Mereenie Loop allows you to visit the gorges along the West Macs, Tnorala (Gosse Bluff) and Watarrka, then travel south to Uluṟu and Kata Tjuṯa, before heading back to Alice Springs via the Stuart Hwy, without retracing your steps. A 4WD is recommended for the Mereenie Loop. The route is becoming popular, however, and within a few years it will be a sealed road all the way. The Loop passes through Aboriginal land and you must buy a permit (see *Fact File*, p. 42).

Watarrka National Park

Tucked away in the George Gill Range, 302 km by road south-west of Alice Springs via the Stuart Hwy and Ernest Giles Road, is Watarrka (formerly Kings Canyon) NP. A longer but more fascinating route to the park is via the West MacDonnells, Hermannsburg and the red-dirt Mereenie Loop road (see above).

The traditional custodians of this region are the Luritja people. Much of the surrounding country has been returned to the Luritja, who are involved in park management. Several Indigenous communities live within the park boundaries.

Unlike Uluṟu and Kata Tjuṯa, Watarrka does not reveal its drama so easily. The extraordinary gorge of Kings Canyon has soaring walls, sheltered valleys and pockets of lush vegetation, but to really experience the gorge, to appreciate its scale and many facets, you need to walk in. There are several options. The Kings Canyon Walk (often called the rim walk), a 6 km loop, takes three to four hours. It starts with 500 steep steps, and there are more steps on the way, but it is an exceptional trail with breathtaking views. Splendid red river gums and ghost gums, with their stark white trunks stand silhouetted against russet-coloured rock and the sky glows blue. The sandstone chasm, where the sheer wall drops more than 270 m to the canyon floor, is slashed with colour.

Ripples in the red stone at your feet recall the shallow sea that once washed over this entire area millions of years ago. Trilobites, fossilised crustaceans, are embedded in the sandy rock. A thin red film of dust coats the white sandstone. The scrubby vegetation includes native mint bushes, traditionally used by Aboriginal people as a bush medicine. If you crush the leaves you can inhale the subtle mint fragrance they give off.

This rim walk leads to the Garden of Eden, a peaceful retreat with cool waterholes and ancient cycads. Further on, the Lost City presents an imposing series of weathered and eroded beehive-like domes.

The Kathleen Springs Walk (around 2.6 km, 1.5 hours return) takes you into a lovely spring-fed waterhole. The Kings Creek Walk (2.6 km, one-hour return) leads to a lookout. Serious walkers might consider the 22 km two-day Giles Track, which traverses the top of the range from Kathleen Springs to Kings Canyon, with entry/exit points at Reedy Creek and Lilla. The Parks and Wildlife Service have detailed walking notes (see *Travel Tips*, p. 30 for contact information).

More than 600 plant species have been recorded in the park, most of them growing in sheltered niches. The only wildlife you will usually see are tiny lizards and occasionally birds, especially in the early morning or at dusk.

Visitors can stay at Kings Canyon Resort or at Kings Creek Station (see *Contacts*, p. 43). There is a ranger's workshop and residence 1 km from the turn-off to the canyon.

Kings Canyon Resort

Kings Canyon Resort, 7 km from the gorge, has fuel supplies, a restaurant, cafes, camping, dormitories and luxury cabins (all relatively expensive, but it is a truly unique location). A range of activities and tours can be arranged from here.

Kings Creek Station

Kings Creek Station, 35 km from the park and part of a working cattle and camel station, is an alternative for an overnight stay. There are camping facilities, a basic general store and fuel supplies, swimming pool and the opportunity to enjoy a helicopter flight (the flight over the canyon is spectacular), ride a camel, a quad bike, or even watch a whip-cracking demonstration. You can also arrange tours to Uluru–Kata Tjuta NP and other activities.

Following page *Mount Conner is an imposing outcrop, on Curtin Springs Station, east of Uluru.*

Below *Sheer rock wall at Watarrka NP.*

Uluru and Kata Tjuta

If the Red Centre is the heart of Australia, then perhaps the vast monolith of Uluru and the many domes of Kata Tjuta are its soul. Nothing can prepare you for the sight of these magnificent landmarks in the desert country.

Lake Amadeus
The largest of Central Australia's salt lakes, stretchin for over 120 km, this dry lake proved a formidable barrier to early explorers. It was named after King Amadeus of Spain, a noted patron of science.

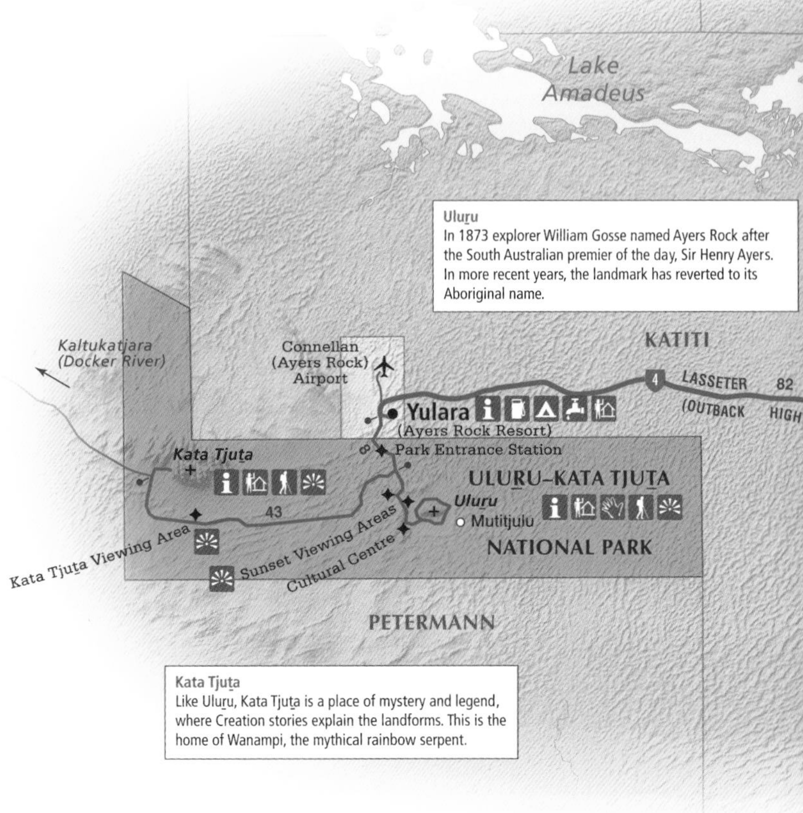

Uluru
In 1873 explorer William Gosse named Ayers Rock after the South Australian premier of the day, Sir Henry Ayers. In more recent years, the landmark has reverted to its Aboriginal name.

Kata Tjuta
Like Uluru, Kata Tjuta is a place of mystery and legend, where Creation stories explain the landforms. This is the home of Wanampi, the mythical rainbow serpent.

The enormous red rock of Uluru (Ayers Rock) and the multiple domes of Kata Tjuta (the Olgas) are powerful spiritual places to the Anangu, who have lived in Central Australia for more than 30 000 years. But Europeans are also drawn to these rare geological outcrops – intrigued by the myths and legends surrounding them, fascinated by their powerful presence, and awed by their majestic scale and intense colours.

Many visitors arrive by road, often via Alice Springs, before visiting these famous sights, but it is possible to fly directly to Connellan airport, which is just 4 km from the Ayers Rock Resort.

A multitude of tour options enable visitors to experience the area in different ways: from luxury resort accommodation to throwing your swag down next to a campfire, and from whistle-stop trips to more leisurely excursions where you have time to savour this unique World Heritage-listed area.

Uluru–Kata Tjuta NP lies some 460 km by road – or about four-and-a-half to five hours' drive – south-west of Alice Springs. On the trip, there are a few dusty but welcome roadside stops, where you can refuel, enjoy a drink, ride a camel or just stretch your legs. Arriving by road does give you the chance to experience the vastness of the landscape surrounding these outback icons.

Join one of the tours organised by the traditional custodians to learn about survival skills in the desert and the surprisingly rich variety of flora and fauna that the arid zone supports. Many creatures, however, only emerge at night. If you watch closely, though, you may see lizards scurrying for cover, or birds flocking to a waterhole.

Must see, must do

- Tour historic Curtin Springs Station and see Mount Conner up close
- Experience Uluru coming to life in the dawn light
- Take a bush tucker tour with an Anangu guide at Uluru
- Walk in Kata Tjuta's majestic Valley of the Winds
- Enjoy some star-gazing in the desert's star-filled skies

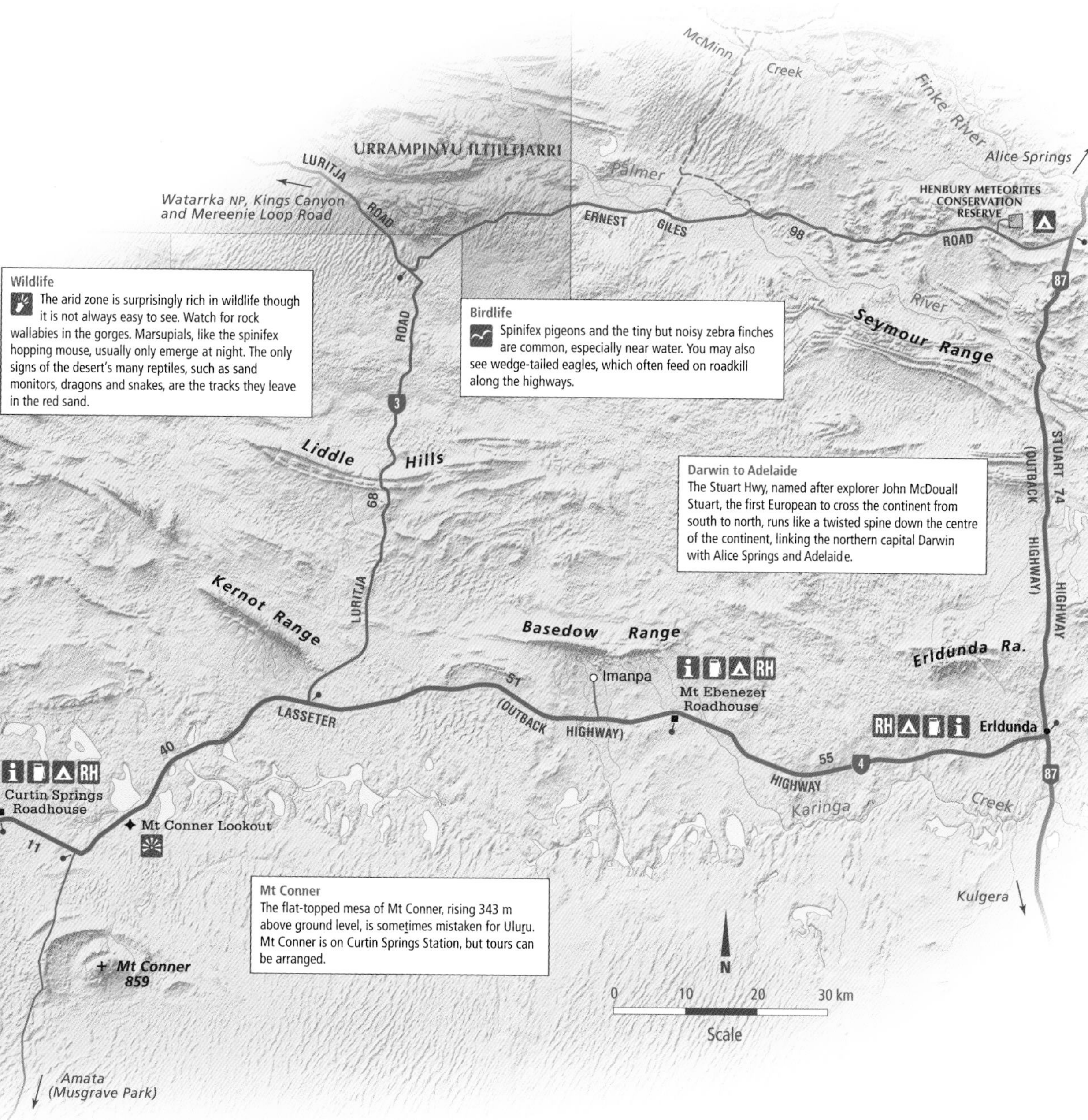

Wildlife

The arid zone is surprisingly rich in wildlife though it is not always easy to see. Watch for rock wallabies in the gorges. Marsupials, like the spinifex hopping mouse, usually only emerge at night. The only signs of the desert's many reptiles, such as sand monitors, dragons and snakes, are the tracks they leave in the red sand.

Birdlife

Spinifex pigeons and the tiny but noisy zebra finches are common, especially near water. You may also see wedge-tailed eagles, which often feed on roadkill along the highways.

Darwin to Adelaide

The Stuart Hwy, named after explorer John McDouall Stuart, the first European to cross the continent from south to north, runs like a twisted spine down the centre of the continent, linking the northern capital Darwin with Alice Springs and Adelaide.

Mt Conner

The flat-topped mesa of Mt Conner, rising 343 m above ground level, is sometimes mistaken for Uluṟu. Mt Conner is on Curtin Springs Station, but tours can be arranged.

Uluṟu–Kata Tjuṯa NP ☎(08) 8956 1128; www.environment.gov.au/parks/uluru

Fact File

Permits and regulations

Aboriginal land If planning to travel to or from the region via the Mereenie Loop road, a permit is needed because the road crosses Aboriginal land. Purchase permits in person from Visitor Information, Gregory Tce, Alice Springs, open daily: (08) 8952 5800; Glen Helen Resort: (08) 8956 7489; Hermannsburg Petrol Station: (08) 8956 7480; Kings Canyon Resort: (08) 8956 7442.

Parks and reserves

Uluru–Kata Tjuta NP The park is administered by the Anangu and Parks Australia. Entry fees are charged, with tickets valid for three consecutive days. One quarter of the fee goes to the Anangu to help maintain their community. The park is open from half an hour before sunrise to sunset daily; tickets are available at the park entrance. There is no ranger station at Kata Tjuta; arrange guided tours at Ayers Rock Resort or Uluru. For further information contact www.environment.gov.au/parks/uluru Visitors cannot stay in the park, but accommodation of various standards, from camping to five-star, is available at Ayers Rock Resort at Yulara (20 km by road from Uluru and 53 km by road from Kata Tjuta). Ayers Rock Resort: (08) 8957 7888; www.ayersrockresort.com.au Cultural Centre Information Desk: (08) 8956 1128; park administration (08) 8956 1100.

Climbing Uluru The Anangu prefer that visitors respect the cultural significance of Uluru and do not climb it. Those who choose to climb should be aware it is a steep, strenuous climb requiring a high degree of fitness. (See *To climb or not*, p. 54.)

Tours

Tours to Uluru–Kata Tjuta NP and surrounds can be arranged in and from Alice Springs as well as at Ayers Rock Resort (see *Contacts*, opposite).

Warnings

Roads Avoid driving at dawn, dusk and at night when wildlife and stock may wander onto roads. The Mereenie Loop is an unsealed road, usually graded every few months, but conditions can vary due to weather and traffic. Although not strictly a 4WD route, it is not recommended for conventional vehicles, caravans and trailers. A permit is required (see *Aboriginal land*, above).

Walking Carry plenty of drinking water. When walking, wear sensible shoes and clothes, a hat, sunblock and insect repellent. If camping in winter, be prepared for extremely cold weather.

See also *On the Road*, p. 246.

Driving south from Alice Springs

Once you leave Alice Springs on the Stuart Hwy, there are only two turns to reach Uluru – one at Erldunda onto the Lasseter Hwy, and one leading into the national park. It's a long, straight drive.

About 50 km west of Erldunda, the Aboriginal-owned Mount Ebenezer Roadhouse has a small gallery with some interesting and reasonably priced artwork.

From the Lasseter Hwy, one of the Red Centre's remarkable but less well-known landforms shimmers on the horizon to the south. Mount Conner, a flat-topped, horseshoe-shaped outcrop or 'mesa' rising 343 m above the surrounding countryside, is surprisingly impressive: on first sighting many people mistake it for Uluru. In fact, this 700 million-year-old tor is geologically more ancient than its landmark cousins Uluru and Kata Tjuta and, although almost exactly the same height is three times the size of Uluru. Its sheer sandstone walls are sculpted by the wind and weather, but the capping of hard silica prevents it from eroding away as quickly as the other tors. It rises abruptly, ringed by tough mulga and spinifex, which are home to euros, dingoes and rabbits.

Mount Conner is on private property, the 4162 sq km working cattle station of Curtin Springs, run by three generations of the Severin family. The station's roadhouse offers fuel and supplies, meals, camel rides, basic accommodation and camping. There is a lookout off the highway, but Mount Conner is about 20 km off the road. If you want to have a better look, book ahead for a half day or full day tour of the station itself, including a visit to Mount Conner, either in a vehicle or as a 4WD tag-along tour. Take your camera – the sunsets are spectacular.

Past the roadhouse, it is another 57 km to the entrance to Uluru–Kata Tjuta NP, 1325 sq km of arid country, dominated by two of the country's most imposing geological forms.

Opposite top *The thorny devil is small but fearsome.*

Opposite below *Uluru looms large in the desert landscape.*

Right *Plump spinifex pigeons can often be seen foraging for food.*

Uluru

Uluru, or Ayers Rock as it was known for many years, looms 348 m above the desert floor. From a distance the vast, dome-like shape seems solid and impenetrable; up close, the surface is grooved and indented, worn down over time by water and wind. Subtly, endlessly, it changes colour as the light falls on it. The Rock, as most locals call it, is composed of a coarse-grained sandstone known as arkose, and as the iron in the sandstone oxidises it creates a rusty red surface.

The first European to visit the rock, explorer William Gosse in 1837, described it as 'an immense pebble rising abruptly from the plain'. Although Uluṟu covers 3.3 sq km, and measures about 9.4 km around its base, what we see is but the tip of the iceberg – geologists believe the rock, the 600 million-year-old peak of a buried mountain range, extends several kilometres below ground.

A mosaic of spinifex, native grasses, mulga, desert oaks, witchetty bushes and red sand surround the monolith. The ground is surprisingly well covered – not lush, but in most seasons cloaked in a mantle of sage green. After a good wet season, a rush of wildflowers creates an incongruous carpet of colour. At times, heavy clouds shroud the Rock; after rain, the run-off glitters silver as it sweeps down the sides; the surface glimmers golden as the dawn's rays strike it, or fades to a monotone in the harsh midday sun. Try to be at the Rock at dawn or at sunset; you may find yourself part of a crowd at the restricted viewing areas – and a large crowd at that – but it is worth the effort and the wait.

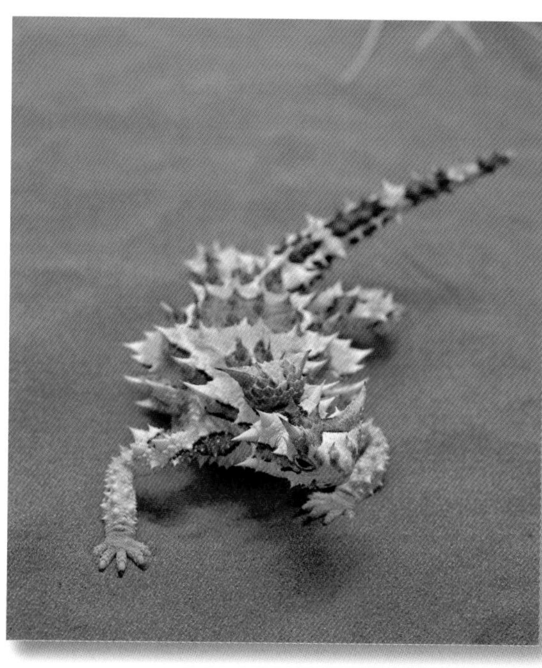

Wildlife-watching

The national park, despite its dry, seemingly hostile environment, is home to many animal species. Reptiles flourish, there are small marsupials and

Contacts

Visitor information

Alice Springs
Gregory Tce
08) 8952 5800 or 1800 645 199
www.centralaustralian tourism.com

Parks and reserves

See *Fact File*, opposite

Resorts, station stays

Ayers Rock Resort
(08) 8957 7888
www.ayersrockresort.com.au

Curtin Springs Station
Tours of Mount Conner and station
(08) 8956 2906
www.curtinsprings.com

Activities

Anangu Tours
Book at Ayers Rock Resort (see above) or direct, (08) 8950 3030
www.ananguwaai.com.au

Witchetty grubs, a traditional bush tucker, are usually found in the roots of the acacia tree.

Desert bush tucker

The countryside around Uluru and Kata Tjuta is classified as desert. It is a harsh and dry environment, but Aboriginal people have lived here for thousands of years. While the men traditionally hunted for kangaroos, wallabies and goannas, women and children gathered native plants as a major food source. Around 140 plant species were considered food by desert people.

Favourite bush fruits included the wild orange vine (*Capparis mitchellii*), which has a large yellow-green berry with a sweetish yellow pulp. It has a lovely creamy white flower, which blooms at night then dies. Bush bananas (*Marsdenia australis*) have a pale green pod, which splits open to reveal silky white hairs with tiny black seeds. Bush bananas were eaten raw when young or sometimes cooked in hot ashes. Native rock figs (*Ficus platypoda*) are a typical fruit in this arid country. The fig bush is often found clinging to a rock face or in sheltered gorges, its roots stretching towards water. The small, heavily seeded fruits turn reddish-brown as they mature and have a slightly tart flavour. Golden-flowering honey grevillea (*Grevillea juncifolia*) provided a special sweet treat. The 'honey', or nectar, was sucked direct from the orange–yellow flowers, or dunked in water to make a sweet drink.

Seeds were also an important part of the desert bush tucker diet. Seeds from acacia trees (*Acacia* spp.) and various grasses were collected, and often roasted then ground into a powder or paste, made into small cakes and baked in hot ashes.

One of the best known of all bush tuckers is the witchetty grub (*Cossidae* sp.). The pale, soft grub is the larva of a large moth; it is usually found in the roots of an acacia (*Acacia kempeana*), more widely known as a witchetty bush. The grubs were eaten raw or lightly roasted, and are still a popular bush food if Aboriginal people go on a bush picnic.

Join an Aboriginal tour to learn more about bush food; remember many bush plants are highly toxic.

To climb or not

The Anangu request that people respect the immense cultural significance of Uluru and do not climb the Rock. Safety is also a concern, as more than 30 people have died on the climb in the last 20 years. Those who choose to make the ascent should be aware that it is a steep, strenuous climb, at a sharp incline; it is 1.6 km return and takes around two hours. It is closed if conditions are unsuitable (for example, predicted high temperatures, high winds and rain). In summer months, anyone attempting the climb should do so as early in the day as possible. Always take sufficient drinking water.

rodents as well as 22 species of native mammal, including dingoes and red kangaroos. Many of these creatures are nocturnal and shy, so even keen wildlife-watchers might only observe animal tracks in the vivid red sand. There are also many bird species – more than 150 species have been recorded – with dawn and dusk the best time to spot them.

Exploring Uluru

The full (but easy) Base Walk, 9.4 km plus short detours into caves and waterholes, enables visitors to experience at close hand the Rock's swellings and curves, the flaking rust-red surface and the mysterious indentations and black holes that loom high along the side. Around the caves and waterholes it is cool and shady and tiny fairy martins dart into their diminutive nests.

The Mutitjulu Walk (1 km return) winds past rock-art sites and then to the peaceful Mutitjulu waterhole (no swimming permitted). The Mala Walk (2 km return), taking in art sites on the north-west side, leads to Kantju Gorge. The Liru Walk (2 km one way) links the Cultural Centre, the Mala Walk and the base of the climbing point. A free, ranger-guided Mala Walk leaves daily (at 8 am from October to April; 10 am from May to September), from the Mala Walk carpark, on the north-west side of Uluru.

Anangu tours and the Cultural Centre

The traditional custodians, the Anangu, run tours offering an Indigenous perspective of this unique land. Guides from the Mutitjula community explain the Creation stories of Uluru, which form the basis of Anangu law. Various tours explore the nearby bush, discuss how tools and implements were traditionally made and used, and explain some of the desert bush tuckers and survival skills. (See *Contacts*, p. 53.)

Located about 1 km from Uluru, the Cultural Centre provides an excellent introduction to the area's landscape, ecology, culture and history. There is a gallery, craft shop and cafe.

Ayers Rock Resort

Visitors cannot stay in the national park, but Ayers Rock Resort, 20 km from Uluru, offers accommodation, from camping to a five-star hotel. The resort – really a small service village – offers a well-stocked supermarket, restaurants, cafes, shops, post office, service station, police station and more. At the information centre numerous tours are offered, om Aboriginal-guided cultural walks and candlelight inners in the desert to helicopter flights, camel trails, ot-air balloons and even Harley Davidson tours. The utback's dense canopy of stars is the perfect place or star-gazing and the Ayers Rock Observatory has ightly sessions. (See *Contacts*, p. 53.)

Nearby, but not open to the public, is the Iutitjulu Aboriginal community – travellers are sked to respect their privacy.

Kata Tjuta

orty-eight km west of Uluru, still within the ational park, is the unique outcrop of Kata Tjuta, r 'many heads', to many people more beautiful nd intriguing than Uluru. Explorer Ernest Giles, e first European to record the landform, in 872, noted: 'The appearance of this mountain is arvellous in the extreme, and baffles accurate escription… it displayed to our astonished eyes ounded minarets, giant cupolas, and monstrous omes'. Giles named the highest point Mount Olga, ter the Queen of Württemberg, and for many years e 36 domes were referred to as the Olgas.

The strangely swollen red rock domes, reaching 46 m, are intersected by canyons and passages. The ock, a conglomerate of granite and basalt, traps the eat of the day and reflects the many warm hues of e setting sun.

There are two main walks. The 7.4 km alley of the Winds walk, winding through the agnificent outcrops to a wonderful lookout, is reasonably demanding, and can take about two to three hours return. Start early in the day in summer, as it can be searingly hot. If the forecast is for 36°C or higher, the walk is closed from the Karu Lookout. The walk to Olga Gorge (Tatintjawiya), around 2.6 km in length and taking an hour, follows the creek to the gorge.

Sunset can be just as spectacular as at Uluru, with brilliant colours glowing off the red domes. There is a viewing area on the south side, on the road between Yulara and Kata Tjuta. Walk to the dunes for wonderful views – Kata Tjuta looming large and the bulky outline of Uluru on the distant horizon. The return walk from the carpark to the viewing area takes about half an hour.

The Tjukurpa

Anangu ('we people') is the collective name for Aboriginal people of this area. The Anangu are made up of several main groups, including the Pitjantatjatjara and the Ankuntjatjara. Central to their way of life, their law and their beliefs is the Tjukurpa, the Creation stories that explain their ancestral beginnings and the features of the land. To them Uluru is sacred – every scar, every cleft and ridge is a mark left by ancient ancestors during the Dreamtime. Visitors are requested not to enter or photograph certain sacred sites, which are clearly signposted.

The giant domes of Kata Tjuta glow red in the desert sun.

The Tanami and Tennant Creek

The Tanami Track heads north-west from Alice Springs, a ragged red-dirt road that cuts 1000 kilometres through arid spinifex country to the Kimberley. Tennant Creek, the site of Australia's last gold rush, is 500 kilometres due north of Alice along the Stuart Highway.

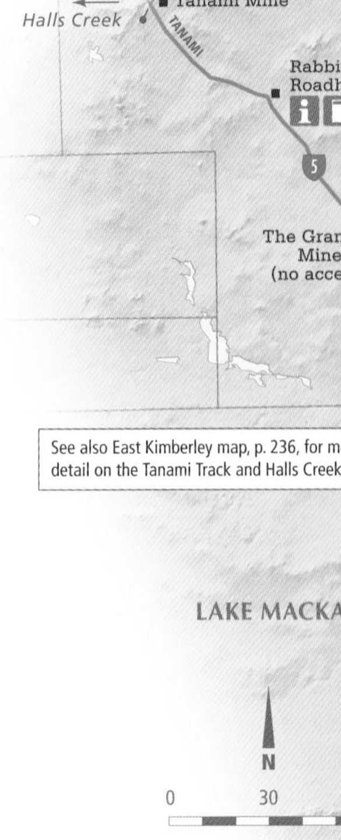
Halls Creek
Tanami Mine
TANAMI
Rabbit
Roadh
5
The Gran
Mine
(no acce
See also East Kimberley map, p. 236, for mo
detail on the Tanami Track and Halls Creek.
LAKE MACKA
N
0
30
Scale
Newhaven Reserve
This 262 sq km reserve, managed by Birds Australia an
Aboriginal custodians, is home to three threatened bird
species and three threatened mammal species. Campin
is available (BYO everything).

The Tanami Track (officially the Tanami Road) is the outback idea of a 'shortcut' – a 1000 km, 4WD red-dirt road across some of Australia's most arid country, the Tanami Desert, linking Alice Springs and the remote Kimberley region in WA. It is an awesome introduction to the immensity of the outback.

The once notorious stock route is becoming increasingly popular for those wanting to get off the beaten track – and so is becoming a little less off the beaten track. It is best driven in a 4WD, though in recent years it has been upgraded. The road is regularly maintained as it is used as a service route for one of Australia's largest gold-producing mines, the Granites. Don't underestimate the trip, however. It is still isolated, fuel and supply outlets are long distances apart and not open at all hours, or even on all days. The road can become heavily corrugated, especially once you reach the WA section, and the causeway at Sturt Creek can flood during the Top End's wet season (usually November to April). It is best to avoid doing this trip in the summer, when it is scorching hot.

For those heading north from Alice, the Stuart Hwy is a first-grade, all-sealed road, but it still wends its way through comparatively remote countryside. Tennant Creek is the largest town between Alice and Darwin, a reasonable-sized town (for these parts) with an interesting history.

Must see, must do

- Marvel at the Tanami's spinifex plains dotted with termite mounds
- Visit the remote Newhaven Reserve, a refuge for birdlife
- Photograph the precariously balanced Devils Marbles rock formations
- Pan for gold at Tennant Creek, site of the country's last gold rush
- Inspect the fortified 1872 telegraph station at the small town of Barrow Creek

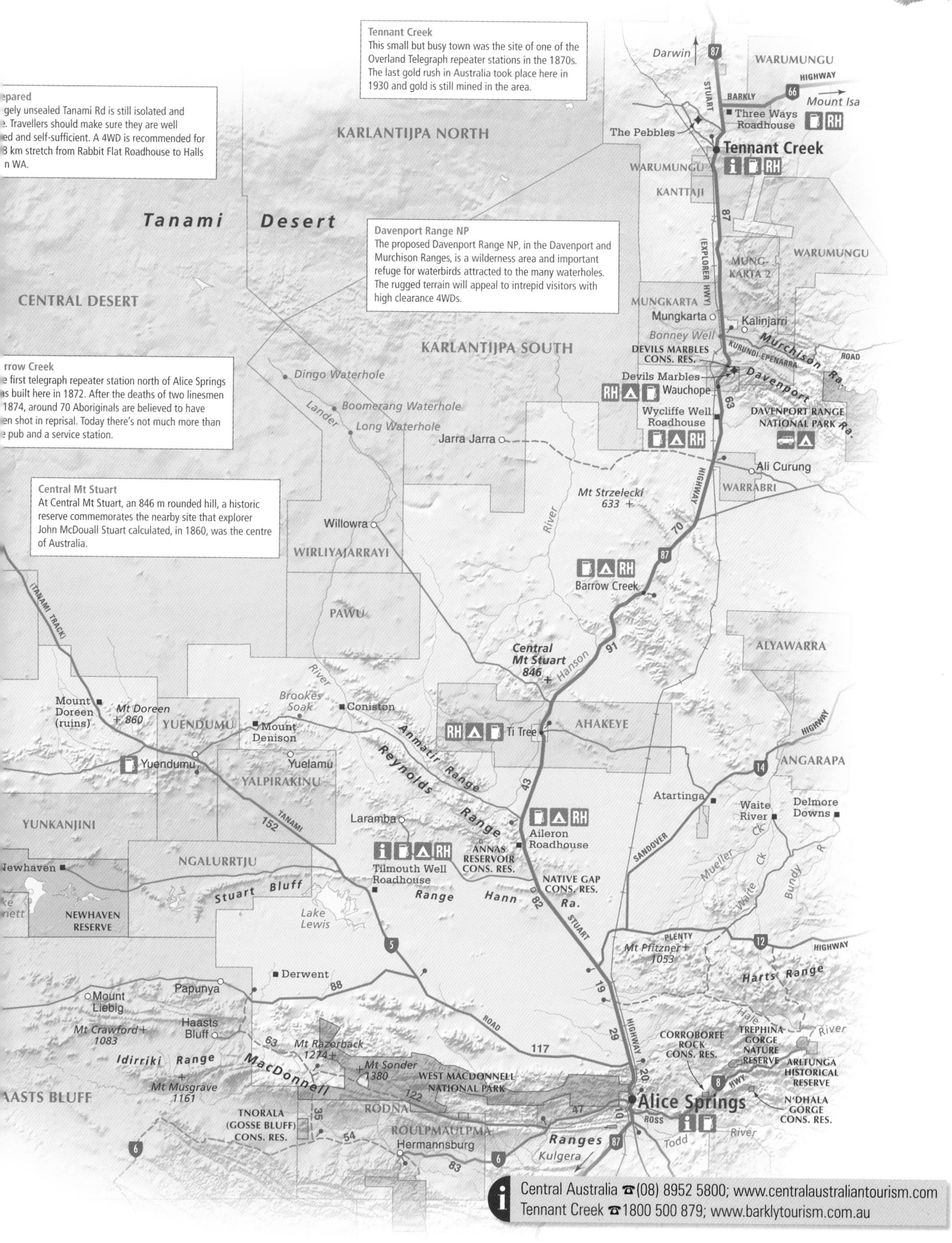

Central Australia ☎(08) 8952 5800; www.centralaustraliantourism.com
Tennant Creek ☎1800 500 879; www.barklytourism.com.au

Fact File

Top events
April *Tennant Creek Rodeo*
May *Tennant Creek Cup*
June *ABC Brunette Downs Races–Rodeo Campdraft*
Aug *Yuendumu Festival*
Sept *Desert Harmony Festival (Tennant Creek)*

Permits and regulations
Aboriginal land Most of the Tanami trip is across Aboriginal land. Note that travellers should not venture more than 50 m off the main road without a permit (see Red Centre *Travel Tips*, p. 30). Access is available to Yuendumu, Yuelumu and Bililluna for fuel and supplies (see also *Warnings* below). Yuendumu is a 'dry' community – no alcohol is permitted. There is no access to Balgo Community without a permit. Visitors are asked to respect the privacy of the communities.

Parks and reserves
For general information regarding parks and reserves in the area contact Parks and Wildlife Service of the NT (PWSNT), Alice Springs: (08) 8951 8250; Tennant Creek: (08) 8962 4599.

Davenport NP 4WD vehicle is essential (high clearance in some areas) and rocky escarpments create challenging driving conditions; stay on the tracks. There are two campsites. For general information contact PWSNT, Tennant Creek: (08) 8962 4599.

Newhaven Reserve This reserve is owned by Birds Australia. It is usually accessible by 2WD vehicle, but road conditions can deteriorate quickly after rain. Check at Tilmouth Well Roadhouse (see *Contacts*, opposite) or phone Newhaven before entering the reserve. BYO everything. Drinking water is available but additional supplies are recommended. Take fuel stove; no fires permitted. Visitors must register at the information shelter on arrival and departure; a small fee is payable for entry and camping. Contact Newhaven ranger: (08) 8964 6000.

Warnings
Fuel and supplies On the Tanami, fuel is available at Tilmouth Well Roadhouse. Yuendumu Store (Aboriginal community, enter for fuel or supplies only), Rabbit Flat Roadhouse (open only Fri–Mon), Mindibungu (Billiluna) (fuel available business hours only) and Halls Creek. For phone numbers see *Contacts*, opposite.

Road access and closures It is recommended that you check road conditions before undertaking the Tanami Track. For the NT contact NT Road Report 1800 246 199; www.ntlis.nt.gov.au/roadreport For WA contact 138 138; www.mainroads.wa.gov.au

Water Carry adequate water supplies. Water from bores and wells along the Tanami route is undrinkable.

See also *On the Road*, p. 246.

The red-dirt track that leads off the Tanami to Newhaven Reserve.

Alice Springs to Halls Gap

The first part of the trip, around 140 km, from Alice Springs to the Papunya turn-off, is on bitumen, then you are on a dirt road, often corrugated and sandy. Another 50 km takes you to the well-maintained Tilmouth Well Roadhouse, which has cabins, a restaurant and even a swimming pool. The roadhouse is part of Napperby Station, a working cattle property; you can buy a pass to drive on the property, or join a tour (see *Contacts*, p. 59). At the roadhouse, a gallery exhibits and sells art and craft by the local Warlpiri people, including some impressive dot paintings.

At Yuendumu, an Aboriginal town 2 km off the road, you can refuel, pick up supplies, or visit the Aboriginal-owned art centre, but if you want to stay longer, you will need a permit.

Newhaven Reserve

A turn-off 22 km past Tilmouth Roadhouse leads 103 km to the former Newhaven cattle station (it's a further 35 km to the old homestead, where visitors can register and pay entrance and camping fees) This is now a conservation reserve, covering 2620 sq km of desert country – an expanse of sand dunes, salt lakes, grasslands, open woodlands and rocky ranges – that is an important refuge for threatened bird and mammal species. Dozens of bird species frequent the park, from emus and egrets to buzzards and bustards. The reserve is managed by Birds Australia in association with local Aboriginal custodians.

Contacts

Visitor information

Alice Springs
Gregory Tce
(08) 8952 5800 or 1800 645 199
www.centralaustraliantourism.com

Tennant Creek
Battery Hill, Peko Rd
1800 500 879
www.barklytourism.com.au

Parks and reserves

See *Fact File*, opposite

Roadhouses, station stays

Mindibungu (Billiluna)
(08) 9168 8988

Rabbit Flat Roadhouse
(08) 8956 8744

Tilmouth Well Roadhouse/ Napperby Station
(08) 8956 8777
www.tilmouthwell.com

Yuendumu
(08) 8956 4006

Other

Nyinkka Nyunya Centre
Paterson St
Tennant Creek
(08) 8962 2699
www.nyinkkanyunyu.com.au

Visitors can camp and enjoy the solitude, but need to be self-sufficient.

Goldmining

Gold has been mined in the area since the 1930s, and old mining relics from the early days are scattered, rusting along the roadside. There is no access to the Granites mine or the now-closed Tanami mine further along.

Spinifex and termite mounds

The vegetation in this part of the country is fairly monotonous – endless spinifex, occasionally relieved by stunted acacia trees and twisted bloodwoods. There are about 30 varieties of spinifex, a native grass that is perfectly adapted to the arid region's harsh conditions and nutrient-poor soils. The spiky leaves grow flat, but soon become tightly rolled into a rigid, needle-like point to conserve moisture. Nothing eats spinifex except termites, and emerging from the sea of spinifex that cloaks the Tanami are vast numbers of termite mounds – sometimes hundreds of mounds in a single hectare.

You won't see very much wildlife in the Tanami, especially if you are flying along in a 4WD, but the wildlife is there. The termites provide a rich source of food for a wide variety of lizards – from the large perentie to tiny geckoes – as well as small insect-eating marsupials.

Mindibungu (Billiluna) to Halls Creek

Mindibungu (Billiluna) Stock Route is still considered a true outback 4WD adventure, though increasing numbers of visitors attempt the drive. Past Mindibungu, it's another 150 km as the Tanami

Above *Spinifex and scrubby she-oaks stretch to the horizon along the Tanami.*

Below *A yellow-spotted monitor, at home in the desert.*

Noisy galahs flock to waterholes around Davenport NP.

leads north into WA, and meets the Great Northern Hwy. From there it is just 16 km to Halls Creek (see *The East Kimberley*, p. 236).

Alice Springs to Tennant Creek

The Stuart Hwy heads north from Alice to Darwin, with just a few wayside stops along its almost 1500 km. At the small settlement of Ti Tree, on Aboriginal land, a mango orchard and even a vineyard bask in the subtropical climate. The town, whose population is mainly Pmara Jutunta people, is a service centre for surrounding Aboriginal communities including Utopia, a renowned source of Indigenous art.

At Barrow Creek visitors stop to have a drink at the quirky Barrow Creek pub ('the Barrow'), where you can refuel, buy food or camp. To the east of the township are the hills of the Forster Range. Just out of town stands the sturdy Overland Telegraph station, the first repeater station built north of Alice Springs, in 1872 (see *The singing wire*, p. 36). The settlement here gained some notoriety when scores of local Aboriginals were apparently shot in reprisal for the fatal attack in 1874 on the officer-in-charge of the station and a linesman.

Forty-four km north of Barrow Creek, a turn-off leads east to the proposed Davenport NP; there is also a turn-off at the Kurundi–Epenarra Road (a high-clearance 4WD is needed for this route) at Bonney Well. The park, covering 1120 sq km and encompassing the Davenport Range, is an ideal destination for 4WD enthusiasts, experienced bushwalkers and nature lovers. The waterholes are home to at least seven species of fish and also attract a wide array of birdlife – galahs cluster in the trees, finches and pigeons flock to the water.

Back on the Stuart, it's roughly 46 km to Wycliffe Well, one of the outback's quirkiest towns. It has gained a reputation for UFO sightings and whether you believe it or not, lots of people do, and make the trip here to see for themselves. The local pub, where you can catch up on the latest sighting, serves a cold beer.

Another stretch of highway takes you to the small settlement at Wauchope (pronounced 'walk-up'). It began its days as a service centre for the workers from the local wolfram (tungsten) mines and for the cattle properties of the Barkly Tablelands to the north. These days, it's not much more than a whistlestop, though some visitors use it as a base for exploring the remarkable rock formations of the Devils Marbles.

Devils Marbles

Just on 9 km north of Wauchope, strewn among scrubby acacia and golden spinifex in a shallow valley, lie thousands of boulders, some of them teetering precariously, known as the Devils Marbles, or in Aboriginal mythology, the eggs of the Rainbow Serpent. These boulders were once part of a single block of stone that lay below ground level. Over millions of years water has seeped through and the stone has eroded along fault lines, breaking into giant slabs. Gradually the softer soil and rock have weathered away, leaving rounded shapes. At sunrise and sunset the massive granite boulders glow golden-red in the light, a photo opportunity not to be missed.

In the surrounding conservation reserve, watch for lizards, including the larger sand goanna, which are occasionally spotted amongst the tufts of sharp-leaved spinifex. Fairy martins can be seen darting to their nests hidden on the shady side of boulders, while flocks of pretty zebra finches and painted finches can be seen, and heard, especially early in the morning and at dusk. There is bush camping, but you will need to take your own water and firewood.

Tennant Creek

Tennant Creek is the largest town between Alice and Darwin, a busy outback settlement of around 3800 people. Explorer John McDouall Stuart named the creek here in 1862 on his trek across the continent. The town itself sprang up after Australia's last gold rush, which took place here in the 1930s. There was a flurry of activity after the first precious finds. Although the peak years were fairly short-lived, it proved to be one of the richest goldmines in Australia. Copper discovered in the 1950s kept the town alive and mining is still carried out, but Tennant Creek also services the surrounding pastoral properties, and those travelling the Stuart Hwy.

Old machinery, early buildings and some intriguing photos recall the town's gold rush heyday at the Battery Hill Mining Centre. The thump of the giant 10-head battery, used to crush gold-bearing ore, whirrs up twice a day and there are underground mine tours or, if you're feeling lucky, you might try your hand at panning for gold. Otherwise, you could enjoy a picnic or head to the lookout for some sweeping views.

The Nyinkka Nyunyu Centre, a distinctive building housing the Barkly region's excellent Aboriginal art and culture centre, offers a glimpse of the region's rich Indigenous heritage. The centre is on a Warumungu sacred site, home of the nyinkka, or spiky-tailed goanna.

Eleven km north of town stand the isolated 1872 stone buildings of the Tennant Creek Telegraph Station, which can be inspected. Just 25 km north of Tennant Creek the Stuart Hwy comes to a road junction and the Three Ways roadhouse. Here, you can turn east to Queensland, or continue north, almost another 1000 km to the NT's capital, Darwin.

Above *The old telegraph station at Tennant Creek.*

Below *Golden light on the Devils Marbles.*

The Top End
a timeless world

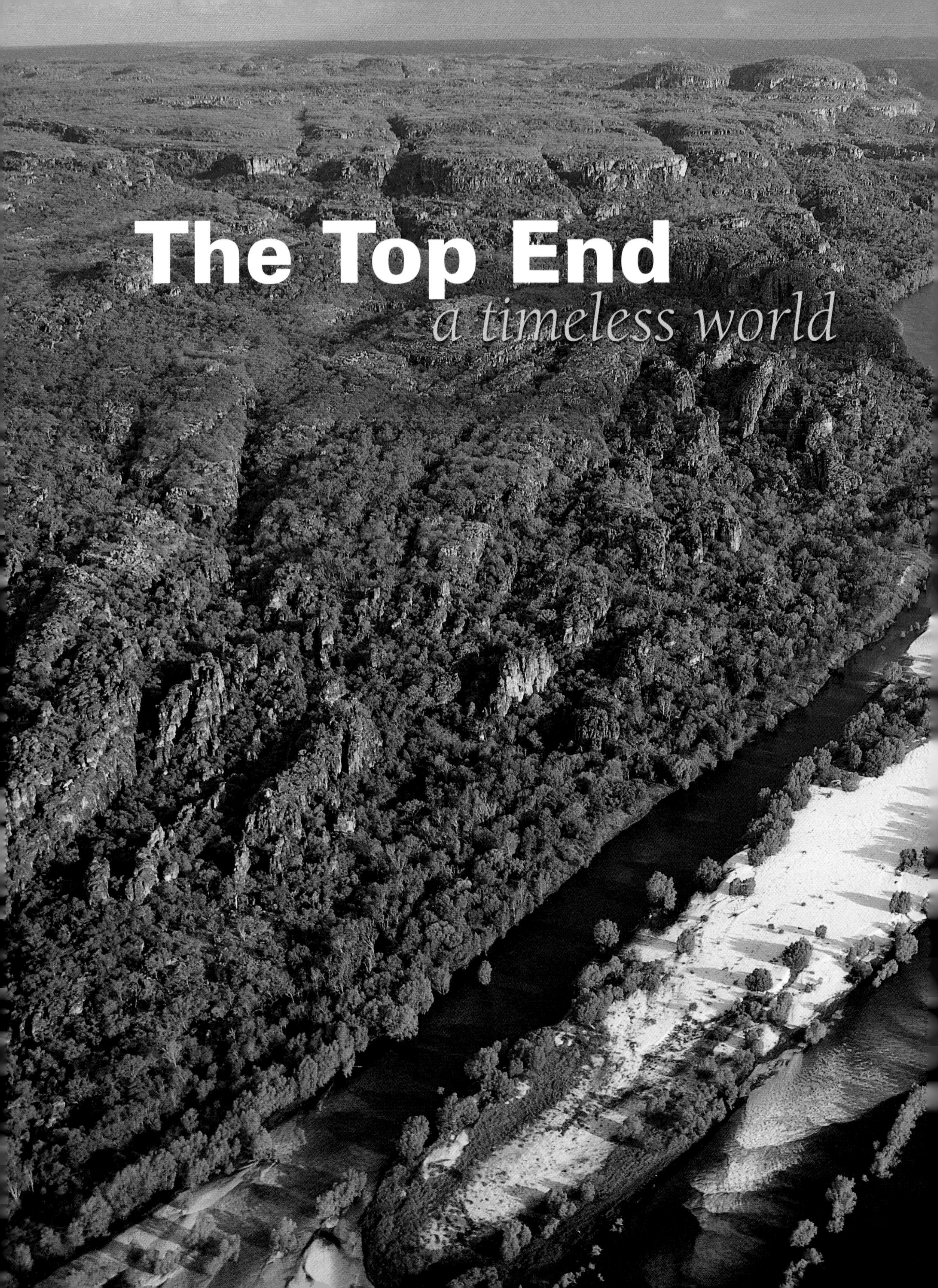

The Top End

The Top End is a world of its own, a unique landscape of shimmering tropical flood plains, weather-scarred escarpments, tinder-dry woodlands, extraordinary wildlife, vast cattle stations and a priceless heritage of ancient Aboriginal rock art.

The Top End Regions

Darwin to Mataranka

The NT capital, Darwin, presides over a series of wild and varied landscapes: the wetlands of the Mary River delta, the waterfalls and sandstone pillars of Litchfield NP and the mighty river gorges of Nitmiluk NP. Fishing for barramundi, bushwalking in the national parks, soaking in thermal pools or exploring the region's pioneering history are just some of the activities in the region. *See p. 68*

Katherine to Keep River

The Victoria River and its knitted tributaries dominate this landscape between the tropics of the north and the deserts of the Red Centre. Historic cattle stations have claimed the region's broad plains, but the escarpment-bound river frontage, arresting natural landscapes and precious rock art in the Territory's far west are protected within two outstanding national parks – Gregory and Keep River. *See p. 76*

Kakadu and Arnhem Land

Heritage-listed Kakadu NP, one of Australia's richest ecological environments, also contains the world's most extensive repository of rock art – more than 5000 sites, dating back tens of thousands of years. East of Kakadu lies Arnhem Land, a remote and little-known wilderness, one of the last strongholds of traditional Aboriginal culture. Garig Gunak Barlu NP protects the pristine landscape of Cobourg Peninsula. *See p. 84*

Leichhardt's grasshopper

Sea

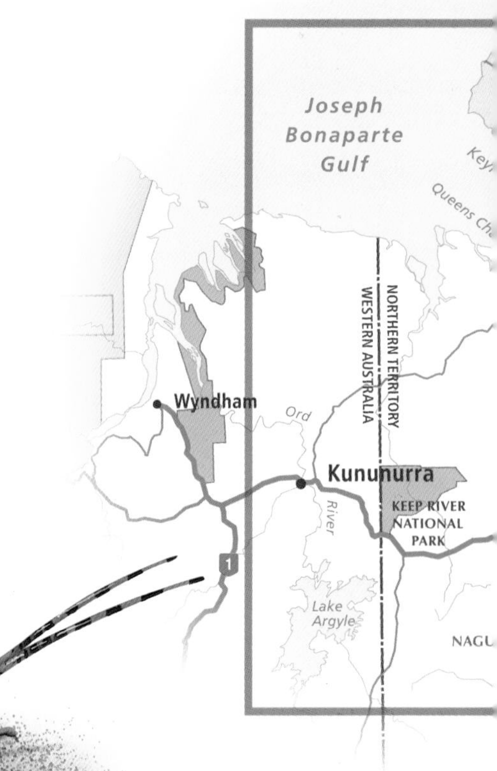

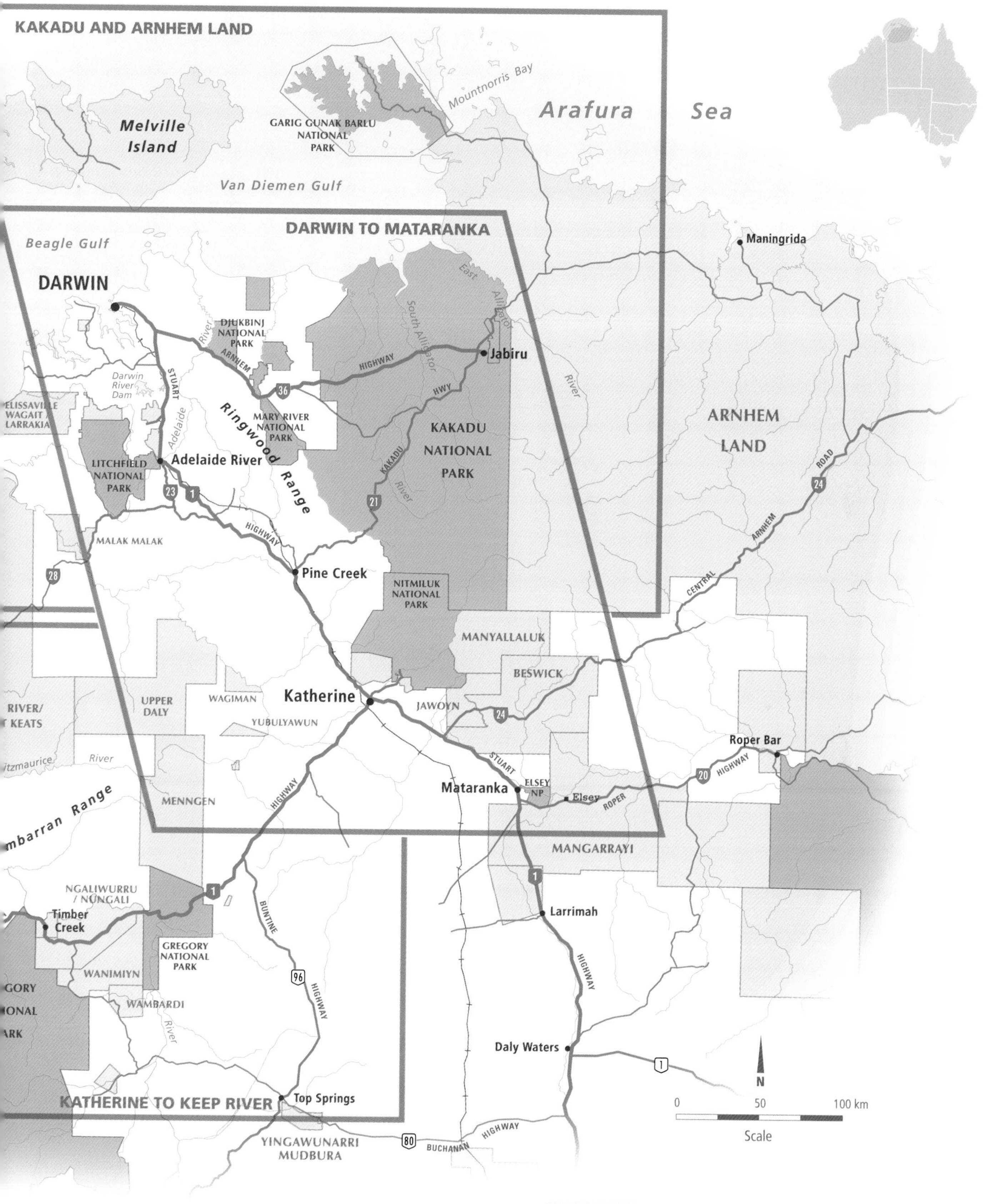

Tourism Top End ☎(08) 8980 6000; www.tourismtopend.com.au

Travel Tips

When to go

The Territory's Top End is subject to a wet/dry tropical weather pattern. The Dry extends approximately April–Oct, when temperatures sit fairly constantly around 30–35°C, but humidity and rainfall are low. May–mid-June is a good time to visit, when it's not too dry or too crowded. June–July is the peak tourist season. During the Wet, the temperature remains much the same, but the region experiences torrential rain and high humidity; roads flood frequently, and some roads are closed to all vehicles. That said, the explosion of flora and fauna and dramatic, storm-scoured skies are attracting increasing numbers of visitors at this time. For further information contact the Bureau of Meteorology (BOM): 1900 955 367; www.bom.gov.au

Aboriginal land

A large part of the Top End is Aboriginal land. In most cases the roads are public and open to general use, although visitors may not deviate more than 50 m from the roadside, or camp without a permit. Some Aboriginal communities have shops selling fuel and supplies, and these may be open to the public. If you do enter communities, respect people's privacy. Also be aware that some communities are 'dry' and no alcohol is permitted at all. Access to Arnhem Land is limited and strictly controlled. All road travel requires a permit (see *Kakadu and Arnhem Land*, p. 84). For all queries relating to Aboriginal land in the Top End, contact the Northern Land Council: (08) 8920 5100; www.nlc.org.au

Parks and reserves

All national parks in the Top End, with the exception of Kakadu NP, are administered by the Parks and Wildlife Service of the NT (PWSNT). Visitors are not required to have a permit or pay a fee to enter these parks, however, small camping fees apply – pay at the nearest ranger station or use the honesty boxes on-site. There are a number of standard regulations (see *On the Road*, p. 246) as well as specific regulations for some parks. For general queries, contact PWSNT: (08) 8999 4555; www.nt.gov.au/nreta/parks See also contact details for individual parks in the *Fact File* for each region.

Kakadu NP is jointly administered by Parks Australia (Commonwealth Dept of the Environment, Water, Heritage and the Arts) and the traditional owners. There are no entry fees but camping fees apply. For queries, contact the park direct: (08) 8938 1121; www.environment.gov.au/parks/kakadu

Walkers Registration Scheme Bushwalkers undertaking overnight walks in parks should register with the PWSNT's Registration Scheme: 1300 650 730. A refundable deposit of $50 (payable by credit card or cash) is required to assist with costs in case help is needed. Not all parks are covered by the scheme.

Opposite, far right *A road train churns up the dirt in the Katherine area, south of Darwin.*

Opposite *A frilled lizard spreads its collar to frighten potential enemies.*

Below *A magpie goose, painted in the X-ray style, from the Mt Borradaile area, western Arnhem Land.*

CLIMATE — DARWIN

	J	F	M	A	M	J	J	A	S	O	N	D
Max °C	32	31	32	33	32	31	30	31	32	33	33	33
Min °C	25	25	24	24	22	20	19	21	23	25	25	25
Rain mm	406	349	311	97	21	1	1	7	19	74	143	232
Raindays	21	20	19	9	2	0	1	1	2	7	12	16

CLIMATE — KATHERINE

	J	F	M	A	M	J	J	A	S	O	N	D
Max °C	35	34	35	34	32	30	30	33	35	38	38	37
Min °C	24	24	23	20	17	14	13	16	20	24	25	24
Rain mm	234	215	161	33	6	2	1	1	6	29	89	195
Raindays	15	14	10	2	1	0	0	0	1	3	8	12

Fishing

Licences are not required for recreational fishing in the NT, but regulations are in place to ensure the quality of recreational fishing is maintained. Note the restrictions that apply to the highly sought after barramundi: a bag limit of five (two in Mary River) and a minimum length of 55 cm. The esturaries of the Mary and Daly rivers are closed to fishing Oct–Jan. For further information contact NT Fisheries: (08) 8999 2144; www.nt.gov.au/d/fisheries Information is also available at: www.fishingtheterritory.com.au

National parks have their own fishing guidelines (see *Parks and reserves*, above, and individual parks in the *Fact File* for each region).

Warnings

Fuel and supplies In some areas long distances separate fuel and supply stops (for example, in Arnhem Land and west of Timber Creek) . Drivers should be well equipped and self-sufficient.

Road access and closures Avoid driving at dawn, dusk and at night, when wildlife and stock can wander onto roads. Most of the major public roads in the Top End are sealed and suitable for 2WD vehicles; a number of minor roads and national park roads are 4WD only; some are suitable for high-clearance, 4WD only. Flooding of both minor and major roads is common in the Wet. For up-to-date road reports and information on closures contact Dept of Planning and Infrastructure (DPI): 1800 246 199; www.ntlis.nt.gov.au/roadreport Or check with local police or national park rangers.

Remote travel Many areas in the Top End are remote and travellers need to be well prepared. Those venturing off major tourist routes should consider carrying an emergency communications device (see *On the Road*, p. 246). In some national parks, walkers need a permit for overnight walks or remote areas.

Maps Maps in this book are guidelines only – carry detailed maps.

Crocodiles Northern Australia has two types of crocodiles. Potentially deadly saltwater or estuarine crocodiles (*Crocodylus porosus*) can be found in salt, brackish and fresh water throughout the Top End. They can be found hundreds of km out to sea, and hundreds of km inland. They are large, well camouflaged and dangerous. Heed all warning signs. Take care when boating and fishing. Only swim where recommended. Do not allow children or dogs to play near the edge of waterways.

Freshwater crocodiles (*Crocodylus johnstoni*) are smaller and recognisable by their long narrow snout. They are less dangerous but will still guard their territory and young fiercely if they need to. Stay well away from these crocodiles.

See also *On the Road*, p. 246.

Images of weathered monoliths, dry skies and endless plains of red dust are commonly associated with the term 'outback', but much the Top End is steamy, well watered and richly getated. Despite this, the region unquestionably nbodies the spirit of the outback, with its laidback, ntamed atmosphere, its vast cattle stations and ioneering past, its long, empty roads and the tonishing grandeur of its landscapes.

Darwin, though streamlined and modern, mains a town of the frontier. It is one of the world's most remote cities. Twice during the 20th century it faced potential destruction – bombings in WW II, and Cyclone Tracy in 1974 – a history that saves it from any hint of suburban complacency. It faces the countries of Asia, rather than the populous cities of Australia's south, and Asian trade ties and eady immigration have infused the tiny metropolis ith vibrancy and diversity.

Immediately beyond the city limits, the natural orld erupts into view. Millions of birds plait the ies; crocodiles inhabit the rivers; barramundi reed to a legendary size. The forces of nature anifest in extraordinary ways: palm-like oases opear in the middle of parched plains; thermal orings bubble up from deep beneath the earth's urface; steep gorges score age-old escarpments; vers spill into vast flood plains choked with opical vegetation. The human settlements that ouch alongside these majestic landscapes seem nall and insignificant, although determined to revail. Culture where it appears is ancient and ndigenous: the 5000 or so rock-art sites in the Vorld Heritage-listed Kakadu NP serve as another ivid reminder of the comparatively brief and fragile nure of modern settlement.

In the Top End, the weather sets the pattern f life and underscores the ascendancy of nature. o Aboriginal people there are six or more finely alibrated seasons, but most people talk of just two. he Dry produces hot clear days, parched blue skies nd relatively cool nights. The Wet is a challenge: a time of storms, soaking rain and cyclone-strength winds, and the thick fug of tropical humidity.

Most visitors come during the Dry, although increasing numbers are drawn by the proliferation of flora and fauna during the Wet, or the 'green season'. Regardless of the season, 4WD adventurers, barramundi anglers, walkers, campers, rockclimbers, and nature lovers are lured by the prospect of relatively untrammelled landscapes and a small, thinly distributed population. Visitors, especially in remote areas, must be prepared to cope with patchy facilities, road closures and dangers such as crocodiles.

Darwin to Mataranka

Fanning out from Darwin, Australia's only tropical capital city, are wildlife-rich wetlands, majestic escarpments and a string of world-class national parks.

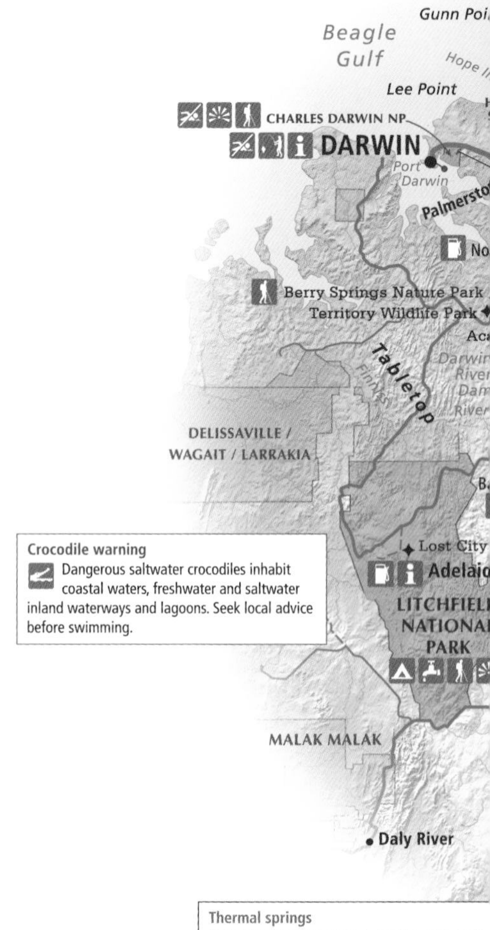

Crocodile warning

Dangerous saltwater crocodiles inhabit coastal waters, freshwater and saltwater inland waterways and lagoons. Seek local advice before swimming.

Thermal springs

Thermal springs, common in the Top End, are th of volcanic activity below the earth's surface. Th can reach 60°C. The springs collect in pools and fringed by shady trees, make ideal spa pools.

Darwin is a vibrant, cosmopolitan capital – geographically closer to cities of Asia than those of southern Australia – where the pattern of urban life is determined by powerful tropical weather patterns. The Dry is the expansive season of tourism and major events. The Wet is when visitors flee to drier climates and residents hunker down to wait out the season, as the humidity and the teeming rain bring renewed vigour to the landscape.

The surrounding landscapes are as dramatic as the weather: estuaries woven with mangroves overlap white-sand beaches; wetlands shimmer, clogged with tropical plants, barramundi and big crocs; strange, prehistoric-looking landforms rise out of the heat-cracked earth. Idyllic tropical features – palms, waterfalls, bubbling thermal springs and pools of exquisitely clear water – appear, oasis-like, amid tinder-dry hills and plains.

To the south of the city is Litchfield NP. Here, a variety of tropical landscapes converge, from monsoonal rainforest to yellow-grass plains stippled with gums. Crocodile-free swimming holes and waterfalls lie between the folds of the bulky Tabletop Range, flanked by campsites and walking trails.

Near the regional centre of Katherine is the celebrated Nitmiluk NP, where the mighty Katherine River washes through a long, ragged line of dramatic gorges, creating the perfect setting for boat cruises and canoeing.

For visitors new to the tropics, perhaps the most amazing places are those east of Darwin. Here, unfolding from the coastal curve of Van Diemen Gulf, is a broad, flat landscape, incised by the flow of eight big, northern rivers. This is adventure territory – tourists come to camp, fish for barramundi and watch the prolific wildlife.

Must see, must do

- Canoe through the gorges of Nitmiluk NP
- Swim in spring-fed rock pools near Mataranka
- Photograph the towering sandstone pillars in Litchfield NP
- Take a cruise on the Adelaide River to see wild crocodiles
- Fish for barramundi in the Mary River delta

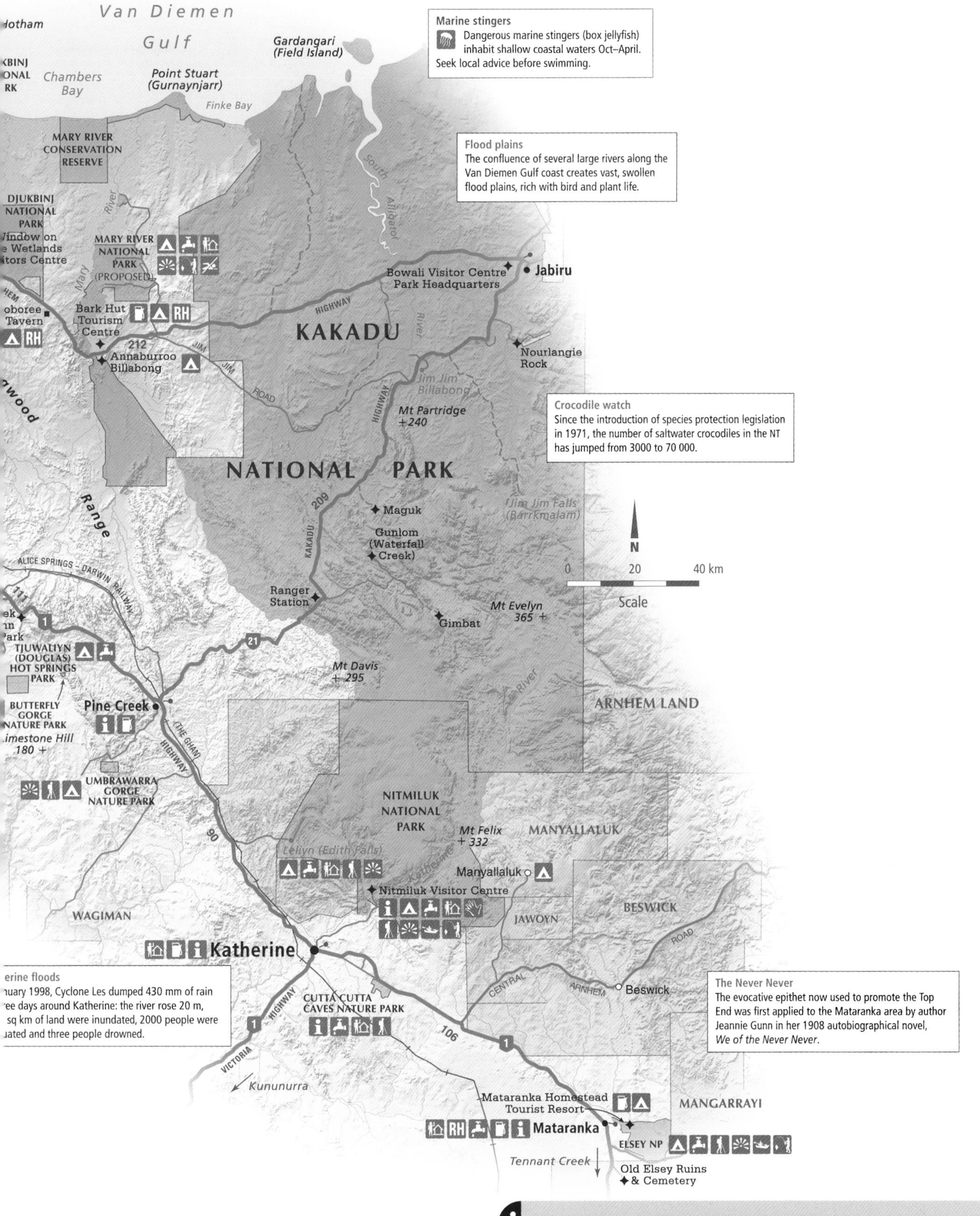

Marine stingers
Dangerous marine stingers (box jellyfish) inhabit shallow coastal waters Oct–April. Seek local advice before swimming.

Flood plains
The confluence of several large rivers along the Van Diemen Gulf coast creates vast, swollen flood plains, rich with bird and plant life.

Crocodile watch
Since the introduction of species protection legislation in 1971, the number of saltwater crocodiles in the NT has jumped from 3000 to 70 000.

erine floods
ıuary 1998, Cyclone Les dumped 430 mm of rain ee days around Katherine: the river rose 20 m, sq km of land were inundated, 2000 people were ıated and three people drowned.

The Never Never
The evocative epithet now used to promote the Top End was first applied to the Mataranka area by author Jeannie Gunn in her 1908 autobiographical novel, *We of the Never Never*.

Darwin ☎1300 138 886, (08) 8980 6000; www.tourismtopend.com.au

Fact File

Top events

Mar *Farm and Garden Day, Katherine*
April/ May *Pine Creek Rodeo and Races*
May *Katherine Country Music Muster*
The Arafura Games, Darwin (biennial sporting festival)
Back to the Never Never Festival (Mataranka)
Katherine Races
June *Red Cross Canoe Marathon (Katherine River)*
July *Territory Day*
Dancing with Spirits Festival (Djilpin Arts Dancers, Beswick)
Darwin Rodeo and Country Music Festival
Darwin Show
Katherine Rodeo
Katherine Show
Aug *Darwin Cup*
Festival of Darwin (arts, culture)
Katherine Flying Fox Art and Cultural Festival
Mataranka Bushman's Carnival
Oct *Mataranka Barra Bash Fishing Competition*

Permits and regulations

Aboriginal land There are areas of Aboriginal land within this region, but no permits are required if travellers stay on main roads.

Parks and reserves

For general information about parks in the Top End, see *Travel Tips*, p.66.

Butterfly Gorge Nature Park Not suitable for 2WD vehicles. Park closes during the Wet. Camping is not permitted. Contact Parks and Wildlife Service of the NT (PWSNT) in Batchelor: (08) 8976 0282.

Charles Darwin NP Park closes at 7 pm; camping is not permitted. Contact PWSNT in Darwin: (08) 8947 2305.

Cutta Cutta Caves Nature Park Tours of one cave run hourly (daylight hours). Caves may flood during the Wet. No camping in the reserve. Contact PWSNT in Katherine: (08) 8973 8888.

Elsey NP Park campsites at 12 Miles Yard (good facilities; no power; generators not permitted). Lure fishing only. Safe swimming is at Bitter Springs and Mataranka Thermal Spring Pool and along the Roper River (heed warning signs). Contact PWSNT at Mataranka: (08) 8975 4560.

Litchfield NP Some areas not suitable for 2WD vehicles. There are a number of campgrounds with facilities; caravan sites at Wangi Falls (no power). Some waterholes are safe for swimming, but always check signs. Contact PWSNT at Batchelor: (08) 8976 0282.

Mary River NP (proposed) Most roads (sealed and unsealed) are suitable for 2WD vehicles in the Dry. During the Wet, all are subject to flooding. Crocodile numbers are high. There are a number of campsites and day-use areas. There are wilderness lodges at Point Stuart: (08) 8978 8914 and Wildman River: (08) 8978 8912. For all other information contact the ranger station: (08) 8978 8986.

Nitmiluk NP Privately owned camping and caravan sites are at the base of the gorge, contact: (08) 8972 3150, and at Leliyn (Edith Falls), contact: (08) 8975 4869. Bookings are not accepted at either site. Basic campsites are scattered along the gorge (access by foot or boat). Fishing (lure only) is permitted in the gorge section of the park, but not at the falls. Canoes for hire at the visitor centre (book ahead). Visitors wishing to use private boats or canoes need to check regulations with the park's visitor centre. Walkers must register for overnight treks. For further information contact park visitor centre: (08) 8972 1886.

Tjuwaliyn (Douglas) Hot Springs Park Access is by gravel road (suitable for 2WD in Dry).The thermal water can be very hot; swim upstream or downstream (200 m either way). Camping is available; there are basic facilities (no power). Visitors are not allowed to enter sacred site areas (observe signs). Contact PWSNT in Batchelor: (08) 8976 0282.

Umbrawarra Gorge Nature Park The gorge is accessible only during the Dry when the river level drops. This park may be closed to 2WD vehicles or closed altogether during the Wet. Rockclimbers and abseilers must register with PWSNT staff at Batchelor: (08) 8976 0282. Camping is allowed (BYO everything).

Fishing

For general information on fishing in this region see *Travel Tips*, p. 66. See also individual park entries.

Warnings

Fuel and supplies The furthest distance between fuel stops in this region is around 100 km. Accommodation and supplies are readily available.

Road access and closures Major public roads in this area are sealed and well maintained. Some roads in some parks and reserves are not suitable for conventional vehicles at any time. All Top End roads are subject to flooding during the Wet. For up-to-date road reports contact DPI: 1800 246 199; www.ntlis.nt.gov.au/roadreport; or check with local police.

Crocodiles Freshwater and dangerous saltwater crocodiles are widespread throughout this region. Be crocodile-wise; heed warning signs; swim only where recommended. Take care when fishing and boating. Do not allow children to play near the edge of waterways.

See also *On the Road*, p. 246.

Opposite *Darwin, Australia's only capital city in the tropics.*

Right *Termite mounds are built on a north–south axis, to minimise the area exposed to the sun at the hottest time of day.*

Contacts

Visitor information

Darwin (Top End)
cnr Bennett and Smith sts
(08) 8980 6000 or 1300 138 886
www.tourismtopend.com.au

Katherine Visitor Centre
cnr Stuart Hwy and Lindsay St
(08) 8972 2650 or 1800 653 142
www.visitkatherine.com.au

Mataranka
Stockyard Gallery, Stuart Hwy
(08) 8975 4530

Pine Creek
Diggers Rest Motel, Main Tce
(08) 8976 1442

Parks and reserves

See *Fact File*, opposite

Activities

Crocodylus Park
(08) 8922 4500

Darwin Crocoile Farm
(08) 8988 1491

Jumping Crocodile Cruises
(08) 8988 8144 or
1800 888 542

Manyallaluk Experience
(08) 8975 4727 or
1800 644 727

Mataranka Homestead Tourist Resort
(08) 8975 4544

Territory Wildlife Park
(08) 8988 7200

Window on the Wetlands
(08) 8988 8188

Other

The *Ghan*
(Great Southern Railway)
13 2147
www.trainways.com.au

Darwin

Unlike other Australian cities, Darwin is scarcely separable from its natural environment. During the Wet (October to April), inundating rains bring to bloom the city's magnificent trees and plants, including poinciana, frangipani and bougainvillea, resulting in a riot of foliage and flower. Abundant populations of birds and reptiles sometimes ignore the boundaries of civilisation, camping on suburban verandahs, invading city plazas and travelling through the plumbing.

Just 5 km from the centre of town lies the ·8 sq km Charles Darwin NP, a tangle of mangrove-threaded estuaries, inlets, islands and bays. On the northern side of the city, rugged red-gold cliffs frame ribbons of white-sand beaches that are beautiful to stroll along, but can be dangerous for swimmers.

Probably Darwin's favourite beach is Mindil Beach on Fannie Bay. Each Thursday and Sunday during the Dry it hosts the perennially popular Mindil Beach Sunset Market. Members of the city's ·5 or so ethnic communities emerge and a fair smattering of tourists gather to eat from the South-East Asian-style food stalls, socialise and marvel at the brilliance of a tropical sunset.

At the northern end of Fannie Bay, East Point Recreation Reserve shelters the popular (and crocodile-free) Lake Alexander, where swimming is year-round. For those who want to see crocodiles, a visit to either Darwin Crocodile Farm or Crocodylus Park, both fairly close to the city, is a must.

Litchfield National Park

The 1430 sq km Litchfield NP protects a series of beautiful tropical environments – pockets of monsoon rainforest, open woodlands, savannah plains – along with some of the Territory's most arresting landforms.

For many, the big drawcard is safe swimming. The assortment of sandy swimming holes, cascades and waterfalls make the park a genuine oasis for visitors to, and residents of, this region. (Temperatures in the Top End hover constantly in the thirties, and the fringing Timor Sea, although beautiful, is awash with crocodiles, sharks and poisonous stingers.) The park's landscape centrepiece, the massive sandstone Tabletop Range, captures and absorbs the wet-season run-off in such a way as to ensure a supply of water year-round; this supply is supplemented by a chain of freshwater springs.

Wangi and Florence falls and Buley Rockhole, the main visitor areas, have camping, walking and picnic areas and great swimming. The large pools attract reptiles such as water monitors. Orange-footed

The Territory Wildlife Park

The Top End's diversity of tropical wildlife is brilliantly showcased at the extensive Territory Wildlife Park, 60 km south of Darwin. In a range of environments, from grasslands to mangroves and paperbark forests, many of the region's most distinctive animals can be viewed. Reptiles such as water monitors and pythons, marsupials including endangered bilbies (in a nocturnal house), bird species (in a walk-through aviary) and a twice-daily raptor display are among the highlights. At the nearby Berry Springs Nature Park, there are spring-fed pools for swimming, shady picnic areas and a well-planned walking trail.

The *Ghan* railway

The 3000 km *Ghan* railway line links the continent from south to north, travelling from the wide, orderly streets of Adelaide to tropical Darwin. En route, it traverses deserts of sand and stone, ancient mountain ranges and steep gorges amid tropical wilderness. It passes through outback towns whose iconic fame exceeds their size many times over – Alice Springs, Tennant Creek and Katherine, to name a few. The *Ghan* was a project on the boil (sometimes just a simmer) from 1878 when work began on the SA section. The Adelaide to Alice track opened in 1929, but it was not until 2004 that the 1420 km extension to Darwin was up and running. It is billed as one of the world's great rail journeys. A return service runs weekly between Adelaide and Darwin (two nights each way); two weekly return services link Adelaide and Alice Springs. For a fee, passengers can take their car along. Passengers can enjoy the luxury of sleeper accommodation, or book the more basic seats. Book well in advance (see *Contacts*, p. 71).

scrub fowl, honeyeaters, fig birds and Torres Strait pigeons share the fruit and berries in the area along with a range of nocturnal mammals – northern quolls, northern brown bandicoots and northern brush-tailed possums.

Other attractions include a rash of giant termite mounds – large, wedge-shaped towers erupting from the surrounding treeless, black-soil plains. The so-called magnetic mounds face north–south. This is a temperature-control mechanism: by positioning their homes thus, the termites ensure that during the hottest, brightest time of day, only a thin strip of the mound is exposed to the sun's direct rays

Equally mesmerising is the Lost City, a collection of 25 m high sandstone pillars. Over thousands of years, alternating bouts of parching heat and torrential rain have carved the pillars into their present shapes from the bulky mass of the Tabletop Range. Early white settlers thought they had stumbled upon the ruins of a lost civilisation. Access to the Lost City is 4WD only.

Adelaide River to Pine Creek

The town of Adelaide River (population 300) lies 112 km south-east of Darwin on the Stuart Hwy. During WW II, the town was a base for 30 000 Australian and American troops. The beautifully kept Adelaide River War Cemetery recalls the trauma of the wartime period: 63 civilians, victims of the air raids on Darwin, are buried here, as are 434 Australian, British and Canadian service personnel.

South of Adelaide River the land is the domain of the Wagiman people. Three small parks, managed jointly by the Wagiman and NT park authorities, enclose a richly patterned landscape of creeks, gorges, woodlands and springs. Tjuwaliyn (Douglas) Hot Springs Park protects a bubbling artesian spring and surrounding creek bed and bushland. The waters of the spring can heat to a scorching 60°C: visitors are advised to swim in cooler waters, 200 m downstream or upstream. The reserve has a very pleasant campground.

Butterfly Gorge Nature Park, 17 km away, features a section of the Douglas Daly River and an abundant population of black-and-white crow butterflies that establish habitats in the crevices of the surrounding gorge. The granite and sandstone walls of the Umbrawarra Gorge Nature Park provide an ideal habitat for short-eared rock-wallabies and ringtail possums – and good sport for rockclimbers.

Pine Creek lies 230 km south of Darwin on the Stuart Hwy. The small town, population 500, thrived as the centre of a gold rush in the 1870s. Museums and other sites preserve relics and reminders of the old days.

Top *The first part of the track for the* Ghan, *was laid in 1878 – the last part was finished in 2004.*

Opposite *Walking horses through the shallows of the Katherine River.*

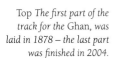

Katherine

Katherine is the NT's third largest settlement, with a population of around 11 000. It services the nearby Mt Todd goldmine, the Tindal RAAF Airbase and the local cattle industry.

The original inhabitants, the Jawoyn people, drew on the rich resources of the Katherine River, around which the town is built. Explorer John McDouall Stuart passed through in 1862, naming the river after the daughter of one of his sponsors, but the area was not settled until 1878, when pastoralist Alfred Giles built his homestead, Springvale, on the banks of the river; the structure stands today as the oldest in the Territory (free guided tours operate weekdays during the Dry). Other historic attractions include the Katherine Museum, with displays charting the district's settlement, and O'Keefe House, a 1942 bush hut fashioned from bark off-cuts, flywire and sheets of corrugated iron.

Katherine has a good range of accommodation and plenty of places to stock-up for forays into more remote areas. It is home to a couple of uniquely outback institutions: a branch of the School of the Air, where lessons are relayed by radio or disseminated via the internet to students in remote locations, and a campus devoted to educating jillaroos and jackeroos – the graduates go to work on northern pastoral properties. To see Katherine at its best, join locals at the annual Katherine Country Music Muster, held over the first weekend in May.

Many travellers to Katherine come to visit the renowned gorges of nearby Nitmiluk NP (see below), but also well worth a look is the Cutta Cutta Caves Nature Park, about 27 km south of the town. This complex of limestone caverns was created 500 million years ago. Guided tours of one of the caves depart hourly during daylight hours in the Dry and there is a peaceful, self-guided woodland walk.

Nitmiluk National Park

In this celebrated 3000 sq km national park, the Katherine River cuts a course through the scenic Arnhem Plateau, creating 13 sheer-walled gorges of red, orange and cream sandstone. The river waters abound with life: short-necked turtles emerge for breath; Merten's water monitors scuttle across sandy beaches or bask on rocks; archer fish patrol close to the banks, shooting insects with of a jet of water. Around 170 species of bird, including the great bower bird, the threatened Australian bustard and hooded parrot, and the rare chestnut-quilled rock pigeon, fill the skies with their colour and song. Ancient livistona palms sprout from faults dissecting the sandstone, along with grasses and shrubs, while monsoon rainforest takes hold in dark, damp gullies.

A gorge cruise that can last from one hour to a whole day, is the way most visitors choose to

Aboriginal culture

The Djilpin Arts Dancers from Beswick, 50 km south of Katherine, perform regularly in Katherine from May to August, featuring three corroborees drawn from the area's main Aboriginal language groups – contact visitor information in Katherine. Manyallaluk, 102 km north-east of Katherine, is an Aboriginal community with a vibrant arts and cultural program. Visitors can participate in activities such as basket weaving, collecting bush tucker, painting and spear throwing. There is a small camping ground nearby with a few powered sites. (See *Contacts*, p. 71).

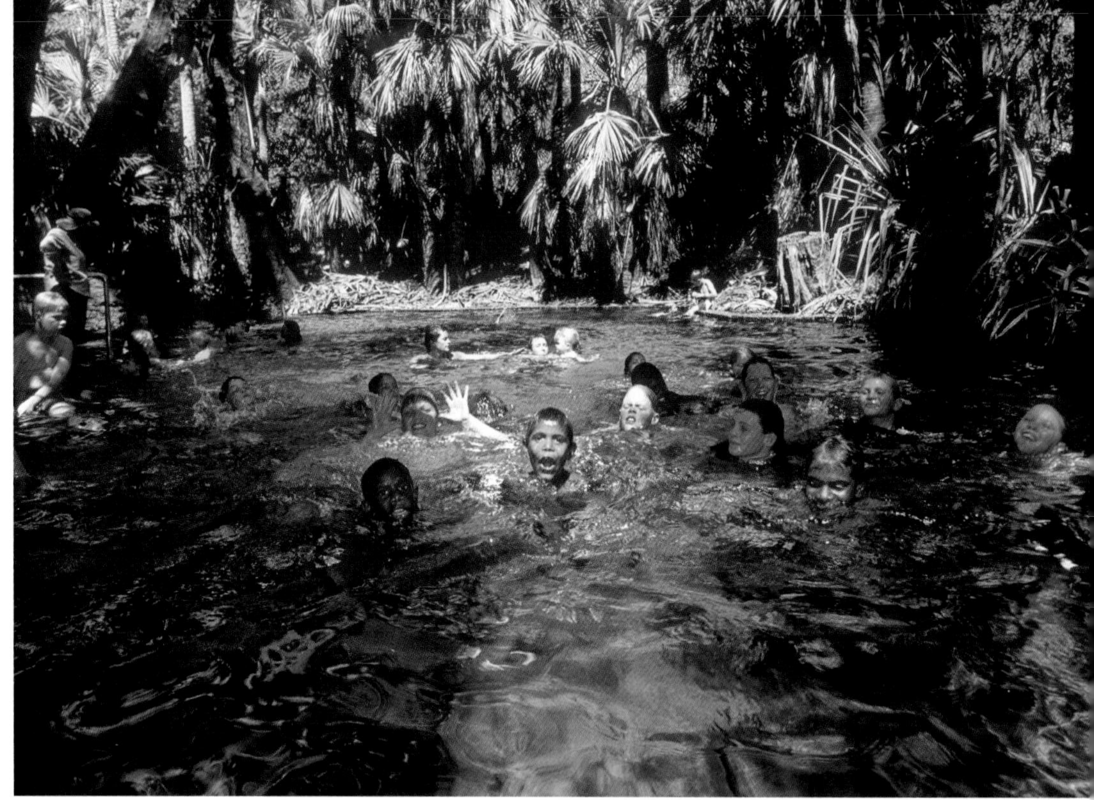

Swimming in the fresh thermal pools at Mataranka.

Never never land

Novelist Jeannie Gunn used the evocative description 'never never' in the title of her landmark book, *We of the Never Never*, a fictionalised account of Gunn's 13-month foray into the vast reaches of the remote region, accompanied by her husband Aeneas. With its tales of adventure, hardship and encounters with the Indigenous population, the novel, published in 1908, fired the imagination of a generation of readers. The Elsey Cemetery, 20 km south of Mataranka, contains the graves of Gunn's husband (Jeannie outlived him by 50 years) and various other characters from her book.

discover the wonders of this landscape – although helicopter rides are an option (check with the park's information centre for details of local operators, see *Fact File*, p. 71). The independent traveller can hire a canoe, or bring their own vessel into the park (these must be registered with park staff). With ranger permission, visitors can canoe to the higher gorges, camping overnight in designated areas.

Ten well-marked walking trails fan out alongside the gorges, ranging from a one-hour stroll to a five-day, 66 km trek north-west to Edith Falls (see below). Stop in at the impressive visitor centre at the park's entrance for information on the walks.

Leliyn (Edith Falls)

This lovely little pocket of Nitmiluk is reached via the Stuart Hwy north of Katherine. A short road leads to a natural pool fringed by pandanus and paperbark, fed by the cascading Edith Falls. Alongside is a private camping area with good facilities and a kiosk (see *Fact File*, p. 71). From here a walking trail leads to the top of the escarpment, where another idyllic pool offers safe swimming in the Dry. Salmon gums, identified by the glow of their rich creamy trucks, are common in the area and, if you are patient, you may spot the rare and brightly patterned Gouldian finch (see also *Gouldian finch*, p. 80).

Mataranka

The climate zone shifts from tropical to semi-arid conditions around the little settlement of Mataranka, with forests of stringybark, woollybutt, bloodwood and salmon gum marking the transition. The big rivers still flow: the mighty Roper River starts its journey here, before surging eastwards to drain into the Gulf of Carpentaria.

Near the township, Elsey NP (138 sq km) protects a meticulous reconstruction of the area's original homestead. It was built in the 1980s as a set for a film based on the book *We of the Never Never* (see side column). The homestead now forms part of the Mataranka Homestead Tourist Resort. The park's main drawcard is its picture-perfect thermal-spring pools. The pools filter 30 million litres of water every day – clear, emerald-green, bubbling to a spa-like 34°C and renowned for its curative and soothing effects. There is a private campsite at the nearby homestead and a park site further east at 12 Miles Yard on the Roper River (swimming and canoe hire are on offer). Walking and fishing are popular throughout the park.

Along the Arnhem Highway

Eight rivers converge along the Van Diemen Gulf coastline, creating vast water-logged plains and myriad billabongs. These swollen waterways are woven together by a dense mat of tropical vegetation. An outstanding array of wildlife, from big saltwater crocs to a plethora of waterbird species, inhabits this lush environment. The Arnhem Hwy, which stretches 249 km from just past Darwin to Jabiru in Kakadu NP (see *Kakadu and Arnhem Land*, p. 84), is a wide, sealed road, ffering numerous opportunities for visitors to top, look and marvel at the richness and beauty f the landscapes.

·ogg Dam and Adelaide River

·ogg Dam, about 35 km past the town of Howard prings, was built in the 1950s to supply water to ice farms. The area is now a conservation reserve nd wildlife sanctuary. Viewing platforms along the am wall as well as walking tracks give an insight nto wetland ecology. The adjacent rainforest is ome to a large colony of rainbow pittas – small, lack birds with green wings and an eye-catching ash of blue feathers.

Less than 10 km away at Beatrice Hill is Window n the Wetlands. This state-of-the-art information and nterpretive centre perches on a high point above the lood plains of the mighty Adelaide River. The centre as interactive displays about the region's ecological rocesses and seasonal changes. The views across he flood plains are superb. Just past the centre, on he opposite side of the highway, Jumping Crocodile Cruises set off for tours of the river, and offer the hance to spot dangerous saltwater crocodiles from he safety of a croc-proof vessel.

Mary River

Vhen the British arrived to settle Cobourg Peninsula (see p. 93) they brought buffalo from Indonesia; when they abandoned the settlement, defeated by isolation, disease and heat, they left the animals to roam free. For a century, hundreds of thousands of wild buffalo trampled the delicate terrain of the Mary River delta. Now protected within the bounds of a proposed national park, the delta's astonishing network of lagoons, canals and billabongs is slowly returning to its former glory. Patches of paperbark and spreading monsoon forests have made complex webs across the waterways, and large populations of sea eagles, egrets, pelicans, jabirus, jacanas, spoonbills and kingfishers thrive. Fishing and camping are the big drawcards – the barramundi are said to be the biggest in the Territory.

Mary River Crossing on the Arnhem Hwy, about 150 km from Darwin, is the easiest place to access the river – there are good picnic facilities and a boat ramp, but no camping. Couzens Lookout, a few kilometres west, does offer camping, along with superb views, particularly at sunset. A number of day-use and overnight visitor areas, along with two well-established wilderness lodges, are tucked away to the north of the highway along unsealed roads (these roads are generally suitable for 2WD travel, but only in the Dry). The most popular area is Shady Camp, a national park campground with boat ramp, boat hire and picnic facilities. Many visitors choose to explore this still very remote region as part of a tour – contact visit information in Darwin (see *Contacts*, p. 71).

Magpie geese thrive in the Top End's wetland areas.

Katherine to Keep River

Between the sultry northern tropics and the central deserts, vast cattle stations sprawl beside national park-protected woodlands and ragged escarpments. Crisscrossing the region is the broad weave of the mighty Victoria River.

From the regional centre of Katherine, the Victoria Hwy forges 550 km south-west to the WA town of Kununurra. The township of Timber Creek, near the western section of the extensive Gregory NP, marks the halfway point. Gregory NP takes in part of several former station properties and its rugged terrain invites 4WD enthusiasts and anglers.

Further west, hugging the state border, is the small but spectacularly scenic Keep River NP. A remote and not especially well-known park, Keep River is rich in wildlife, attracts a fascinating range of birds to its waterholes and also shelters some fine rock art. A number of walks in the park lead to some of the outstanding, and sometimes startling, landforms: beehive-shaped mounds, turreted outcrops and soaring gorges. Winding its way towards the Joseph Bonaparte Gulf is the mighty Victoria River, the NT's largest waterway, renowned for its bounty of prized barramundi. As you travel further west you will begin to see the twisted limbs of the iconic boab tree, so typical of WA's Kimberley region.

The region's main roads are sealed, which means 2WD travellers can experience much of the landscape, including key national parks. Walking, river cruises, fishing for barramundi, rock art, camping, and wonderful touring scenery are among the attractions and activities.

The area experiences two main seasons – a wet and a dry season – much like the more northern regions of the Top End, but with lower rainfall. The best time to visit is during the Dry, from April to October, when the sun shines, the sky is relentlessly blue and the crystal-clear atmosphere highlights the magnificence of the Top End's landscape.

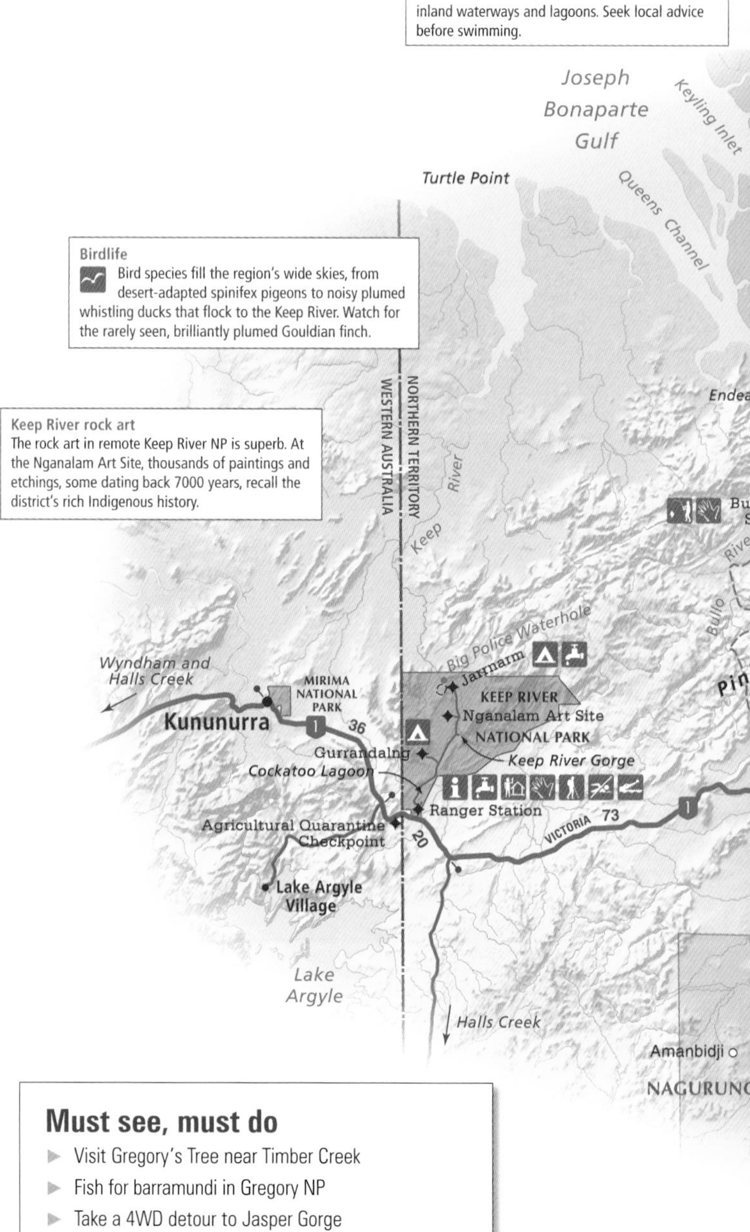

Crocodile warning
Dangerous saltwater crocodiles inhabit coastal waters, freshwater and saltwater inland waterways and lagoons. Seek local advice before swimming.

Birdlife
Bird species fill the region's wide skies, from desert-adapted spinifex pigeons to noisy plumed whistling ducks that flock to the Keep River. Watch for the rarely seen, brilliantly plumed Gouldian finch.

Keep River rock art
The rock art in remote Keep River NP is superb. At the Nganalam Art Site, thousands of paintings and etchings, some dating back 7000 years, recall the district's rich Indigenous history.

Must see, must do

- Visit Gregory's Tree near Timber Creek
- Fish for barramundi in Gregory NP
- Take a 4WD detour to Jasper Gorge
- Cruise the magnificent Victoria River
- View rock art in remote Keep River NP

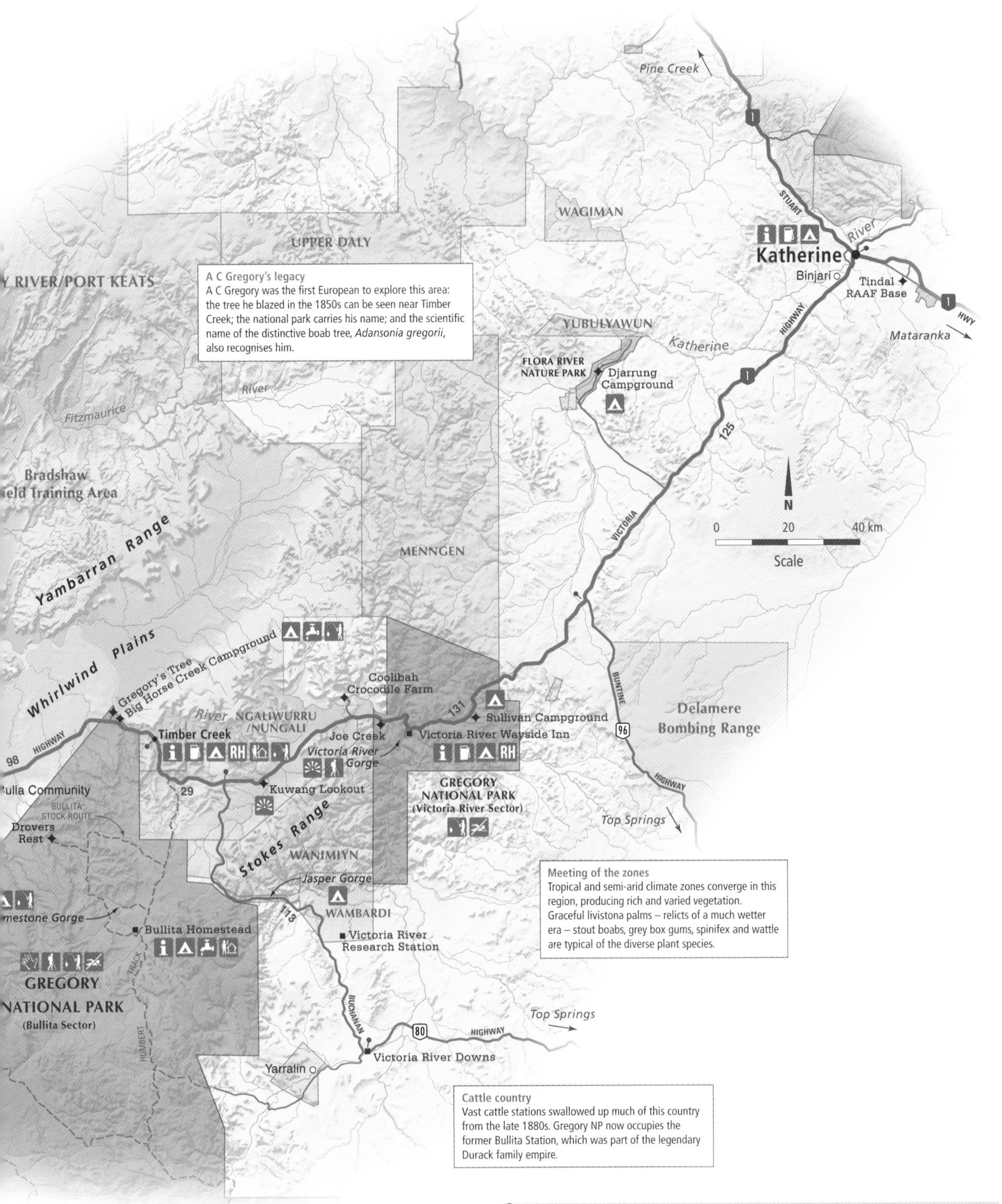

A C Gregory's legacy

A C Gregory was the first European to explore this area: the tree he blazed in the 1850s can be seen near Timber Creek; the national park carries his name; and the scientific name of the distinctive boab tree, *Adansonia gregorii*, also recognises him.

Meeting of the zones

Tropical and semi-arid climate zones converge in this region, producing rich and varied vegetation. Graceful livistona palms – relicts of a much wetter era – stout boabs, grey box gums, spinifex and wattle are typical of the diverse plant species.

Cattle country

Vast cattle stations swallowed up much of this country from the late 1880s. Gregory NP now occupies the former Bullita Station, which was part of the legendary Durack family empire.

Katherine ☎1800 653 142, (08) 8972 2650; www.visitkatherine.com.au

Fact File

Top events

Easter *Easter Barra Fishing Competition (Timber Creek)*
May *Big Horse Barra Classic Fishing Competition (Timber Creek)*
Aug *Timber Creek Camp Draft*

Permits and regulations

Aboriginal land Aboriginal land is private land. Timber Creek is on Aboriginal land, which extends east towards the Victoria River Wayside Inn. However, permits are not required to enter the town or use public roads in the area. Visitors must observe the normal restrictions applying to private property, including cattle stations.

Parks and reserves

For general information on parks in the NT, see *Travel Tips*, p.66.

Gregory NP The campgrounds in both sections are very busy during the Dry (April–Oct); bookings are not accepted; small camping fees apply (honesty boxes on site). Fishing is permitted throughout the park, but no nets or traps. Fresh and saltwater crocodiles inhabit most of the park's waterways – be crocodile wise; heed warning signs. A swimming hole at Limestone Gorge is considered 'croc free', but always check first. 4WD is recommended to reach Limestone Gorge and Bullita. Bullita Stock Route is 4WD only. Visitors planning to walk or 4WD in remote areas of the park are strongly advised to register: 1300 650 730. Drinking water is available in Timber Creek and at Victoria River Wayside Inn, but always carry supplies. For inquiries, contact ranger station at Timber Creek on (08) 8975 0888 or Bullita on (08) 8975 0833.

Keep River NP There are two campgrounds, both with basic facilities; generators are not permitted; small overnight fees apply; running water is available. No fishing is allowed in the park. The main park roads are gravel, but are suited to 2WD vehicles during the Dry. A permit is required to walk the overnight trail between Gurrandalng and Jarrnarm campgrounds; visitors must apply two days in advance and prove that they have suitable walking and navigation equipment (a GPS device is required – see *On the Road*, p. 246). For all queries contact on-site rangers: (08) 9167 8827.

Fishing

For general information on fishing in the NT see *Travel Tips*, p. 66. See also entries for individual national parks.

Warnings

Fuel and supplies Long distances separate fuel stops along the Victoria Hwy. There is no fuel between Timber Creek and Kununurra (225 km). Travellers along the Buchanan Hwy may be able to get fuel at the Victoria River Downs store (hours are limited); if store is closed, the next stop is 100 km away at Top Springs (see *Contacts*, opposite).

Road access and closures The main route, the Victoria Hwy, is sealed, but may be impassable during the Wet. The Buchanan Hwy (a dirt road) is considered suitable for conventional vehicles, but 4WD vehicles are recommended. For road conditions check NT Road Report: 1800 246 199. Many of the touring routes in Gregory NP are for high-clearance 4WD only; contact the ranger station at Timber Creek: (08) 8975 0888.

Boating Changing tides and hidden snags can make the Victoria River dangerous for boating, particularly around popular Big Horse Creek.

Crocodiles Freshwater and dangerous saltwater crocodiles inhabit many waterways throughout this region. Be crocodile-wise; heed warning signs; swim only where recommended. Take care when fishing and boating. Do not allow children to play near the edge of waterways.

See also *On the Road*, p. 246.

Above A water monitor suns itself near Wickham River, in Gregory NP.

Opposite A magnificent salmon gum in the Timber Creek district.

Katherine

Katherine is the place to stock-up before heading into more remote parts. This is the NT's third largest centre with a population of 11 000, servicing the surrounding pastoral district as well as travellers visiting nearby Nitmuluk NP or passing through on the Sturt Hwy. (For more about Katherine, see *Darwin to Mataranka* p. 68.) Victoria Hwy heads south-west from Katherine to Kununurra in WA, crossing the Victoria River and winding past Gregory NP. The road is sealed and well maintained, although past Timber Creek the remote countryside and lack of fuel stops mean travellers must be well prepared.

Victoria River

Just past Katherine, the vast pastures of legendary Top End cattle stations, many established in the late 1800s, sprawl in all directions. These stations are measured in square kilometres, not hectares, and cattle mustering is by helicopter rather than horse. The scenery is on a grand scale too, the wide plains ribbed by steep red escarpments, deep valleys and gorges. The Victoria River, which dominates the landscape between the Victoria River roadhouse, also known as the Wayside Inn, and Timber Creek, has carved its way through the sandstone over millions of years. The river was named after Queen Victoria by royalist sailors who arrived at its mouth in HMS *Beagle* in 1839 (the entrance is called Queens Channel).

These days, the 'Vic' can be enjoyed by a boat cruise from Timber Creek, especially at sunrise and sunset when spectacular colours are reflected on the water surface. Anglers come for the North's most-prized fighting fish, the great barramundi, as well as blue salmon, threadfin, and mudcrabs in the river's tidal sections. Ask about fishing tours at the visitor centres in Katherine or Timber Creek, or at the Victoria River roadhouse (see *Contacts*, opposite). Turtles, saltwater crocodiles and smaller freshwater crocodiles can also be observed.

;regory National Park

;regory NP spans two large areas, in all about 3 000 sq km. Most visitors, particularly those ı 2WDs, access the attractions in the immediate icinity of Victoria River crossing and Timber :reek. Those with the right equipment, including a igh-clearance 4WD vehicle, can explore the park's ıore rugged terrain and wilderness areas (register t the ranger station in Timber Creek and check ɔad conditions before heading off – see *Fact File* pposite).

The Victoria River Wayside Inn, 194 km west of :atherine, can be surprisingly busy during the Dry s tourists pull in and out to eat, camp and fuel up efore exploring the gorges and cliffs of the eastern ector of Gregory NP.

Impressive red cliffs form a 250 m high scarpment, with the river surging through a valley elow, and the vegetation a rich mix of tropical and emi-arid species. There are several walking trails. 'he 3 km return Escarpment Walk, which starts just ff the road near the Victoria River crossing, leads ɔ sensational river and escarpment views. Further vest, a 1.7 km walk sets off from the pretty Joe Creek icnic area; it features more escarpment scenery, tands of palms and Aboriginal art. There's camping t Sullivan Campground, east of the crossing.

Crocodile-spotting tours on the Victoria r a visit to the local crocodile farm, which has ıousands of saltwater crocs, are other activities ask at the roadhouse, or in Timber Creek – see :*ontacts*, above).

Jasper Gorge to Victoria River Downs

About 62 km west of the roadhouse, there is a turn-off onto the Buchanan Hwy (actually a dirt road) and another 40 km takes you to magnificent Jasper Gorge. There is a bush camping spot here on Jasper Creek. Eighty-six km south is Victoria River Downs – VRD or the 'Big Run' – which, with its 100 000 cattle, is still one of Australia's largest working stations. Its original homestead and former bush hospital are listed on the National Estate; there is no public access, though visitors can buy fuel at the station's small store.

The land between the roadhouse and Timber Creek is the traditional country of the Nungali

Explorer A C Gregory

In 1855 surveyor Augustus Charles Gregory arrived at the mouth of the Victoria River by sea. His brief from the British Government was to find grazing land and look for traces of explorer Ludwig Leichhardt's party, missing since 1848. Gregory, the first European to explore the Victoria River area, journeyed up the river with a small team, establishing a base at Timber Creek before heading further into the interior. Sheep died, rations ran out, men came down with scurvy and horses drowned in mangrove swamps and were eaten by crocodiles, but the party survived without losing a single man. They eventually traversed around 8000 km of land – west to what is now the WA/NT border, east to Cape York, and south to Moreton Bay (Brisbane).

Contacts

Visitor information

Katherine
cnr Stuart Hwy and Lindsay St
(08) 8972 2650 or
1800 653 142

Kununurra
Coolibah Dr
(08) 9168 1177

Timber Creek
Victoria River Cruise
Victoria Hwy
(08) 8975 0850

Parks and reserves

See *Fact File,* opposite

Roadhouses, station stays

Bullo River Station
(08) 8354 2719

Top Springs Roadhouse
(08) 8975 0767

Victoria River Wayside Inn
(Victoria River Roadhouse)
(08) 8975 0744

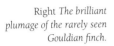

Right *The brilliant plumage of the rarely seen Gouldian finch.*

Below *Plumed whistling ducks take off in a flurry.*

Gouldian finch

Gouldian finches (*Erythrura gouldiae*) were once widespread throughout the tropical savannahs of northern Australia. Now listed as threatened, they are confined to a handful of areas in the NT, including Gregory NP, and the Kimberley in WA. The birds' fashion-plate looks have made them popular with aviary keepers and the species has thrived in captivity, but not in the wild.

Renowned 19th-century ornithologist John Gould named the species after his wife and fellow bird enthusiast, Elizabeth. The birds are known for their stunning plumage: mature male adults have a bright purple head, yellow breast and green back; the face colour can be red, black or yellow. The females have more subdued colouring and the young are a dullish green. During the Dry, the finches often nest in eucalypt woodlands. During the Wet, they move to lowland areas, and can occasionally be spotted feeding on perennial native grasses.

and Ngaliwuru peoples, along with a number of other closely related groups. Kuwang Lookout, 57 km west of the Victoria River roadhouse and on Aboriginal land, provides memorable views of the northern face of Stokes Range, and interpretative material on the area's Aboriginal history.

Timber Creek

There is not much in the tiny town of Timber Creek (population around 500) but it is rich in history – drovers, stockmen and early settlers all used this river port. Visit the park headquarters in the town, where you can pick up maps and other information and chat with rangers before exploring this sector of the park.

The 1856–57 exploration of the area by A C Gregory and colleagues is recorded on the trunk of a heritage-listed boab tree, 15 km north-west of Timber Creek. The western or Bullita sector of Gregory NP fans out south and west of Timber Creek. The land was formerly part of Bullita Station, which was part of a network of properties owned by the Australian pastoral family, the Duracks.

Most visitors head for the Big Horse Creek campground, a few kilometres west of town, where facilities include a boat ramp for the many keen barramundi anglers who holiday here. Campgrounds at Limestone Gorge and historic Bullita Homestead both offer fantastic walking trails and fishing. Challenging 4WD routes include the 90 km Bullita Stock Route. Wherever you are, keep an eye out for the superb local birdlife, which includes the rare and elegantly plumed Gouldian finch.

About 100 km west of Timber Creek is the turn-off to Bullo River Station, a vast working cattle property, which sprawls across 2000 sq km in the north-west corner of the Top End. The property is circled by the Victoria River and stretches to the horizon, freckled with gouty boabs, and taking in hidden gorges and waterfalls. There are hundreds

Above *Dramatic sandstone escarpment country in Keep River NP.*

Following page *An egret flies across still waters at Nourlangie Rock.*

of bird species, including many waterbirds, and prolific wildlife. The fishing is some of the Territory's best, with fresh water and tidal saltwater species (barramundi, of course, but also threadfin salmon, black bream and others). Cultural tours of the station's rock art, the chance to join mustering in season (the station runs 9000 cattle) and helicopter rides for an eagle's-eye view of the landscape are other possibilities. Hosted accommodation is available, but there is no camping (see *Contacts*, p. 79).

Keep River National Park

European settlement has had little impact on the remote, wild and ruggedly beautiful landscape protected within the Keep River NP (700 sq km). The park is reached along the Victoria Hwy, 150 km west of Timber Creek; the entrance is just 3 km from the NT/WA border.

This is the traditional preserve of the Mirriwung and Gadjerong peoples. Towering sandstone escarpments and rock formations, echoing the beehive shapes of WA's Bungle Bungle Range, rise from a mix of tropical and semi-arid vegetation, a diverse landscape of slender livistona palms, gouty boabs, grey box gums, bloodwoods, spinifex, desert grevilleas, wattle and kapok trees. The walls of a deeply incised river gorge chart the geological history of the area, while a rich repository of rock art speaks of the long history of Aboriginal occupation. Visitors – only about 10 000 a year – come to camp and to savour this tranquil wilderness. Although the Dry is peak season, some travellers arrive during the Wet – the green season – when the plains and woodlands become lush and the waterways swollen with seasonal rains.

Birdlife here is remarkable – around 190 species have been recorded, from desert species to waterbirds. The ephemeral Keep River, a raging torrent in the Wet, shrinks to a series of waterholes during the Dry, providing some wonderful birdwatching opportunities. At Cockatoo Lagoon, herons, brolgas, jabirus and whistling ducks swoop around the semi-permanent waterhole.

Thousands of rock paintings and etchings can be seen at the Nganalam (Little Corella) Art Site, north of Keep River Gorge. The works are believed to date back as much as 7000 years. One painting is of a 6 m long rainbow serpent, swaying languidly across the rock face. There are smaller art sites in the park – respect the sites and do not touch or disturb any artwork.

The park is accessible to 2WD vehicles, with camping at Gurrandalng, 15 km north of the park entrance, and Jarrnarm, 28 km north. Fascinating walking trails include the 4 km Keep River Gorge – definitely take a camera.

Kakadu and Arnhem Land

Kakadu National Park is a magnificent wilderness – waterlilies flower on serene billabongs, birds throng the waterways, the sun-scorched stone country, towering escarpment and woodlands stretch into the distance. East of the park lies the remote and pristine world of Arnhem Land.

Marine stingers
Dangerous marine stingers (box jellyfish) inhabit shallow coastal waters Oct–April. Seek local advice before swimming.

Crocodile warning
Dangerous saltwater crocodiles inhabit coastal waters, freshwater and saltwater inland waterways and lagoons. Seek local advice before swimming.

Kakadu, at almost 20 000 sq km, is Australia's largest national park. Classified as a World Heritage area, it is valued for its immense range of natural wonders and rich cultural heritage. Around 220 000 visitors a year come to marvel at the ancient Aboriginal rock art, cruise the Yellow Water billabong, and observe the masses of birdlife and predatory saltwater crocodiles at close range.

East of Kakadu, the vast wilderness of Arnhem Land sprawls across 97 000 sq km, edged by Van Diemen Gulf, the warm waters of the Arafura Sea and the Gulf of Carpentaria. The landscape of Kakadu and Arnhem Land is dominated by the Arnhem Land Plateau, an ancient sandstone plateau rising to 300 m, its escarpment extending 500 km or more at its western edge, weather-worn yet majestic.

Marking the north-west tip of Arnhem Land, jutting into the Timor Sea, is the isolated and scarcely touched wilderness of Cobourg Peninsula, protected within Garig Gunak Barlu NP.

Almost all of Arnhem Land is Aboriginal land and one of the last strongholds of traditional Aboriginal culture. To safeguard this unique area, access is strictly limited.

The intense tropical climate dictates the rhythm of life. During the long, hot Dry the land becomes parched, the heat is searing, smoke from bushfires smudges the horizon and man and animal retreat, waiting for relief. When relief comes it is life-giving – torrential rain washes the land, streams in sheets off the plateau, billows from waterfalls, and refreshes, renews and regenerates. And then the cycle begins again.

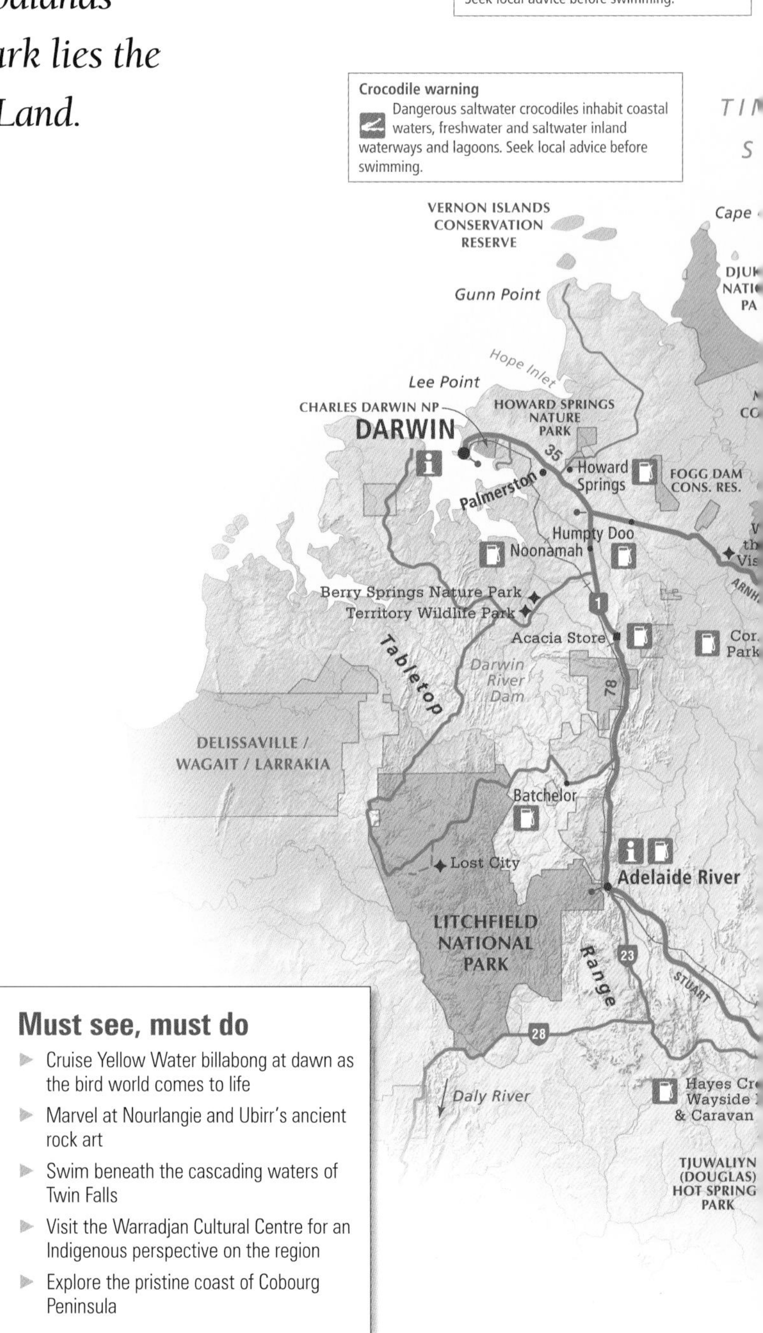

Must see, must do

- Cruise Yellow Water billabong at dawn as the bird world comes to life
- Marvel at Nourlangie and Ubirr's ancient rock art
- Swim beneath the cascading waters of Twin Falls
- Visit the Warradjan Cultural Centre for an Indigenous perspective on the region
- Explore the pristine coast of Cobourg Peninsula

Smith Point
Black Point (Algarlarlgarl)
Danger Point
Port Essington
Croker Island
Grant Island
Seven Spirit Wilderness Lodge
Fort Wellington (ruins)
Cobourg Peninsula
Victoria Settlement (ruins)
GARIG GUNAK BARLU NATIONAL PARK
Greenhill Island
Morse Island
Endyalgout Island
Mountnorris Bay
Murgenella
Cape Cockburn
De Courcy Point
ARAFURA SEA
Brogden Point
North Goulburn Island
South Goulburn Island
Aurari Bay
Braithwaite Point
Junction Bay
ARNHEM LAND
(4WD only)
Umorrduk
Mt Borradaile
Diemen Gulf
Gardangari (Field Island)
West Alligator Head
Finke Bay
POINT STUART COASTAL RESERVE
East Alligator
Maningrida and Nhulunbuy
Gunbalanya (Oenpelli)
Ubirr
Border Store
Merl
Cahills Crossing
0 20 40 km
Scale
KAKADU
South Alligator River
West Alligator River
Jabiluka Mineral Lease
Ranger Mineral Lease
Ranger Mine
Arnhem Land
Four Mile Hole
Two Mile Hole
Aurora Kakadu
Mamukala Wetlands
Bowali Visitor Centre
Jabiru
Mt Brockman 289
HIGHWAY
NATIONAL
Muirella Park
Nourlangie
Yellow Water
Gagudju Cooinda Lodge
Mardugal
Warradjan Aboriginal Cultural Centre
Jim Jim Billabong
JIM JIM ROAD
Mt Partridge 240
PARK
Jim Jim Falls (Barrkmalam)
Twin Falls (Gungkurdul)
Maguk
Gunlom (Waterfall Creek)
KAKADU HIGHWAY
Mary River
Gimbat
Mary River Roadhouse
Mt Davis 295
Katherine
NITMILUK NATIONAL PARK

Arnhem Land
Arnhem Land was named by Abel Tasman after the Dutch ship, *Arnhem*, which made the first known European contact with this area's coast in 1623.

Permits essential
Visitors must have a permit to drive across Arnhem Land, and to enter Garig Gunak Barlu NP. Permits are extremely limited. See *Aboriginal land, Fact File*, p. 86.

Wildlife abounds
Kakadu NP is literally teeming with wildlife – 280 or so bird species, more than 50 freshwater fish species, 60 mammal, at least 120 reptile, 25 frog and an estimated 10 000 insect species call this home.

Ancient rock art
In the caves and rock overhangs of Kakadu NP and Arnhem Land, thousands of Aboriginal paintings and etchings, dating back tens of thousands of years, provide a unique record of the world's oldest living culture.

Birdwatchers' paradise
One-third of Australia's bird species have been recorded at Kakadu NP and during the wet season 2.5 million birds congregate around the wetlands.

Camping
Key campsites are shown, but there are others. Check with the Bowali Visitor Centre (see *Fact File*, p. 86) for a full list.

Darwin ☎(08) 8980 6000; www.tourismtopend.com.au
Kakadu ☎(08) 8938 1121; www.environment.gov.au/parks/kakadu

Fact File

Top events

Aug *Wind Festival (Jabiru)*
Oenpelli Open Day (culture and bush tucker, Gunbalanya)

Permits and regulations

Aboriginal land Arnhem Land is controlled by the Arnhem Land Aboriginal Land Trust and access is strictly controlled. A permit is required to travel across Arnhem Land and to enter Garig Gunak Barlu NP (formerly Garig NP). Only a limited number of vehicles are permitted to cross each week. Travel across must be made in a single day. Apply up to one year in advance. Permits and bookings: (08) 8999 4814. Black Point Ranger Station: (08) 8979 0244. Cobourg Peninsula Sanctuary and Marine Park Board: PO Box 469, Palmerston, NT 0831; (08) 8999 4814; www.nt.gov.au/nreta/parks (go to Permits). For other travel to Arnhem Land contact the Northern Land Council: (08) 8920 5100; www.nlc.org.au

Parks and reserves

For general information about parks in the Top End, see *Travel Tips*, p. 66 For information about Kakadu NP contact Parks Australia: www.environment.gov.au/parks/kakadu For general information about Garig Gunak Barlu NP contact Parks and Wildlife Service of the NT (PWSNT): (08) 8999 4555;www.nt.gov.au/nreta/parks

Garig Gunak Barlu NP Visitors must purchase a permit. Apply well in advance (see details under *Aboriginal land* (above). The park includes marine park areas; some areas are off-limits for fishing.

Kakadu NP Camping fees apply. Access to some parts of the park in the south is only by 4WD during the Wet. 4WD access roads to Jim Jim and Twin Falls and to West Alligator Head are closed during the Wet. Permits are needed for overnight walks and for camping outside campsites. Some areas in Kakadu NP are off-limits for fishing; fishing for crabs is not permitted. For information contact Bowali Visitor Centre: (08) 8938 1121; www.environment.gov.au/parks/kakadu

Fishing

For general information on fishing in this region see *Travel Tips*, p.68. See also individual park entries.

Warnings

Fuel and supplies There are fuel stops between Jabiru and Black Point (Algarlargarl) at the Border Store at East Alligator River and at Gunbalanya (formerly Oenpelli).

Road access and closures The Arnhem Hwy and Kakadu Hwy are sealed roads but may be cut by floods during the wet season. Some areas of Kakadu NP are 4WD only. Arnhem Land is extremely remote – travellers must carry adequate supplies and be self-sufficient. A 4WD vehicle is necessary for the trip from Jabiru to Garig Gunak Barlu NP, and within the park. The road across Arnhem Land from Gunbalanya to Garig is usually closed during the Wet, Nov–April. Seek local advice about road and weather conditions. For up-to-date road reports contact Dept of Planning and Infrastructure (DPI): 1800 246 199; ww.ntlis.nt.gov.au/roadreport; or check with local police.

Crocodiles Freshwater and dangerous saltwater crocodiles are widespread throughout this region. Be crocodile-wise; heed warning signs; swim only where recommended. Take care when fishing and boating. Do not allow children to play near the edge of waterways.

See also *On the Road*, p. 246.

Jabiru and uranium mining

One of the world's richest uranium deposits is buried in Kakadu, and many believe the mining that takes place there jeopardises the park's pristine environment and its cultural heritage. The town of Jabiru was built for the workers of the Ranger mine. In 1992 it was agreed that a second mine, Jabiluka, would proceed only with the agreement of the Mirrar people, the traditional custodians; to date no such agreement has been given. Around 5000 tonnes of uranium oxide are produced by the Ranger mine each year. The traditional custodians receive a royalty on sales. Tours of the mine are available from May to September.

Above *Magpie geese nest on the water.*

Opposite *Light gleams off a towering wall of the Kakadu escarpment.*

Kakadu National Park

The Arnhem Land Plateau and its escarpment cut dramatically south-east across Kakadu. Deep gorges slashed through the escarpment shelter pockets of lush monsoon forest. Grass, scrub and open eucalypt forest spread across the plains that make up most of Kakadu, broken by dramatic rocky outcrops, or outliers. During the torrential rains of the tropical monsoon season, waterfalls plunge over the crumbling escarpment, channelling vast amounts of water into the river systems, creating extensive wetlands. Pandanus, cycads and

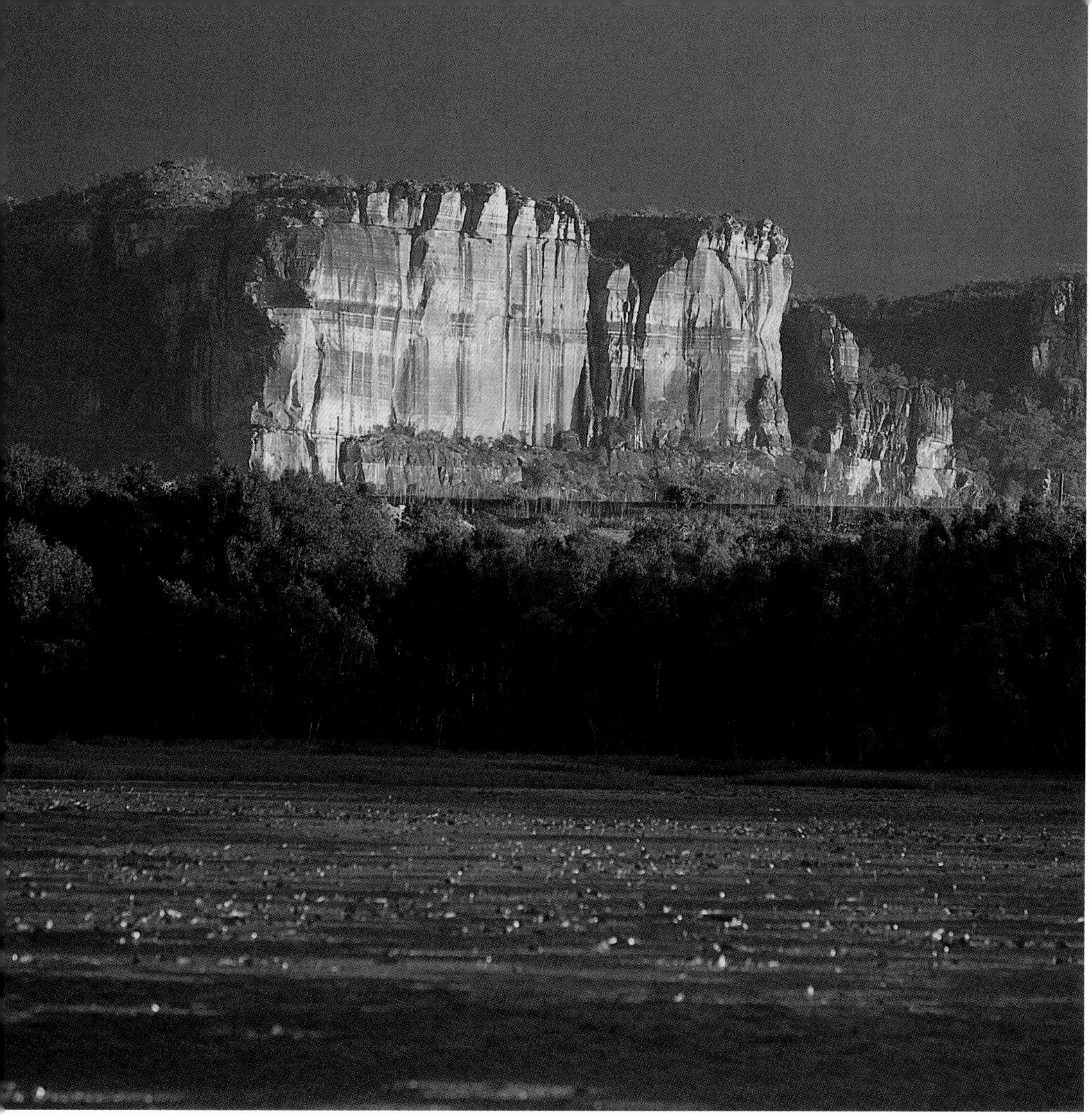

Contacts

Visitor information

Darwin (Top End)
cnr Bennett and Smith sts
(08) 8980 6000 or 1300 138 886
www.tourismtopend.com.au

Kakadu NP
Bowali Visitor Centre
(08) 8938 1121

Cultural centres

Injalak Arts and Crafts Centre
Gunbalanya
(08) 8979 0190

Warradjan Aboriginal Cultural Centre
(08) 8975 0051

Parks and reserves

See *Fact File,* opposite

Activities

Cruises

Guluyambi Cruises
1800 089 113

Yellow Water Cruises
(08) 8979 0145

Tours

Check with Tourism Top End or at the Bowali Centre, Kakadu NP (see above)

Ranger Mine Tours contact Kakadu Tours: 1800 089 113

agrant flowering paperbarks fringe tannin-stained llabongs. Beyond this, estuaries, tidal flats and ense mangrove forests rim the coast.

he original inhabitants

his area has been home to Aboriginal people r at least 50 000 years. For them, Kakadu is a vered cultural landscape, indivisible from their reation-time history and the ancestors who named d shaped the land, establishing their law. For enerations, these people sheltered in the caves and verhanging rock platforms during the long wet asons, leaving an unparalleled legacy of rock art d a precious record of their life and culture.

Kakadu NP is on Aboriginal land and is jointly anaged by the traditional custodians, the Bininj/ ungguy, and Parks Australia. The name Kakadu is erived from the Gagudja flood-plain language.

isiting the park

akadu NP is 170 km east of Darwin at its closest oint, stretches 210 km from north to south, and as two entry points. The northern entrance is 170 km by road, about two and a half hours' drive on the Arnhem Hwy from Darwin. The southern entrance is 300 km by road via Pine Creek, on the Stuart and Kakadu highways. There are also daily flights between Darwin and Jabiru.

Hotel or lodge accommodation is available at Jabiru, Cooinda, South Alligator and Ubirr. There are more than 20 separate camping areas (four with full facilities) and you can apply for a permit to camp outside these areas. The hub of the park is Jabiru, a neat, well-ordered town of about 1700 people, with a golf course, tennis courts and the famous crocodile-shaped Gagudju Holiday Inn.

Call at the Bowali Visitor Centre, 2 km from Jabiru, for an excellent introduction to the park's ecology from both European and Indigenous perspectives. The park's headquarters are also located here.

Cooinda, on the banks of Yellow Water billabong, is a popular place to stay, with a lodge, campsites, fuel, groceries, a cafe and an airport. Near Cooinda, the Warradjan Cultural Centre, architecturally designed to symbolise the area's

Saltwater crocodiles, or 'salties', can be found all across the Top End.

Ancient predator – the saltwater crocodile

Saltwater crocodiles (*Crocodylus porosus*), also known as estuarine crocodiles or 'salties', are widespread across the Top End and their fearsome reputation is justified – they are ferocious predators. They inhabit both salt and brackish water, living mostly in tidal estuaries, coastal swamps and mangrove forests, but can be found hundreds of kilometres out to sea, and hundreds of kilometres inland in tidal rivers, billabongs and swamps. Salties can also be found in fresh water. Male and female crocodiles are said to make ritual trips from salt to fresh water in areas such as Black Point (Algarlarlgarl) on the Cobourg Peninsula. According to rangers, this weekly ritual of gargling fresh water clears the build-up of grit in their teeth from hunting in brackish waters.

Female crocodiles lay about 50 eggs in huge reed nests during the wet season but less than one per cent survive. Once established, however, they are awesome, growing to 7 m in length (though the average is 4 m) and living for 70 or more years.

In the early 20th century saltwater crocodiles were hunted nearly to extinction for their prized skins. Although still listed as threatened, conservation programs have seen numbers in northern Australia recover to an estimated 80 000. Crocodile farms have also become big business.

Lilies

In season, from around March to November, a carpet of flowering waterlilies spreads across Kakadu's flood plains. The red or pink lotus lily is especially striking, with its fragrant deep-pink flowers on long green stems up to 2 m tall. Others are the snowflake lily, and the blue lily, which grows along billabong fringes, its violet-tipped white blooms appearing between January and July. Waterlilies were traditionally an important bush food for Aboriginal people of the area – the roots, stalks and seed heads were eaten either cooked or raw, and the seeds ground into flour.

distinctive pig-nosed turtle, presents the culture of the Aboriginal people.

What to do

Kakadu is huge and the options for exploring are plentiful – cruises on the broad rivers and waterways, bushwalking, fishing safaris, exceptional birdwatching, light plane and helicopter flights over the park, ancient rock-art sites to visit, picnics near lily-covered billabongs, drifting beneath magnificent waterfalls, and Aboriginal-guided tours. During the Dry, rangers run a series of free walks and talks that provide an insight into the park's many facets.

Birdwatching

Kakadu is one of the first stops for migratory waterbirds from the north. This, together with the variety of habitats, makes the park a paradise for birdwatchers. One-third of Australian species have been recorded here. At the end of the Dry, millions of birds congregate around shrinking creeks, billabongs and waterholes – the 2 m tall jabaru or black-necked stork, stately brolgas, gangly egrets, ibis, whistling ducks, cormorants and more. Head for Mamukala and other wetlands or join a Yellow Water cruise (see below) for closer viewing.

During the wet season huge numbers of magpie geese spread across the flood plains, building their breeding platforms on woven swamp grasses. Their eggs in particular were traditionally considered excellent bush tucker. The birds often perch high in trees, their plaintive 'honking' echoing across the plains.

Bowerbirds, grass wrens and owls nest in the drier plateau country. Red-tailed black cockatoos and parrots prefer open forest, especially after fire when seeds are dispersed. During the Dry, when fires flush out small wildlife, falcons and kites can often be seen swooping in search of food. The ish- and crustacean-dense mangrove forests and ivers provide rich pickings for many species, ncluding kingfishers and herons. Along the coast andpipers, curlews and plovers thrive and majestic vhite-breasted sea eagles nest.

Vildlife-watching

'he extreme climate and rich and varied habitats nean Kakadu is home to an astonishing variety of lora and fauna – as well as 280 or so bird species, nore than 50 freshwater fish species, 60 mammal, 20 reptile, 25 frog and thousands of insect species all this home.

Most of the mammals (including the 28 species f bat) are nocturnal, shy, or only come out to feed n the cool of the morning or evening, but you may limpse wallaroos, wallabies and kangaroos.

Amongst the abundant reptiles, the saltwater rocodile is certainly the most dangerous, although isitors shouldn't underestimate the freshwater rocodile. Smaller, and recognisable by its long, arrow snout, it can defend its territory aggressively. 'here are 36 land snakes (including four venomous pecies) and a wealth of lizards, with the intriguing rilled lizard often spotted on the roadside during he Wet.

Of the estimated 10 000 insect species, the mosquito sometimes seems the most prevalent (take plenty of insect repellent) while termites – or at least their towering mounds – are the most visible. The most brilliant insect is the rarely seen orange-and-blue Leichhardt's grasshopper. If you're lucky you might encounter one in the escarpment country, especially near the end of the Dry – their presence is said to herald the wet season.

Bushwalking

Marked walking trails, most of them relatively easy, range from 1 km to 12 km, though the adventurous can strike out in other directions across more challenging terrain. Pick up walking notes at the Bowali Visitor Centre, or at the start of walks. Permits are needed for overnight walks (see *Fact File* p. 66) and walkers should carry a topographic map and drinking water.

Fishing

Kakadu's network of tidal rivers, creeks, coastal estuaries and beautiful billabongs are fishing heaven. More than 50 native freshwater species swim the park's rivers, and a range of saltwater fish such as threadfin salmon and snapper are popular catches.

Perfectly balanced, a jacana walks across lily pads.

Water thunders down at Jim Jim Falls during the wet season.

But the famed fighting barramundi is the most talked-about catch, especially during the 'run-off', in the months after the wet season. Make sure to check park restrictions on fishing.

Ubirr and Nourlangie

Kakadu's two great rock-art sites are at Ubirr and Nourlangie. At Ubirr, 39 km north of Jabiru, X-ray paintings of wildlife, sprayed hand stencils, Creation beings such as the powerful Rainbow Serpent, delicate 'mimi spirits' and contact art showing balanda, or 'whitefellas', reveal the complexity of styles and subjects.

At Nourlangie Rock, 35 km south-east of Jabiru, the black-and-orange stained sandstone outcrop looms large. Around 60 art sites provide a continuous record of Aboriginal lifestyle and art over 20 000 years. There are three main sites, reached by a 1.5 km circular walk from the carpark. The main Anbangbang gallery focuses on Namarrgon, the Lightning Man, an important Creation Ancestor, considered responsible for the wet season's vivid lightning storms. A short walk from the gallery leads to a magnificent view of the escarpment.

The Nourlangie area is also a favourite with bushwalkers.

Cruises

A dawn cruise on the waterlily-covered Yellow Water, part of the South Alligator flood plain, is a magical experience as corellas, cockatoos, jacanas, sea eagles and brolgas start their day in a cacophony of sound. Sunsets here are spectacular too. This is also perfect croc-watching territory, but stay well within the boat. Cruises run all year, leaving from Cooinda, but access may be limited during the Wet. Bookings are essential (see *Contacts*, p. 87).

The Aboriginal-guided Guluyambi Cruise on the East Alligator River, with a focus on Aboriginal traditions, is also recommended. Cruises depart several times daily from East Alligator, near the Border Store (see *Contacts*, p. 87).

Jim Jim Falls and Twin Falls

During the wet season and the beginning of the Dry, the thunder of waterfalls adds another dimension to the Kakadu environment. Two of the most spectacular falls are Jim Jim (Barrkmalam) and Twin Falls (Gungkurdul), which are 45 km south of Jabiru, then about 2 hours' drive off the Kakadu Highway on a dry-season only track. Twin Falls is a further 10 km and you'll need a 4WD fitted with a snorkel to cross Jim Jim Creek. A certain amount of walking and rock-scrambling is also needed to reach the falls.

When Jim Jim is flowing at the end of the Wet, a curtain of white water plummets 200 m to a tree-fringed pool (check it is croc-free before even considering a swim, and do not swim downstream of the pool). Jim Jim often dries to a trickle by July, the peak tourist season. Twin Falls, however, flows all year, the water spilling endlessly into a crystal-clear pool. During the Wet the only way to enjoy the spectacle of these isolated falls is from the air.

Some of Kakadu's finest rock art can be seen at Nourlangie Rock, in Arnhem Land.

Rock art – myths, legends, law

For Aboriginal people, art expresses a profound, spiritual relationship with the land and its creation by ancestral beings. Myths, legends and law were handed down through their rock paintings, but the paintings also recorded their daily lives. During the wet season, people would shelter in caves and rock platforms and would paint and draw using red and yellow ochres, charcoal and white pipeclay.

Rock art at Kakadu and in Arnhem Land spans thousands of years, layer upon layer of history, culture and style. The earliest rock art depicts Creation beings, such as the mythical Rainbow Serpent, said to have created many landforms in the wake of its journeys. Food items were often painted, to ensure bountiful harvests and hunts. Barramundi have been depicted for up to 10 000 years.

The freshwater period, dating back 1500 years, includes the X-ray style, where humans and animals were depicted with their organs shown. One painting depicts a thylacine or Tasmanian tiger, thought to have become extinct on the mainland 3000 years ago. The so-called Contact art depicts the visits of Macassan traders, coming in search of trepang or sea cucumbers, and the arrival of European ships and explorers.

In Kakadu itself, 5000 art sites have been recorded so far and many more are known to exist.

Arnhem Land

Arnhem Land extends from Port Roper on the Gulf of Carpentaria to the East Alligator River in the north and the border of Kakadu NP. This is a timeless landscape, where paperbark-lined creeks meander across the central plateau through a patchwork of rocky outcrops and woodlands.

This is Aboriginal land, home to 18 000 traditional owners, and its privacy is closely guarded to protect its culture and environment. Although it is possible to fly to Nhulunbuy on Gove Peninsula, in eastern Arnhem Land, or to the isolated world of Garik Gunag Barlu NP on Cobourg Peninsula, road access is strictly limited. Day permits are relatively easy to obtain to make the trip to Gunbalanya (formerly Oenpelli) in western Arnhem Land, to visit the arts centre. A permit to drive across Arnhem Land to Garig Gunak Barlu NP, however, must be arranged well in advance. A limited number of vehicles a week are permitted to make the trip (see *Fact File*, p. 86) and the road is closed for several months during the Wet, usually November to April.

Jabiru to Gunbalanya (Oenpelli)

The small Aboriginal community at Gunbalanya focuses on arts and is well worth visiting. The town, 60 km north of Jabiru, is reached by 4WD, crossing the notoriously dangerous East Alligator River at the tidal Cahills Crossing. Day permits to enter Arnhem Land can be arranged through the Northern Land Council, Jabiru (see *Fact File*, p. 86).

Aboriginal seasons

Up to seven 'seasons' are recognised by Aboriginal clan groups in the Top End, sensitive to the nuances of different bush food harvesting times and the subtleties of seasonal variations. These seasons shaped the lifestyle of traditional owners, dictating when to move camp, when to look for certain foods, when to start burning grassy areas. The Kakadu Bininj/Mungguy people, for example, recognise six seasons: Gunumeleng, pre-monsoon storm season; Gudjewg, monsoon season; Banggerreng, 'knock 'em down' storm season, when pounding rains flatten the fresh grass; Yegge, cooler but still humid season; Wurrgeng, cold weather season; and Gurrung, hot, dry weather.

The flood plains meet the escarpment country, near Mt Borradaile.

The drive past the flood plains of the East Alligator River reveals stunning red lily lagoon country and the burnt-orange of the rugged sandstone escarpment. There is some superb rock art at Injalak Hill behind the community, with local guides taking tours. Gunbalanya's contemporary art is showcased at the non-profit Injalak Arts and Crafts Centre.

Mt Borradaile and Umorrduk

Commercial tours take visitors deeper into Arnhem Land, to natural galleries at Mt Borradaile and Umorrduk. At Mt Borradaile a labyrinth of caverns contain paintings detailing the spiritual and daily life of Aboriginal people over 50 000 years. An impressive Rainbow Serpent, a Creation being, writhes more than 6 m across the roof of the main sandstone gallery. The escarpment galleries overlook rivers, flood plains and woodlands, with crocodiles, barramundi, and clouds of magpie geese and sea eagles wheeling overhead. Iridescent water pythons, which still inhabit the flood plain, are believed to have been the model for the Creation serpent.

At Umorrduk, 15 km north-west of Mt Borradaile, the rock art is characterised by a plethora of paintings of women, colourful examples of the famous X-ray style and contact art (see *Rock art – myths, legends, laws*, p. 91).

Gunbalanya to Cobourg Peninsula

A permit is needed to cross western Arnhem Land to reach Cobourg Peninsula and to enter Garig Gunak Barlu NP. This is remote, 4WD territory, so make sure you are self-sufficient and well supplied (see *Fact File*, p. 86, and *On the Road*, p. 246).

Fire – cool burns

Aboriginal people traditionally used fire to regenerate growth, to flush out game and for ceremonial purposes. Today, the Parks and Wildlife Commission of the NT has its own controlled burning practices, conducted early in the dry season, to prevent the build-up of natural fuel that would allow ravaging, damaging bushfires. Spread in a mosaic burn pattern following the Aboriginal practice, these 'cool' burns limit the spread of major bushfires, or wildfires, when they do inevitably occur.

harter flights fly into Garig, and are the only way
during the Wet.

As you drive north from Gunbalanya you ave the flood plains and stone country of the scarpment and cross open woodland, with sombre ringybark and messmate trees. Wild banteng ndonesian cattle), wild boar and buffalo roam e country, more visible than any native wildlife s you reach one of the country's last frontiers, obourg Peninsula.

:obourg Peninsula and Garig ;unak Barlu National Park

arig Gunak Barlu NP (formerly Gurig NP and obourg Marine Park), 570 km by road north-east f Darwin, occupies the entire Cobourg Peninsula. he park, covering 4500 sq km, is on Aboriginal nd, administered by the traditional custodians nd the NT Parks and Wildlife Commission. he name derives from the language of the four vaidja-language clans who share custodianship: arig, their cultural name; Gunak, land; and Barlu, eep water.

Patches of paperbark, swamp and eucalypt orest and serene billabongs are highlights of the nterior. Ribbons of yellow and white sand and tangle of mangroves fringe the pale, turquoise vaters of the Arafura Sea. Here, coral reefs, eagrass meadows and abundant marine life thrive, ncluding the threatened dugong, giant manta rays nd six species of marine turtle. Swimming is not ecommended – saltwater crocodiles, poisonous tonefish and, in season, potentially lethal marine tingers also frequent these waters.

The legendary fishing lures anglers to the eninsula, but walking the pristine beaches, bird- nd wildlife watching are other favourite pastimes.

Above *A water python in the flood plains north of Kakadu.*

Below left *A wild water buffalo enjoys some choice greens.*

Black Point (Algarlarlgarl)

First stop on the peninsula is the small community of Black Point (known as Algarlarlgarl to the traditional custodians), to register your permit with the rangers, stop in at the general store and cultural centre. Accommodation ranges from self-contained cabins at Smith Point and two camping grounds at Black Point (BYO everything) to the luxury, eco-sensitive Fishing Lodge at historic Cape Don lighthouse, and the serene surrounds of Seven Spirit Wilderness Lodge.

What to do

Garig is a feast for birdwatchers, with the internationally recognised wetlands attracting a huge migratory population of waterbirds, including the jacana, jabiru, spoonbill and brolga. There are plenty of crocodiles to spot for; or, after seeking ranger guidance, observe marine turtles nesting at night on Black Point beach during June and July. Watch for wallabies, grey kangaroos and bandicoots.

For fishing enthusiasts, the prized catch is barramundi, but anglers head offshore for mackerel, barracuda, queenfish, snapper and more. Giant clams, rock oysters, crayfish and succulent mud crabs can also be caught (check fishing regulations as these waters are part of the marine park). Local clans have permission to hunt some protected species using traditional hunting methods – ask the rangers about joining one of these trips (see *Fact File*, p. 86).

Visit the historic outpost of Victoria Settlement. In 1838 the British established the colony at Port Essington, 'to defend the North'. The settlement struggled for 11 years, doomed to failure by isolation, food shortages, fever and the totally alien climate and environment. The eerie ruins are today a poignant memorial to those early settlers.

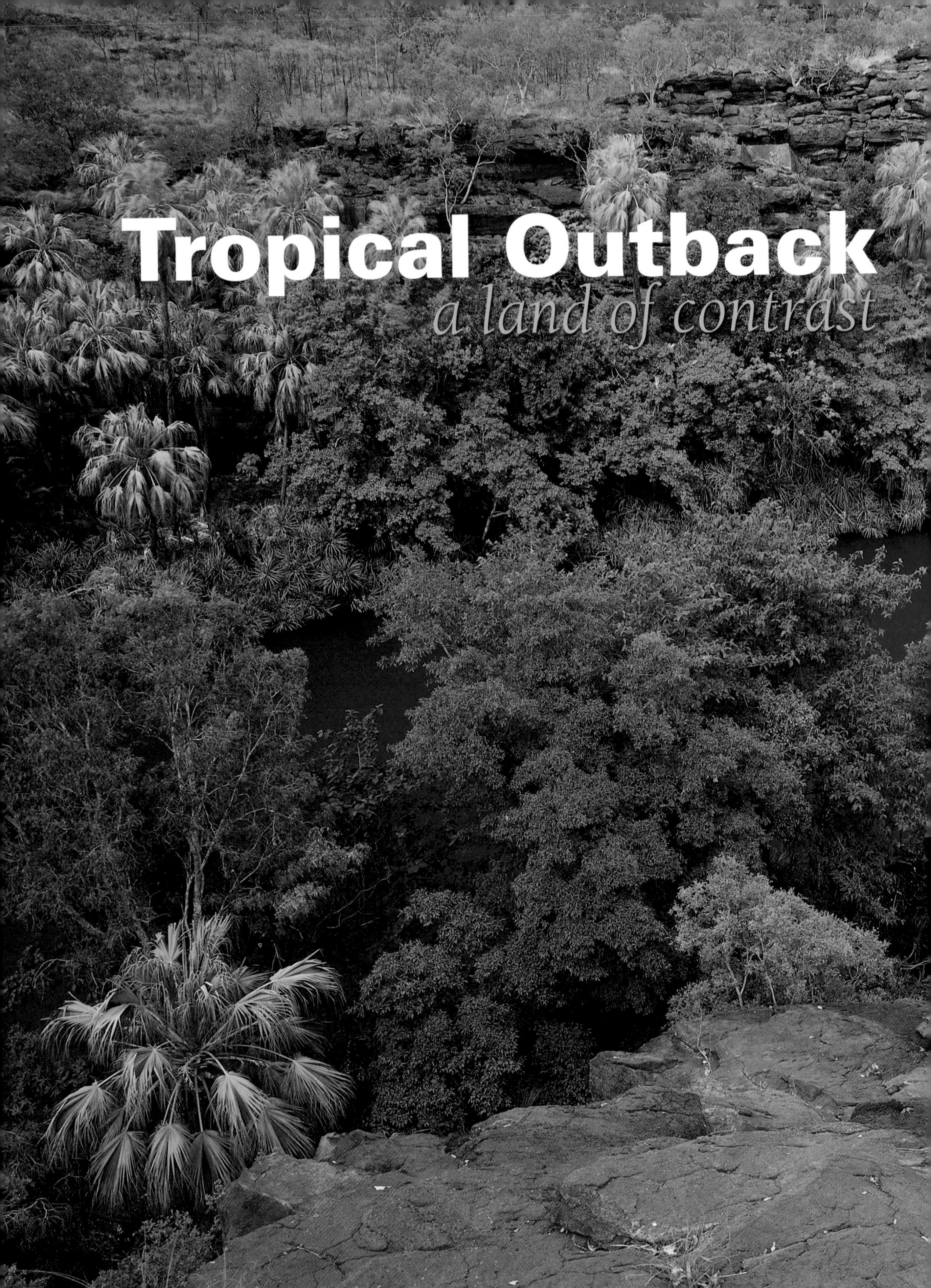

Tropical Outback

a land of contrast

Tropical Outback

The Tropical Outback stretches from the heat-cracked plains of western Queensland, past the Gulf Country's savannah plains and maze of coastal rivers to the dry woodlands and virgin rainforest of Cape York Peninsula, as it pushes deep into the tropics.

Tropical Outback Regions

Mossman to Lakefield National Park

Cape York Peninsula's south-eastern coastal region is busy with tourists exploring the World Heritage-listed forests of Daintree NP. Further north, cultural tourists travel to Laura for the intriguing Quinkan rock art, while anglers, walkers and campers with a predilection for doing it rough target the remote Lakefield NP. *See p. 100*

Coen to the Cape

Far north Queensland's isolation, its woodland country, pockets of heavily woven rainforest, tangled mangroves and extreme weather conditions entice adventure travellers. The tiny population is dispersed among a few towns and traditional Aboriginal communities. Visitors enjoy the fishing, the scenery and the sheer sense of escape and adventure. *See p. 106*

Gulf Country

This big, flat area lies in the broad scoop of the Gulf of Carpentaria coastline and includes the south-east coastal corner of the NT. Most visitors come for the exceptional river and ocean fishing, to explore the savannah plains by 4WD, and to enjoy the oasis-like gorges of Boodjamulla (Lawn Hill) NP. *See p. 114*

Outback Queensland

On remote stations, down mines and in the frontier towns of this wide, dusty land, many an Australian icon has been born. *Waltzing Matilda* was inspired, the Royal Flying Doctor Service, Qantas, and even the union arm of the Labor movement began their days here. Museums document these events, while the countryside offers excellent outback touring. *See p. 122*

Ulysses butterfly

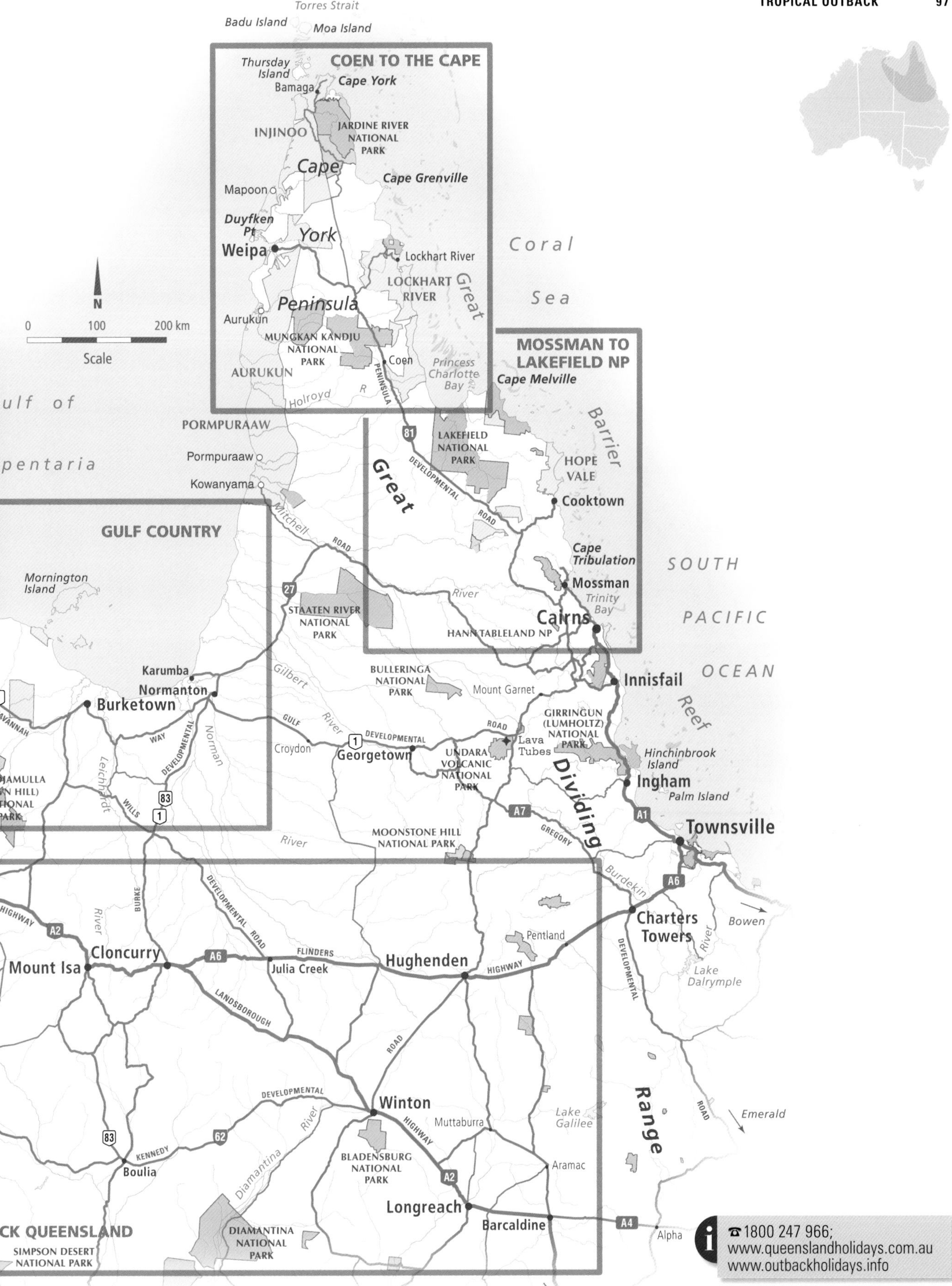

Torres Strait
Badu Island
Moa Island
COEN TO THE CAPE
Thursday Island
Bamaga
Cape York
INJINOO
JARDINE RIVER NATIONAL PARK
Cape
Cape Grenville
Mapoon
Duyfken Pt
York
Weipa
Lockhart River
LOCKHART RIVER
Peninsula
Aurukun
MUNGKAN KANDJU NATIONAL PARK
Coen
AURUKUN
Princess Charlotte Bay
Holroyd
PENINSULA
Coral
Sea
Great
N
0 100 200 km
Scale
MOSSMAN TO LAKEFIELD NP
Cape Melville
Barrier
LAKEFIELD NATIONAL PARK
HOPE VALE
Cooktown
Great
DEVELOPMENTAL ROAD
PORMPURAAW
Pormpuraaw
Kowanyama
ulf of
pentaria
GULF COUNTRY
Mitchell
ROAD
Cape Tribulation
Mossman
Trinity Bay
Cairns
SOUTH
PACIFIC
OCEAN
Mornington Island
STAATEN RIVER NATIONAL PARK
River
HANN TABLELAND NP
Karumba
Normanton
Burketown
Gilbert
River
BULLERINGA NATIONAL PARK
Mount Garnet
Innisfail
Reef
GIRRINGUN (LUMHOLTZ) NATIONAL PARK
Lava Tubes
GULF DEVELOPMENTAL ROAD
WAY
DEVELOPMENTAL
Norman
Croydon
Georgetown
UNDARA VOLCANIC NATIONAL PARK
Dividing
Hinchinbrook Island
Ingham
Palm Island
Leichhardt
WILLS
River
MOONSTONE HILL NATIONAL PARK
A7
GREGORY
A1
Townsville
Burdekin
A6
HIGHWAY
A2
River
BURKE
DEVELOPMENTAL ROAD
Charters Towers
Bowen
River
Pentland
Cloncurry
A6
FLINDERS
Julia Creek
Hughenden
HIGHWAY
Mount Isa
LANDSBOROUGH
DEVELOPMENTAL
Lake Dalrymple
ROAD
Range
ROAD
Emerald
DEVELOPMENTAL
Winton
River
Muttaburra
HIGHWAY
Lake Galilee
KENNEDY
Boulia
Diamantina
BLADENSBURG NATIONAL PARK
Aramac
A2
Longreach
Barcaldine
A4
Alpha
CK QUEENSLAND
SIMPSON DESERT NATIONAL PARK
DIAMANTINA NATIONAL PARK
Charleville
☎ 1800 247 966;
www.queenslandholidays.com.au
www.outbackholidays.info

Travel Tips

When to go

Except for Outback Queensland, the regions described in this section are subject to a tropical wet/dry weather pattern. The Dry, the main tourist season, runs April–Oct, give or take a few weeks: temperatures sit fairly constantly in the 30–35°C range, but humidity and rainfall are low. During the Wet, the region experiences torrential rain and high humidity; roads flood frequently and tourist facilities, particularly in the far north, close. The Outback Queensland area, which occupies the mid-section of the state, can catch the edge of the Wet, but the problem here in the summer months is extreme heat rather than torrential rain: daily maximums Dec–Jan sit at around 37°C. For further information, contact the Bureau of Meteorology (BOM): 1900 955 360 (Qld); 1900 955 367 (NT); www.bom.gov.au

CLIMATE												LONGREACH
	J	F	M	A	M	J	J	A	S	O	N	D
Max °C	37	36	35	31	27	24	23	26	30	34	36	37
Min °C	23	23	20	16	12	8	7	8	12	17	20	22
Rain mm	58	68	43	10	13	5	4	3	3	16	16	44
Raindays	7	7	5	3	3	2	2	2	2	4	4	6

CLIMATE												WEIPA
	J	F	M	A	M	J	J	A	S	O	N	D
Max °C	32	31	32	32	32	31	30	32	33	35	35	33
Min °C	24	24	24	23	21	20	19	19	20	21	23	24
Rain mm	421	401	338	82	6	2	1	1	1	14	98	256
Raindays	22	21	20	10	3	2	1	1	1	3	8	16

Aboriginal land

Large areas in northern Qld, particularly on Cape York and over the border in NT, are Aboriginal land. This land is private property and travellers should respect the rights of the traditional owners. In many cases, particularly along the western coast of the Cape, the owners encourage campers and anglers to come and enjoy their land, but permits and fees apply (see *Fact File* in individual regions for details, where applicable). If you do enter communities, respect people's privacy. Some Aboriginal communities are 'dry' and no alcohol is permitted at all. To find out more about the land and its communities around Cape York, contact Atsip: www.atsip.qld.gov.au For all queries relating to Aboriginal land in the NT, contact the Northern Land Council: (08) 8920 5100; www.nlc.org.au

Parks and reserves

Permits are required to camp in national parks in Qld. For some parks, bookings for campsites need to be made well in advance; in others, it's first come, first served. Many campsites have self-registration sites. Most of the very remote parks in northern Qld have an on-site ranger station; visitors are encouraged to advise staff of their length of stay, planned activities and so on. Many parks either do not allow fishing or allow it only in certain areas; others have specific instructions, for example, to do with lighting of fires and the use of generators.

Check the *Fact File* for each region; however, it is a good idea to ring and check requirements before travelling as this information does change. For general information on parks and reserves in Qld contact Queensland Parks and Wildlife Service (QPWS) 1300 130 372; www.derm.qld.gov.au

Fishing

Licences are not required for recreational fishing in Qld or NT, but regulations are in place to ensure the quality of recreational fishing is maintained. Worth noting are the restrictions that apply to the highly sought after barramundi. In Qld, there is a bag limit of five, a maximum length of 120 cm, and minimum lengths of 58 cm (east coast) and 60 cm (Gulf of Carpentaria). For further information contact the Dept of Primary Industries: 13 2523; www.dpi.qld.gov.au/fishweb In the NT, there is a bag limit of five and a minimum length of 55 cm. For further information contact NT Fisheries: (08) 8999 2144; www.nt.gov.au/d/fisheries Information is also available at www.fishingtheterritory.com.au National parks have their own fishing guidelines (see *Parks and reserves,* above).

Warnings

Fuel and supplies Many areas in these regions are remote and drivers should be well equipped and self-sufficient. In some areas long distances separate fuel stops.

Road access and closures Avoid driving at dawn, dusk and at night, when wildlife and stock can wander onto roads. During the Wet, especially Jan–Mar, many roads, particularly in the Gulf country and north of Cairns, are subject to flooding. In some areas 4WD roads may be closed for several months. Many national parks have unsealed roads; some require 4WD vehicles, some require high-clearance 4WD. Check road conditions in Qld with the RACQ: 13 1905; www.racq.com.au Check conditions in NT with the Dept of Planning and Infrastructure (DPI): 1800 246 199; www.ntlis.nt.gov.au/roadreport Or check with local police, national park rangers or at roadhouses.

Remote travel Drivers and walkers need to be aware of the remote nature of many areas of outback Qld and NT. Those venturing off major tourist routes should consider carrying an emergency communications device (see *On the Road*, p. 246).

Maps Maps in this book are guidelines only – carry detailed maps.

Crocodiles Northern Australia has two types of crocodiles. Potentially man-eating saltwater or estuarine crocodiles (*Crocodylus porosus*) can be found in salt, brackish and fresh water on Cape York and across the Gulf country. They can be found hundreds of km out to sea, as well as in inland waterways. They are large, well camouflaged and dangerous. Heed all warning signs. Take care when boating and fishing. Only swim where recommended. Do not allow children or dogs to play near the edge of waterways.

Freshwater crocodiles (*Crocodylus johnstoni*) are smaller and recognisable by their long, narrow snout. They are less dangerous but will still guard their territory and young fiercely if they need to. Stay well away from these crocodiles.

See also *On the Road*, p. 246.

Opposite top *Dense rainforest at Kennedy Inlet, Cape York.*

Opposite below *Waterlilies bloom on the Cape's wetlands.*

Below *A sheepdog cools off.*

Despite the existence of busy towns, and of major industries such as mining and farming, particularly further south, the entire region, stretching from the Tropic of Capricorn to the tip of Cape York, has the feel of a place that has yet to be fully explored.

The most settled section is the wide belt of farming and mining land that runs westwards from the coastline between Rockhampton and Townsville – the Outback Queensland. It catches the edge of the tropical wet/dry weather pattern, but lies too far inland to benefit from seasonal downpours. It is hot, dry, vast and flat. But out here the climate has helped guard ancient treasures – dinosaur fossils from millions of years ago, and metals that have formed the basis of mining empires. Sealed roads connect well-serviced towns, but the area retains a world's-end feel with its dusty horizons, deep silences, huge skies and occasional crop of rugged, low-slung hills.

The southern half of Cape York Peninsula, from Mossman to Lakefield NP, protects the World Heritage-listed rainforests known as the Wet Tropics. Large numbers of tourists arrive to experience the dense and tangled beauty of one of the world's most ecologically rich environments, with its ancient plant species and rare wildlife. But, once you venture beyond the end of the sealed road at Cape Tribulation, it is still largely a wilderness area; if you plunge into the riverine and woodland country protected by Lakefield NP you'll leave all but the most intrepid travellers behind you.

The furthest point north is the tip of Cape York. Here the last vestiges of anything approximating modern urban life disappear amid the rainforest and mangrove thickets. This is a place where roads vanish beneath water in the Wet, fuel supplies dry up, the weather can be fierce and nothing is predictable.

In terms of facilities, or lack thereof, things are not dissimilar in the Gulf country, where an area the size of Victoria is serviced by a handful of small fishing towns. Poet Banjo Paterson described this as 'a great grey chaos'. Boundaries cease to exist. Grasslands meld with mudflats; in the Wet, flooded rivers slosh across the plains, too swollen to drain; the coastline is vague, its definition obscured by the snarl of mangroves and maze of tributaries. But anglers love the Gulf for their chance to hook prized fish, while adventurers get hooked on the intoxicating scenery and sense of space – the horizon-to-horizon skies and hypnotic flatness of the sea and land.

Apart from small pockets of luxury lodging around the Daintree NP, this region remains one of the frontiers of Australian tourism. Distances are long, accommodation is often basic and travellers can still experience landscapes much as they were hundreds or even thousands of years ago.

Mossman to Lakefield National Park

The ancient Daintree rainforest, fringing reef, eco-resorts, rivers teeming with barramundi and a fascinating collection of rock art are features of this region on the eastern side of Queensland's Cape York Peninsula.

Australia's tropical outback is at its most accessible just beyond the unofficial capital of the north, Cairns. Here lie the World Heritage-protected wonders of the Wet Tropics: ancient rainforest, gorges, waterfalls and mist-shrouded mountains. The adjoining coast has a string of tropical beaches, which face the Coral Sea and the World Heritage-protected Great Barrier Reef. The area is fragmented, with cities, towns and sugarcane fields replacing rainforest, but not all has been lost. Within the remaining rainforest, in particular the famed Daintree area, there are plants found nowhere else on earth and a range of habitats for equally rare wildlife.

The Daintree region is well set up for exploring, with eco-tours, walking excursions, sea-kayaking, crocodile-spotting and more. The Kuku Yalangi, the region's traditional custodians, lead tours within the park sharing their knowledge and understanding of this precious environment.

Further north and west, more remote and less well known, the landscape flattens, opening out into woodland and dry grassland, patterned by swollen rivers and lily-clogged billabongs during the Wet. The myriad rivers and waterholes of Lakefield NP mean great fishing (this is one of the few parks in Queensland where fishing is allowed) and also spectacular birdwatching. Lakefield NP is a favourite for those looking to get further off the beaten track, to watch for wildlife, to enjoy some peaceful fishing or simply to camp beneath the star-filled skies. The isolation and serenity bring with them responsibility. Travellers to this sparsely populated area need to be self-sufficient and well prepared. Don't forget that these rivers are home to saltwater crocodiles.

Must see, must do

- Fish for barramundi in the wilds of Lakefield NP
- Visit the outstanding James Cook Museum in a former convent
- Bush camp in tropical rainforest at Cedar Bay (Mangkal–Mangkalba) NP
- See the dramatic Quinkan rock art, with its spirit figures of the Dreamtime, at Laura
- Take a boardwalk tour through the mangroves around Cape Tribulation

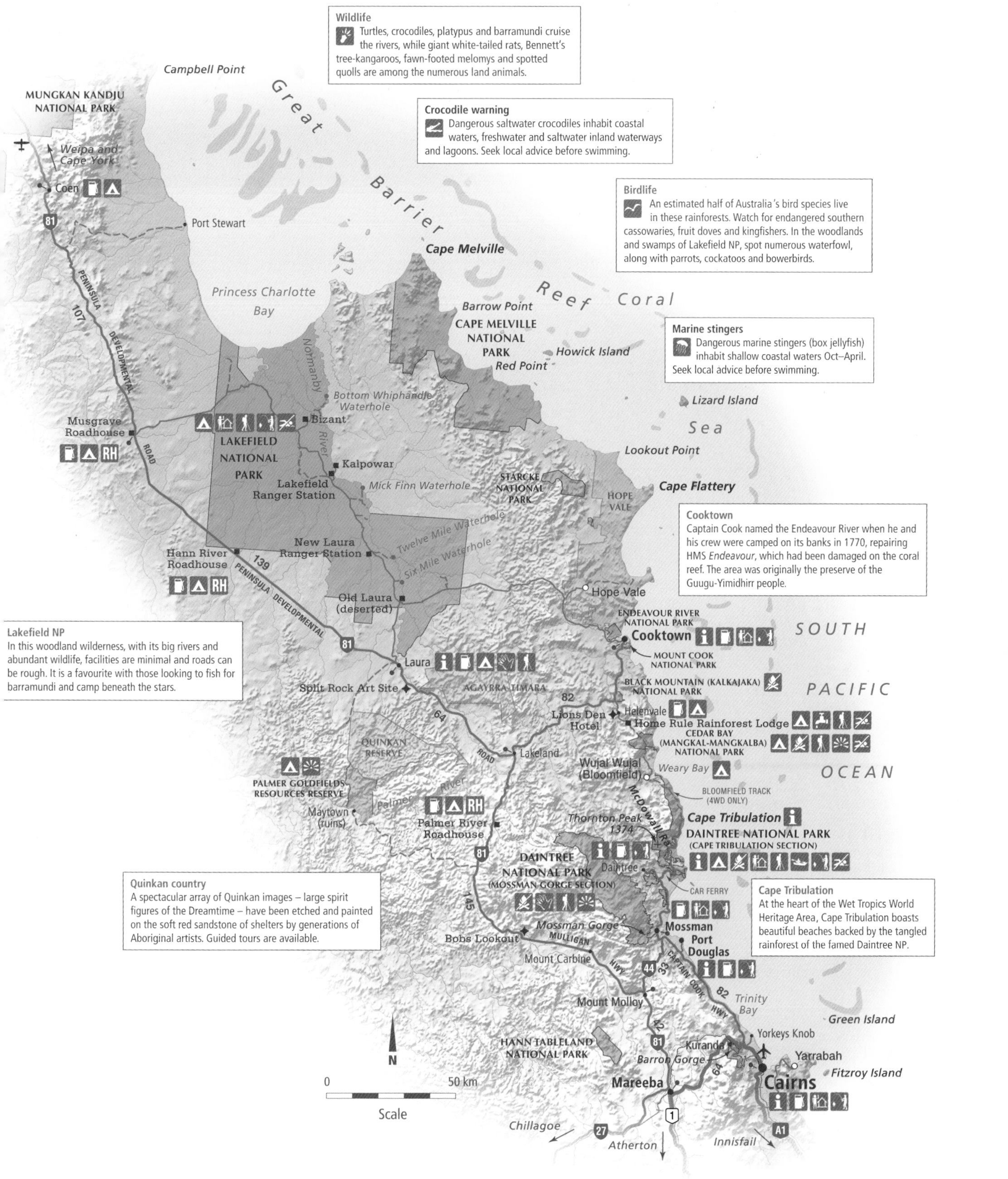

Wildlife

Turtles, crocodiles, platypus and barramundi cruise the rivers, while giant white-tailed rats, Bennett's tree-kangaroos, fawn-footed melomys and spotted quolls are among the numerous land animals.

Crocodile warning

Dangerous saltwater crocodiles inhabit coastal waters, freshwater and saltwater inland waterways and lagoons. Seek local advice before swimming.

Birdlife

An estimated half of Australia's bird species live in these rainforests. Watch for endangered southern cassowaries, fruit doves and kingfishers. In the woodlands and swamps of Lakefield NP, spot numerous waterfowl, along with parrots, cockatoos and bowerbirds.

Marine stingers

Dangerous marine stingers (box jellyfish) inhabit shallow coastal waters Oct–April. Seek local advice before swimming.

Cooktown

Captain Cook named the Endeavour River when he and his crew were camped on its banks in 1770, repairing HMS *Endeavour*, which had been damaged on the coral reef. The area was originally the preserve of the Guugu-Yimidhirr people.

Lakefield NP

In this woodland wilderness, with its big rivers and abundant wildlife, facilities are minimal and roads can be rough. It is a favourite with those looking to fish for barramundi and camp beneath the stars.

Quinkan country

A spectacular array of Quinkan images – large spirit figures of the Dreamtime – have been etched and painted on the soft red sandstone of shelters by generations of Aboriginal artists. Guided tours are available.

Cape Tribulation

At the heart of the Wet Tropics World Heritage Area, Cape Tribulation boasts beautiful beaches backed by the tangled rainforest of the famed Daintree NP.

Campbell Point
MUNGKAN KANDJU NATIONAL PARK
Weipa and Cape York
Coen
Port Stewart
Great Barrier Reef
Coral Sea
Cape Melville
Princess Charlotte Bay
Barrow Point
CAPE MELVILLE NATIONAL PARK
Howick Island
Red Point
Normanby River
Bottom Whiphandle Waterhole
Bizant
Lizard Island
Musgrave Roadhouse
LAKEFIELD NATIONAL PARK
Kalpowar
Lookout Point
Lakefield Ranger Station
Mick Finn Waterhole
STARCKE NATIONAL PARK
HOPE VALE
Cape Flattery
Twelve Mile Waterhole
Six Mile Waterhole
New Laura Ranger Station
Hann River Roadhouse
PENINSULA DEVELOPMENTAL ROAD
Old Laura (deserted)
Hope Vale
ENDEAVOUR RIVER NATIONAL PARK
Cooktown
MOUNT COOK NATIONAL PARK
SOUTH PACIFIC OCEAN
Laura
Split Rock Art Site
AGAYRRA TIMARA
BLACK MOUNTAIN (KALKAJAKA) NATIONAL PARK
Lions Den Hotel
Helenvale
Home Rule Rainforest Lodge
CEDAR BAY (MANGKAL-MANGKALBA) NATIONAL PARK
QUINKAN RESERVE
Lakeland
PALMER GOLDFIELDS RESOURCES RESERVE
Wujal Wujal (Bloomfield)
Weary Bay
BLOOMFIELD TRACK (4WD ONLY)
Palmer River
Maytown (ruins)
Palmer River Roadhouse
Thornton Peak 1374
McDowall Ra
Cape Tribulation
DAINTREE NATIONAL PARK (CAPE TRIBULATION SECTION)
DAINTREE NATIONAL PARK (MOSSMAN GORGE SECTION)
Daintree
CAR FERRY
Mossman Gorge
Mossman
Port Douglas
Bobs Lookout
MULLIGAN HWY
Mount Carbine
CAPTAIN COOK HWY
Mount Molloy
Trinity Bay
Green Island
HANN TABLELAND NATIONAL PARK
Yorkeys Knob
Kuranda
Barron Gorge
Yarrabah
Fitzroy Island
Cairns
Mareeba
Chillagoe
Atherton
Innisfail
N
0 50 km
Scale

Cairns ☎(07) 4051 3588; www.tropicalaustralia.com.au

Fact File

Top events

June *Discovery Festival (Cooktown)*
July *Cooktown Races*
Laura Aboriginal Dance and Cultural Festival (odd-numbered years)

Permits and regulations

Aboriginal land Permits are not required when visiting the Aboriginal town of Wujal Wujal on the Bloomfield River, although some areas around the town may be off-limits to campers. Wujal Wujal is a 'dry' community; no alcohol is permitted (see *Travel Tips*, p. 98). For more information contact the Community Council: (07) 4060 8155. Travellers to Quinkan country, Laura, should make a courtesy registration for any activities beyond visiting the open rock-art sites. Contact the Ang-Gnarra Aboriginal Corporation: (07) 4060 3214.

Parks and reserves

National Parks in Qld are administered by the Parks and Wildlife Service (QPWS). For general information see *Travel Tips*, p. 98.

Black Mountain (Kalkajaka) NP Camping is not permitted. Contact QPWS in Cooktown: (07) 4069 5777.

Cedar Bay (Mangkal–Mangkalba) NP Bush camping is allowed (access to sites is by foot only); fishing and collecting marine life in the marine park-protected coastal waters are prohibited. Contact QPWS in Cooktown: (07) 4069 5777. There is a private campground, Home Rule Rainforest Lodge, south of Helenvale (see *Contacts*, opposite).

Daintree NP The Mossman Gorge section is accessible at the southern end near Mossman; camping is not permitted. Fishing is not permitted in Cooper Creek or Mossman Gorge. Contact QPWS in Mossman: (07) 4098 2188. The Cape Tribulation section has camping at Noah Beach (bookings essential; contact the national park booking service: 13 1304; www.derm.qld.gov.au/parks). No fires permitted; take a fuel stove and water; campground is closed during the Wet; contact QPWS in Mossman (see above) or the ranger station at Cape Tribulation: (07) 4098 0052.

Lakefield NP Bush camping and a number of campsites are available; some have basic facilities (booking recommended; contact the national park booking service: 13 1304; www.derm.qld.gov.au/parks). Fishing and boating are allowed. Bring your own water and firewood. The park is usually closed during the Wet, often Nov–April. For information contact park rangers direct: (07) 4060 3260 (New Laura Ranger Station); (07) 4060 3271 (Lakefield Ranger Station). Information also available from QPWS in Cooktown: (07) 4069 5777.

Palmer Goldfields Resources Reserve Bush camping is permitted; BYO everything. Prospecting is not permitted. Roads are rough and remote; a 4WD vehicle is essential. For information contact QPWS in Cairns: (07) 4046 6600.

Fishing

For general information on fishing in Qld see *Travel Tips*, p. 98. See also individual park entries.

Warnings

Fuel and supplies Beyond Cooktown, fuel, food and accommodation is limited; travellers need to plan ahead. A number of roadhouses in the area have campsites (see *Contacts*, opposite).

Road access and closures A car ferry services the river crossing north of Daintree (6 am–midnight). The stretch between Mossman and Cape Tribulation is sealed and suitable for conventional vehicles. The road north from Cape Tribulation to Helenvale is 4WD only. Cape Tribulation to Wujal Wujal (the Bloomfield Track) is particularly rugged; definitely not suitable for trailers or caravans. Roads throughout the region may close during the Wet. Check road conditions with the RACQ: 13 1905; www.racq.com.au

Crocodiles Dangerous saltwater crocodiles inhabit coastal waters, freshwater and saltwater inland waterways and lagoons in this region. Be crocodile-wise; heed warning signs; swim only where recommended; take care when fishing and boating.

See also *On the Road*, p. 246.

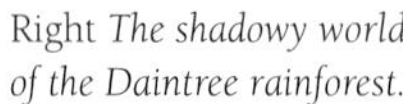

Right *The shadowy world of the Daintree rainforest.*

Opposite *Green tree frog.*

Mossman and Mossman Gorge

Mossman, 82 km north of Cairns, is Queensland's most northerly sugar town, hemmed by fields of sugarcane and framed by forested mountains. Nearby attractions include diving, reef cruises and fishing along the stunning Coral Coast and the World Heritage riches of the Mossman Gorge section of the Daintree NP.

Large swaths of this section of Daintree NP are without tracks or facilities, and are therefore suitable for experienced walkers only. However, at the southern end of the Mossman Gorge an access road, walking trail and picnic area enable sightseers to catch a glimpse of Queensland's famed tropical forests. Wander alongside a pristine forest creek and spot resident platypus and turtles, and explore thickets of lowland rainforest. For an Indigenous perspective on this remarkable landscape, take a tour with a Kuku Yalanji guide. Walkers intending to travel beyond this southern area should contact park staff (see *Fact File*, opposite).

Daintree to Cape Tribulation

Daintree, a small township of around 200 people, lies at the heart of the Daintree River catchment basin, surrounded by the McDowall Ranges. A wide variety of visitors, but especially international backpackers, make the trip here, fascinated by the abundant native plant life, birds and tropical butterflies, and keen to glimpse one of the huge prehistoric-looking saltwater crocodiles that lurk in the forest-fringed estuaries. Here it is possible to experience the density, antiquity and richness of Queensland's tropical rainforest. Eco-tours ply the river and eco-lodges feature treetop rooms and natural therapies.

The Daintree River is crossed by car ferry, which operates daily from 6 am to midnight. North of the river the Cape Tribulation section of Daintree NP begins, a 170 sq km narrow coastal strip running as far as Bloomfield River. Lowland and upland rainforest, mangrove swamps and heathlands weave a rich, tropical tapestry across the serrated contours of the surrounding hills and alongside steamy mudflats and estuaries. Immediately offshore, in the near-pristine waters of the Coral Sea, lie the wonders of the Great Barrier Reef, making this the only place on earth where two World Heritage areas collide. Hundreds of animal species – including rare creatures such as the giant white-tailed rat, the southern cassowary and Bennett's tree-kangaroo – inhabit the area's fern gullies, matted canopies and swamps (see also *Wet Tropics – World Heritage* p. 104).

Cape Tribulation, 36 km north of Daintree, is the park's focal point. The Kuku Yalanji people call the landmark Kulki; its European name provides a clue to Captain James Cook's state of mind when his ship the *Endeavour* struck a coral reef nearby on his momentous 1770 voyage of discovery. Camping is at Noah Beach, 8 km south of Cape Tribulation, and supplies are available at Cape Tribulation and at Cow Bay to the south. Rainforest and mangrove ecology is evident along boardwalk tracks: Dubuji and Kulki, near Cape Tribulation; Marrdja, just south of Noah Beach; and Jindalba, south of Cow Bay. Local operators based in Daintree, Cow Bay, Thornton Beach (south of Noah Beach) and Cape Tribulation offer 4WD tours, trekking, sea-kayaking, diving and reef-viewing. Swimming is not recommended either along the coast or in the estuaries, due to the year-round presence of crocodiles, and marine stingers from October to April.

On to Cooktown

Cooktown can be reached by the sealed Peninsula Developmental Road from just south of Mossman, but many – those with 4WD vehicles – prefer the attractions and excitement of the unsealed coast road. Both routes offer some wonderful views. Wujal Wujul, on the Bloomfield River, is about 33 km past Cape Tribulation. The town, the preserve of the Kuku Yalanji, was formerly known as the Bloomfield River Mission. Walking tours with Indigenous guides are a feature of the area, as are the thundering Bloomfield Falls. Accommodation is at nearby Weary Bay and ranges from luxurious resort-style to camping and cabins.

Contacts

Visitor information

Cairns
51 The Esplanade
(07) 4051 3588

Cape Tribulation
Cape Tribulation Rd
(07) 4098 0070

Cooktown
Nature's PowerHouse,
Botanic Gardens
(07) 4069 5446 or
1800 174 895

Daintree
5 Stewart St
(07) 4098 6120
www.pddt.com.au

Laura
Quinkan and Regional
Cultural Centre
(07) 4060 3457

Port Douglas
Reef Anchor House
(07) 4099 4588

Parks and reserves

See *Fact File*, opposite

Roadhouses, lodges

Hann River Roadhouse
(07) 4060 3242

Home Rule Rainforest Lodge
(07) 4060 3925

Musgrave Roadhouse
(07) 4060 3229

Palmer River Roadhouse
(07) 4060 2020

Aboriginal tours

Ang-Gnarra Tours (Laura)
(07) 4060 3214

Kuku Yalanji (Mossman)
(07) 4098 2595

Quinkan and Regional Cultural Centre (Laura)
(07) 4060 3457

Walker Family Tours
(Wujal Wujal)
(07) 4060 8069

One of Cooktown's grand buildings, a legacy of its goldmining past.

Gold fever

Gold lured the first white settlers onto Cape York Peninsula. William Hann, a squatter from the Townsville area, found traces of the precious metal in the Palmer River in 1872. Among the early prospectors was the miner James Mulligan, who found around 3 kg of gold in just three heady months. Government officials arrived at Endeavour River (Cooktown) in October 1873 to establish a port and secure an overland route to the goldfield. By November there were 200 miners on-site. During the Wet, these men endured appalling conditions: temperatures and humidity soared and rising waters threatened to leave them isolated without supplies. Many retreated to the coastal settlement of Cooktown, but returned in the Dry.

Over time, the field proved itself the richest in Queensland, producing £5.5 million of gold. In the peak years, the mid-1870s, the population of the main settlement, Maytown, numbered tens of thousands. The glory days, however, were short-lived: by the mid-1880s the gold had dried to a trickle. Reminders of this rich history are now preserved within Palmer Goldfield Resources Reserve. Visitors travel from Cairns or Cooktown along remote, 4WD tracks and camp within the park, and perhaps dream of those golden days.

Wet Tropics – World Heritage

The lush vegetation of this 8940 sq km World Heritage-classifed area is mostly wet tropical rainforest: deep, dense thickets that contain a near-complete record of the evolutionary stages of plant life. Many species originated when Australia was still part of the land mass known as Gondwana, over 65 million years ago. The diversity of plant life is extraordinary: around 1161 species of higher plants have been documented; 710 species are endemic to Australia and 500 are peculiar to the area. Animal life is similarly varied: the forests contain one-third of the country's marsupial species, nearly half of its bird species and almost 60 percent of its butterfly species.

The road north skirts the forests of Cedar Bay (Mangkal–Mangkalba) NP, covering almost 57 sq km of rainforest wilderness, 40 km south of Cooktown. A private campground on the edge of the park, Home Rule Rainforest Lodge, provides friendly accommodation (see *Contacts*, p. 103). From here there is access by foot to Cedar Bay (17 km). Bush camping is allowed at the bay, but hikers need to be well equipped. Further north is tiny Black Mountain (Kalkajaka) NP, its name derived from its centrepiece – a 470 m high mound of loose granite boulders, some of them as big as houses. Myth and legend surround the eerie outcrop. Camping is not permitted and there are no walking tracks, although visitors can explore the area around the carpark. Schedule a stop at the tiny community of Helenvale, about 30 km south of Cooktown, to enjoy a drink at the Lion's Den Hotel, one of Queensland's true outback pubs – and reputedly the oldest, dating from the 1880s.

Cooktown has a character all its own. A smattering of grand Victorian buildings grace the wide streets, tropical forest cloaks the hills and the Endeavour River flows languidly into the ocean, its banks a tangle of mangrove forest. Captain Cook's crew repaired the *Endeavour* here in 1770, but it was not until gold was discovered at Palmer River in 1873 (see *Gold fever*, above) that the town was properly established. During its heyday it boasted around two dozen hotels, several banks and a transient population of up to 20 000 (the current population is around 1400). Life is pretty easygoing this far north. Visitors and locals alike enjoy a beer watching the sun set over the Coral Sea. Don't miss the first-rate James Cook Museum with displays on Cook's life and travels, a Chinese temple commemorating the thousands of Chinese goldminers who made the trip here, and traditional Aboriginal tools and weapons, housed in a handsome Victorian-era convent. Gamefishing is big around Cooktown, as are reef-cruises and diving

Laura

Laura, at the heart of Quinkan country, was established in the 1870s as a stop en route to the Palmer River goldfields. A tiny town with a mostly Aboriginal population of around 100, it is widely known for the extraordinary rock art that is painted and etched on the red sandstone shelters of the area

The name Quinkan refers to the large, semi-human figures that appear in many of the artworks Opinions vary as to what the Quinkan figures represent, but they are most likely spirit beings, with a role in magic rituals. The figures often appear horizontal or inverted, and are painted in solid colours, most commonly red ochre. Animals,

ncluding kangaroos, emus and crocodiles, are also lepicted; many of these forms are patterned with tripes and spots. It is thought that members of he various local clans decorated the shelters while aking refuge during the Wet.

Within Quinkan Reserve, a walking track leads o the richly detailed Split Rock Art Site, and there re also private tours conducted by local Ang-Gnarra (see *Contacts*, p. 103). The Quinkan and Regional Cultural Centre provides visitor and tour nformation, along with displays on the creation nd meaning of the art. Many visitors schedule heir trip to this area to coincide with the Laura Aboriginal Dance and Cultural Festival, a rich and aried event celebrating Cape York's Indigenous history and culture. The event is staged biennially n July, in odd-numbered years.

Lakefield National Park

Queensland's second largest national park, covering 5370 sq km, is remote – at least seven hours' drive rom Cairns – but is well patronised by an itinerant band of adventurers: anglers, campers and 4WD xplorers. This is a tropical landscape, but rather han rainforest it is open tropical woodland country. There is a sense of expansiveness here, a precursor o the flat plains and wide skies of the Gulf Country o the west (see *Gulf Country*, p. 114).

Rivers trace a course across the park, fracturing nto a string of billabongs and lakes before draining nto the Coral Sea. During the Wet the waterways lood, creating shimmering plains; during the Dry hey can shrink to a trickle, leaving waterholes marooned in the middle of large stretches of dry and. There is plenty of wildlife: at least 181 bird, 18 mammal and 38 reptile species – including saltwater and freshwater crocodiles – are resident, but not always easy to spot.

Fishing lures a steady stream of enthusiasts to Lakefield during the Dry. The park's lakes flood and restock with barramundi each season. A couple of strategically placed boat ramps allow anglers to put a 'tinnie' into the water – watch for crocodiles. There are campsites throughout the park, although facilities range from minimal to non-existent. Check with park staff ahead of travelling, as bookings may be necessary (see *Fact File*, p. 102).

In the south of the park, on the track to the Palmer River goldfields, the Old Laura Homestead, built from termite-resistant timbers in the 1880s, gives an idea of just how basic living standards were for early settlers. Further north lies the New Laura Station, an essential stop for information on where to camp and fish. In the northern part of the park are clustered cities of 'magnetic' termite mounds: tall, thin structures with broad sides and a narrow axis, angled north–south to optimise temperature control in these well-insulated insect colonies.

Above *Quinkan rock art at the Giant Horse Gallery, near Laura.*

Below *Old Laura homestead at Lakefield NP.*

Coen to the Cape

Cape York, Australia's most northerly mainland region, is home to just a few thousand people, who live scattered among tiny towns, rural stations and remote Aboriginal communities. The roads are few and the facilities patchy, but there is wonderful scenery including pockets of virgin rainforest, unspoilt beaches, abundant wildlife, great fishing and, above all, the chance to make 'the trip to the Tip'.

Cape York is a true adventure destination. The further north you travel, the more difficult things become – roads are rough, the human population thins, mosquitoes and crocodiles proliferate and fuel supplies are scarcer. But many travellers – thousands each year – come precisely for the challenge of the journey.

The rewards, en route, are rich and varied. There are remote national parks knitted with dense jungles of rainforest, where the camping is bush-style, the walking is tough and the birdwatching is extraordinary. In particular, the jungle-like rainforest of Iron Range NP is home to many unusual species, from rare parrots and birds of paradise to tree kangaroos.

In these parts, adventure anglers gain access to some of the cleanest and least-fished waters in Australia, both coastal and river; and scattered historic sites bear evidence of repeated attempts to settle this difficult land. Aboriginal communities go about their business, too remote to be much affected by development. For travellers, the luxuries of modern life – a hot shower and a soft bed – are confined to a couple of isolated settlements, including the well-serviced mining town of Weipa.

Travellers should have a high-clearance 4WD vehicle, and be well prepared with equipment and supplies (see *On the Road*, p. 246). Those unwilling to go it alone can join one of the many tours or tag-along convoys that operate in the region. Conditions during the Wet are extreme; many roads are impassable, especially beyond Weipa. Travel is not advised, not just for tourists' safety, but because driving on these roads in the Wet can tear them up for the locals.

Must see, must do

- Cast a line from Seisia's famous fishing pier
- Catch a ferry to Thursday Island
- Awake to the sound of trumpet manucode birds of paradise in Iron Range NP
- Tour Comalco's vast bauxite mine at Weipa
- Camp and fish in remote Aboriginal communities

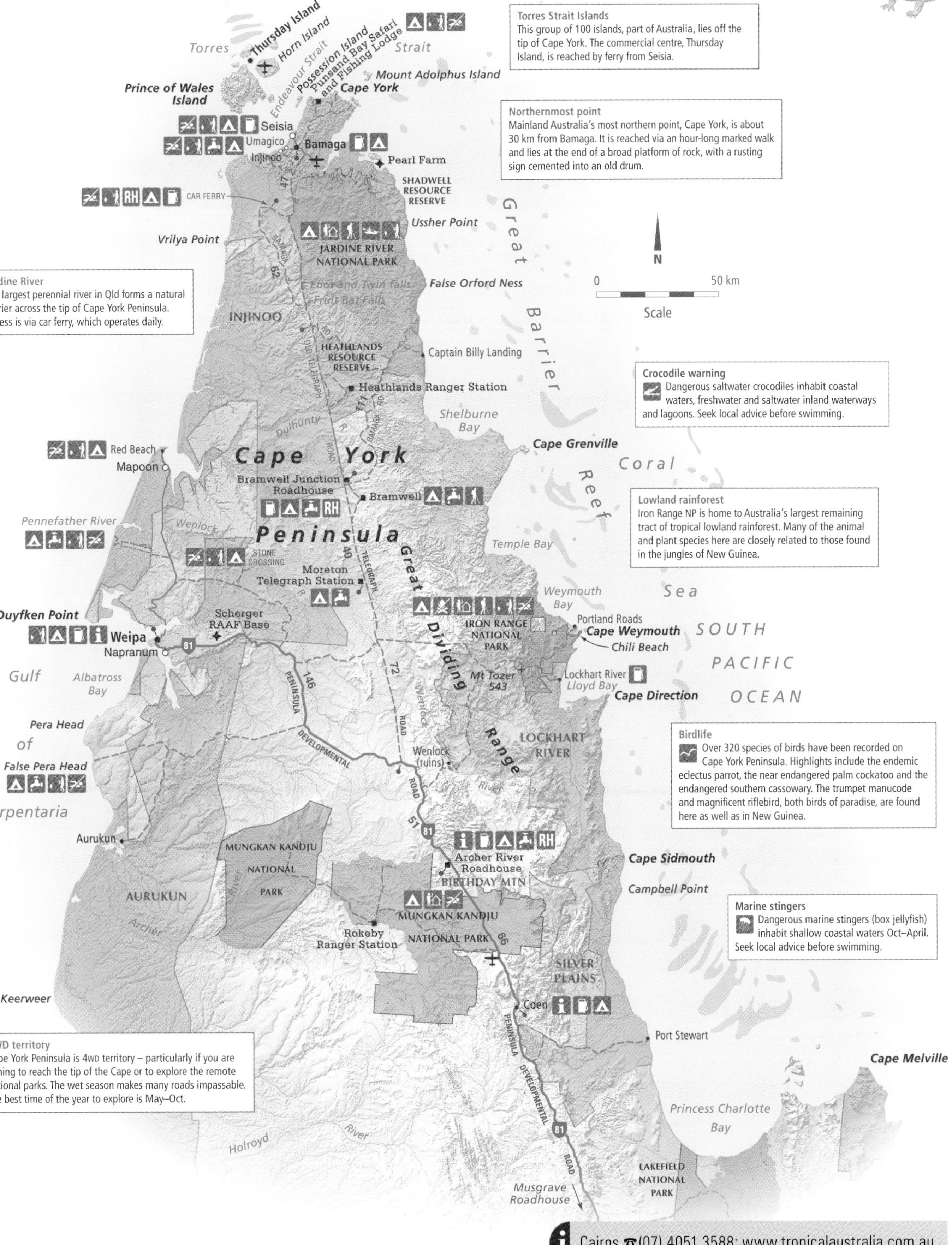

Torres Strait Islands
This group of 100 islands, part of Australia, lies off the tip of Cape York. The commercial centre, Thursday Island, is reached by ferry from Seisia.
Northernmost point
Mainland Australia's most northern point, Cape York, is about 30 km from Bamaga. It is reached via an hour-long marked walk and lies at the end of a broad platform of rock, with a rusting sign cemented into an old drum.
dine River
largest perennial river in Qld forms a natural rier across the tip of Cape York Peninsula. :ess is via car ferry, which operates daily.
Crocodile warning
Dangerous saltwater crocodiles inhabit coastal waters, freshwater and saltwater inland waterways and lagoons. Seek local advice before swimming.
Lowland rainforest
Iron Range NP is home to Australia's largest remaining tract of tropical lowland rainforest. Many of the animal and plant species here are closely related to those found in the jungles of New Guinea.
Birdlife
Over 320 species of birds have been recorded on Cape York Peninsula. Highlights include the endemic eclectus parrot, the near endangered palm cockatoo and the endangered southern cassowary. The trumpet manucode and magnificent riflebird, both birds of paradise, are found here as well as in New Guinea.
Marine stingers
Dangerous marine stingers (box jellyfish) inhabit shallow coastal waters Oct–April. Seek local advice before swimming.
VD territory
pe York Peninsula is 4WD territory – particularly if you are ning to reach the tip of the Cape or to explore the remote tional parks. The wet season makes many roads impassable. best time of the year to explore is May–Oct.
Torres
Strait
Thursday Island
Horn Island
Endeavour Strait
Possession Island
Punsand Bay Safari and Fishing Lodge
Mount Adolphus Island
Prince of Wales Island
Cape York
Seisia
Umagico
Bamaga
Injinoo
Pearl Farm
SHADWELL RESOURCE RESERVE
CAR FERRY
Ussher Point
Vrilya Point
JARDINE RIVER NATIONAL PARK
Great Barrier Reef
N
0
50 km
Scale
False Orford Ness
INJINOO
HEATHLANDS RESOURCE RESERVE
Captain Billy Landing
Heathlands Ranger Station
Shelburne Bay
Red Beach
Mapoon
Cape York Peninsula
Cape Grenville
Coral Sea
Bramwell Junction Roadhouse
Bramwell
Pennefather River
Weipa
Temple Bay
STONE CROSSING
Moreton Telegraph Station
Great Dividing Range
Weymouth Bay
Duyfken Point
Scherger RAAF Base
IRON RANGE NATIONAL PARK
Portland Roads
Cape Weymouth
Chili Beach
SOUTH PACIFIC OCEAN
Napranum
Gulf of Carpentaria
Albatross Bay
Mt Tozer 543
Lockhart River
Lloyd Bay
Cape Direction
Pera Head
False Pera Head
PENINSULA DEVELOPMENTAL ROAD
TELEGRAPH ROAD
LOCKHART RIVER
Wenlock (ruins)
Aurukun
MUNGKAN KANDJU NATIONAL PARK
Archer River Roadhouse
BIRTHDAY MTN
Cape Sidmouth
Campbell Point
AURUKUN
Archer River
Rokeby Ranger Station
SILVER PLAINS
Keerweer
Coen
Port Stewart
Cape Melville
Princess Charlotte Bay
Holroyd River
LAKEFIELD NATIONAL PARK
Musgrave Roadhouse

Cairns ☎ (07) 4051 3588; www.tropicalaustralia.com.au

Fact File

Top events

June *Torres Strait Cultural Festival (even-numbered years, Torres Strait Islands)*

July *Coming of the Light Festival (Torres Strait Islands)*

Permits and regulations

Large areas of land on Cape York are owned and administered by Aboriginal communities. These areas should be treated as private property. Some communities allow visitors; in many cases entry is by permit only.

Injinoo (around Bamaga) The Injinoo community has jurisdiction over much of the land around the tip of Cape York. To travel, camp and fish in the area a permit is needed. Permits are issued when you pay to use the Jardine River Ferry (see *Road access and closures,* below). For information contact the Northern Peninsula Area Regional Council: (07) 4069 3252.

Lockhart River Visitors are welcome to buy fuel and other supplies in this small township. For other activities contact the Lockhart River Aboriginal Shire Council: (07) 4060 7144.

West Cape (around Weipa) There are three communities in this area. Permits to travel to Napranum and Mapoon can be obtained from the Weipa Camping and Caravan Park: (07) 4069 7871. For travel to Aurukun contact the community direct: (07) 4060 6800; www.aurukun.qld.gov.au

Parks and reserves

National parks and reserves in Qld are administered by the Qld Parks and Wildlife Service (QPWS). For general information see *Travel Tips*, p. 98. All parks in this area are extremely remote. Contact the relevant ranger ahead of travelling to check road conditions and the availability of campsites. Generally, facilities are minimal and visitors should be prepared to BYO everything, including firewood and drinking water.

Iron Range NP There are several bush-camping sites; very few facilities (BYO everything). Fires and generators not permitted. Fishing permitted only at Chili Beach. The ranger station is near Lockhart River: (07) 4060 7170.

Jardine River NP and reserves There are two camping areas in the park as well as bush-camping spots; facilities (toilets, tables, fireplace) at Eliot Falls camping area only. There is fishing on the coast at Camp Billy and Ussher Point camping areas. Bring all supplies including drinking water and firewood. Generators are not permitted. A ranger is located at Heathlands Resource Reserve: (07) 4060 3241.

Mungkan Kandju NP Bush camping allowed, but no facilities (BYO everything). Generators are not permitted. A ranger station is located 66 km west of the park's entrance (off Peninsula Developmental Rd). Visitors are asked to notify the ranger when they are leaving the park or travelling to the Archer Bend section of the park. For further information contact the ranger: (07) 4060 1137.

Fishing

For general information on fishing in this region see *Travel Tips*, p. 98. See also individual park entries.

Warnings

Fuel and supplies This area is extremely remote and travellers need to be self-sufficient. Expect distances of up to 200 km between fuel stops. Remote petrol supplies are at Archer River Roadhouse, (07) 4060 3266; Lockhart River Store, (07) 4060 7192; Bramwell Junction Roadhouse, (07) 4060 3230; Jardine River Ferry (availability of fuel varies), (07) 4069 1369. Fuel is also available in Coen, Bamaga, Seisia and Weipa.

Road access and closures This is 4WD territory; many of these roads are impassable or inaccessible during the Wet (see *When to go*, p. 98). Check road conditions before travelling, particularly at the beginning or end of the Dry. Contact on-site rangers at national parks (see above); the RACQ on 13 1905; or police in Coen on (07) 4060 1150, Bamaga on (07) 4069 3156 or Weipa on (07) 4069 9119. A vehicle ferry provides access across the Jardine River; it operates 8am–5pm, daily; the charge of $88 includes the cost of a permit to access Injinoo lands around Bamaga (see *Contacts*, opposite).

Crocodiles Dangerous saltwater crocodiles inhabit coastal waters, freshwater and saltwater inland waterways and lagoons in this region. Be crocodile-wise: heed warning signs; swim only where recommended; take care when fishing and boating.

See also *On the Road*, p. 246.

Opposite *The white sands of Chili Beach, on the edge of Iron Range NP.*

Below *Waterlilies flowering at Mungkan Kandju NP.*

Contacts

Visitor information

Cairns
51 The Esplanade
(07) 4051 3588

Cooktown
Nature's PowerHouse,
Botanic Gardens
(07) 4069 5446 or
1800 174 895

Weipa
Weipa Camping and Caravan Park
(07) 4069 7871
www.weipa.biz

Parks and reserves

See *Fact File*, opposite

Station stays, lodges

Bramwell Station
(07) 4060 3300

Morton Telegraph Station
(07) 4060 3360

Punsand Bay Camping Resort
(07) 4069 1722

Other

Ferries

Peddell's Thursday Island Ferry
(07) 4069 1551

Jardine River Ferry
(07) 4069 1369

:oen to Iron Range

oen's population is just 200, but it's a large town y local standards, boasting a school, hospital, shops ıd, of course, an outback pub. A former gold ɔwn, Coen now services the surrounding pastoral ıdustry and adventure tourists passing through on ıeir way to the wilderness reaches of Queensland's xtreme north.

About 24 km north of the town, the Peninsula ›evelopmental Road skirts the eastern edge of Iungkan Kandju NP (formerly Rokeby). This :mote 4570 sq km park is a largely undeveloped weep of eucalypt and melaleuca woodlands. It ɔntains Aboriginal and pastoral heritage sites ıd wonderful opportunities for birdwatching, :mote hiking and camping – there are no facilities, owever, so be well prepared.

Just before the Archer River crossing is the rcher River Roadhouse. Here, in typical outback)ueensland fashion, you'll find a cold beer and ood company to break your journey. You can lso camp, refuel and stock-up on supplies. :amping is permitted along the sandy banks of ıe Archer, where magnificent paperbarks cast deep, sheltering canopy even when the sun is : its most fierce.

A road 20 km north of the roadhouse leads to ıe community of Portlands Roads, the coast (Chili each) and Iron Range NP. The road passes through ockhart River Aboriginal Land. No permits are :quired to travel the public roads and visitors can top at the settlement of Lockhart River for fuel and ıpplies (see *Fact File*, opposite).

Iron Range National Park

Iron Range preserves a veritable jungle of lowland rainforest, the largest surviving remnant in Australia, along with heathland and woodland. These habitats protect many uncommon species of bird and at least 1500 plant species. The park spreads across the ragged rise of the Janet and Tozer ranges, which reach their peak at Mount Tozer (543 m).

The area is the traditional preserve of the Kuuku-ya'u people, who were forced into missions with the expansion of European settlement in the early 1900s. Descendants of the tribe now live at Lockhart River, along with Indigenous people from other parts of Cape York. Captain William Bligh visited the area in 1789, when he and his ragged crew stopped at Restoration Island, just offshore from Chili Beach (see *Captain Bligh – master mariner*, p.110). Gold was mined here in the 1930s and 1940s, and during WW II the area served as an important post for Allied troops.

The park has an extraordinary collection of animal and plant life. Many species you'll find only here, such as the beautiful, vividly coloured eclectus parrot, which makes its home in the park's scrubland. Other unusual bird species are the endangered southern cassowary, the fawn-breasted bowerbird and the red-bellied pitta. The park is home to around 25 species of butterfly; many of these species are not found further south. The rivers are well stocked with fish and wildlife, but fishing is only permitted on the coast at Chili Beach.

Most visitors head for Chili Beach, where there is camping, fishing and a line of coconut

Captain Bligh – master mariner

Captain Bligh landed on, and named Restoration Island, off the coast of what is now Iron Range NP, in 1789. He had just sailed 4000 km in an open boat with 18 other men and a limited cache of supplies. He had lost command of his ship, HMS *Bounty*, near Tahiti, when the crew mutinied. Bligh was said to be quick-tempered, sometimes brutal, but he was also an extraordinary navigator and seaman. He plotted his course using his memory of Captain Cook's original charts, some nautical tables and a sextant. On reaching the island, Bligh and his men filled up with water, and dined on fresh oysters and other bush tucker before heading a further 2000 km north to Timor.

Aboriginal Cape York

Before the arrival of Europeans, the Aboriginal people of Cape York established themselves across two regions: the East Cape and the West Cape. The people of the East Cape were further divided into around 13 language groups, linked by kinship systems. So abundant were the resources of this region that the East Cape people were able to maintain a semi-sedentary existence, in contrast to the nomadic lifestyle of Aboriginal people across much of the rest of the continent. They built huts and sturdy outrigger canoes (technology possibly borrowed from the Torres Strait Islanders) from which they hunted turtle and dugong. The distinctive art of the southern tribes of the East Cape region survives in the rock shelters around Laura (see *Mossman to Lakefield National Park*, p. 100).

The lands of the West Cape people extend north from the base of the Gulf of Carpentaria to the Jardine River. The people here established themselves across 18 groups, and include the Wik people (now based at Aurukun), whose famous land rights claim went before the High Court in 1996. Overall, the West Cape has proved resistant to large-scale modern settlement – the environmental and geographical challenges have proved too great. Many areas remain the preserve of the traditional communities. Visit the Western Cape Cultural Centre in Weipa for an overview of the West Cape communities.

trees planted by missionaries. Nearby lies the tiny settlement of Portland Roads (there are no facilities, but good offshore fishing if you have a boat). There are a few rainforest bush campsites in other parts of the park. All visitors should visit the ranger station, located on the road to Lockhart River.

To the tip of Cape York

Old Telegraph Road, leading to the tip of Cape York, starts about 44 km north of Archer River. It is prized by adventurers for its degree of difficulty. Diehards follow the route all the way through; those wanting to save time take the maintained bypass, the Bamaga Road, which branches off to the east. Early in the journey there is private camping at Moreton Telegraph Station, Bramwell Junction Roadhouse and Bramwell Station (see *Contacts*, p. 109), as well as bush camping on the roadside. Jardine River NP has several campsites, while camping and other tourist facilities are available around Bamaga.

Jardine River National Park

Jardine River NP, together with Heathlands and Shadwell Resource reserves, covers 4000 sq km of pristine wilderness and protects the catchment area of the Jardine River, the largest perennial stream in Queensland. Vegetation in this northern pocket includes stretches of woodland, open forest and scrubland, and what early explorers called the 'Wet Desert' – a sandy region of stunted heath vegetation, springs, lakes and swamps. The park is home to many bird species including the yellow-billed kingfisher and the rarely seen palm cockatoo, an impressive black cockatoo with a long, straggly crest.

A number of campsites in the park cater for visitors, including two on the coast, Ussher Point and Captain Billy Landing, where beach fishing is allowed. The most popular and scenic site is Eliot Falls, in the south. From here you can access the scenic Fruit Bat Falls and Twin Falls, where the swimming is safe (but heed warning signs).

Fruit Bat Falls, a favourite swimming spot in Jardine River NP.

Above *A sizeable catch at Pajinka Beach, at the top of the Cape.*

Following page *A peaceful beach at the tip of Cape York.*

amaga

ımaga, Australia's most northerly mainland town, ıs a population of around 2000, made up of ainland Aboriginals and Torres Strait Islanders om the island of Saibai, 4 km off the Papua New uinea mainland. The latter group arrived in the ea in the late 1940s, having been forced from ıeir traditional home by the scarcity of water and gh monsoonal tides. The town bears the name of ıe chief who led the first wave of immigrants, and ow it serves as the administrative centre for nearby boriginal communities.

The township, reached via car ferry across the rdine River (see *Fact File*, p.109), has all basic rvices, while the tourist hub is at the nearby shing settlement of Seisia, with camping and w-key resort style accommodation. Seisia's jetty is nown by anglers as the 'pier without peer', and the fshore fishing opportunities are also difficult to eat. Fishing charter services operate.

Seisia is the departure point for ferries to hursday Island, the administrative centre of the orres Strait Islands, traditional home of Australia's nly non-Aboriginal indigenous population.

Mainland Australia's most northerly point lies bout 30 km from Bamaga, along a turn-off to the rmer Pajinka Wilderness Lodge. From here you ın stroll for a few minutes to reach the continent's ıost northerly beach, and for another hour or so reach the rocky platform that marks the actual p of the cape. A few kilometres to the west, by ad, is Punsand Bay Camping Resort, a small-scale sort with camping and lodge accommodation nd fishing and island tours. The beach is glorious, ut swimming is not an option, with sharks and ocodiles patrolling the waters. Heritage sites in the rea include the ruins of the settlement at Somerset, stablished in the 1860s.

Weipa and the West Coast

The western side of Cape York Peninsula remains one of Australia's most remote regions. The mining centre of Weipa is the only town of size. Surrounding it are small Aboriginal settlements – Aurukun, Napranum and Mapoon – and extensive areas of Aboriginal land. The landscape is wild and unsettled – a maze of mangrove swamps, winding tidal channels and barren salt flats.

Weipa lies 145 km north-west of Archer River Roadhouse, along a continuation of the Peninsula Developmental Road. In 1955 geologist Harry Evans discovered that the red cliffs surrounding the old Weipa Mission were almost pure bauxite. In the 1950s, Comalco established a bauxite mine, which is now the world's largest. Miners work shifts that run 24 hours a day, 365 days a year, extracting 15 million tonnes of bauxite a year, used in the production of alumina.

The township was built from scratch in the 1960s, with all the facilities needed to attract miners and their families: schools, hospital, water, power, golf course, parks and ovals. It now has a population of 2500.

This is a company town through and through, but tourism is encouraged. Anglers come for the excellent river and offshore angling; there are mine tours and the chance to explore the local landscape. The Uningan Nature Reserve, on the town's northern border, protects rich mangrove habitats along with giant cockleshell middens, a reminder of the region's ancient Aboriginal heritage. For those with a permit, there is superb fishing and camping along the coast and rivers of neighbouring Aboriginal communities; particularly popular is Red Beach at Mapoon. The riverside Western Cape Cultural Centre in Weipa offers a look at the history, culture and lifestyle of these communities.

BAM 101

Gulf Country

Most visitors come to this region for the fishing, but the landscapes have their own allure: huge horizon-to-horizon skies and a kingdom of grassy plains unfurling from the calm waters of the Gulf of Carpentaria.

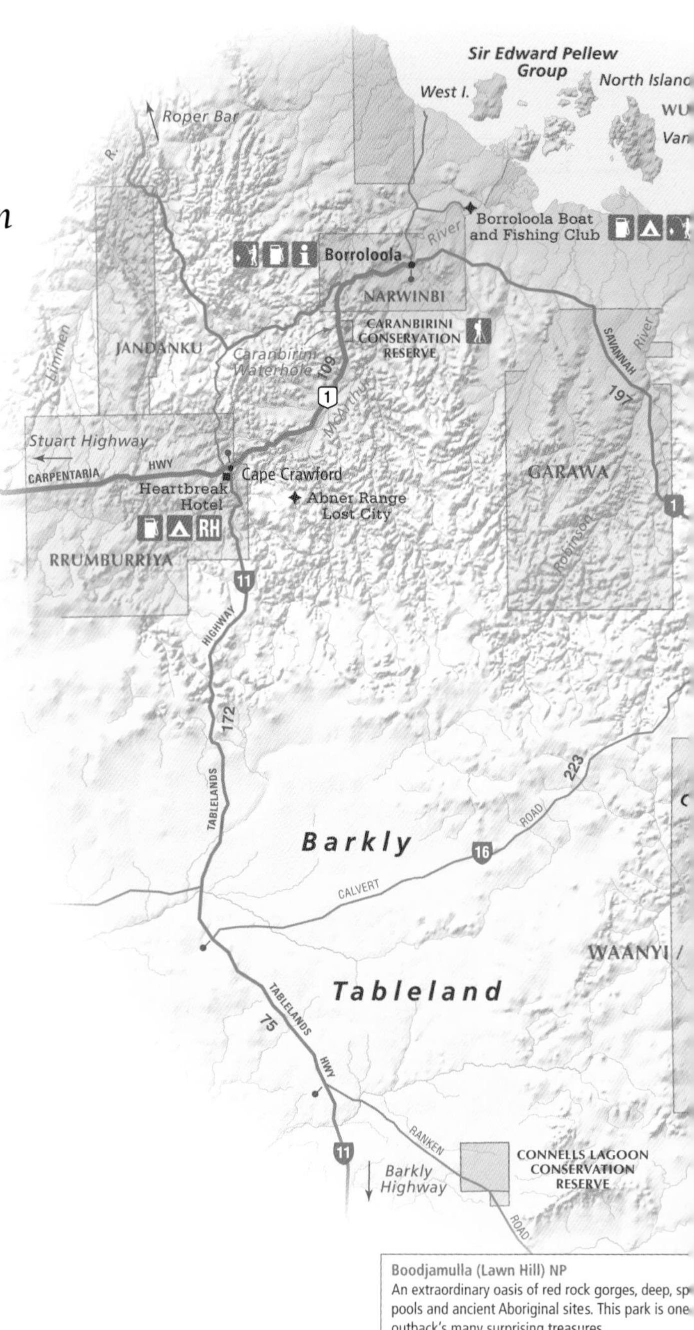

Boodjamulla (Lawn Hill) NP
An extraordinary oasis of red rock gorges, deep, sp pools and ancient Aboriginal sites. This park is one outback's many surprising treasures.

The Gulf Country seems to stretch as far as the eye can see. The sea is flat – a calm, protected expanse mirroring vast, overarching skies; and the land is flat – a jigsaw of grassy plains, salt flats and mudflats, crisscrossed by the flow of many rivers. During the Wet the rivers flood, creating a single saturated surface that swallows the lightly etched outline of the coast along with most other distinguishing features. Inland, sandstone outcrops form an occasional ripple in the plains, most notably at Boodjamulla (Lawn Hill) NP, where oasis-like vegetation and emerald green waterholes are remnants of the rainforest that once covered the area. There are other signs of the landscape's history – million-year-old fossils have been unearthed at Riversleigh Fossil Site in Boodjamulla's southern section.

Normanton in the east marks the start of the region. From here the towns become progressively smaller and the distances between them greater. While facilities are limited in Queensland, they are positively sparse over the border in the NT – confined to a couple of far-flung settlements and a few station properties.

Any travel to these parts is an adventure. The roads are mostly unsealed and a heavy fall of rain can make them impassable within minutes. The Wet is an impossible season for all but seasoned adventurers. The Dry brings its own challenges, not least the competition for limited tourist resources. Barramundi anglers account for most of the 100 000 or so visitors who come each year, with Boodjamulla (Lawn Hill) NP drawing another 20 000 or so enthusiasts.

Must see, must do

- Canoe the emerald waters at Boodjamulla (Lawn Hill) NP
- Explore the giant lava tubes at Undara Volcanic NP
- Wander amid the 'lost cities' of the NT
- Fish for barra in the big Gulf rivers
- Rattle your way across grassy plains aboard the *Gulflander*

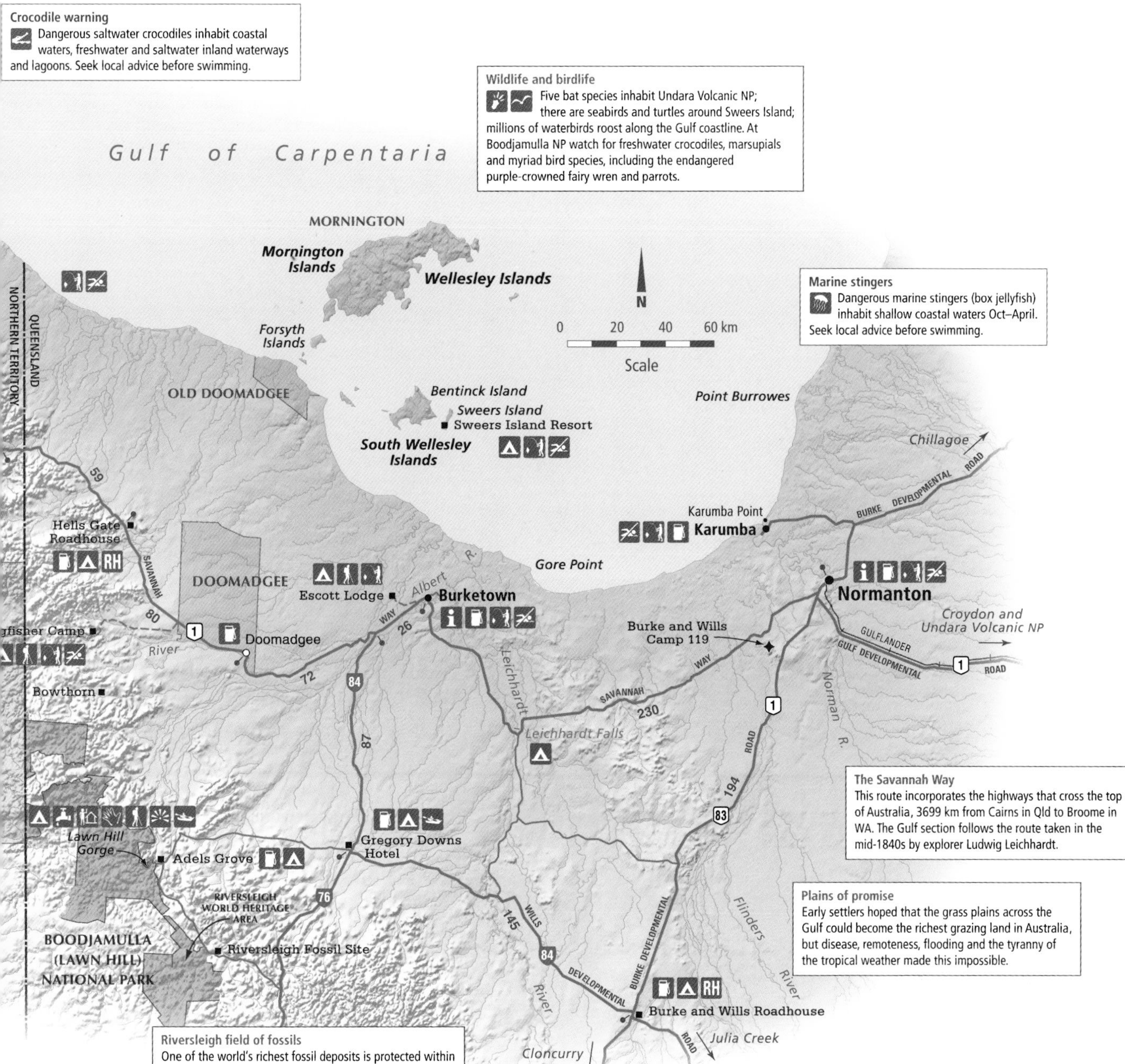

Crocodile warning
Dangerous saltwater crocodiles inhabit coastal waters, freshwater and saltwater inland waterways and lagoons. Seek local advice before swimming.

Wildlife and birdlife
Five bat species inhabit Undara Volcanic NP; there are seabirds and turtles around Sweers Island; millions of waterbirds roost along the Gulf coastline. At Boodjamulla NP watch for freshwater crocodiles, marsupials and myriad bird species, including the endangered purple-crowned fairy wren and parrots.

Marine stingers
Dangerous marine stingers (box jellyfish) inhabit shallow coastal waters Oct–April. Seek local advice before swimming.

The Savannah Way
This route incorporates the highways that cross the top of Australia, 3699 km from Cairns in Qld to Broome in WA. The Gulf section follows the route taken in the mid-1840s by explorer Ludwig Leichhardt.

Plains of promise
Early settlers hoped that the grass plains across the Gulf could become the richest grazing land in Australia, but disease, remoteness, flooding and the tyranny of the tropical weather made this impossible.

Riversleigh field of fossils
One of the world's richest fossil deposits is protected within this World Heritage-listed area. Fossils of more than 100 animal species provide vital clues to the evolution of the landscape, fauna and flora over 20 million years.

Queensland ☎(07) 4031 1631; www.gulf-savannah.com.au
Northern Territory ☎(08) 8975 8799; www.tourismtopend.com.au

Fact File

Top events

Easter *Borroloola Easter Barra Classic*
Normanton Barra Classic
Burketown Barramundi World Fishing Championships
May *Burketown Campdraft and Horse Sports*
Gregory Downs Canoe Race
June *Gregory Campdraft and Horse Sports*
Normanton Rodeo and Campdraft
June/ July *Karumba Fishing Competition*
Aug *Borroloola Campdraft Show and Rodeo*

Permits and regulations

Aboriginal land Borroloola township is located on Narwinbi Aboriginal Land Trust, but no permits are needed to enter or stay. Doomadgee is on Aboriginal land but no permit is needed to drive through Doomadgee or to stop for fuel and supplies (weekend opening is limited to Sat morning.) For other activities (camping, fishing), contact Doomadgee Community: (07) 4745 8188.

Parks and reserves

National parks and reserves in Qld are administered by the Qld Parks and Wildlife Service (QPWS). For general information see *Travel Tips*, p. 98.

Boodjamulla (Lawn Hill) NP There is a limited number of campsites available; book well ahead of travelling, particularly for the Easter period. A private campground is located at Adels Grove, just outside the park (see *Contacts*, opposite). For travellers in conventional vehicles and those pulling caravans and trailers, the most reliable access is via Cloncurry, 425 km south-east. There is no camping in the Riversleigh section of the park; tours of this section are run by the proprietors of Adels Grove. For further information contact park staff on (07) 4748 5572, or QPWS at Mount Isa on (07) 4744 7888.

Undara Volcanic NP This is a day-use park only; there are picnic areas and walking trails, but no camping. Commercial operators run tours of the Undara lava tubes (see *Contacts*, opposite). For general information contact QPWS at Mt Surprise: (07) 4097 1485.

Fishing

For general information on fishing in Qld and the NT see *Travel Tips*, p. 98 See also entries for individual national parks.

Warnings

Fuel and supplies Long distances separate towns and roadhouses in this area. If travelling outside of weekdays and daylight hours, ring roadhouses to check opening times (see *Contacts*, opposite). Note that there are no petrol facilities between Burketown and Normanton (228 km). Visitor accommodation is in towns and at roadhouses. Camping is permitted throughout the region (observe signage). Make bookings ahead of travelling.

Road access and closures Most of the roads are unsealed; main roads are graded and maintained and generally suitable for 2WD vehicles (check close to travelling). All roads are subject to flooding in the Wet, and may be impassable even with a 4WD vehicle. Travel is not recommended Jan–Mar. To check road conditions in Qld contact the RACQ: 13 1905; www.racq.com.au To check road conditions in the NT contact: 1800 246 199; www.ntlis.nt.gov.au/roadreport

Crocodiles A few inland rivers and creeks offer safe swimming, including Boodjamulla (Lawn Hill) NP. Dangerous saltwater crocodiles inhabit coastal waters, freshwater and saltwater inland waterways and lagoons in this region. Be crocodile-wise; heed warning signs; swim only where recommended: take care when fishing and boating.

See also *On the Road*, p. 246.

Explorers turn back

Burke and Wills set out from Melbourne in 1860, intent on being the first to cross the continent from south to north. They reached the Gulf in February 1861, established a camp near present-day Normanton (a memorial off the highway marks the spot), and then made their dash to the coastline. But it was the height of the Wet; the mangrove-matted rivers were flooding and the mosquito-ridden mudflats were swollen and glue-like. The explorers failed to penetrate this maze-like terrain, deprived of a clear view of the northern ocean, a view they had struggled 3000 km to see (see also *Birdsville and Beyond*, p. 134).

Opposite top *Egrets strut through wetlands.*

Opposite below *Normanton Railway Station is home to the* Gulflander.

Right *The Savannah Way cuts across the savannah plains, from Burketown to Normanton.*

Normanton to Burketown

etween the Gulf towns of Normanton and urketown lie grassy plains, mudflats and salt lains, incised by the flow of numerous broad vers. In the Wet these plains turn into an immense land lake, attracting millions of waterbirds such s jabirus, brolgas and herons. When explorer hn Lort Stokes sailed up the Albert River in 1841 e declared the landscape the Plains of Promise, onvinced that within a short time the grassy ingdom would be well populated, stocked with rming animals and liberally strewn with towns nd villages.

It was not to be. Pioneering pastoralists were ampered by disease, the curse of remoteness and e demented force of the tropical climate. The iscovery of gold in the 1870s at Croydon, 150 km ast of Normanton, accelerated the pace of ttlement, but when the supply petered out in the rly 20th century, the miners left the region along ith most of the businesses and services. These ays, the population remains light and thinly ispersed. The mostly modest-sized mining, cattle, shing and tourism industries serve as the onomic mainstays.

A bitumen road loops south between ormanton and Burketown, but the more teresting – and shorter – route is across the top via the Burketown–Normanton Rd (part of the Savannah Way). This road skirts a 40 km wide maze of salt flats, mangroves and tidal channels. En route is the Leichhardt River crossing, where a short stroll leads to a pretty waterfall (during the Dry it may not flow). You can camp here, but there are no facilities. The road is suitable for all vehicles in the Dry, but is often closed for weeks on end in the Wet.

Normanton

Normanton, with a population of around 1500, sits on a high ridge on the banks of the Norman River. It was established in the late 1860s as an inland port and became the most important town along the Gulf after gold was discovered in Croydon.

The town's few historic buildings, products of the 19th-century gold rush, are grand in style. Points of interest include the restored former Bank of New South Wales built in 1896, and the 1880s Burns Philp trading emporium. The grandiose 1889 Normanton station (see *The* Gulflander *– train to nowhere,* p. 118) reflects the optimism of the early founders, who believed that a steady traffic of settlers from the south would fill the arrival hall for decades to come. Other distinctive attractions include the pub, painted various hues of purple, and the life-size replica of the largest crocodile ever caught (8.54 m), which sits outside the council offices. The croc, known as Krys the Savannah King, was one of 5000 shot by female crocodile hunter Krys Pawlowski, in the 1950s.

Karumba

Karumba lies at the mouth of the wide Norman River, 79 km north-west of Normanton along a sealed road. In the 1990s its sleepy, fishing-village ambience was challenged with the building of a major port to serve the Pasminco (now Zinifex) Century Zinc mine, near Lawn Hill, about 300 km to the south-west. That said, Karumba remains one

Contacts

Visitor information

Burketown
Musgrave St
(07) 4745 5100

Borroloola
(08) 8975 8799

Normanton
cnr Landsborough and Caroline sts
(08) 4745 1065

Parks and reserves

See *Fact File*, opposite

Hotels, roadhouses, station stays

Adels Grove
(07) 4748 5502

Borroloola Boat and Fishing Club
(08) 8975 8763

Kingfisher Camp
(Bowthorn Station)
Camping, fishing tours
(07) 4745 8212

Gregory Downs Hotel
(07) 4748 5566

Heartbreak Hotel
(08) 8975 9928

Hells Gate Roadhouse
(07) 4745 8258

Sweers Island Resort
(07) 4748 5544
www.sweers.com.au

Activities

Riversleigh Tours
Adels Grove
(07) 4748 5502

Undara Volcanic NP Tours
Undara Experience
1800 990 992

For other tours to Riversleigh and Undara Volcanic NP
(07) 4031 1631
www.gulf-savannah.com.au

Other

The *Gulflander*
(07) 4745 1391
http://thegulflander.com.au

The *Gulflander* – train to nowhere

The historic *Gulflander*, a 'tin hare' rail motor introduced in 1922, is known as the train from 'nowhere to nowhere'. It runs 152 km on the 1891 rail track linking the remote town of Normanton with the equally remote Croydon, to the east, and offers no connection to the rest of the Queensland rail network. In the late 19th century, however, this was not an issue – the railway provided a vital link between the river port and the rich goldfields. Now the burgundy and gold rattler is mostly for tourists. It runs once a week, leaving Normanton on Wednesday and returning on Thursday. The journey takes four hours each way, with stops at a few points of interest en route.

Undara Volcanic National Park detour

The Undara lava tubes are an extensive cave system in a national park-protected expanse of savannah woodland, fringed with rainforest. The tubes formed around 190 000 years ago when a giant volcano erupted sending a wave of lava across the surrounding plain. The lava was channelled north and west by a series of dry riverbeds. As the lava cooled, a crust formed creating an insulating tunnel through which molten lava continued to flow. Volcanic activity slowed then ceased, and the lava drained, leaving a series of black basalt tunnels. Undara's longest tube, the impressive Bayliss, is about 20 m high and stretches at least 1350 m, making it the longest in the world. Undara Volcanic NP is located 300 km south-west of Cairns (due east of Normanton). Visitors can picnic, walk up the volcano or through the forests and vine thickets, or join a tour to explore the lava tubes (see *Contacts*, p. 117).

of the best recreational fishing spots in this region. Thousands of visitors arrive each year, drawn by the access to the coast and by the promise of barramundi, prawns, salmon, sooty grunter and mackerel. Most visitors head for Karumba Point, 4 km from town, where there is excellent caravan park accommodation and boat hire. Swimming is not really an option, with saltwater crocodiles enjoying the waters. Birdwatching along the coast on surrounding wetlands is brilliant. Offshore lies Sweers Island, where a low-key resort (see *Contacts*, p. 117) accommodates anglers (the offshore fishing here is legendary) and nature lovers (myriad bird species and marine turtles are among the attractions).

Burketown to Gregory Downs

Burketown, 25 km inland on the Albert River, was established as a port in 1865 and named after explorer Robert Burke. North of the town are wetlands, to the south lie savannah plains. In 1866 'Gulf plague', possibly yellow or dengue fever, hit the fledgling settlement, wiping out many of its residents (some relocated, temporarily, to Sweers Island). About 20 years later two cyclones hit, killing seven people and destroying most of the buildings (the 1866 Customs House still stands, though in the guise of the local pub). Today, Burketown shows few scars of its chaotic past. It is a sleepy place of around 250 people, a pub, a general store and a post office – not dissimilar to how it looked in the 1950s, when Neville Shute used it as the inspiration for the imaginary Willstown in his novel *A Town Like Alice*.

Visit in late May, when the Burketown Campdraft is held, or in October, when the Morning Glory clouds appear – peculiar tubular formations that stretch for hundreds of kilometres across the sky, signalling the build-up to the Wet. Anglers should make a point of turning up at Easter for the Burketown Barramundi World Fishing Championships. The event helps support the Royal Flying Doctor Service and community groups, and is held annually in the Albert, Nicholson and Leichhardt rivers surrounding Burketown. The competition has open, junior and family sections, and daily weigh-ins are followed by entertainment, food and prizes.

Some 117 km south of Burketown is the tiny settlement of Gregory Downs. Camp here and hire a canoe for a trip along the Gregory River, said to offer some of the best inland canoeing in Queensland. Further west is Boodjamulla (Lawn Hill) NP.

Boodjamulla (Lawn Hill) National Park

This jewel-like national park is not just a diversion from the Gulf coastline, but a place to be savoured and explored over several days. It lies about 220 km south of Burketown, along unsealed roads that may be impassable during the Wet.

Covering nearly 2820 sq km, Boodjamulla NP preserves an oasis of remnant rainforest, gorges, ranges and palm-fringed creeks and spring-fed pools – a landscape all the more extraordinary for the flat, featureless plains that surround it. The Waanyi, who have lived in the area for at least 17 000 years,

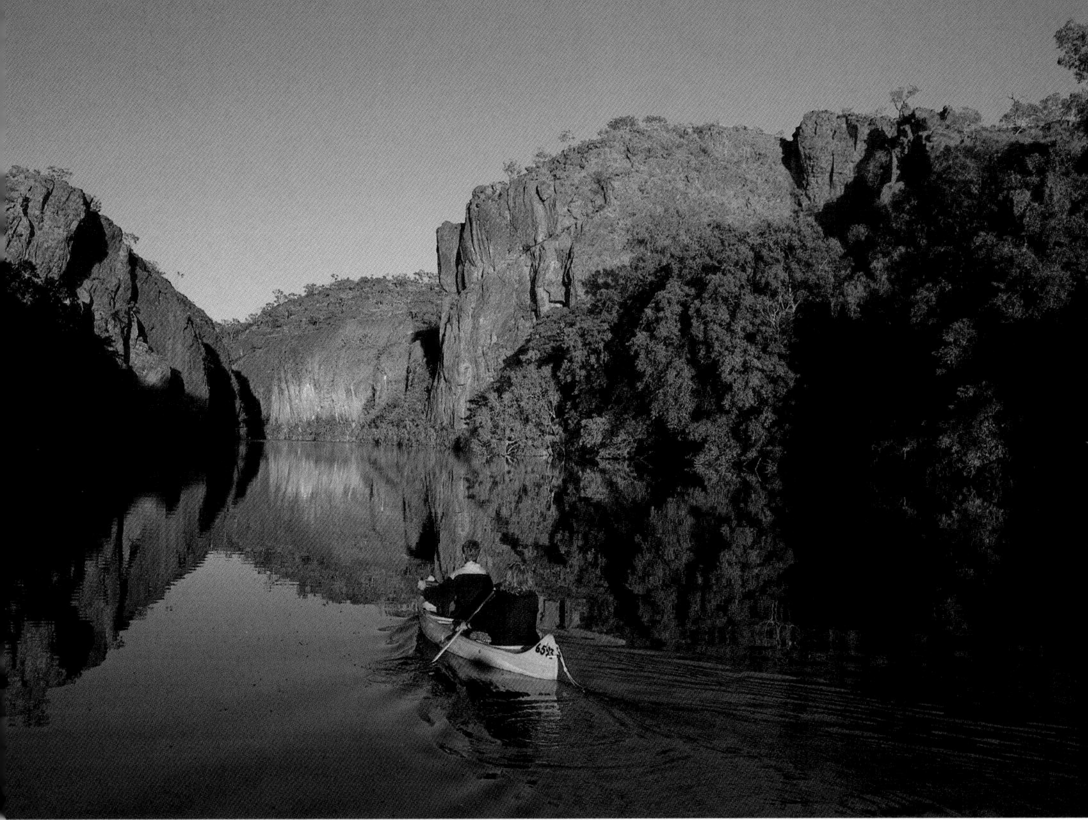

Left *Canoeing in peace at remote Boodjamulla (Lawn Hill) NP.*

Opposite *The brilliant yellow flowers of the kapok tree.*

now this place as Rainbow Serpent country – oodjamulla. With the arrival of Europeans, it ecame part of the huge pastoral property, Lawn Hill.

The centrepiece of the park is Lawn Hill Gorge, its 0 m high, reddened walls sculpted by the flow of the awn Hill Creek. The waters of the creek are fed by network of underground springs. Vegetation grows uickly and densely in these oasis-like conditions. here are thickets of pandanus, paperbacks and luster figs. Lilies float serenely on the creek's surface. ut the signature species is a livistona palm, or abbage palm, a tall fan-leaved palm with a thin, traight trunk and a shock of needle-like fronds.

Wildlife is abundant. Freshwater crocodiles – nore benign than their saltwater cousins – plump arramundi, salmon-tailed catfish, turtles and triped archer fish glide in the deep, velvety waters f the creek. On land, agile wallabies feed at dawn nd dusk, carefully avoiding the olive pythons, for vhich they are prey. The air carries the sound of irds – there are endangered purple-crowned fairy vrens, dozens of parrot species, lorikeets, oneyeaters and darters.

Much of this park is wild and inaccessible. Most isitors are content to spend their time canoeing, wimming and walking in the gorge area. Canoes an be hired for a relaxing 3 km paddle into the Jpper Gorge, or you can cool off in the emerald reen waterholes and beneath the Indarri Falls, vhich tumble into a natural pool. Walking tracks nclude the 4.5 km trail to see Aboriginal rock art along the Wild Dog Dreaming Track. There is a grassed campsite with facilities at the gorge. It is very popular and visitors are asked to book well in advance, particularly for Easter (see *Fact File*, p. 116). Additional camping is adjacent to the park at Adels Grove.

Riversleigh Fossil Site

The southern section of Boodjamulla protects the World Heritage-listed Riversleigh Fossil Site. The limestone cliffs of this 100 sq km area, the former Riversleigh Station, have yielded fossils dating back 20 million years, to a time when the landscape lay beneath a blanket of rainforest, with numerous rivers, lakes and billabongs. When some of these waterways developed a calcium crust, many animals were entombed and their remains preserved. Fossil finds include marsupial moles and feather-tailed possums; extinct mammals such as marsupial lions; and oversized versions of living creatures, such as 3 m high cassowaries. Visitors to the area must be part of an organised tour. Tours come down from nearby Adels Grove and north from Mount Isa (see *Contacts*, p. 117).

West to the Border

Beyond Burketown, the Savannah Way traverses a remote and lonely landscape. Great flat plains stretch out in all directions, beneath vast skies. Woodland plains and coastal swamps dominate. Towards the NT border, the landscape is relieved of

The outback's most prized catch – the silvery barramundi.

The great barramundi

Barramundi (*Lates calcarifer*), an Aboriginal word meaning 'fish with large scales', is northern Australia's most prized sport fish. Small towns and remote fishing lodges survive on the back of barra tourism, with keen anglers jetting in from across Australia and around the world to experience the thrill of the chase and the taste of the catch – barramundi are respected angling opponents, and their sweet flesh makes good eating.

Barramundi can grow up to 40 kg, but most fish caught weigh less than 6 kg. The best fishing is just before and after the Wet.

Barra are warm-water animals, found in the tropics in both fresh and salt water, and they inhabit a diverse range of habitats including rivers, creeks and mangrove-fringed estuaries. The fish grow to maturity upstream and then move into coastal waters and tidal estuaries for spawning. While in salt water, their scales turn a distinctive silvery bronze. In the ocean, they can be found at depths to around 40 m. Barramundi feed on smaller fish and crustaceans.

One interesting feature of the barramundi is its hermaphrodite breeding pattern. Barramundi less than five years old are male, and then some become female on reaching a certain size. These fish lay large numbers of eggs and are vitally important as brood stock. Fishing regulations apply to barramundi in both NT and Queensland (see *Travel Tips*, p. 98).

its persistent flatness as sandstone and limestone outcrops and weathered ranges take form.

West of Burketown, the only town before the NT border is the Aboriginal community of Doomadgee. It's not possible to stay overnight or camp, but visitors can refuel and stock-up on supplies. There is camping, however, on the cattle property Bowthorn Station, at Kingfisher Camp – the turn-off is 30 km past Doomadgee, then about 40 km south along an unsealed track. The campsite is on shady lawns beside a large waterhole on the Nicholson River. You can birdwatch, hire a boat, spot for crocs or, of course, fish for barra.

Hells Gate, 70 km past Doomadgee, sounds grim but in fact is a friendly roadhouse on part of a working cattle station. The settlement had a fearsome reputation in the 1860s and 1870s. Travellers en route to Katherine could rely on police protection from local Aboriginal tribes as far as Hell Gate, after which they were on their own. These days the roadhouse is a camping spot; tours of the country to the north may also be on the agenda (ring ahead – see *Contacts*, p. 117).

From here it's 53 km to the NT border. Straddling the border is the 6900 sq km Wollogorang Station. The on-site roadhouse is no longer open to the public but Wollogorang still operates as a meteorological station.

The Territory Gulf

The most remarkable thing about the NT's Gulf country is its incredible emptiness. Just 2800 people live here, either in Borroloola or in isolated traditional communities. In the 1890s, the Eastern Steamship Company sponsored Banjo Paterson to travel to the district and pen a few words that might promote the area as a travel destination. In his poem *By the Grey Gulf-water*, an awed Paterson wrote of a land where 'the soul of a man will recoil, afraid, from the sphinx-like visage that Nature weareth'. These words failed to incite a tourist stampede at the time, although a century on a small but steady stream of anglers pass through, as do travellers on the trail of the NT's extraordinary 'lost cities'.

Borroloola

The word borroloola, said to mean 'land of the paperbarks', aptly describes some of the shaded sites along the fish-rich McArthur River, but the town itself, about 50 km inland, is fairly basic. Borroloola, with a population of around 500, lies at the centre of the Narwinbi Aboriginal Land Trust area. The town was established in 1885 to open up more pastures for the cattle industry. Although it never really boomed, its reputation for rowdiness and a propensity to attract eccentrics – including well-read hermits – spread far. These days, it is best known as a top destination for barramundi fishing.

About 30 km downstream, at King Ash Bay, the Borroloola Boat and Fishing Club attracts a stream of recreational anglers and campers; many come at Easter for the Borroloola Easter Barra Classic. For those who can resist the lure of the barra for a day or so, there are charter tours of the fertile waters of the Sir Edward Pellew Group of islands, just offshore from the McArthur River estuary.

Lost Cities

The sealed Carpentaria Hwy runs west from Borroloola and forms part of the Savannah Way. The main attraction here is the series of landscapes referred to as lost cities – eerie, cylindrical pillars of sandstone jutting out of the surrounding scrub-covered escarpment. The Caranbirini Conservation Reserve, 500 m from the highway, about 46 km south-west of Borroloola, protects pillars up to 25 m high, good examples of this type of formation which is the result of millions of years of weathering and erosion. An easy, 60-minute walk leads visitors around the maze of outcrops. Another 60 km west, is Cape Crawford. Rumour has it that this modest, weathered rise was mistaken for a headland by an early navigator, hence its name. A roadhouse and motel complex known, unforgettably, as Heartbreak Hotel, provides visitors with fuel, supplies, accommodation and helicopter tours of the otherwise inaccessible Abner Range, where the most dramatic of the region's geological lost cities lie in ancient and undisturbed splendour.

Above *'Lost City', a strange world of rocky outcrops in the Abner Range.*

Below *Sunrise at Borroloola.*

Outback Queensland

Queensland's mining and cattle country cuts a broad swath across the state's mid-section, extending west to meet the Northern Territory border. Wide plains stretch to dusty horizons, broken here and there by low-slung hills laced with minerals and fossils.

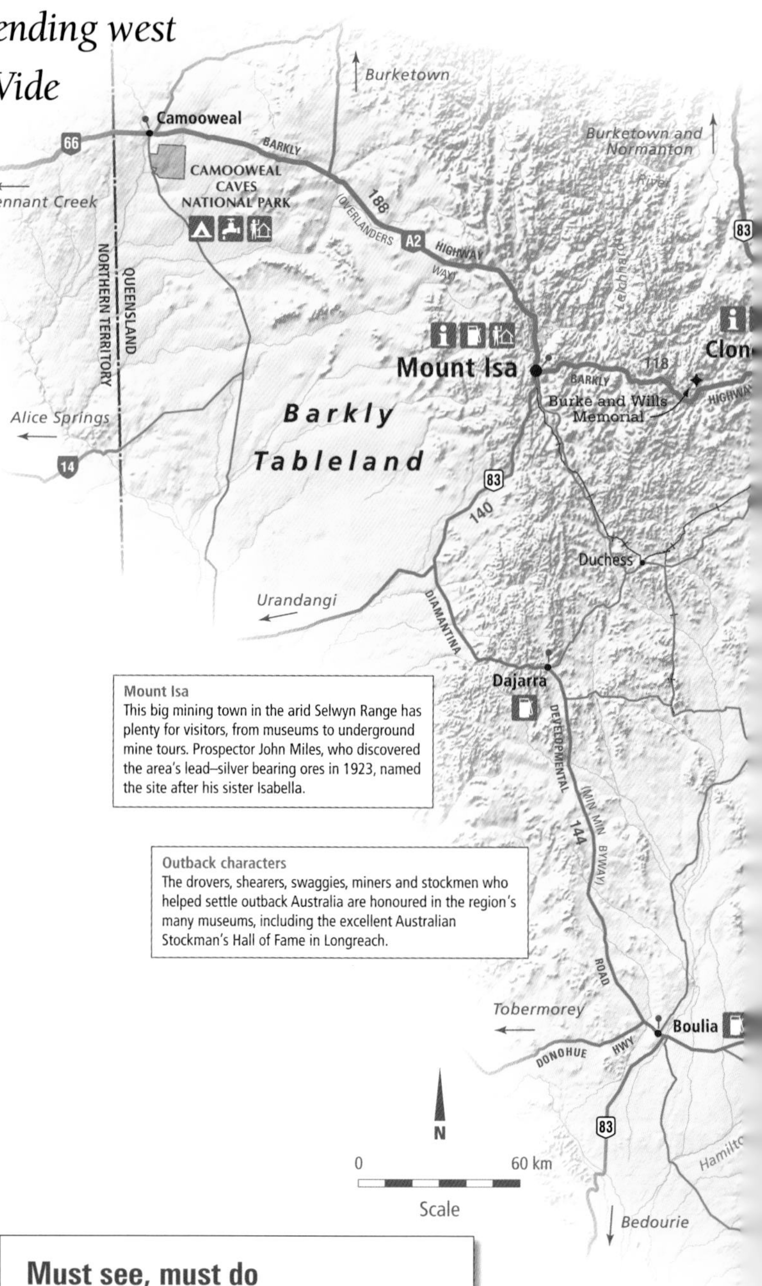

Burketown
Camooweal
BARKLY
CAMOOWEAL CAVES NATIONAL PARK
66
Tennant Creek
188
OVERLANDERS
A2
HIGHWAY
WAY
Burketown and Normanton
83
QUEENSLAND
NORTHERN TERRITORY
Mount Isa
118
BARKLY
HIGHWAY
Burke and Wills Memorial
Barkly Tableland
Alice Springs
14
140
Duchess
Urandangi
DIAMANTINA
Dajarra
DEVELOPMENTAL
MIN MIN BYWAY
144
ROAD
Mount Isa
This big mining town in the arid Selwyn Range has plenty for visitors, from museums to underground mine tours. Prospector John Miles, who discovered the area's lead–silver bearing ores in 1923, named the site after his sister Isabella.
Outback characters
The drovers, shearers, swaggies, miners and stockmen who helped settle outback Australia are honoured in the region's many museums, including the excellent Australian Stockman's Hall of Fame in Longreach.
Tobermorey
Boulia
DONOHUE HWY
N
0
60 km
Scale
Bedourie

Travellers can explore Outback Queensland along sealed, well-maintained roads. There are two key touring routes: the Flinders and Barkly highways, also known as the Overlanders Way, which run west from Townsville to the NT border; and the Matilda (Landsborough) Hwy, which runs in a north-west direction connecting towns such as Longreach and Winton. Many visitors head due west from Rockhampton along the Capricorn Hwy, then pick up the Matilda at Longreach.

Some of the great characters of the Australian outback hail from this area and many an outback myth has taken root in the dusty soil. Pastoralists established properties here on a scale unthinkable in England or Europe. Gold rushes in the 19th century settled pockets along the east coast, while the discovery of lead and silver in the arid hills of Mount Isa saw the birth of one of the country's biggest mines. The men and women who came to work in these industries were pioneers, enduring all manner of hardship. The region's museums pay tribute to their efforts and to qualities that emerged from the sweat and tears of those early years – egalitarianism, courage, mateship and enterprise.

As an outback touring destination, it's hard to beat this area. Roads and facilities are good; cattle stations unfurl from either side of the road; stretches of natural landscape appear, rough and scrubby, but wonderfully expansive; towns flick by, sometimes substantial places, other times a collection of rickety buildings framing the town pub. Best of all, there are long, straight stretches of road heading for – but never quite reaching – distant horizons.

Must see, must do

- Ride one of Queensland's great outback rail routes
- Find out about fossils at one of three fossil museums
- Discover dinosaur footprints in their original state
- Celebrate outback Australia at the Australian Stockman's Hall of Fame
- Camp among the vine forests in Porcupine Gorge NP

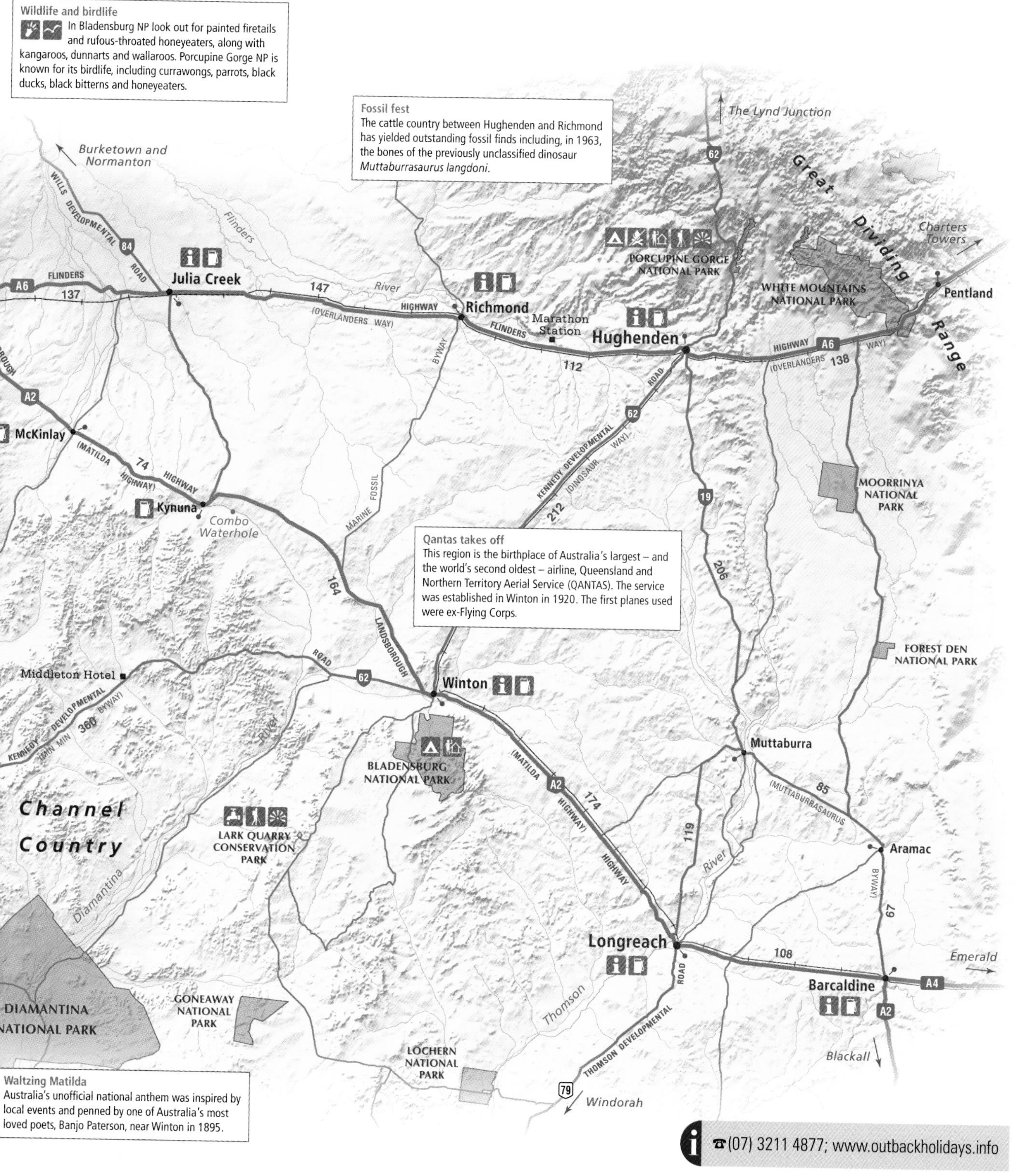

Wildlife and birdlife
In Bladensburg NP look out for painted firetails and rufous-throated honeyeaters, along with kangaroos, dunnarts and wallaroos. Porcupine Gorge NP is known for its birdlife, including currawongs, parrots, black ducks, black bitterns and honeyeaters.

Fossil fest
The cattle country between Hughenden and Richmond has yielded outstanding fossil finds including, in 1963, the bones of the previously unclassified dinosaur *Muttaburrasaurus langdoni*.

Qantas takes off
This region is the birthplace of Australia's largest – and the world's second oldest – airline, Queensland and Northern Territory Aerial Service (QANTAS). The service was established in Winton in 1920. The first planes used were ex-Flying Corps.

Waltzing Matilda
Australia's unofficial national anthem was inspired by local events and penned by one of Australia's most loved poets, Banjo Paterson, near Winton in 1895.

☎(07) 3211 4877; www.outbackholidays.info

Fact File

Top events

Easter *Easter in Outback Queensland (Longreach)*
Hughenden Country Music Festival
April/ May *Dirt and Dust Triathlon (Julia Creek)*
June *Waltzing Matilda Festival (Winton)*
July *Drovers Camp and Reunion Festival (Camooweal)*
Aug *Mount Isa Rodeo*
Sept *Diamantina Rodeo (Winton)*
Hughenden Dinosaur Festival
Richmond Country Music Festival

Permits and regulations

Large pastoral properties cover much of this region. Visitors are asked to respect private property and seek permission to enter.

Parks and reserves

National parks and reserves in Qld are administered by the Qld Parks and Wildlife Service (QPWS). For general information see *Travel Tips*, p. 98.

Bladensburg NP Not suitable for 2WD vehicles during wet weather. Bush camping only; take firewood and water. There are no walking tracks, so experienced hikers only. For information contact the ranger: (07) 4657 1192.

Camooweal Caves NP 4WD recommended (2WD may be ok in dry weather). Campsites available, but bookings required; take firewood, and water as supply not guaranteed. Only experienced cavers with suitable equipment should attempt to explore the caves. For information contact the QPWS at Mount Isa: (07) 4744 7888.

Lark Quarry Conservation Park Walking trails, picnic area and lookouts, but no camping. Contact visitor information in Winton (see *Contacts*, opposite).

Porcupine Gorge NP Campsites available, but bookings must be made several weeks in advance (phone the QPWS booking line: 13 1304); take water and fuel stove (no fires). For general information contact (07) 4741 1021.

Warnings

Fuel and supplies Long distances separate some towns in this region. Check you have adequate fuel and water before proceeding.

Road access and closures Major roads are sealed and maintained. Some minor roads and roads in national parks may not be suitable for 2WD vehicles. The region catches the edge of the tropical Wet; at this time roads can become impassable. Check conditions with the RACQ: 13 1905; www.racq.com.au

See also *On the Road*, p. 246.

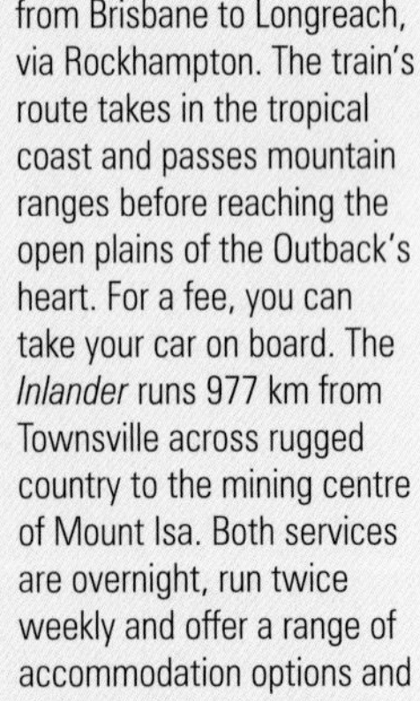

On track

A trip on the *Spirit of the Outback* is one of Queensland's great train journeys, covering 1300 km from Brisbane to Longreach, via Rockhampton. The train's route takes in the tropical coast and passes mountain ranges before reaching the open plains of the Outback's heart. For a fee, you can take your car on board. The *Inlander* runs 977 km from Townsville across rugged country to the mining centre of Mount Isa. Both services are overnight, run twice weekly and offer a range of accommodation options and dining facilities (see *Contacts*, opposite).

Opposite *An arid landscape of Mitchell grass and low rocky outcrops.*

Below *Australian Stockman's Hall of Fame, Longreach.*

Matilda (Landsborough) Highway

The Landsborough Hwy forms part of the road-train route from Brisbane to Darwin. It connects with the Capricorn Hwy, which heads west from the coastal town of Rockhampton, and runs between Barcaldine and Longreach. Sealed and well maintained, for much of its distance the Matilda sweeps through a low-slung landscape, with Mitchell grass spreading across the poor soil, treeless plains and, in the heat, a shimmering haze. Here and there, bands of mesas (flat-topped hills with steep sides) break the monotony. The landscapes are flat, the horizons distant, and the townships prosperous, interesting places with plenty of attractions and facilities for travellers.

Barcaldine

In 1887 Barcaldine, known as the 'Garden City of the West', was the first Australian town to tap the waters of the Great Artesian Basin, an event that is commemorated by the town's giant windmill. Fittingly, Barcaldine's leafy, well-watered streets are all named after trees.

The town sprang to fame in the early 1890s as the meeting place for shearers protesting the use by pastoralists of non-union labour. The shearers gathered beneath a ghost gum, the 'Tree of Knowledge', which survived until 2006, when it was poisoned. When they lost their battle in 1891, the strikers realised that future industrial action would benefit from a strong political base; a membe of the strike committee later became the first labour representative to be elected to parliament. His success eventually led to the formation of the Australian Labor Party. This history is celebrated in the town's Australian Workers' Heritage Centre.

Longreach

Wide, airy streets and a pleasant, ordered ambienc greet visitors to Longreach, a well-serviced country town (population 4000). Since 1988, its name has been synonymous with its chief attraction, the Australian Stockman's Hall of Fame and Outback Heritage Centre. Housed in a magnificent contemporary building, a symphony of corrugated iron, sweeping curves, stonework and earthy colours, the museum is a tribute to those men and women whose experiences have shaped the

The Royal Flying Doctor Service

Presbyterian minister Reverend John Flynn was sent bush in 1910. From then until his death in 1951, Flynn worked tirelessly to provide 'a mantle of safety' for the people of the outback. He established bush hospitals and hostels in remote places, providing medical services where none had previously existed. He then turned his attention to the fledgling aviation industry to extend his care and, in 1928, helped found the Aerial Medical Service at Cloncurry, later to become the Royal Flying Doctor Service (RFDS).

The RFDS is now one of the world's most unusual and respected medical services. It has 20 bases that cover an area the size of Europe. It has pioneered and advanced techniques in the provision of medicine to remote areas, such as consultation and diagnosis by radio and the design of a medicine chest for remote households. Less well known is the role the RFDS has played in the social settlement of the outback. The widespread installation of radios saw social contact between remote households flourish, creating communities where none had existed before. The network also enabled the establishment of the education service School of the Air and, later, provided a safety net for travellers and played a major role in opening up to tourism some of Australia's most remote regions.

legends and history of the Australian outback. Examine transport wagons and an 1860s slab hut, read period diaries and letters, listen to oral histories and view an extraordinary range of items salvaged from the homes and farms of Australia's pastoral adventurers.

The Qantas Founders Outback Museum and Qantas Hangar can be seen at the airport. Two ex-Flying Corp officers, Hudson Fysh and Paul McGinness, established the now famous international carrier in nearby Winton (see *Winton to Cloncurry*, below), in 1920. The headquarters were moved to Longreach in 1922, where they remained until 1934. The museum features a full-size replica of the first type of passenger aircraft, tours of a fully equipped Boeing 747, along with audiovisual displays, documents and photographs.

Winton to Cloncurry

Winton, about 170 km north of Longreach, is celebrated as the site of the first performance of Banjo Paterson's *Waltzing Matilda*, which took place at the North Gregory Hotel in 1895. The song, which tells of a swagman stealing a sheep, is the spiritual anthem of Australia; its melancholy lyrics better known and more enthusiastically voiced than the verses of the official anthem, *Advance Australia Fair*. To find out more, visit the town's excellent Waltzing Matilda Centre, where displays detail the history of Paterson and his famous ode to the outback.

The township of Kynuna (population around 20) lies 160 km north-west of Winton. Once an important staging post for Cobb & Co, it still turns on the hospitality at its famous Blue Heeler Hotel. Another town best known for its watering hole is McKinlay (population 30), where the Walkabout Creek Hotel, along with other town buildings, featured in the film *Crocodile Dundee*.

Cloncurry sits at the junction of the Matilda Hwy and the Overlanders Hwy. This sizeable town (population 4000) serviced a huge copper mining industry in the early 1900s and is now a centre for the region's cattle industry and railhead for transporting stock. In 1922, the first commercial airline flight in Australia, operated by Qantas, landed here from Charleville, 1000 km south. In

Contacts

Visitor information

Barcaldine
Oak St
(07) 4651 1724

Cloncurry
McIlwraith St
(07) 4742 1361

Hughenden
37 Gray St
(07) 4741 1021

Julia Creek
cnr Burke and Quarrell sts
(07) 4746 7690

Longreach
Qantas Park, Eagle St
(07) 4658 4150

Mount Isa
19 Marian St
(07) 4749 1555

Richmond
Flinders Hwy
(07) 4741 3429

Winton
50 Elderslie St
1300 665 115

Parks and reserves

See *Fact File*, opposite

Museums

Australian Stockman's Hall of Fame
Longreach
(07) 4658 2166
www.outbackheritage.com.au

Outback at Isa Centre
Mount Isa
1300 659 660
www.outbackatisa.com.au

Qantas Founders Outback Museum
Longreach
(07) 4658 3737
www.qfom.com.au

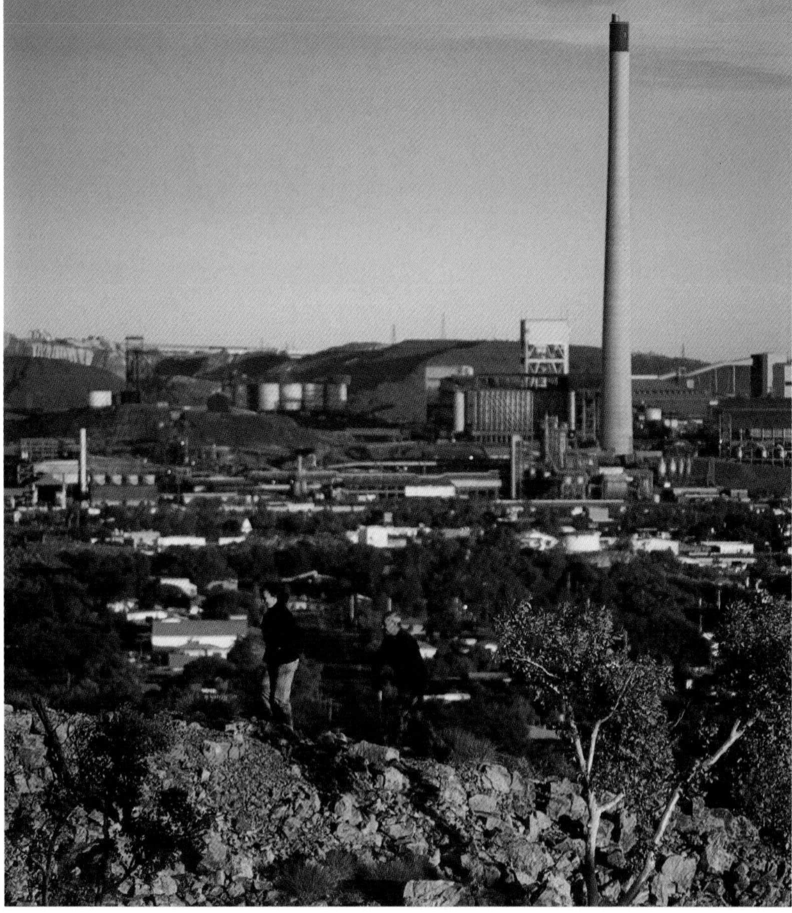

Above *Mt Isa township.*

Opposite *Mustering by helicopter on an outback station.*

1928, the town become the first base for the Royal Flying Doctor Service (RFDS) (see p. 125) – the history and achievements of this remarkable organisation are on display at the RFDS Museum.

The Overlanders Way

This remarkable 1150 km route traces the journey of the drovers who moved huge herds of cattle across the continent and the pioneers who established western Queensland's cattle and mining industries. The route, along the Flinders and Barkly highways, heads south-west from the coastal city of Townsville and passes through Charters Towers, where a collection of elaborate Victorian-era buildings survive as a legacy of the gold rush of the late 19th century.

Hughenden and Richmond, beef and wool towns set 100 km apart, have come to mark the start of the outback. The surrounding area has yielded extraordinary fossil finds. In 1963, the owner of Muttaburra Station discovered the bones of the previously unnamed land animal, the *Muttaburrasaurus langdoni*, embedded in the rocks of a riverbank. A replica of this 7 m high herbivore, along with other local discoveries, is on display at Hughenden's Flinders Discovery Centre. In 1989, the owner of Marathon Station stumbled across Australia's most complete large-animal fossil – a 4 m long swimming reptile. The find was the catalyst for the establishment of the Richmond Marine Fossil Museum. The specialty here is the display of local fossils from the Cretaceous inland sea, which covered a large slab of Queensland 120 million years ago.

Visitors should consider a detour to the popular Porcupine Gorge NP (54 sq km) 60 km north of Hughenden. The park protects a stunning steep-walled gorge known as the 'Little Grand Canyon', and thickets of vine forest. Facilities include camping, walking tracks and picnic areas. The small cattle town of Julie Creek lies about 165 km west, and then it's on to Cloncurry (see *Winton to Cloncurry*, p. 125) and the large mining centre of Mount Isa.

Grasslands and dinosaur prints

About 17 km south-west of Winton is Bladensburg NP, spreading across 850 sq km. The region's spacious landscapes – grasslands, woodlands, low sandstone escarpments, mesas and river flats – can be experienced on this former pastoral property. There are picnic spots and a campground, but visitors must be self-sufficient in what is fairly remote country. Another 100 km further south-west lies Lark Quarry Conservation Park, where you can see 100 million-year-old dinosaur footprints preserved in sandstone (entry to see track prints is by guided tour only).

Mount Isa

Mount Isa, with a multicultural population of 23 000, is the most important industrial, commercial and administrative centre in north-west Queensland, an oasis – albeit somewhat suburban and industrial in character – at the heart of the cattle and spinifex country of the Barkly Tableland.

The original inhabitants were the Kalkadoon (see opposite). Pastoralists and miners were in the district from the 1860s, but the town was not founded until 1923, when prospector John Campbell Miles pegged two leases by the Leichhardt River, after discovering an outcrop of silver–lead carbonate ore. Mount Isa Mines commenced operation in 1931 and now runs Australia's largest mine. In addition to silver and lead, rich deposits of copper and zinc have been found. Visit the Outback at Isa Centre, where miners conduct tours of an underground mine (hardhats included). Mining heritage is displayed at the National Trust-listed Tent House, a structure built of hessian, canvas, wood and iron, an example of the town's early miner accommodation.

Outback at Isa is also home to the Riversleigh Fossil Centre. Fossils have been uncovered throughout the Gulf and the Outback, with a concentration at Riversleigh, at the tail end of Boodjamulla (Lawn Hill) NP (see *Riversleigh Fossil Site*, p. 119). The fossil centre in Mount Isa showcases many of the Riversleigh discoveries and provides information on fossil formation and techniques for discovery and excavation.

Among the town's other attractions is the School of the Air centre, which services the educational needs of Queensland students in remote locations such as desert-bound Birdsville (see *Birdsville and Beyond*, p. 134).

A great time to visit The Isa is in the blessedly cool weather of early August, when the folks – and their steers – kick up their heels at the Mt Isa Rodeo – one of the largest and richest events of its type in Australia.

Camooweal

Down the road in Camooweal, rodeo fever flares in July with the Drovers Camp and Reunion Festival, which celebrates the town's glory days as a resting place for drovers moving cattle across the Barkly Tableland. Now huge road trains thunder down the main street, but a few reminders of those earlier days survive, including the shire hall, with its display of photos, and Freckleton's Historic Store, which is home to the Barkly Tableland Heritage Centre.

About 20 km south of the town lies Camooweal Caves NP (138 sq km). Water percolating through 500 million-year-old dolomite created this landscape with its honeycombed network of underground caverns. These caves are for experienced and well-equipped cavers only. Other visitors can enjoy some beautiful scenery and a pleasant campsite alongside Caves Waterhole.

The Kalkadoon

The Mount Isa district was originally the preserve of the Kalkadoon people. Pastoralists and miners began to take up land here in the 1860s and at first the situation was peaceful, with the Kalkadoon working as labourers and guides. But in the late 1870s, when it became clear that the whites were not moving on, the Kalkadoon launched a series of attacks. The white retaliation culminated in a battle in 1884 at a place known as Battle Mountain, to the north-east of Mt Isa.

The Kalkadoon resisted white settlement more ferociously than many other Indigenous Australian tribes. An estimated 900 men, women and children lost their lives at the hands of white settlers between 1878 and 1884. The descendants of the Kalkadoon have retained many of the rich traditions of their forebears. Visitors can learn about their history and experience their culture at the Kalkadoon Tribal Centre in Mount Isa.

Corner Country

desert tracks

Corner Country

The Corner Country is sparse – sometimes the only testament to civilisation is a long mesh fence or a marker left by an explorer. But the natural features – like Cooper Creek, Lake Eyre and the chain of artesian springs – leap out.

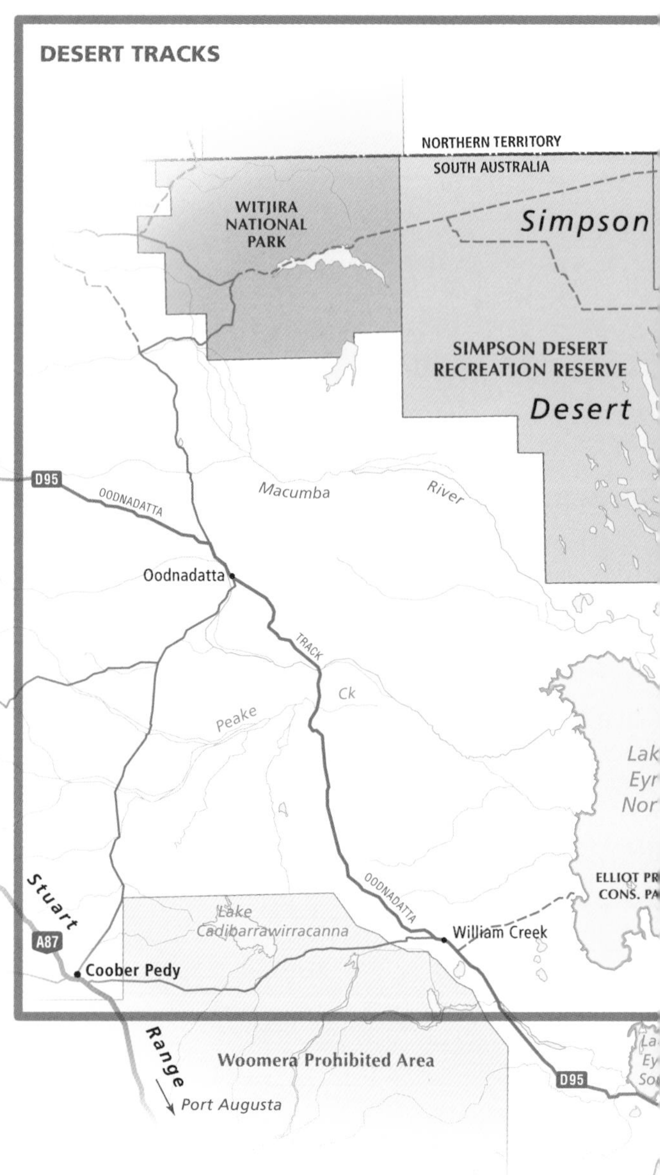

Corner Country Regions

Birdsville and Beyond

The Birdsville Track is regarded as one of Australia's essential 4WD treks – a journey through deserts of changing colours, following in the historic tracks of some of the country's toughest drovers. The Strzelecki Track is the way to Innamincka and Cooper Creek, which together form one of the most evocative sites in the Australian desert – a small community surrounded by bright red plains and a beautiful river tinged with the memory of Burke and Wills. Linked with the Cooper are the Coongie Lakes, oases of fish and waterbirds. *See p. 134*

Desert Tracks

The melaleuca-fringed pool at Dalhousie Springs is a paradise for weary travellers, and good for a moment of quiet relief at the beginning or end of a journey across the Simpson Desert, the world's largest sea of dunes. Here the predominant colour is red, temperatures can reach above 50°C, and the mode of travel is strictly 4WD. To the south-west, the Oodnadatta Track sidles past Lake Eyre, overlapping with the historic routes of the Overland Telegraph Line and the original *Ghan* railway, two of the greatest engineering feats in Australia's outback history. *See p. 142*

Emu chick

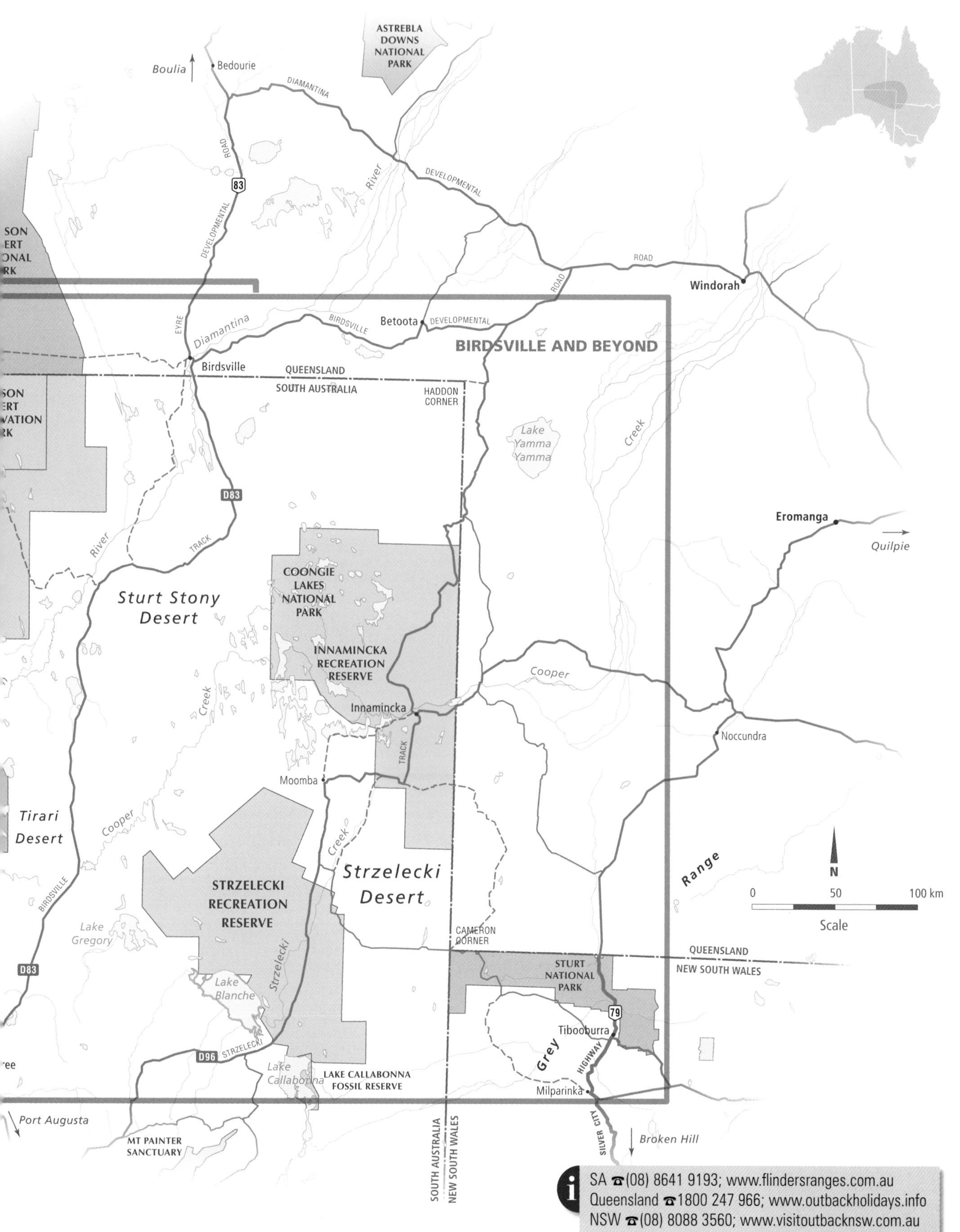

SA ☎(08) 8641 9193; www.flindersranges.com.au
Queensland ☎1800 247 966; www.outbackholidays.info
NSW ☎(08) 8088 3560; www.visitoutbacknsw.com.au

Travel Tips

When to go

Many people head to this region in winter to escape the cooler coastal centres, as June–Aug temperatures hover around a pleasant 20°C. April–Oct are the best months to travel, while the hotter months (Nov–Mar) are not recommended, with some days above 40°C. In the Simpson Desert, summer temperatures can top 50°C. Winter nights can be cold, even freezing. For further information contact the Bureau of Meteorology (BOM): 1900 926 113; www.bom.gov.au

CLIMATE												MARREE
	J	F	M	A	M	J	J	A	S	O	N	D
Max °C	38	37	34	28	23	20	19	21	26	29	33	36
Min °C	21	21	18	13	9	6	5	6	10	13	17	20
Rain mm	18	21	14	11	14	14	10	9	10	13	11	16
Raindays	2	2	2	2	3	3	3	3	2	3	3	3

CLIMATE												BIRDSVILLE
	J	F	M	A	M	J	J	A	S	O	N	D
Max °C	39	38	35	30	25	22	21	24	28	32	35	38
Min °C	24	24	21	16	11	8	7	8	12	16	20	23
Rain mm	25	30	17	10	12	10	11	6	6	12	14	16
Raindays	3	3	2	1	2	2	2	1	1	2	2	3

Aboriginal land

At the time of publication there were no declared areas of Aboriginal land in this region.

Government land

While visitors are permitted in the township of Woomera, entry to the Woomera Prohibited Area is by permit only, except in the immediate corridors of the Stuart Hwy and the road from Coober Pedy to William Creek. Camping is not permitted in the area.

Parks and reserves

South Australia All SA national parks, conservation parks and regional reserves in this region are part of the state's Desert Parks. All are subject to a total fire ban 1 Nov–30 April. Campfires are allowed outside these times, though a fuel stove is preferred. Bring your own firewood. Don't expect campsites to have water. If you intend to visit more than one desert park or to stay for more than a few days in a single park, then it is worthwhile obtaining a Desert Parks Pass. This covers entry and camping fees to all parks and includes a handbook, park maps and wildlife information. The pass is valid for 12 months. To purchase one or for further information on any of the parks, ring the Desert Parks Hotline: 1800 816 078. Passes are also available from regional agencies, including the Marree Outback Roadhouse, Innamincka Hotel or Trading Post, William Creek Roadhouse, Pink Roadhouse (Oodnadatta), and Mount Dare Homestead. 24-hour passes are also available from these places. The online *Desert Parks Bulletin* is regularly updated with information on road conditions throughout the parks; www.environment.sa.gov.au/parks/visitor/latest.html

New South Wales For general information on NSW parks, contact NSW National Parks and Wildlife Service (NPWS): 1300 361 967; www.environment.nsw.gov.au/nationalparks For specific information on Sturt NP, see also *Fact File* p. 136.

Queensland For general information on Queensland parks and reserves, contact Queensland Parks and Wildlife Service (QPWS); 1300 130 372; www.derm.qld.gov.au For specific information on Simpson Desert NP, see also *Fact File* p. 144.

Fishing

Licences are not required for recreational fishing in SA; however, bag and size limits apply. Contact Primary Industries and Resources South Australia PIRSA (Fisheries) for information: 1800 065 522; www.pir.sa.gov.au

Warnings

Fuel and supplies This is a remote region and long distances separate towns and fuel stops. In some instances travellers will need to carry reserves of fuel; for example, if planning to cross the Simpson Desert. Always carry plenty of water.

Road access and closures Some roads in this region are 4WD only, while others require at least a high-clearance vehicle. Rain can make roads impassable. For NSW road reports contact the Roads and Traffic Authority: 13 2701; www.rta.nsw.gov.au For SA road reports contact Transport SA: 1300 361 033; www.transport.sa.gov.au In the Oodnadatta area, the Pink Roadhouse has a toll-free number and offers information on regional road conditions and outback travel advice: 1800 802 074. For information on road conditions within SA parks and reserves, check the *Desert Parks Bulletin* (see *Parks and reserves*, above).

Remote travel Those venturing off the major tourist routes, for example crossing the Simpson Desert, should consider carrying a long-range communications device (see *On the Road*, p. 246).

Maps Maps in this book are guidelines only – carry detailed maps.

See also *On the Road*, p. 246.

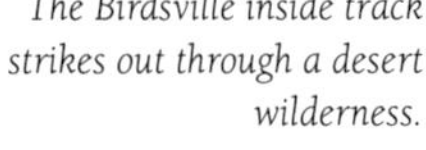

The Birdsville inside track strikes out through a desert wilderness.

Three tracks head north through the Corner Country like splayed, twisting fingers – the Oodnadatta, the Birdsville and the Strzelecki acks. Each reveals just a little more about a ndscape that mystifies and defies definition at ery chance. This is a place dotted not with hills ıt with jump-ups, channelled with rivers and eeks that for the most part are dry, and scattered ith salt lakes that are most often inhospitable astelands, but are sometimes transformed into ind-rippled jewels filled with life.

This region registers the lowest rainfall on the ntinent, and yet so many of its features have to do ith water. In the east is Cooper Creek – a far-flung mnant of Queensland's Channel Country – whose rene, brown expanse and coolibah-fringed banks ve been awing travellers for decades. And in e west along the Oodnadatta Track is a chain of rings that feature water so blue and grass so green at they don't look quite real.

Lake Eyre is the largest lake in the country. s shoreline includes bays, peninsulas, headlands d canyons – names that convey something of grandeur when full – but despite a catchment ne covering 15 percent of Australia, Lake Eyre is

only partially filled around once every eight years. For the rest of the time it is the domain of desert creatures such as the Lake Eyre dragon, which totters across the salty surface on its heels to protect itself from the heat.

Towns and stations are sometimes separated by mind-numbing distances, but for four-wheel drivers this is part of the attraction. Across a swath of sand dunes you can arrive at a tree blazed by ill-fated explorers Burke and Wills, or a marker left by a lonely government surveyor, and feel that they were here just yesterday.

Above *Lake Eyre when full – a vista of blue water and sky.*

Left *A desert flower blooms in the Simpson's rusty red sand.*

Birdsville and Beyond

Around the Birdsville and Strzelecki tracks the word 'desert' seems to live up to its reputation – flat, dry, hot and dangerous. But out of such adversity come some of Australia's bravest tales and loveliest sights.

This is a land of many textures – sandy and rippling, coarse and rock-strewn, fuzzy and grass-covered, with only dunes and a few flat-topped hills to interrupt the view. But after a while in this region, where NSW, Queensland and SA meet, you come to see that the space that lies between you, the horizon and the arching blue sky is far from empty.

Life exists here in a style alien to the continent's soft, bountiful edges, the land of the coast. Here, life is less certain. Birds and animals cluster around bores, water tanks and the few lakes. Creatures live in the cracks of the earth or between the leaves of a clump of spinifex. Homesteads cling to features that are optimistically called gorges, mountains or creeks, but which rarely live up to their name.

A captivating history goes with the tough landscape. Charles Sturt ended an ambitious expedition to discover the centre of the continent here in 1845, beaten by the endless sand dunes. In 1860, at Cooper Creek, Burke and Wills began the most fearsome leg of their journey to the north of Australia. The trip would slowly leach the life out of them, and back on the Cooper's banks they would eventually die of malnutrition. Two old droving routes, the Birdsville and Strzelecki tracks, are now among Australia's best-known 4WD treks.

Cooper Creek is this region's true jewel, a creek that even Sturt, the man who named it, thought could have been called a river. From its braided beginnings in Queensland's Channel Country, it forges a self-assured path through bone-dry desert. Here the fish seem like miracles and the birds, draped across the sprawling limbs of a coolibah, kind enough to let you in on their secret.

Birdsville Track
Many men and cattle were lost to sand storms, thirst a starvation as the legendary Birdville Track was being p into existence. Today four-wheel drivers replace drove many time their trip in September for the Birdsville Ra

Desert Parks Pass
All SA national parks and reserves in this region are covered by the annual Desert Parks Pass, which includes all entry and camping fees as well as maps and information; for more details see *Travel Tips*, p. 132.

Wildlife and birdlife
The region around Cooper and Strzelecki creeks is reported to have one of the highest concentrations of raptors in the country, while Coongie Lakes can support up to 20 000 waterbirds at full capacity. Red kangaroos and emus are ever present, but many other creatures lie hidden from view in the cracks in the earth, like the marsupial known as the narrow-nosed planigale.

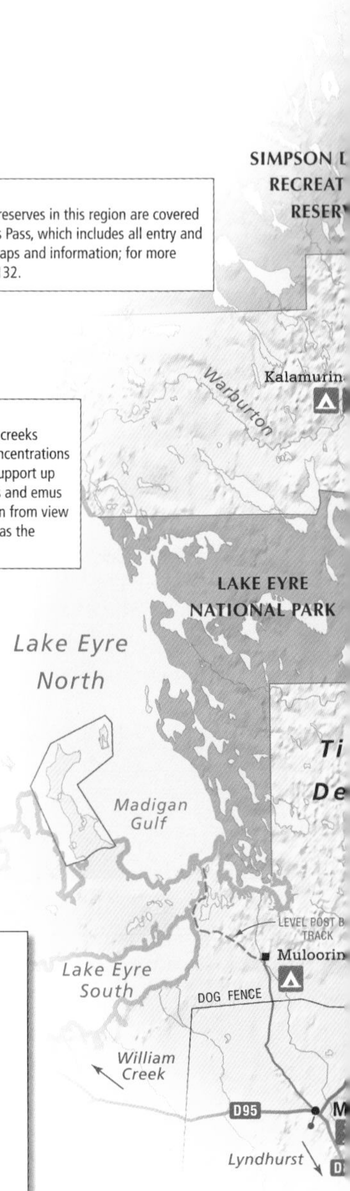

Must see, must do

- Travel the Birdsville Track, once the route of hardened outback drovers
- Drive the Strzelecki Track, a route made famous by a cattle rustler in 1870
- Witness the incredible diversity of birdlife at Coongie Lakes
- Visit the Burke and Wills Dig Tree near Innamincka
- Survey the plains from a jump-up in Sturt NP

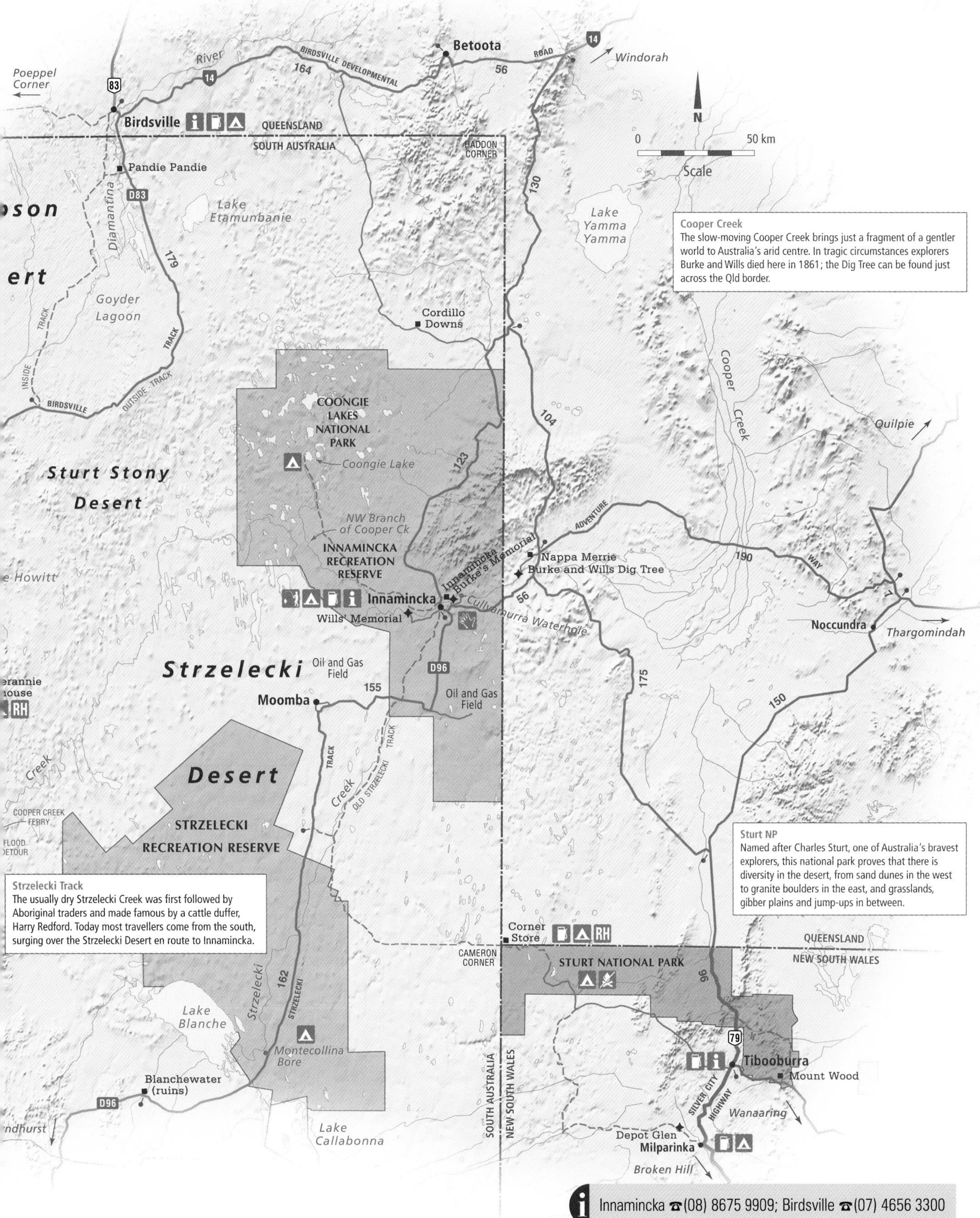

Cooper Creek
The slow-moving Cooper Creek brings just a fragment of a gentler world to Australia's arid centre. In tragic circumstances explorers Burke and Wills died here in 1861; the Dig Tree can be found just across the Qld border.

Sturt NP
Named after Charles Sturt, one of Australia's bravest explorers, this national park proves that there is diversity in the desert, from sand dunes in the west to granite boulders in the east, and grasslands, gibber plains and jump-ups in between.

Strzelecki Track
The usually dry Strzelecki Creek was first followed by Aboriginal traders and made famous by a cattle duffer, Harry Redford. Today most travellers come from the south, surging over the Strzelecki Desert en route to Innamincka.

Innamincka ☎(08) 8675 9909; Birdsville ☎(07) 4656 3300

Fact File

Top events

June *Marree Picnic Races and Gymkhana*
July *Marree Camel Cup*
Aug *Innamincka Races*
Sept *Birdsville Races*
Oct *Gymkhana (Marree)*

Parks and reserves

For information on access, camping and campfires in the desert parks, see *Travel Tips* p. 132.

Innamincka Regional Reserve Speed limit on all roads in the reserve is 40 km an hour; drivers should beware of wandering stock and of approaching vehicles on dune crests. No fishing or power boating is allowed at Coongie Lakes. For details on fishing and boating in Cooper Creek see below. For more information contact the reserve visitor's centre: (08) 8675 9909.

Strzelecki Regional Reserve This reserve is a wilderness of dunes and the ephemeral Lake Blanche, which fills on average every 10–15 years. Most of the time Strzelecki Creek is dry. The only access road in the reserve is the Strzelecki Track. Although the park is covered by the Desert Parks Pass (see *Travel Tips* p. 132), if this is the only outback park you are visiting then you do not need this or any other pass. Camping at Montecollina Bore is free.

Sturt NP For general information or to book accommodation at Mount Wood Homestead or shearers' quarters contact the park visitor centre in Tibooburra: (08) 8091 3308. Wood fires are prohibited at all campsites. Campgrounds have only untreated water. A vehicle day pass and camping permit is required.

Fishing and boating

While no fishing licence is required, there are bag and size limits. Contact Primary Industries and Resources SA (Fisheries) on 1800 065 522 or visit www.pir.sa.gov.au for information. Motorised boats are allowed along Cooper Creek provided the motor is under 10 hp and speed is kept below 10 knots.

Warnings

Fuel and supplies The longest distance without fuel is 459 km (the Strzelecki Track, from Lyndhurst to Innamincka). On all roads travellers need to be adequately prepared with fuel and water.

Road access and closures When crossing dunes be wary of oncoming traffic. All roads can become impassable after rain. For NSW road reports contact the Roads and Traffic Authority: 13 2701; www.rta.nsw.gov.au For SA road reports contact Transport SA: 1300 361 033; www.transport.sa.gov.au For information on road conditions within SA parks and reserves, you can check the *Desert Parks Bulletin*: www.environment.sa.gov.au/parks/visitor/latest.html

See also *On The Road*, p. 246.

Sidney Kidman – cattle king

'Cattle king' Sidney Kidman was one of the first to realise the rich potential of the Channel Country, where cattle fatten beautifully on the grasses and clover that flush green across the flood plains. He snapped up an empire of properties on the Georgina and Diamantina rivers and Cooper Creek in a buying spree in the late 1800s and early 1900s. Because of the sheer amount of land he owned, he could ride out droughts by moving cattle to wherever the conditions were best. Today many of his stations are still owned by S Kidman and Co, including Innamincka Station, which became Innamincka Regional Reserve in 1988 but, uniquely, remains operating and is involved in the reserve's management.

Birdsville Track

The Birdsville Track, stretching 517 km from Birdsville south to Marree, is inextricably linked with Queensland's Channel Country. It began as a droving route and an answer to the problems of a region that contained some of Australia's best cattle land but also lay far, far away from any market.

The closest ports were Brisbane, 1600 km east, and Port Augusta, 900 km south. When the railway line reached Marree in SA it added extra incentive to drive cattle south, even though it involved striking out through the Sturt Stony and Tirari deserts without – until bores tapped the Great Artesian Basin – reliable sources of water. Drovers like Jack Clarke in the 1890s must have truly felt that they faced the unknown. Clarke's mob of 500 bullocks was reduced to just 72 in a fierce sandstorm as they trekked towards the railhead.

Opposite *The Strzelecki Track bumps its way between Lyndhurst and Innamincka.*

Right *The Birdsville Track stretches across some of Australia's most desolate country.*

Today, the time it takes to travel the Birdsville Track (a day, if you wish) eliminates much of the danger, but the landscape you pass through is still some of the most desolate in the country. En route to Birdsville, Mulka – south of Mungerannie Roadhouse – boasts the continent's lowest annual rainfall (around 100 mm), and apart from the clusters of sandhills that form long, wind-rippled channels, the landscape is amazingly flat.

At Mungerannie Roadhouse a bore-water pool provides an opportunity for both birdwatching and swimming, while a detour to Kalamurina Station on the Warburton River offers camping and good fishing when the river is flowing. But the real reward for travellers is Birdsville – more specifically, the Birdsville Hotel. Just north of the SA–Queensland border, Birdsville's prosperity peaked in the days before Federation, when a border tax was charged on stock and goods crossing state borders. The town once boasted, among other things, three hotels and a cordial factory.

Each September a line of people links the now solitary pub with the town's dusty racetrack – the annual Birdsville Races attract around 5000 people, and most of them are partial to a cold beer.

Strzelecki Track

Harry Redford may not have been the first man to travel down the Strzelecki Track, but he was the one who made it famous. He drove 1000 stolen cattle along this route in 1870, having realised that some Channel Country stations were so big that their owners wouldn't miss a few here and there. He and some mates began collecting stray cattle in the back blocks, slowly moving south. They followed the Strzelecki Creek from the current-day site of Innamincka and sold the cattle at Blanchewater Station, 1300 km from their starting point, for £5000.

Redford was eventually arrested and tried in Roma in Queensland, but the jury was so taken by his incredible feat across virtually uncharted land that they declared him not guilty. Redford caused public outrage and admiration in almost equal amounts, and was a source of inspiration for Rolf Boldrewood's novel *Robbery Under Arms* and the character Captain Starlight.

Today the Strzelecki is a 459 km dirt track climbing north-east in tiers from Lyndhurst to Innamincka. It roughly follows the path of usually dry Strzelecki Creek, named by Charles Sturt in 1845 after the Polish explorer Paul Strzelecki. Between Lakes Blanche and Callabonna the track bumps its way across the dunefields of the Cobbler Desert, in the middle of which is Montecollina Bore, where many travellers camp. In droving days Montecollina was the only government-sunk artesian bore along the track and the only reliable source of water.

Along the Strzelecki Track towards Innamincka is the Moomba gasfield, a desert cityscape of giant refining towers and accommodation for up to 500 staff. Moomba (closed to the public) is the headquarters of mining in the Cooper Basin, the largest onshore gas- and oilfield in Australia. Pipelines from here channel natural gas to Sydney and Adelaide.

Innamincka

Innamincka almost ceased to exist once, in 1952. Drought and erosion had rendered the Cobbler Desert virtually impassable to traffic from the south and station owners were either gaining independence with their own airstrips or shutting-up shop. After years of decline, the town gradually closed down. For 20 years Innamincka lay like a ghost town on the banks of Cooper Creek.

However, a new style of traffic – people in 4WDs, seeking out Australia's wildest places – led to Innamincka II. Today it has a population of around 15 as well as a store, the Innamincka Hotel and the restored Elizabeth Symon Nursing Home, now the Innamincka Regional Reserve Visitor Centre. This distinctive two-storey building was a branch of the Australian Inland Mission from 1929 to 1951, its nurses visiting far-flung patients on horseback until the Royal Flying Doctor Service took over.

Today Innamincka's attraction is entwined with the beauty and isolation of Cooper Creek, which meanders south and spills into the north of the 13 800 sq km Innamincka Regional Reserve.

Contacts

Visitor information

Birdsville
Wirrari Centre
(07) 4656 3300

Innamincka
Innamincka Regional Reserve Visitor Centre
(08) 8675 9909

Marree
Marree Outback Roadhouse and General Store
(08) 8675 8360

Tibooburra
National Parks and Wildlife Service
(08) 8091 3308

Parks and reserves

See *Fact File*, opposite

Hotels, roadhouses

Birdsville Hotel
(07) 4656 3244

Corner Store
Cameron Corner
(08) 8091 3872

Innamincka Hotel
(08) 8675 9901

Mungerannie Roadhouse
(08) 8675 8317

Station stays

Kalamurina Station
(08) 8675 8310

Right *Sprawling river red gums on the banks of Cooper Creek.*

Opposite top *Sturt NP's plains suit red kangaroos.*

Opposite below *Jewel in the desert – the Coongie Lakes.*

Burke and Wills – a tragic tale

The tale of Robert O'Hara Burke and William John Wills' pioneering journey across the continent from south to north has all the elements of a good drama – in fact, you might be forgiven if you thought it was fiction.

The pair set out from Melbourne in 1860 with a party of men, 21 tonnes of equipment and food, and enough animals and wagons to match. Under Burke's erratic command, the journey was a magnificent shambles. At Menindee their second-in-command left after a disagreement, and the party split in two. Burke went on to Cooper Creek, where he established a base camp. From there Burke, Wills, John King and Charles Gray pressed on for the Gulf of Carpentaria. Eventually they reached the Gulf – or as close as they could get but for a tangle of mangroves – before heading back towards the Cooper. En route, Gray died.

William Brahe, in charge of the base camp at present-day Nappa Merrie Station, waited four months, then – convinced that the leaders had perished – left just eight hours before Burke, Wills and King staggered into camp in April 1861. They dug up the supplies Brahe had buried and then set out for the nearest station, 300 km away. In their dazed state, however, they had forgotten to mark the tree. Brahe returned for one last look, but finding the site apparently just as he had left it, returned to his men.

Burke and Wills were too weak to travel far and in June died back on the banks of the Cooper. King, helped by the Yandruwandha people, was the only one to survive. The famed Dig Tree, the coolibah Brahe inscribed with 'DIG 3FT NW', can be found 85 km east of Innamincka, just across the Queensland border.

Jump-ups and gibbers

These two landforms – one of low, flat-top hills and the other of rock-strewn plains – are closely related, gibbers being eroded pieces of the hardened silcrete crusts of jump-ups. Where the rocks are large, gibber plains are formidable, something that even four-wheel drivers avoid. Your view of the rocks really depends on whether you're facing the sun or have your back to it. Facing the sun, their coating of 'desert varnish', containing black manganese and red iron bound to them by micro-organisms, brings out the black, rendering the landscape a rocky wasteland. In the other direction the sun brings out their rich ochre tones, rendering them characteristically Australian.

Innamincka Regional Reserve

Cullyamurra Waterhole lies 16 km east of Innamincka – a waterhole that, in the middle of the desert, has never been known to be dry. It is thought to be Australia's largest (8 km long and up to 100 m wide), created by the Innamincka Choke at the eastern end of the waterhole, where the rocky banks allow only a narrow passage of water. As the floodwaters of the Cooper attempt to squeeze through, pressure builds up; over time, the force of the water spilling out has gouged out a basin 28 m deep.

When the Cooper dries up Cullyamurra remains, a rippling jewel sheltered with river red gums and coolibahs, awash with brilliant colours at sunset. In its depths are fish species such as yellowbelly, catfish and grunter, making this (and al of the Cooper when flowing) a popular fishing spot You can camp at various sites along its banks. Once Aboriginal people, including the Yandruwandha, lived all along the banks of the Cooper, and at the choke Aboriginal engravings speckle the rocks.

North-west of Innamincka are the Coongie Lakes, where the Cooper overflows into a series of shallow pans that make up one of the most important and pristine wetlands in central Australia Late summer and autumn rains in Queensland arriv in the Innamincka region in winter, filling the lakes in succession, depending on the volume of water. First in the line is Coongie, which is seldom empty.

The lakes are a magnet for birdlife, luring many species into an area that could otherwise never sustain them. Coongie Lakes can support over 20 000 birds – teams of fish-hungry pelicans patrol the depths, long-beaked waders poke around in the shallows, and ducks weave in and out of the lignum bushes. Some species, like the whimbrel, hail all the way from the Arctic.

The Innamincka Hotel (see *Contacts*, p. 137) hires canoes for paddling on the Cooper or taking out to Coongie Lakes (no fishing or motorboats are permitted on the lakes); there are also unmarked walking trails and a campsite at the lakes. At the time of publication the lakes region was in the process of being made a national park; contact the reserve visitor centre (see *Fact File*, p. 136) for an update on facilities.

Tibooburra and Sturt National Park

High up on stilts in a park in dusty Tibooburra lies an upturned whaleboat, a 9 m replica of the one explorer Charles Sturt carried on his 1844–46 journey into the outback. He had hoped to find an inland sea and, to go with it, perhaps a swath of fertile farming land. But from nearby Depot Glen, a waterhole where Sturt's party remained for six months during a drought and where the boat was finally abandoned, it must have seemed an unlikely prospect.

Tibooburra sprang to life with the discovery of gold, almost 40 years after Sturt passed through, and its survival today is thanks to outlying properties and tourists. It is the gateway to the 3250 sq km

Sturt NP, a land of jump-ups, gibbers, grassy plains and red kangaroos.

In the park's east is the old Mount Wood Station, with shearers' quarters and homestead accommodation (see *Fact File,* p. 137), while in the west is Fort Grey where Sturt, after leaving Depot Glen, built a stockade to protect his party's supplies and secure their sheep. When he arrived the land was alive and green and Sturt made the comment, perhaps only slightly desert-crazed, that he 'never saw a more beautiful spot'.

There are four campsites in the park, each with short walking trails, and loop drives that take in rolling downs, creek beds and jump-ups. From Fort Grey it is just a short drive to Cameron Corner, where NSW and Queensland meet SA. The aptly named Corner Store is the only fuel stop between Tibooburra and Innamincka, a drive of 410 km.

The Dog Fence

In normal circumstances, Queensland's fertile Darling Downs and SA's rugged Nullarbor coast have little in common, but since 1946 they have been linked by one of the longest man-made structures on earth – the 5400 km Dog (or Dingo) Fence. The fence divides the land into two giant paddocks – one for cattle in the north and the other for sheep in the south. Dingoes prey on sheep, and until they could be contained they thwarted the progress of the wool industry. A team of maintenance workers patrols the fence, which can be seen at Cameron Corner or along the Birdsville, Strzelecki and Oodnadatta tracks. Always remember to shut the gate.

Following page *Australia's largest lake, the salty Lake Eyre, appears mirage-like in the desert.*

Desert Tracks

In this rugged region the white, crackled expanse of Lake Eyre abuts the swelling red-ochre sands of the Simpson Desert. In the west, the Oodnadatta Track follows a fascinating line of natural springs and historic sites.

Boom or bust is a catchcry of the Australian outback, a way of describing the fickle pattern of life. It has particular resonance in this region that centres on Lake Eyre, which is Australia's largest lake, but is often just a sea of salt. Even history here has an all-or-nothing style – along the Oodnadatta Track a tangle of events converge, while elsewhere it's hard to pick up a single thread of the past.

Spanning three state borders is the Simpson Desert, a giant canvas of fiery-red dunes, some up to 500 km long. For explorers this was one of Australia's final frontiers. Today it is a challenging 4WD route for the adventurous.

The ultimate contrast lies in Witjira NP, with the small window of blue and green that is Dalhousie Springs. Dalhousie lies at the head of a trail of artesian springs that arcs around the south-west of Lake Eyre. The Oodnadatta Track, as it is known today, began as an Aboriginal trail following this chain of springs. For thousands of years it provided tribes with a safe passage between the Flinders Ranges and the Simpson Desert. Explorer John McDouall Stuart followed the trail when he crossed Australia; the Overland Telegraph Line and the *Ghan* followed, making the track today one of Australia's most interesting historical journeys.

Lake Eyre is the region's focal point, the place where all the rivers and creeks across an area of 1.2 million sq km drain in times of flood. Around once every eight years water fans out across the lake's salty crust; dormant shrimp eggs hatch, the sky blurs with birdlife, and Lake Eyre is catapulted into a time of growth and activity. But this region's vast landscapes and desert-adapted creatures hold just as much intrigue in the quiet times.

Dalhousie Springs
Forty percent of all natural water flow from the Grea Basin comes to the surface in Witjira NP. The largest refreshed with 150 litres of water per second, and its temperature makes it a superb setting for a swim.

On the Oodnadatta Track
The 617 km Oodnadatta Track takes in a panorama of historic and natural sights – old railway sidings, crumbling telegraph stations and a series of artesian springs. Stretch the journey across a week with an interlude at Lake Eyre or a camel trek.

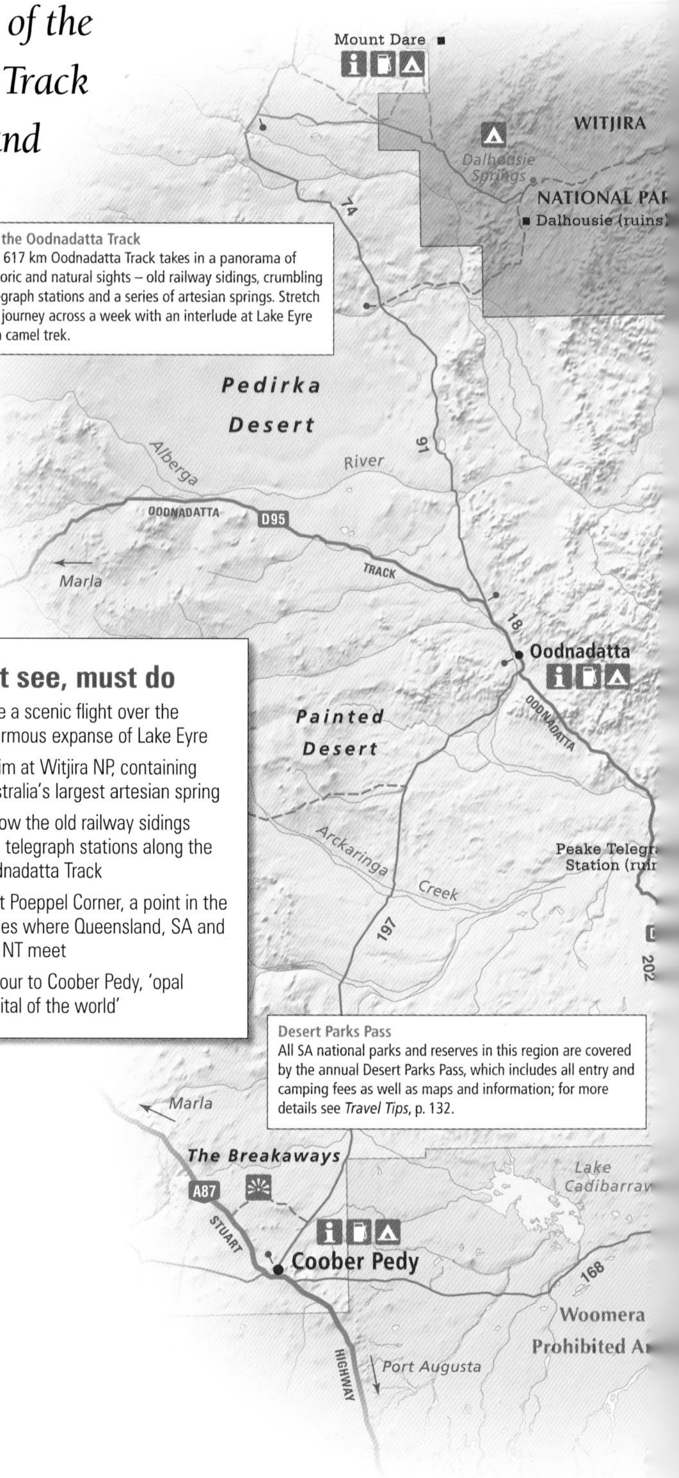

Must see, must do

- Take a scenic flight over the enormous expanse of Lake Eyre
- Swim at Witjira NP, containing Australia's largest artesian spring
- Follow the old railway sidings and telegraph stations along the Oodnadatta Track
- Visit Poeppel Corner, a point in the dunes where Queensland, SA and the NT meet
- Detour to Coober Pedy, 'opal capital of the world'

Desert Parks Pass
All SA national parks and reserves in this region are covered by the annual Desert Parks Pass, which includes all entry and camping fees as well as maps and information; for more details see *Travel Tips*, p. 132.

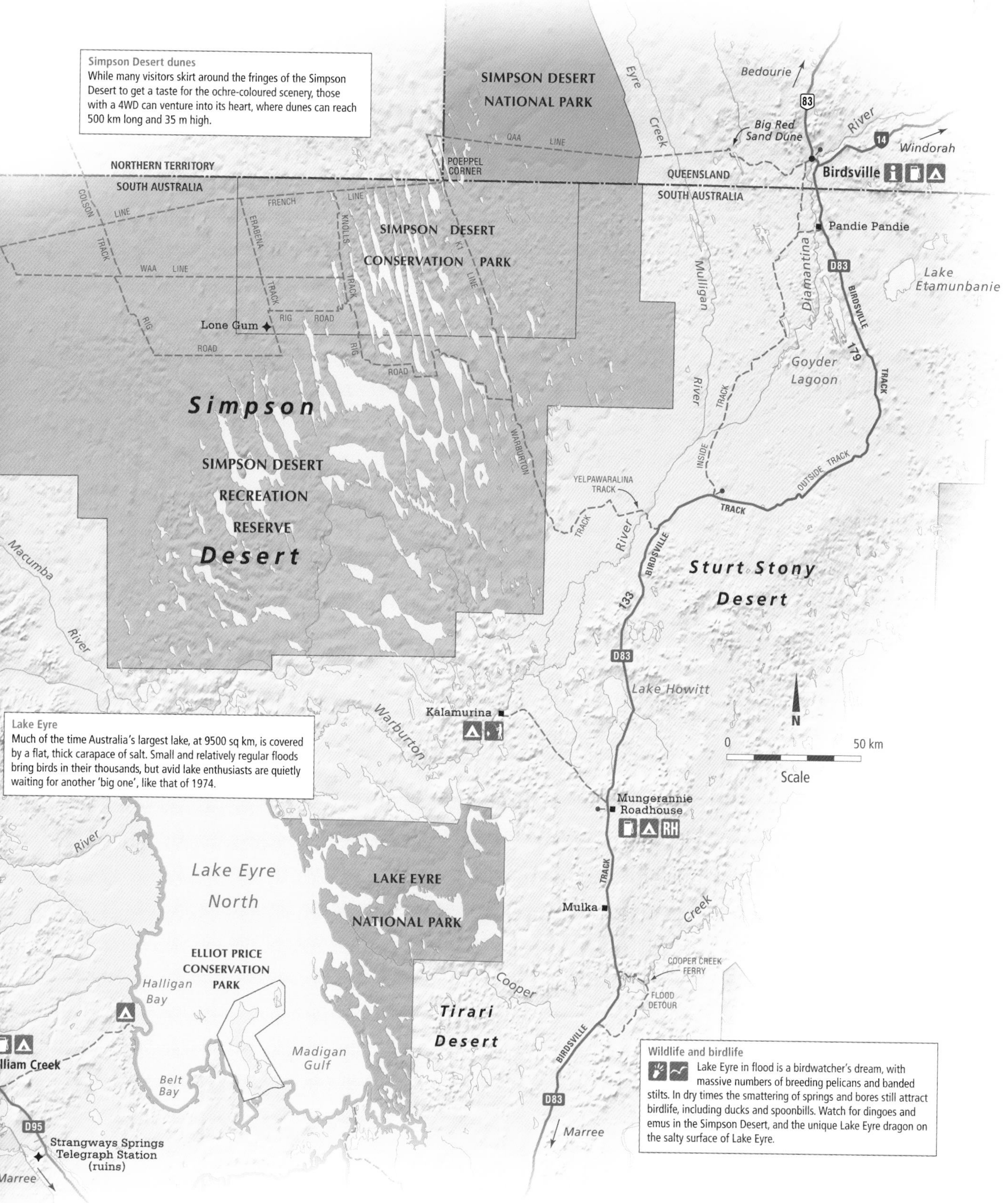

Simpson Desert dunes

While many visitors skirt around the fringes of the Simpson Desert to get a taste for the ochre-coloured scenery, those with a 4WD can venture into its heart, where dunes can reach 500 km long and 35 m high.

Lake Eyre

Much of the time Australia's largest lake, at 9500 sq km, is covered by a flat, thick carapace of salt. Small and relatively regular floods bring birds in their thousands, but avid lake enthusiasts are quietly waiting for another 'big one', like that of 1974.

Wildlife and birdlife

Lake Eyre in flood is a birdwatcher's dream, with massive numbers of breeding pelicans and banded stilts. In dry times the smattering of springs and bores still attract birdlife, including ducks and spoonbills. Watch for dingoes and emus in the Simpson Desert, and the unique Lake Eyre dragon on the salty surface of Lake Eyre.

SA Outback ☎ (08) 8641 9193; www.flindersranges.com.au
Oodnadatta, Pink Roadhouse ☎ (08) 8670 7822

Fact File

Top events

Mar *William Creek Gymkhana*
Easter *Coober Pedy Opal Festival*
May *Oodnadatta Races and Gymkhana*
June *Marree Picnic Races and Gymkhana*
July *Marree Camel Cup*
Oodnadatta Bronco Branding
Coober Pedy Greek Glendi (Greek celebration)
Sept *National Bronco Branding Championships (William Creek)*
Birdsville Races
Oct *Gymkhana (Marree)*

Parks and reserves

For information on access, camping and campfires in SA's desert parks, see *Travel Tips*, p. 132.

Lake Eyre NP The access tracks from William Creek and Muloorina are 4WD only. Bush camping only; there are no facilities; wood fires are not permitted; take water. Camping at Muloorina Station is via a donation to the Royal Flying Doctor Service; no bookings required.

Witjira NP Camping is available at Dalhousie Springs, 3 O'clock Creek (no facilities), Purnie Bore and Mount Dare Homestead. A 4WD is necessary if heading out to Purnie Bore and the Simpson Desert.

Simpson Desert Conservation Park and Regional Reserve
A 4WD is essential throughout. Crossing the desert from west to east is recommended as the dunes have a more gentle upsweep. Beware of oncoming vehicles on dune crests (see also *On the Road*, p. 246). Towing trailers is not recommended.

Simpson Desert NP A 4WD is essential; beware of oncoming vehicles on dune crests. Camping is possible anywhere along the access road (called the QAA line), but not more than 500 m from the track. A permit is required in advance from the QPWS office in Birdsville: (07) 4656 3249.

Warnings

Fuel and supplies Fuel is available at Marree, William Creek, Oodnadatta, Mount Dare Homestead (Witjira NP), Birdsville, Coober Pedy and Marla. The longest distance without fuel is Birdsville to Mount Dare Homestead (507 km). Carry reserves of fuel if planning extended travel, especially across the Simpson Desert. Always carry plenty of water.

Road access and closures All roads can become impassable after rain. For SA road reports contact Transport SA: 1300 361 033; www.transport.sa.gov.au The Pink Roadhouse, Oodnadatta, offers information on regional road conditions and outback travel advice: 1800 802 074. See also *Desert Parks Bulletin*: www.environment.sa.gov.au/parks/visitor/latest.html

See also *On the Road*, p. 246.

Overland Telegraph Line

The construction workers of the Overland Telegraph Line followed quickly on the heels of explorer John McDouall Stuart, using his 1861–62 diary of his trek across the continent as a map. They even made a few discoveries of their own, like Dalhousie Springs, first sighted by a survey party in 1870. The ambitious project, a telegraph line linking Adelaide to Darwin, then via submarine cable to Asia, Europe and England, was completed in 1872. It reduced the time it took to communicate with Britain from months to just hours. The crumbling Peake and Strangways Springs repeater stations can be visited along the Oodnadatta Track.

Simpson Desert

In the Simpson Desert you get a true sense of Australia's red centre – the vast scale, the unchanging scenery, the heat, the sand, the lack of water. Here lies a sea of parallel dunes 170 000 sq km in area and a part of Australia so singular in character that even a tree becomes a feature – like the Lone Gum on the Rig Road.

The Simpson Desert extends north from Lake Eyre into the NT and Queensland. Large swaths of it are protected within Queensland's Simpson Desert NP and SA's Simpson Desert Regional Reserve and Simpson Desert Conservation Park. Right across the desert temperatures can exceed 50°C in summer, making it the domain of creatures specially adapted to this harsh environment – nocturnal marsupials, reptiles, raptors and dingoes.

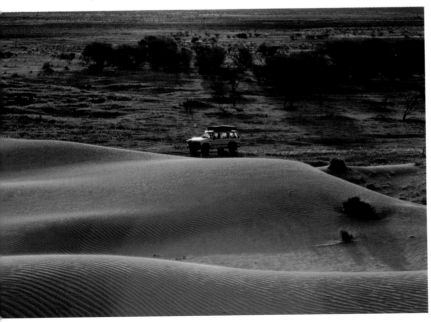

Evening light in the Simpson Desert.

A chain of salt lakes unfolds from the NT border like a concertina, and the chequerboard of 4WD tracks that run through the Simpson today – mostly south of the NT border – are virtually all owing to oil exploration in the 1960s. There are two main routes to choose from – the French Line and the Rig Road. Each runs roughly east–west between Birdsville and Dalhousie Springs.

The French Line, at 438 km, is the most direct route across the desert, but is also the most difficult owing to its constant dune crossings, beginning (or ending) just outside Birdsville with the formidable Big Red, around 90 m high. The 703 km Rig Road is a little easier, built to accommodate large oil-drilling rigs. It diverges from the Birdsville Track, although you can also reach it via the K1 Line from Poeppel Corner.

Poeppel Corner, the junction of Queensland, NT and SA, is proof that government surveyors were a unique brand of explorers. Augustus Poeppel was the first European to penetrate the Simpson Desert when he reached the corner with his surveyor's chain in 1880 and marked it with a coolibah post dragged in from Eyre Creek (now replaced by a concrete one). Around 2000 travellers add their names to the visitors' book here each year. For Simpson Desert travel advice see *Fact File*, above.

Contacts

Visitor information

Birdsville
Wirrari Centre
(07) 4656 3300

Coober Pedy
Hutchison St
1800 637 076 or (08) 8672 5298
www.opalcapitaloftheworld.com.au

Marree
Marree Outback Roadhouse
and General Store
(08) 8675 8360

Mount Dare Homestead
(08) 8670 7835
www.mtdare.com.au

Oodnadatta
Pink Roadhouse
(08) 8670 7822
Road conditions and travel advice
1800 802 074
www.pinkroadhouse.com.au

Parks and reserves

See *Fact File*, opposite

Activities

Explore the Outback Camel Safaris
Near William Creek
(08) 8634 7079
www.austcamel.com.au

Mail Run Tour
Coober Pedy
1800 069 911 or (08) 8672 5226
www.desertdiversity.com

Scenic flights

Marree
C/O Marree Hotel
(08) 8675 8344

William Creek
Wrightsair
(08) 8670 7962
www.wrightsair.com.au

Other

Coward Springs campground
(08) 8675 8336 (April–Oct)
www.cowardsprings.com.au

Lake Eyre Yacht Club
www.lakeeyreyc.com

Great Artesian Basin

The Great Artesian Basin underlies 1.7 million sq km of outback Queensland, SA and NSW. This bed of porous sedimentary rock has most of its catchment in Queensland, where the aquifers (water-bearing layers) tilt skywards and catch rain falling on the Great Dividing Range.

The natural springs are known as 'mound springs'. Many sit atop stumpy grey–white hillocks, created by minerals in the water building up around the edges.

Around 3000 bores tap the basin – they plunge to varying depths of up to 2000 m and see the water emerge at different temperatures, sometimes close to boiling. For many years, the volume being drained from the basin was slowly reducing the pressure that pushed the waters to the surface. The water, mainly used by pastoralists grazing cattle was often wasted, so the flow from most bores is now regulated. See also *Witjira National Park*, below.

Witjira National Park

Witjira NP, a tract of 7700 sq km abutting the NT border and the Simpson Desert 120 km north of Oodnadatta, is one of the outback's many pleasant surprises. Here, the shimmering arid plains give way to a cluster of 70 natural springs, bubbling with water from the Great Artesian Basin. An estimated 500 litres of water per second – potentially up to million years old – flows into the basin's natural springs, with 40 percent of the flow accounted for in Witjira NP alone.

Dalhousie Springs is the park's focal point, with its main kidney-shaped pool measuring 150 m long, fringed with a scruffy rim of melaleucas. There are good camping facilities here, and visitors are free to swim – the constant water temperature of around 8°C means you can float around all night if you wish, soaking up the starry desert sky.

Just south of the main spring lie the ruins of old Dalhousie Homestead, once the headquarters of the region's first station. In the north of the park are the coolibah-dotted flood plains of the Finke River. Mount Dare Homestead, near the NT border, sells fuel and supplies and offers camping (see *Contacts*, opposite).

Oodnadatta Track

The 617 km Oodnadatta Track, from Marree to Marla, is one of Australia's best known outback treks. The remains of the old *Ghan* railway (see p. 146) appear at intervals along the roadside, along with an occasional splintered stump from the Overland Telegraph Line (see opposite page). But strip away these layers and you'll see that the road follows a simple chain of springs.

Like Dalhousie Springs in Witjira NP, these small blue pools with fuzzy green edges have their source in the Great Artesian Basin. Two typical springs are found in Wabma Kadarbu Conservation Park, 127 km west of Marree. These are for viewing only, but the prospect of swimming lies just 6 km north-west at Coward Springs, where there is

Above Water gushes from Purnie Bore in the Simpson Desert.

Above Oodnadatta Station now houses a museum.

Below right Spoonbills are just one of the species that take advantage of inland waterways.

a campground and a permanent pool created by a bore.

William Creek is roughly halfway along the track and gives access to Lake Eyre. From the air this town of around 15 people looks little different from nearby Anna Creek Homestead – the headquarters of the world's largest cattle station, covering 26 000 sq km. At ground level, however, it presents itself as a worldly metropolis – a street sign in the 'town square' points you in the direction of Paris and Los Angeles, and there is a parking meter outside the pub (collecting funds for the Royal Flying Doctor Service). The town offers scenic flights over Lake Eyre and multi-day camel treks into the desert (see *Contacts*, p. 145).

At Oodnadatta the road now curves west to Marla and the Stuart Hwy (historically it continued north, with the Overland Telegraph Line and the *Ghan*). A former railhead, Oodnadatta is now a strong Aboriginal community and the home of the Pink Roadhouse, run by two local identities also responsible for the smattering of hand-painted road signs and mud maps in the area. Stop in at the roadhouse for information on track conditions or call their toll-free number before you leave (see *Contacts*, p. 145). At the roadhouse you can also get the keys to the adjacent Railway Station Museum.

The *Ghan*

The Oodnadatta Track follows the original *Ghan* line almost to the curve, passing a series of sidings, bridges and old railway bores. First known as the Great Northern Railway, it reached Marree in 1883, Oodnadatta in 1891 and Alice Springs in 1929, and closed for business in 1980. A new line was built via Tarcoola, and now continues through to Darwin.

Coober Pedy

Coober Pedy, 166 km west of William Creek, is the self-proclaimed opal capital of the world. It is a title that no one is contesting – an estimated 80 percent of the world's precious opal is mined in SA, with most of it happening here.

Australia's opal fields are found around the fringes of the Great Artesian Basin, an area that once was also covered by an inland sea. The sediment deposited on the seabed and around the shores was rich in silica, and when a change in climate caused the sea to dry up, the silica dissolved and seeped into cracks in the earth. It became opal, whose small, silica spheres reflect a rainbow of colours.

Many of Coober Pedy's 2500 residents live in dugouts to escape the intense desert heat. Visitors can wander through the underground museums and galleries, 'noodle' for opal in the surrounding mullock heaps (for advice contact the visitor centre, see *Contacts*, p. 145), or take in some of the spectacular scenery nearby, including the ancient, sun-hardened mesas called the Breakaways, and the Painted Desert. If the idea of covering 600 km on dirt roads in one day is appealing, then there is also the Mail Run Tour every Monday and Thursday (see *Contacts*, p. 145).

Lake Eyre

For most of the time Lake Eyre lies dormant, a 9500 sq km expanse of luminous salt. The sight of it is almost repellently plain – or at least it was for Edward John Eyre, who in 1840 became the first white man to happen upon its banks, describing the area as 'one vast, low, and dreary waste'.

But obviously Eyre didn't see Australia's largest lake in flood, for when its tributaries simultaneously spill into it the event holds all the wonder and awe of a solar eclipse. Hundreds of thousands of birds rush in to feed and some, like pelicans and banded stilts, to breed. The lake last filled to capacity in 1974, but it is partially filled on average once every eight years, generally thanks to heavy rain in Queensland funnelled south through the Channel Country.

Lake Eyre in flood seems to attract more than its fair share of eccentrics, and high on the scale are the founders of the Lake Eyre Yacht Club. Members of this exclusive club sail on the lake whenever they get the chance; they also monitor the area's fragile environment and aim to dispel myths surrounding the lake, such as its often wrongly reported water levels. Their website is a wealth of information, including the lake's current status (see *Contacts*, p. 145).

Lake Eyre actually consists of two lakes – Lake Eyre South dips right down to the Oodnadatta Track, while the much larger Lake Eyre North is accessed from either Marree in the south or William Creek in the west. Both lakes are protected within the 13 492 sq km Lake Eyre NP, which includes Elliot Price Conservation Park. On the west side of the upper lake there is a campsite at Halligan Point and in the south, camping at Muloorina Station along Frome Creek (see *Fact File*, p. 144). While the Frome is naturally dry for most of the time, a station bore fills a small section of it here, creating a permanent coolibah-fringed oasis. There are no facilities in the park and the access tracks from William Creek and Muloorina are 4WD only.

Scenic flights give visitors the opportunity to appreciate the lake's immense scale, whether it is holding water or resigned to its usual salty crust. The flights operate from William Creek and Marree (see *Contacts*, p. 145).

Lake Eyre dragon

When Lake Eyre is dry, the solitary Lake Eyre dragon (*Ctenophorus maculosus*) makes its home in the cracks in the crust. This tiny reptile, found only on Lake Eyre and a few surrounding salt lakes, has adapted to the severe heat by walking on its heels, and manages to cut out some of the glare of its bright-white environment with eyelash-like scales around its eyes. When the lake fills, it joins other reptiles around the shoreline.

Following page *Golden grass and palm trees against an evening sky at Witjira NP, on the edge of the Simpson Desert.*

Below *Banded stilts and silver gulls on Lake Eyre when it is holding water.*

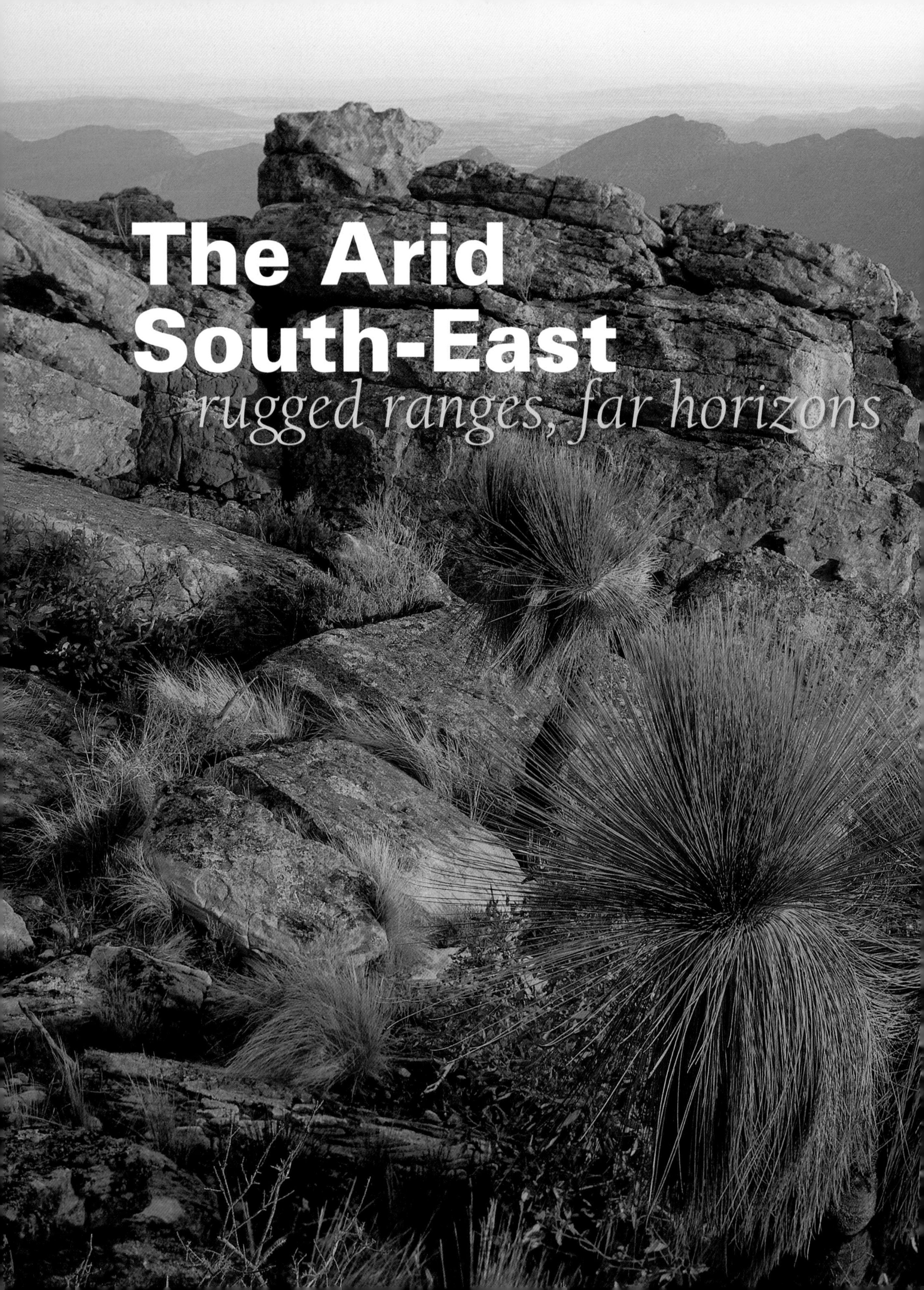

The Arid South-East

rugged ranges, far horizons

The Arid South-East

The gently undulating rangelands that stretch west of Bourke and Cobar are a prelude to South Australia's lofty Flinders Ranges. Linking both is a canvas of rich, earthy hues and rugged, rock-strewn surfaces.

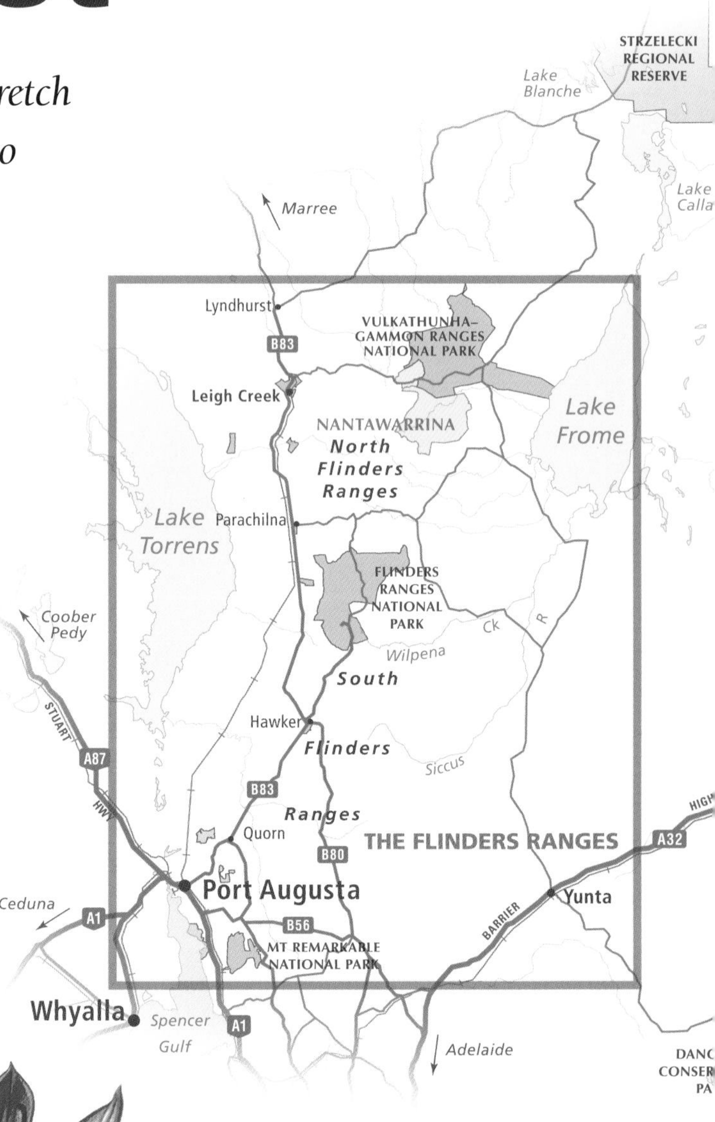

The Arid South-East Regions

Broken Hill and Beyond

This region was founded on sheep stations, and later on came the mining industry in Broken Hill, but it also takes in some prominent national landscapes. Slicing through is the Darling River – once a route for the river trade and a muse for writers and poets, and today a crucial artery for Australian agriculture. Ancient bones, burials and artefacts found within the lunettes of Mungo NP have helped piece together Australia's evolutionary and human history, while Mutawintji NP has a prolific gallery of Aboriginal rock art – engravings, paintings and stencils. *See p. 156*

The Flinders Ranges

Three national parks protect the Flinders Ranges, each just a little more rugged and remote as the mountains push further north. Mount Remarkable NP is close enough to Adelaide to be an easy camping retreat. Flinders Ranges NP takes in awe-inspiring Wilpena Pound, its ridges crisscrossed with walking trails. Vulkathunha–Gammon Ranges NP is a swath of rock-encrusted hills favoured by hikers and 4WD enthusiasts. In between you'll find evocative pastoral ruins, hotels that serve up bush tucker-inspired meals, and an Indigenous centre that invites you into an age-old culture. *See p. 166*

Sturt's desert pea

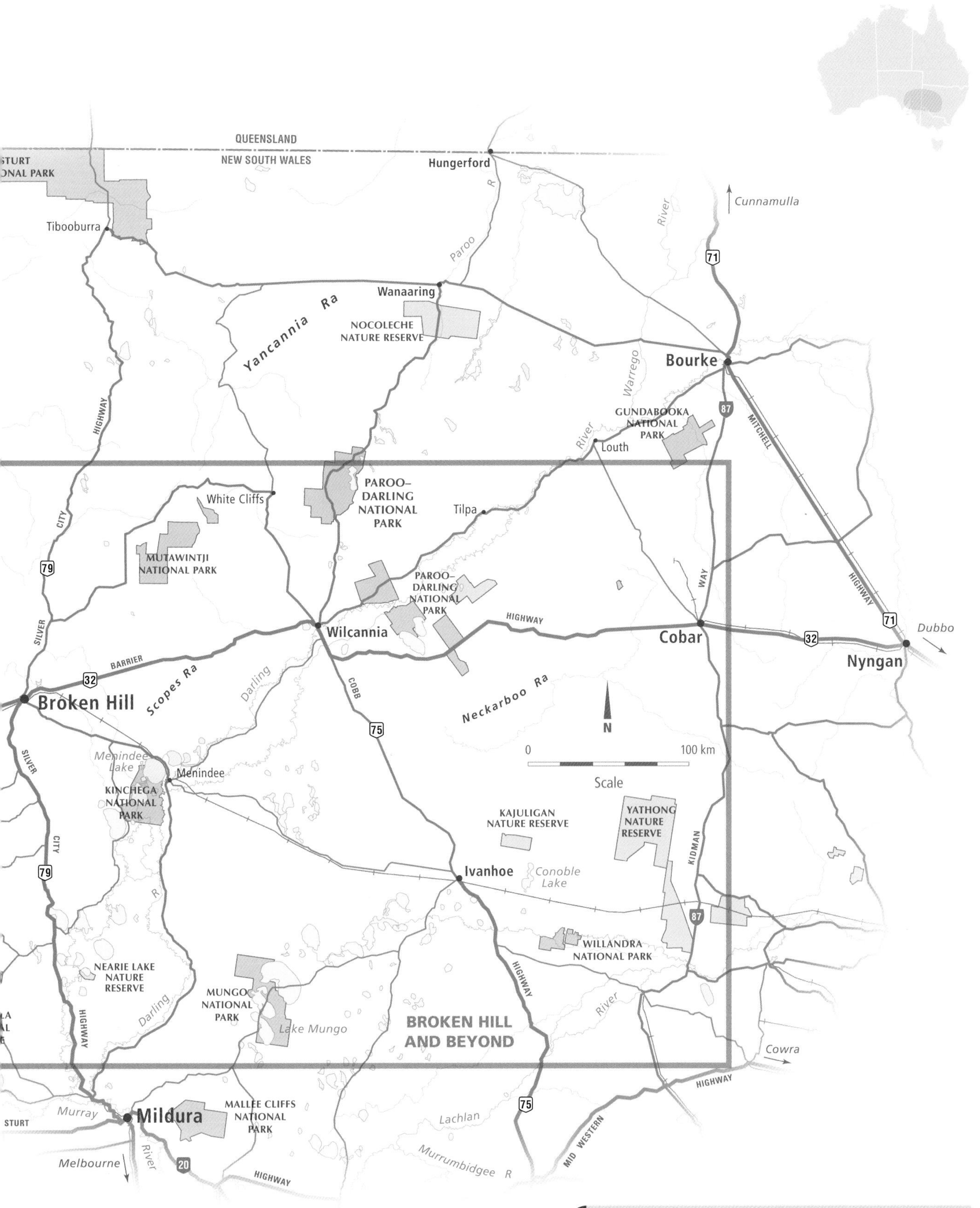

Port Augusta ☎ (08) 8641 9193; www.flindersranges.com.au
Broken Hill ☎ (08) 8088 3560; www.visitoutbacknsw.com.au

Travel Tips

When to go

Temperatures soar in this region in summer, making the cooler months of April–Oct the most popular time to travel, when daytime temperatures usually hover between 15°C–25°C. This is also when most events, festivals and tours are scheduled. This region has typically chilly desert nights. For further information, contact the Bureau of Meteorology (BOM): 1900 926 113; www.bom.gov.au

Aboriginal land

There are two areas of Aboriginal-owned land in this region – the Nantawarrina Indigenous Protected Area in the northern Flinders Ranges (permit required for access, see *Fact File* p. 168), and Mutawintji Historic Site within Mutawintji NP (access by tour only, see *Fact File* p. 158).

Parks and reserves

NSW and SA parks have similar systems – visitors travelling by vehicle are charged entry fees in the parks with the highest visitations, to go towards the upkeep of roads and other facilities. These parks include Mungo NP, Kinchega NP, Willandra NP and all three Flinders Ranges national parks. Payment is generally via a self-registration system; in SA if you are also camping in the park the entry fee is waived; in NSW the camping fee is additional. You can purchase annual passes in both states – in SA the Flinders Parks Pass is well suited to travellers who intend to visit several parks in the ranges. For NSW information contact: 1300 361 967; www.environment.nsw.gov.au/nationalparks; for SA information contact: (08) 8648 5300; www.environment.sa.gov.au/parks

Warnings

Fuel and supplies Some parts of this region are remote and drivers should be well equipped and self-sufficient. In some areas long distances separate fuel stops. Travellers should always carry plenty of water.

CLIMATE — BROKEN HILL

	J	F	M	A	M	J	J	A	S	O	N	D
Max °C	33	32	29	24	19	16	15	17	21	25	29	31
Min°C	18	18	16	12	9	6	5	6	9	12	15	17
Rain mm	23	25	20	18	23	21	19	19	21	25	20	22
Raindays	3	3	3	3	5	5	6	5	4	5	4	3

CLIMATE — HAWKER

	J	F	M	A	M	J	J	A	S	O	N	D
Max °C	34	33	30	25	20	16	16	18	22	26	29	32
Min °C	18	18	15	11	7	5	4	4	7	10	13	16
Rain mm	19	21	17	20	31	39	35	33	28	25	22	21
Raindays	3	3	2	3	5	7	7	7	6	5	4	3

Road access and closures Avoid driving at dawn, dusk and at night, when wildlife and stock can wander onto roads. Some outback routes are 4WD only, including in some of the national parks. Roads through the region are subject to closure during the winter months, owing to flooding. For NSW road reports contact the Roads and Traffic Authority: 13 2701; www.rta.nsw.gov.au For SA road reports contact Transport SA: 1300 361 033; www.transport.sa.gov.au

Remote travel Those venturing off major tourist routes should consider carrying an emergency communications device (see *On the Road*, p. 246).

Maps Maps in this book are guidelines only – carry detailed maps.

See also *On the Road*, p. 246.

White cypress trees near Moralana Road, South Wilpena Pound.

Left *The old Mungo Woolshed, once the centre of an enormous station.*

Below *A sleepy lizard, also known as a shingleback lizard, puts on a fierce display.*

Beyond Bourke, the old port town at the head of the Darling River, the 'outback' historically begins. Over 150 years ago explorer Charles turt passed through, filled with the hope of finding n inland sea, but in reality he was standing on the dge of Australia's vast arid south – the next real reening lay thousands of kilometres west on the dge of the Indian Ocean.

Australia's arid south-east is the immediate ɔack o' Bourke': in the Australian vernacular the nknown, the formidable, the dry and desolate. ut it is everything besides.

On the western edge of the region, the linders Ranges are one of the continent's most nesmerising mountain landscapes. Tucked away n the folds are steep gorges and silent chasms; rom the peaks, views extend to shimmering alt lakes in the distance. The area draws ushwalkers of all abilities, 4WD enthusiasts, nd history buffs seeking out the tragic ruins of nce-promising stations.

Broken Hill appears like a mirage in the desert, city clinging to a body of ore that has proved the vorld's richest concentration of silver, lead and zinc. Iere the rough-and-ready meets the genteel, and plethora of pubs sit comfortably with a growing umber of art galleries.

South-east of Broken Hill lies Mungo NP, with its surreal natural sculptures on the surface and its treasure trove of bones and artefacts within – miraculous both for their age and preservation against the odds for thousands of years.

Away from 'the Hill' and the handful of national parks, the NSW landscape is flatter and, perhaps, lonelier, but the simple colour and simplicity of it heartens you. In both regions – the Flinders Ranges and Broken Hill – you can almost always count on a long, arcing line up ahead on the horizon, of shaggy river red gums edging a brilliant red creek bed, quietly waiting for water.

Broken Hill and Beyond

Outback New South Wales is an area of startling colour – vibrant orange earth and soft purple dusk skies. Recent history has seen sheep stations and mines, but the ancient burial sites that have emerged from the drifting sands are the region's true wealth.

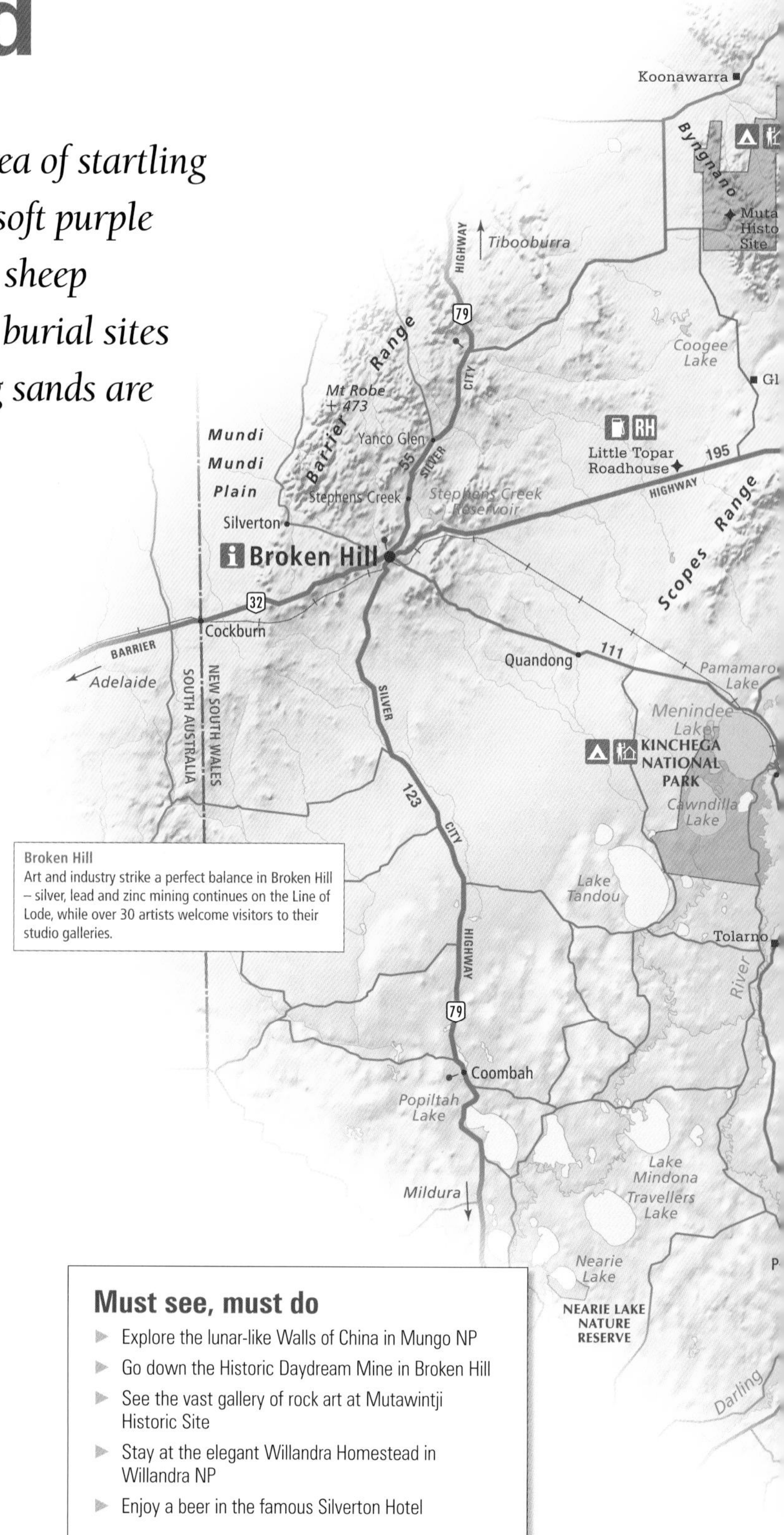

Broken Hill
Art and industry strike a perfect balance in Broken Hill – silver, lead and zinc mining continues on the Line of Lode, while over 30 artists welcome visitors to their studio galleries.

Here, in far west NSW, 'the outback' has many different guises. To a Broken Hill artist it may be in the rugged red Barrier Ranges, which stretch north of this city of over 20 000 people. To station owners on the eastern banks of the Darling it begins just over the river, across the threshold of the Murray–Darling Basin. But to visitors it is everywhere you look – in the sparse Mundi Mundi Plain beyond Silverton or the red, sandy soils and open woodlands of Mungo NP.

This area wasn't always so dry. Mungo NP records astounding evidence of climate change, species extinction and Aboriginal occupation stretching back 50 000 years. Burial sites have been found in the eroding dunes, preserved in the alkaline sands.

More recent history can be found in the remnants of 'Big Willandra', once one of the region's largest sheep stations. Stations are still a huge part of the economy, but the backbone for over a century has been mining in Broken Hill, where the lode of silver, lead and zinc is still going strong.

One of the country's richest rock-art galleries is found in the north at Mutawintji NP, and an equally precious site lies east of the ramshackle opal-mining town of White Cliffs, in Paroo–Darling NP. Here, in the vistas of vast, rippling lakes and hidden, rich-brown billabongs, is proof that the outback is not always monotone and sometimes not even dry.

Must see, must do

- Explore the lunar-like Walls of China in Mungo NP
- Go down the Historic Daydream Mine in Broken Hill
- See the vast gallery of rock art at Mutawintji Historic Site
- Stay at the elegant Willandra Homestead in Willandra NP
- Enjoy a beer in the famous Silverton Hotel

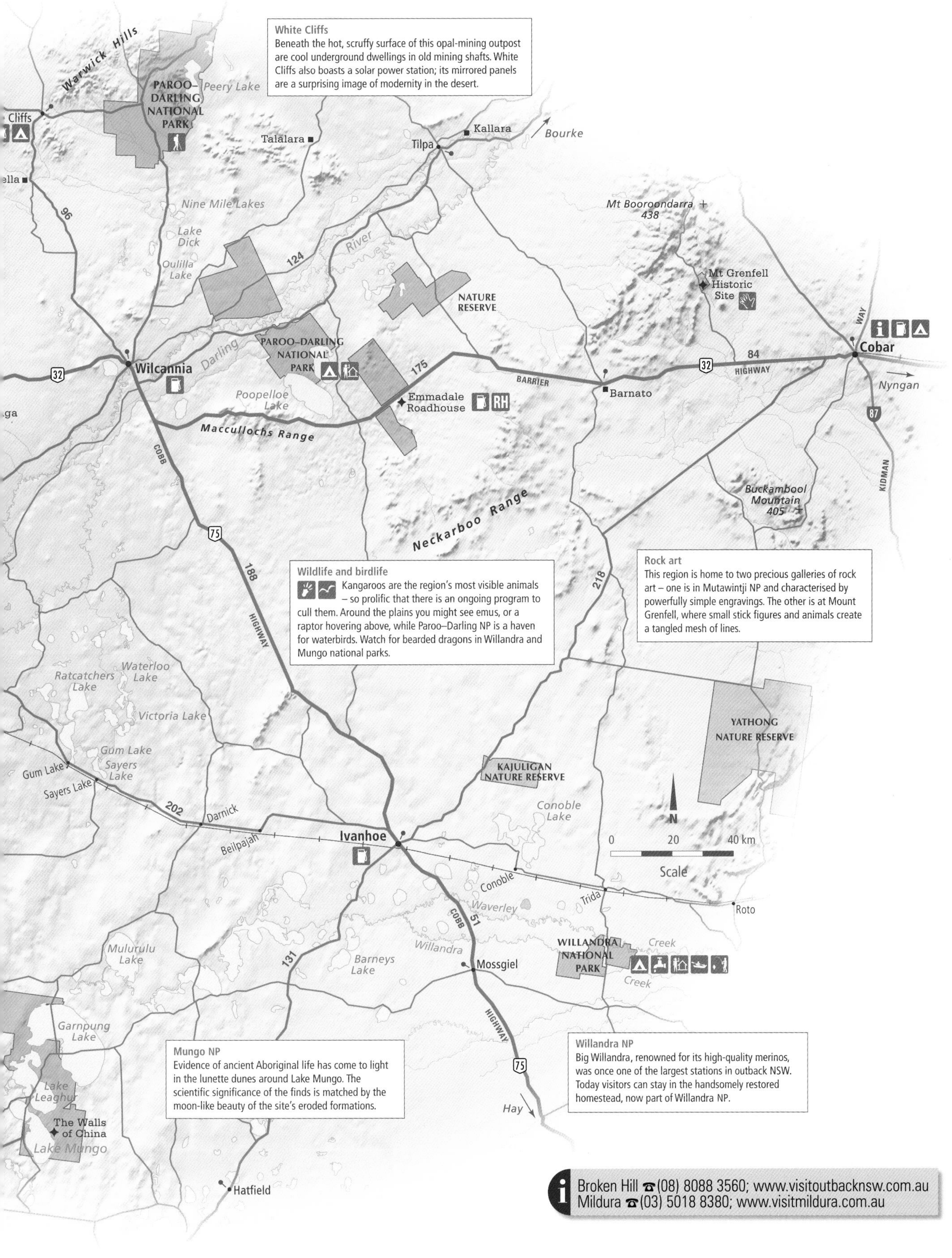

White Cliffs

Beneath the hot, scruffy surface of this opal-mining outpost are cool underground dwellings in old mining shafts. White Cliffs also boasts a solar power station; its mirrored panels are a surprising image of modernity in the desert.

Wildlife and birdlife

Kangaroos are the region's most visible animals – so prolific that there is an ongoing program to cull them. Around the plains you might see emus, or a raptor hovering above, while Paroo–Darling NP is a haven for waterbirds. Watch for bearded dragons in Willandra and Mungo national parks.

Rock art

This region is home to two precious galleries of rock art – one is in Mutawintji NP and characterised by powerfully simple engravings. The other is at Mount Grenfell, where small stick figures and animals create a tangled mesh of lines.

Mungo NP

Evidence of ancient Aboriginal life has come to light in the lunette dunes around Lake Mungo. The scientific significance of the finds is matched by the moon-like beauty of the site's eroded formations.

Willandra NP

Big Willandra, renowned for its high-quality merinos, was once one of the largest stations in outback NSW. Today visitors can stay in the handsomely restored homestead, now part of Willandra NP.

Broken Hill ☎(08) 8088 3560; www.visitoutbacknsw.com.au
Mildura ☎(03) 5018 8380; www.visitmildura.com.au

Fact File

Top events

Mar *St Patrick's Race Meeting (Broken Hill)*
Outback and all that Jazz (Broken Hill)

May *4x4 Outback Challenge (Broken Hill)*
Inland Speedboat Championships (depending on water levels, Menindee)
White Cliffs Gymkhana and Rodeo

Permits and regulations

Aboriginal land Mutawintji Historic Site, within Mutawintji NP, is owned by Mutawintji Aboriginal Land Council. The area protects significant rock art, and through Mutawintji Heritage Tours the owners offer tours at 11 am Wed and Sat, April–Oct, departing Homestead Creek campground (no bookings required). For further information contact Broken Hill NPWS Office: (08) 8080 3200.

Parks and reserves

For general information on parks in this region see *Travel Tips*, p. 154. Carry drinking water; a fuel stove is recommended for parks in this region.

Kinchega NP Vehicle entry fees apply. Bring firewood. Bookings required for shearers' quarters accommodation. Contact Broken Hill NPWS Office: (08) 8080 3200.

Mungo NP Vehicle entry fees apply. Firewood can be purchased at park visitor centre. Bookings required for shearers' quarters accommodation. Contact Buronga NPWS Office: (03) 5021 8900.

Mutawintji NP Bring firewood. For information contact Broken Hill NPWS Office: (08) 8080 3200. For information on Mutawintji Historic Site see *Aboriginal land*, left.

Paroo–Darling NP Bring firewood. Contact the park's visitor centre in White Cliffs: (08) 8083 7900.

Willandra NP Vehicle entry fees apply. Firewood supplied. Bookings recommended for accommodation. Contact Griffith NPWS Office: (02) 6966 8100.

Warnings

Road access and closures Unsealed roads, including those to national parks, may become impassable after rain; phone ahead to check conditions or get a road report from the NSW Roads and Traffic Authority: 13 2701; www.rta.nsw.gov.au Major roads and main national park access roads in this region are generally suitable for conventional vehicles; others may require a 4WD. Always carry plenty of water and plan ahead with fuel, particularly on remote routes.

See also *On the Road*, p. 246.

Mungo National Park

Opposite *The barren, otherworldly dunes around Lake Mungo.*

Below *An old iron bedstead, from the days when Mungo was a sheep station.*

The Mungo lakes have not held water for 15 000 years, but when you cross an old lake bed there can be no mistaking it. Suddenly the road dips down, the vegetation thins out to low, salt-resistant scrub, and vision stretches to the edges of the shallow pan.

Mungo NP protects over 880 sq km of this dry-lake environment, including most of Lake Mungo and the southern belly of Lake Leaghur. There are 17 lakes in total, all protected by the Willandra Lakes World Heritage Area.

Along the eastern edge of Lake Mungo are the Walls of China, a long, curving sand dune known as a lunette, dotted with ridged, moon-like formations. Formed of layers of sand, dust, soil and buried vegetation, this dune was stabilised with a thick covering of trees and shrubs until the arrival of Europeans and their itinerant

Lake Mungo – history in the sand

What makes the Willandra Lakes so archaeologically significant is a simple alignment of events. The lunettes were formed when the lakes were full, which is also when Aboriginal tribes lived here permanently, sustained by a diet of fish, reptiles, marsupials, eggs, seeds and fruit. As a result, artefacts have been buried in the lunettes and preserved for thousands of years by the alkalinity of the sand and soil.

The first middens and tools were discovered accidentally in 1968, slowly emerging from the eroding Mungo lunette. A year later an archaeological team discovered the cremated remains of Mungo Woman. In 1974 the skeleton of Mungo Man was found in one piece, stained with ochre. Both are dated at around 40 000 years old, making them the oldest evidence of ritualised burial on earth.

Also preserved within the lunettes are the remains of megafauna, including the wombat-like diprotodon. Megafauna became extinct around 46 000 years ago, just a few thousand years after humans reached the continent.

Contacts

Visitor information

Broken Hill
cnr Blende and Bromide sts
(08) 8088 3560
www.visitbrokenhill.com.au

Cobar
Barrier Hwy
(02) 6836 2448
www.cobar.nsw.gov.au

Menindee
Menindee St
(08) 8091 4274

White Cliffs
Keraro Rd
(08) 8091 6611

Parks and reserves

See *Fact File*, opposite

Station stays

Kallara Station (near Tilpa)
(02) 6837 3963
www.kallarastation.com.au

Tolarno Station
(south of Menindee)
(08) 8091 7403
www.tolarnostation.com.au

Trilby Station (near Louth, north-east of Tilpa)
(02) 6874 7420
www.trilbystation.com.au

Activities

Harry Nanya Outback Tours
Shop 10 Sandwych St
Wentworth
(03) 5027 2076
www.harrynanyatours.com.au

Historic Daydream Mine
Silverton Rd
(08) 8088 5682

Silverton Camel Farm
Silverton Rd
(08) 8088 5316

-heep, goats and rabbits; soon the Mungo lunette was virtually bare. Rain and wind have dislodged he loose sand, uncovering the miniature peaks nd gullies carved out in storms thousands of ears ago.

The visitor centre has excellent displays on ne archaeological and Indigenous significance of ne lakes and lunettes (see *Lake Mungo – history in he sand*, above). Nearby is Mungo Woolshed, an npressive structure of white cypress pine, once the usy shearing headquarters of Gol Gol Station. You an camp at one of two sites in the park or stay in e shearers' quarters. To thoroughly explore the ark take the 70 km self-guide drive tour. Harry 'anya Outback Tours offers trips to Mungo NP ith a Barkindji guide (see *Contacts*, opposite).

Menindee and Kinchega National Park

To many, the Menindee Lakes are the plainest evidence of an ecological crisis on the Darling River. When the floodwaters of the Darling spilled into them, these lakes attracted hundreds of thousands of waterbirds, but now, with a dam built here and irrigators pumping from upstream, some of them scarcely know water. Strangely, the black box woodlands that were flooded and killed when the capacity of the lakes was extended are now Menindee's biggest attraction, casting their eerie shadows at sunset.

For explorers Burke and Wills, Menindee was the last stop at something resembling civilisation on their doomed journey across the continent

River red gums shade the banks of the Darling River.

The Barkindji

The Barkindji people lived around the Darling River, from its junction with the Murray north to Menindee and Wilcannia. While their territory extended into the arid surrounds, the river was their true lifeblood – they made canoes from the bark of river red gums (scar trees can be found along the river banks) and fish traps like those that still remain at Brewarrina (past Bourke). By the 1850s paddlesteamers were churning up the Darling, and Europeans were fencing off their land at a relentless pace. Today many Barkindji people live in Wilcannia. The streetscape of this old port is European, with its pink sandstone buildings, but the town's name, appropriately, is Barkindji; it refers to a gap in the riverbank where floodwaters escape.

The Darling river run

The Darling River cuts a bold path through arid inland NSW. At 2740 km it is Australia's longest river and part of the vast basin that drains one-seventh of the continent. Still, you won't always find a rushing torrent of water within its steep, pale-grey banks, for even before the days of damming and irrigation the river was known as completely fickle.

Paddlesteamers carting wool from the great grazing empires of outback NSW in the 1800s and early 1900s stood at the mercy of wildly varying water levels. Sudden floods could carry them miles across a plain to be stranded once the water dropped, and in the dry season they would be lucky to find a passage through the muddy, snag-ridden trickle.

Today the 'Darling River Run' is better known as a 4WD trek of over 700 km from Bourke to Wentworth. While the most adventurous route is on the west bank, a road on both sides for the most part means you can switch at the handful of crossings en route. Stations such as Kallara near Tilpa (west bank), Trilby beyond Tilpa near Louth (west bank), and Tolarno south of Menindee (east bank) offer accommodation, camping and fishing (see *Contacts*, p. 159).

(see *Burke and Wills – a tragic tale*, p. 138). When they passed through in 1860, Menindee consisted of a store, a police station, a few shacks and a pub where they stayed (that pub, rebuilt after a fire in 1999, survives as the Maidens Menindee Hotel). Today little seems to have changed, but in the intervening years Menindee, like Wilcannia and Bourke, was a hub of river transport.

Extending from the southern banks of Menindee Lake is 440 sq km Kinchega NP, with 62 km of Darling River frontage. Campsites dot the river red gum-lined banks in the north. The park was once part of Kinchega Station, whose sheep fattened on the fertile lake beds. The old Kinchega homestead and woolshed remain a centrepiece of the park and visitors can stay in the old shearers' quarters.

Boating is not permitted in the national park, but you can head to Copi Hollow north of Menindee Lake for watersports. Fishing and birdwatching are also fairly reliable on the upper lakes.

Broken Hill

The hill that explorer Charles Sturt referred to as 'broken' – a long, jagged ridge curved like a boomerang – has turned out to be the largest body of high-grade silver, lead and zinc-bearing ore in the world.

It is now an ominous pile of black rubble in the centre of the city, but the city itself is at once grand and rugged. Broken Hill is a mix of cast-iron, lace-bedecked hotels and illustrious civic buildings, and humble corrugated-iron miners' cottages. It is equally good

r a pub-crawl (visit Mario's Palace, made famous in *he Adventures of Priscilla, Queen of the Desert*) or gallery tour (see *Brushmen of the Bush*, opposite).

To see the 'real Broken Hill – the one lit by ie light of a head torch – take an underground id surface tour of the Historic Daydream Mine ee *Contacts*, p. 159). Mining giant Broken Hill roprietary (BHP) was formed from the original yndicate of seven', the group of men who staked ut the first mining claims in 1883. Following a erger in 2001, BHP Billiton became the largest iining company in the world.

Overlooking Broken Hill, perched on top of the mullock heap, is the Line of Lode Miners' Memorial and Visitor Centre. The memorial appears in almost any view of the city like a set of giant, rust-red teeth. Inside are the names of more than 800 workers who have died in the mines.

To get a feel for the landscape that so inspires the artists of Broken Hill, head to the Living Desert Reserve, 11 km north. Up close this 'desert' is anything but featureless. At sunset the rocky hills turn the colour of glowing embers; euros hop about and birds chatter in the mulga. There is a 2 km walking trail, but the most popular feature lies at the top of Sundown Hill, where 12 hand-hewn sandstone sculptures, completed in a 1993 symposium, are reminiscent of Stonehenge.

Silverton

It is hard to believe that Silverton was once a bustling town of 3000 people. Old photographs in the Silverton Gaol Museum show the main street, Burke Street, lined with impressive two-storey hotels, while the town survey depicts a busy mini-metropolis. What is left today seems completely random – an old church here, a cottage converted into a gallery there, all strewn across the dusty town site like meteorites.

Brushmen of the Bush

While mining in Broken Hill was founded by the 'syndicate of seven', art in Broken Hill was kick-started by a syndicate of five – the Brushmen of the Bush, who brought fame to the town with a run of national and international exhibitions in the 1970s. Among the painters were Pro Hart and Jack Absalom. Pro Hart was one of Australia's most successful artists – his oil paintings ranged from colourful outback scenes to abstract portraits – and the local gallery he established boasts a significant private collection. There are over 30 private galleries in Broken Hill today along with the Broken Hill Regional Art Gallery, the oldest regional gallery in the state.

Above *Hand-hewn stone sculpture in the Living Desert Reserve.*

Left *Some of the grand buildings that line Broken Hill's main street.*

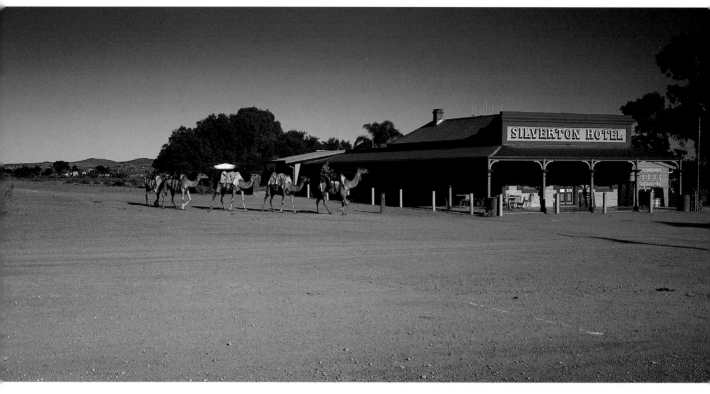

Stark scenery, a quirky pub and camels in outback Silverton.

Mining began in the Silverton area around 1880, several years before Broken Hill. But unlike Broken Hill, the sources of silver had run out of steam by the 1900s.

Today most visitors come for a drink in the bar of the Silverton Hotel, where the walls are lined with photos from the movie sets that have made use of the stark surrounds, including *Mad Max II* and *Dirty Deeds*. Nailed up under the side verandah are the hotel's alter egos – the signs that have been stuck over the real 'Silverton Hotel' sign when the pub itself has played a role in a film or commercial. A replica of Mad Max's black 'interceptor' is often parked out the front.

Silverton Camel Farm, on the eastern outskirts of town, offers camel treks of varying lengths (see *Contacts*, p. 159). To the west is Mundi Mundi Lookout, with views across a plain so flat that on a clear day you can see the curve of the earth, and sometimes the Flinders Ranges in the distance.

Bush mail run

For the outlying stations of Broken Hill the mail is delivered just twice a week, by 4WD. The mail man drives a circuit of 550 km and welcomes passengers on his whirlwind tour. It includes morning tea in a homestead and a BYO lunch on the banks of the Darling. The tour runs on Wednesdays and Saturdays. For bookings call the mail man himself: 0411 102 339.

Mutawintji National Park and Historic Site

The burnt-red Byngnano Range cuts through the south-west of Mutawintji NP, and creek beds spread through the gullies like veins. It also contains the tracks of several ancestral spirits, which since ancient times have made Mutawintji neutral ground for a number of Aboriginal tribes. Together they met here for initiation and rainmaking ceremonies and left behind a rich concentration of paintings, engravings and stencils.

The majority of these are found within Mutawintji Historic Site, an Aboriginal-owned area within the 689 sq km park accessed by guided tour (see *Fact File* p. 158). There are also a handful of sites with unrestricted access on some of the walking trails.

The walking trails range from short wanders through rock pool-dotted gorges to lengthy scrambles along the ridges, for views across the hill and valleys of rock. There is also the 10 km Old Coach Road Drive, which takes in the ruins of an old hotel and gives access to the impressive outcrop of Split Rock. The campground at Homestead Creek is nestled among sprawling river red gums.

White Cliffs

Miners have been living underground at White Cliffs from as early as the 1890s, just a few years after the first opals were discovered here. It made perfect sense: it was hot – an average of 35°C in summer; building materials were expensive and few and far between; and there was an alternative to above-ground living right where the miners were working: the disused mine shafts carved out of solid sandstone. These dark cavities offered a constant temperature of 22°C.

Today these underground dwellings, motels, galleries and showrooms are White Cliffs at its most

:autiful. You can visit Jock's Place, an old mine on ırleys Hill converted into a home and museum ın by one of White Cliff's quirkiest characters, stay in an underground motel or B&B (contact sitor information, see *Contacts*, p. 159).

You can also try your luck fossicking void any pegged claims). An estimated) 000 abandoned opal digs surround the town ke giant white pockmarks, but locals say there is ısily as much opal remaining as has been taken ıt. White Cliffs' population swells from around)0 to 500 in the cooler months of the year for ıis very reason.

aroo–Darling National Park

ıroo–Darling NP covers 1950 sq km, spreading own to the Darling River and beyond, but it is ıe section east of hot and dusty White Cliffs that ntains the most surprises. Here, just when you ought the outback had finally taken hold, is a ries of expansive lakes that form the Paroo River verflow. Unlike the Darling, the Paroo is one of ıe last pristine rivers in the Murray–Darling Basin, ıd finding the lakes full is not unusual – as well as king overflow from the 640 km Paroo, they can be led by local rains. Peery Lake, the largest, is 30 km ng and can retain water for two or three years.

Waterbirds descend on the lakes at the very nt of water; they include brolgas, black swans and ıe endangered freckled duck. The rocky shores of ery Lake are also culturally significant, laden with iddens and stone-tool workshops. It is thought ıat this area was once permanently inhabited.

Facilities in the park include a campground, alking trails and a visitor centre in White Cliffs ee *Fact File*, p. 158).

:obar and Mount Grenfell

he word Cobar comes from the word 'gubar', hich in the local Aboriginal language means d ochre. This modern mining town is located ı the site of an old ochre mine and the pigment as used at local art sites, including the low rock verhangs of Mount Grenfell Historic Site nearby. ount Grenfell rock art is a vibrant display: small ick figures cover the rock faces in layers; they are unting emus and kangaroos, wielding boomerangs ıd axes. The Wongaibon tribe were attracted to the te because of the nearby waterhole, and the scenes ıey painted on the rocks were thought to ensure ıccessful hunting.

Willandra National Park

Many national parks throughout the outback have their origins as former stations – they include pastoral relics and often offer accommodation in old shearers' quarters. Willandra NP even retains the *feeling* of a station. Indeed, the 193 sq km park is split down the middle so that surrounding stations can still move their stock through, and the shearing shed was still in use until just a few years ago.

Willandra Station, covering 400 000 acres, or 1600 sq km, in its heyday, was renowned for fine merino wool. The 1918 homestead and its sprawling gardens are now restored. The homestead has 26 rooms, with wide verandahs and French doors designed to beat the heat of the riverine plains. Visitors can stay in the homestead – it is a decidedly ritzy experience in these environs – or in the nearby cottage, men's quarters or campground. From the homestead explore Willandra Creek, with its reedy banks and waterbirds, or take the Merton Motor Trail across the plains; look out for emus and kangaroos.

Following page *Ridged lunettes present a surreal landscape in the Willandra Lakes World Heritage Area.*

Below *White-necked herons and other waterbirds flock to the reedy banks of Willandra Creek.*

The Flinders Ranges

The Flinders Ranges rise abruptly from the plains, with rugged, rocky peaks and streaked, rich colours. Within their folds lie fern-filled chasms, fossil-strewn gorges, and features of immense cultural and geological significance.

At Crystal Brook, 200 km north of Adelaide, the Flinders Ranges begin as a gentle ripple across the landscape, a backdrop to the sun-drenched wheatfields. Their distant purple shapes lend an enchanting air to the matter-of-fact town of Port Augusta, but it is just a hint of what is to come – magnificent gorges and rock formations, lush waterholes and valleys, Aboriginal rock art and crumbling pastoral ruins. By the time the ranges reach their rocky end on the Mawson Plateau in the north, they have covered over 400 km.

These are the traditional lands of the Adnyamathanha – the 'people of the rocks' – eight Aboriginal groups who have lived in the region for at least 15 000 years. For them the landscape is resonant with the stories of the Muda – their particular version of the Dreamtime. These stories live on, ascribing meaning to the existence of every animal, the shape of every mountain, the placement of every boulder.

The marks of European settlement are scattered throughout the ranges – occasionally in character-filled towns like Blinman and modern operations like the Leigh Creek coalmine, but mostly in the ruins of old homesteads, built by settlers who believed the ranges could be turned over to agriculture. Chimneys, windmills and water tanks conjure the days of giant sheep runs and overland explorers passing through, and the unmistakable hardship of living in such isolation.

Millions of years of wind, water and sun have chiselled these ranges into their current shapes. The area is popular with bushwalkers, wildlife enthusiasts and photographers during the cooler months, and for good reason. When you're standing on the top of Wilpena Pound, or squeezing your way through Bunyip Chasm, it can feel that these hills are as old as the world itself.

Must see, must do

- Marvel at the age of the ranges on the Brachina Gorge Geological Trail
- Take a Ridgetop Tour in an open-topped 4WD from Arkaroola
- Dine on 'Flinders feral food' in the Prairie Hotel at Parachilna
- Hike to the top of Wilpena Pound
- Sample local bush tucker with an Adnyamathanha guide at Iga Warta

Pichi Richi Railway
The old carriages of the *Ghan* and the *Transcontinental* run on the Pichi Richi railway line between Quorn and Port Augusta. The journey through rock cuttings and across ravines operates April–Nov.

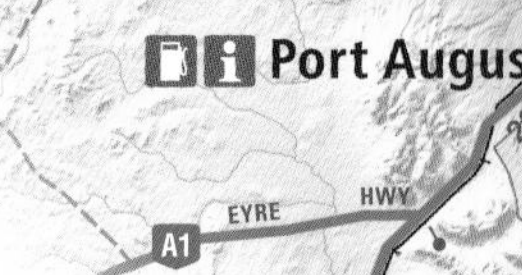

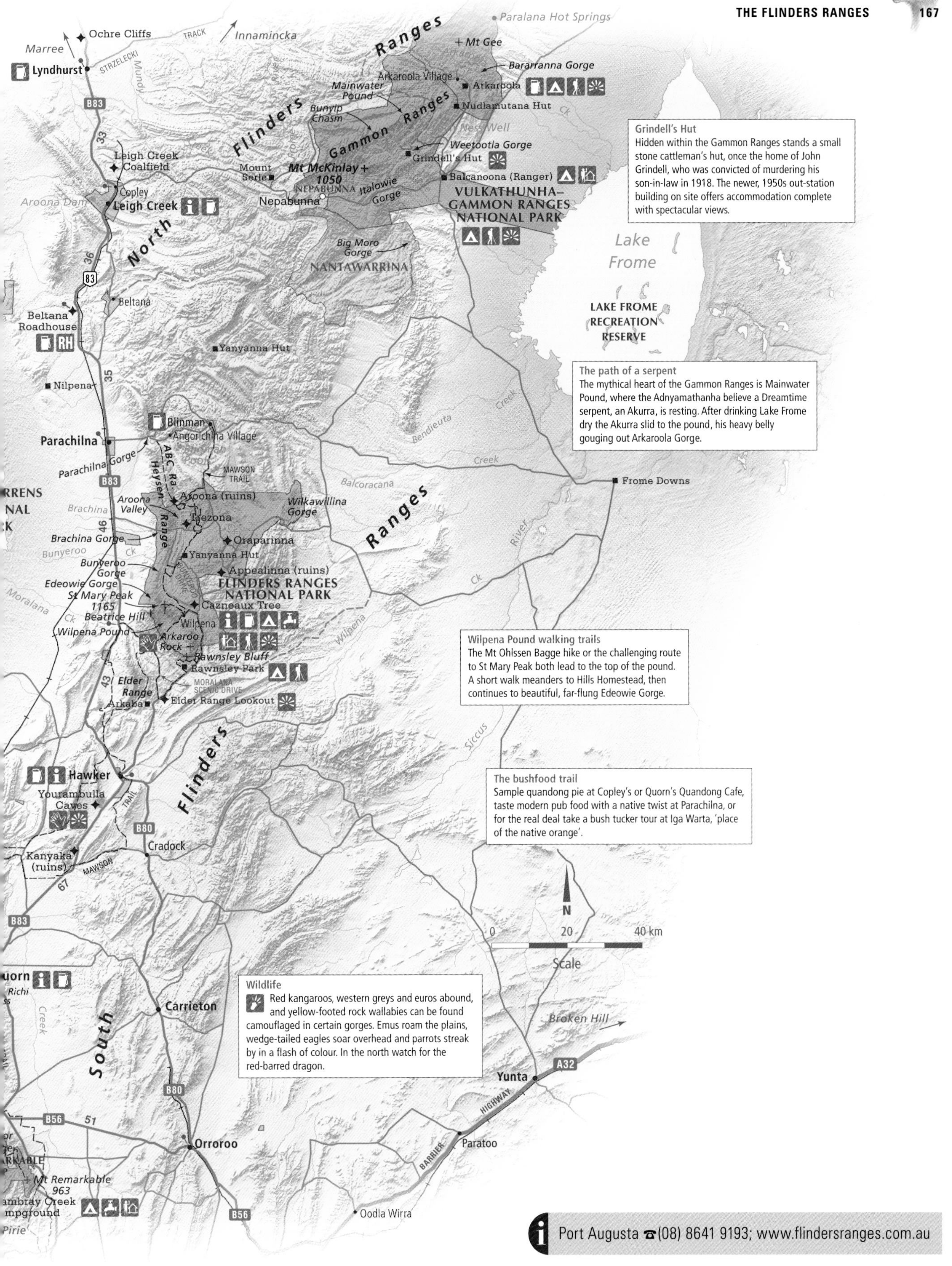

Grindell's Hut
Hidden within the Gammon Ranges stands a small stone cattleman's hut, once the home of John Grindell, who was convicted of murdering his son-in-law in 1918. The newer, 1950s out-station building on site offers accommodation complete with spectacular views.

The path of a serpent
The mythical heart of the Gammon Ranges is Mainwater Pound, where the Adnyamathanha believe a Dreamtime serpent, an Akurra, is resting. After drinking Lake Frome dry the Akurra slid to the pound, his heavy belly gouging out Arkaroola Gorge.

Wilpena Pound walking trails
The Mt Ohlssen Bagge hike or the challenging route to St Mary Peak both lead to the top of the pound. A short walk meanders to Hills Homestead, then continues to beautiful, far-flung Edeowie Gorge.

The bushfood trail
Sample quandong pie at Copley's or Quorn's Quandong Cafe, taste modern pub food with a native twist at Parachilna, or for the real deal take a bush tucker tour at Iga Warta, 'place of the native orange'.

Wildlife
Red kangaroos, western greys and euros abound, and yellow-footed rock wallabies can be found camouflaged in certain gorges. Emus roam the plains, wedge-tailed eagles soar overhead and parrots streak by in a flash of colour. In the north watch for the red-barred dragon.

Port Augusta ☎(08) 8641 9193; www.flindersranges.com.au

Opposite *The natural amphitheatre of Wilpena Pound.*

Below right *The golden Wonoka Plains, north of Hawker.*

Fact File

Top events

Feb *Wilpena under the Stars (black-tie dinner and dance)*
April *Tastes of the Outback (food events across the Flinders)*
Beltana Outback Ball
May *Hawker Races*
Land Rover Jamboree (Blinman)
June *Quorn Races*
July *Pichi Richi Railway Marathon (Port Augusta to Quorn)*
Sept *Hawker Art Exhibition*
Beltana Picnic Races and Gymkhana
Oct *Cook Outback (camp oven cook-off, Blinman)*

Permits and regulations

Aboriginal land Abutting Vulkathunha–Gammon Ranges NP to the south is the 580 sq km Nantawarrina Indigenous Protected Area, including the community of Nepabunna. No permit is needed to drive through to the national park, but permission is required to explore sites such as Big Moro Gorge. Contact Nepabunna Community Council: (08) 8648 3764. Permits can be faxed in advance, or arranged in Nepabunna (office open Mon–Fri, mornings only).

Parks and reserves

National parks and reserves in SA are managed by National Parks and Wildlife SA (NPWSA). For general information see *Travel Tips*, p.154. Campfires are banned in Mount Remarkable, Flinders Ranges and Vulkathunha–Gammon Ranges national parks 1 Nov–31 Mar.

Mount Remarkable NP For general information and campsite bookings for Mambray Creek (necessary during school holidays and long weekends), contact Mambray Creek ranger headquarters: (08) 8634 7068.

Flinders Ranges NP For general information and bookings for campsites and other accommodation at Wilpena (stongly advised during the main holiday periods) contact Wilpena Visitor Centre: (08) 8648 0048.

Vulkathunha–Gammon Ranges NP For general information or to book accommodation in Grindell's Hut, Nudlamutana Hut or Balcanoona Shearers' Quarters contact Hawker Parks and Wildlife office: (08) 8648 4244. To contact the Balcanoona ranger headquarters: (08) 8648 4829.

Warnings

Road access and closures Roads to Wilpena and Leigh Creek are sealed, but other roads through the ranges are unsealed. A 2WD vehicle is adequate for most of Flinders Ranges NP, but in more remote areas, including Vulkathunha–Gammon Ranges NP and Arkaroola Wilderness Sanctuary, a 4WD vehicle is required.

Bushwalking Bushwalkers should carry plenty of drinking water, and maps if the track is not clearly defined. People undertaking a walk of more than three hours within Flinders Ranges NP should use the Bushwalkers Register at Wilpena; for extended hikes in Flinders Ranges NP and other parks, obtain a trip intentions form in advance to let the park ranger know your movements (phone the park on the number listed above).

See also *On the Road*, p. 246.

Mount Remarkable National Park

Explorer Edward John Eyre named 960 m Mount Remarkable for the way it jutted out of the otherwise flat landscape, but there are many other remarkable things about this 160 sq km park in the southern Flinders. One is the range of animal species found here – southern and northern habitats converge, uniting creatures such as brush-tailed possums, typical of wetter, forested regions, and red kangaroos, characteristic of the desert. Much of the park is inaccessible by road, but walkers can explore it on a range of bushwalks, from short saunters to multi-day hikes. To the north is Alligator Gorge, where tall, jagged walls close into a narrow opening filled with rock pools. There is a popular campsite at Mambray Creek in the park's south-west.

Port Augusta

The industrial city of Port Augusta is located at the head of Spencer Gulf, but its character derives more from the ranges and the outback than it does from the coast. Two major attractions take the outback as their theme: at the fascinating Wadlata Outback Centre displays explore the geology, Aboriginal culture and European history of the ranges and desert plains; while the Australian Arid Lands Botanic Gardens, set against a breathtaking mountain backdrop, reveal the subtle wonders and beauties of Australia's arid flora (see *Contacts*, opposite).

Quorn

A dramatic stretch of road leads into Quorn, twisting around the stony, eucalypt-covered hills. This path across the Flinders, known as the Pichi Richi Pass, was once a crucial rail route heading

Pichi Richi Railway

If you happen to spot one of the old steam locomotives ambling through the hills near Quorn you might for a second forget you're driving a car and reach down for the reigns – the sight of steam trains weaving in and out of this typical Australian-bush landscape comes straight out of the 19th century. Since 1973 a team of Quorn volunteers has restored the historic line and many of the original locomotives, and operates various weekend and school holiday rides from April to the end of November between Quorn and Port Augusta. Bookings can be made at the Port Augusta Visitor Centre (see *Contacts*, opposite).

orth to Alice Springs and, for a shorter period, or trains bound for the west. Eventually the lines ere rerouted, stopping only at Port Augusta, but he four stately two-storey hotels that line Quorn's ailway Terrace remain and continue to do business lmost 50 years after the last *Ghan* passed through. isitors can take the charming Pichi Richi train n the original narrow-gauge line (see *Pichi Richi ailway*, opposite).

Kanyaka and Yourambulla

Of all the lonely ruins scattered across the Flinders, erhaps the most evocative are those of Kanyaka Homestead, 40 km north of Quorn. The sandstone uildings lie above a creek bed, a jagged line of walls ear an incongruous palm tree. The homestead once erviced a 945 sq km sheep and cattle station, stablished in 1851. At its peak, the station sheared 1 000 sheep a year, but a severe drought in the iid-1860s spelt its eventual break-up.

Further north, high up on a hill 10 km before Hawker, is a record of another world and time, when he ranges were the undisturbed domain of the ribes of the Adnyamathanha. Many of the charcoal, chre and clay markings in the three Yourambulla Caves relate to the initiation of young men and were efreshed with each new ceremony. Ask at the visitor entre about Aboriginal-guided tours.

Hawker and Beyond

Like Quorn, Hawker is a former rail town, its station ow a restaurant and gallery. Both towns have alleries, but Hawker's Jeff Morgan Gallery stands ut for its impressive 30 m long painting of the view rom St Mary Peak, Wilpena Pound.

There are various lookouts in the surrounding hills, and 19 km north is historic Arkaba Station, set at the base of the rugged Elder Range. Arkaba woolshed has been used continuously for 150 years and the station still runs around 8000 merinos. The owners offer luxury accommodation and 4WD treks for those wanting to sample life on a station or explore the region's wildlife and geology (see *Contacts*, opposite).

Just beyond Arkaba is the beginning of Moralana Scenic Drive. This 27 km route runs between the Elder Range and the south-west wall of Wilpena Pound, across gentle pine-dotted hills. The drive is best at early morning or late afternoon, and the river red gum-lined creek beds make natural picnic spots. In spring, wildflowers carpet the hills (although the most prolific variety – the purple blooms of Salvation Jane – is not a native at all, but a pest imported from Europe).

Flinders Ranges National Park

The scenery of this 950 sq km park is some of SA's best. Its two prominent mountain ranges – the Heysen and ABC – create peaks with panoramic views and gorges with subtle treasures, while in the south is magnificent Wilpena Pound.

Wilpena Pound and Surrounds

From the air Wilpena Pound looks like a giant bird's nest, or perhaps a hand forming the shape of a cup (the word 'wilpena' comes from an Aboriginal word thought to mean 'place of bent fingers'). It is in fact a remnant valley 14 km long and 7 km wide, the surrounding ridges of which are the eroded stumps of large mountains.

Contacts

Visitor information

Hawker
Hawker Motors
cnr Wilpena and Cradock rds
(08) 8648 4014

Leigh Creek
Shop 13, town centre
(08) 8675 2723

Port Augusta
Wadlata Outback Centre
41 Flinders Tce
(08) 8641 9193

Quorn
3 Seventh St
(08) 8648 6419

Wilpena Pound Resort
(08) 8648 0048
www.wilpenapound.com.au

Parks and reserves

See *Fact File*, opposite

Accommodation

Angorichina Village
(08) 8648 4842

Arkaroola Wilderness Sanctuary
(08) 8648 4848 or 1800 676 042
www.arkaroola.com.au

Prairie Hotel
Parachilna
(08) 8648 4844
www.prairiehotel.com.au

Station stays

Arkaba Station
1300 790 561
www.arkabastation.com

Nilpena Station
(08) 8648 4844

Rawnsley Park Station
(08) 8648 0030 (units) or
(08) 8648 0008 (caravan park)
www.rawnsleypark.com.au

Other

Australian Arid Lands Botanic Gardens
Stuart Hwy, Port Augusta West
(08) 8641 1049

Heysen Trail, Mawson Trail
www.southaustraliantrails.com

Iga Warta
(08) 8648 3737
www.igawarta.com

Climbers relish the challenge of tackling the Great Wall near Blinman.

According to the Muda it was created by two serpents, Akurra, who intruded on an initiation ceremony being held at the site. Their long bodies surrounded the ceremony, and when they had eaten their fill of the people attending – all but the initiate – they died, forming the pound walls. St Mary Peak and Beatrice Hill, on either side of Edeowie Gorge, are the serpents' heads.

From the outside the pound is a fortress, but it is a different world from the top. The slopes fall gently towards the valley floor, a green paradise of native pines and river red gums. European settlers saw the natural enclosure as prime real estate and used it for breeding stockhorses and growing wheat but a drought and then a flood soon reinstated the natural order.

From Wilpena Pound Resort (see left) various walking trails lead up and into the pound. The most challenging is the hike up 1170 m St Mary Peak, the highest point of the pound and the ranges. From the top walkers can see shimmering, usually dry Lake Torrens on the horizon, and the 'backbone' of the ranges (the narrow corridor between the Heysen and ABC ranges) twisting away to the north. In one of the great contradictions of the Australian outback, winter occasionally covers St Mary Peak with a light dusting of snow.

Rawnsley Bluff is another popular hike up the pound, reached from the tourist village at Rawnsley Park Station (see *Contacts*, p. 169) to the south. The village offers similar activities and facilities to Wilpena Pound Resort, with the added attraction of horseriding treks into the hills.

Just north of Rawnsley Park on the edge of the pound is Arkaroo Rock, perhaps the best accessible rock-art site in the ranges. The markings, estimated to be 6000 years old, cover the underside of a hidden boulder.

Another site nearby is the Cazneaux Tree, a great grandpa of a river red gum, standing alone on a plain beyond the pound. It bears the name of renowned photographer Harold Cazneaux

Wilpena Pound Resort

Wilpena Pound Resort offers a range of accommodation and facilities, powered in part by a $2.5 million solar station. Campsites sprawl beneath the native pines, and at holiday times the atmosphere is the equal of any summer beach resort. The park visitor centre is located on site for all information on bushwalking, camping in other parts of the park, 4WD tours and scenic flights. A seasonal events program runs in autumn and spring, offering everything from wildlife and rock-art tours to stargazing.

·ho immortalised the tree in his famous 1937 hotograph, *Spirit of Endurance*. Access is along the ırn-off to Blinman from Wilpena Pound Resort.

lorth of Wilpena

eyond the pound the silence of the ranges ıtensifies, engulfing the hills, gorges and ;aterholes. Bunyeroo Drive, one of the park's ıost scenic roads, leads to many of the northern ttractions including Bunyeroo Gorge, with its rching river red gums. The drive culminates at the ıost spectacular gorge in the park, Brachina Gorge.

Brachina Creek slices through the Heysen, ABC nd Trezona ranges, forming gorge walls that are ıagnificent cross-sections of rock. A 20 km road, alled the Brachina Gorge Geological Trail, traces the ourse of the creek, and each of the gorge's 12 istinct sedimentary layers. These layers were ›rmed beneath an ocean 650–500 million years go. Later the layers were thrust up, folding into ıountains as high as Everest before eroding into umps of quartzite and sandstone.

At certain sites along the trail you'll also see ıe fossils of early life forms imprinted in the rocks: ːromatolites and ancient creatures resembling ponges and corals. To the west where the walls are highest, Brachina Gorge is also a fantastic place to simply rest and watch the sunset turn the rubbly cliffs a golden red. Sunrise and sundown are the best times to spot the gorge's yellow-footed rock wallabies.

North of Brachina is a valley that painter Hans Heysen once knew well – he stayed in the Aroona Valley, as a guest at Oraparinna Station, in the 1925 pug and pine hut that still survives today. Many of his paintings depict the valley's giant river red gums, and the views to the Heysen and ABC ranges. The heritage site (including the ruins of an older homestead) is the starting point of three walks, including one to magnificent Red Hill Lookout. For details on these trails and others within the park, pick up the *Bushwalking in Flinders Ranges National Park* brochure from the Wilpena Visitor Centre.

Parachilna to Blinman

In the last decade or so the Prairie Hotel at Parachilna has been transformed from a local watering hole to the toast of Australia's outback pubs. At the back of the establishment are new, environmentally sensitive rooms sunk into the ground to beat the desert heat, while out the front they serve food with a native twist – 'Flinders feral food', which might include

Yellow-footed rock wallabies

With their thick fur, yellow forearms, legs and eyelids, and long, striped tails, yellow-footed rock wallabies are surely one of the most attractive members of the kangaroo and wallaby family. They inhabit rocky outcrops, where they clamber from ledge to ledge with incredible agility. One hundred and fifty years ago they ranged right across arid and semi-arid inland Australia, but in recent times their numbers have dropped perilously low.

In the last decade a conservation program in the Flinders Ranges called Bounceback has focused on every element in the ecosystem, from feral-animal control to strategic revegetation, and has seen an increase in rock wallaby numbers from a declining population of hundreds to a regenerating population of thousands. Brachina and Wilkawillina gorges in Flinders Ranges NP and Weetootla Gorge in Vulkathunha–Gammon Ranges NP are the best places to see them.

Yellow-footed rock wallabies can be spotted in the Flinders Ranges.

Yurlu's coal

Europeans discovered coal at Leigh Creek in 1888, and mining began in earnest in the 1940s, but Leigh Creek coal actually figures in an Adnyamathanha Dreamtime tale many thousands of years old. It is the charcoal left from a giant fire lit by Yurlu the Kingfisher to signal that he was heading to Wilpena to oversee an initiation ceremony. Yurlu left a trail of coal all the way to the pound. The initiation ceremony was eventually interrupted by two serpents, whose bodies are said to form the pound walls. (See *Wilpena Pound and Surrounds*, p. 169.)

anything from emu pâté to roo-tail soup. But this is essentially still an outback pub – at sunset you can sit on the verandah with a beer and delight in the simple magic of the nightly Leigh Creek coal train passing on its way to Port Augusta. The couple responsible for reinventing the pub live on nearby Nilpena Station (see *Contacts*, p. 169) on the edge of Lake Torrens, where they also offer cottage and shearers' quarters accommodation. The station also has self-guide 4WD tracks across desert dunes.

The road east of Parachilna leads back into the ranges to Parachilna Gorge, where giant river red gums dot the rocky creek bed. A little further on is Angorichina Village, once the unlikely spot for a tuberculosis sanatorium and now offering accommodation (see *Contacts*, p. 169). A four-hour walking trail to the spring-fed Blinman Pools begins from here.

Further on, at the intersection of the road heading south into Flinders Ranges NP, is the old mining town of Blinman. From a shepherd's discovery of copper in 1859 to the mine's closure in 1918, Blinman produced a hefty 10 000 tonnes of copper. Proof of this can be found in the three rust-red boilers that lie on a sun-scorched hill above town, and in the gaping open-cut entrance shaft nearby. In an otherwise quiet township, the North Blinman Hotel is the centre of most of the action (as testified by the business card-adorned walls of the front bar).

Leigh Creek, Copley and Lyndhurst

The landscape north of Flinders Ranges NP seems to become drier, dustier and more isolated with every passing kilometre. The modern town of Leigh Creek, with its population of over 500 and its green, tree-lined streets, can come as a bit of a surprise. Perhaps even more surprising is nearby Aroona Dam, a deep, dark-blue body of water that seems improbable against the burnt-orange hills.

The town owes its existence to the giant coalmine that lies 22 km north, a tiered, black bowl descending into the earth. A viewing area lies off the road to Lyndhurst (the turn-off is around 10 km north of Copley), but the tours from Leigh Creek give an even better idea of the scale of the operation (book at the visitor centre, see *Contacts*, p. 169). Each year 2.7 million tonnes of coal are transported by train to Port Augusta, where a power station converts it into electricity. Leigh Creek is responsible for around 40 percent of SA's power.

Grindell's Hut, one of two huts in Vulkathunha–Gammon Ranges NP.

Iga Warta tours take visitors to sacred art sites, which are otherwise inaccessible.

Copley, 6 km north, has what Leigh Creek .cks: a wonderful sense of heritage. The centrepiece f this town is an old two-storey pub, confusingly amed the Leigh Creek Hotel (this was once the il stop for the original Leigh Creek township, ow engulfed by the mine). Also in town is the uandong Cafe, famous for its fruit pies made om the native quandong.

Lyndhurst is where the desert begins – where avellers decide to head east along the Strzelecki rack (see p. 137) or north to the Birdsville (see . 136) or Oodnadatta tracks (see p. 145). Nearby e some magnificent ochre cliffs that the dnyamathanha mined for use in rock art and eremonies. The ochre, along with prized Parachilna chre, was used locally and made its way via trade outes across the country. This is not the only ochre ine in the area, but it is the only one with access. ead a short distance east of Lyndhurst to visit omething altogether different – the Talc Alf Gallery, ith its talc-stone sculptures and healthy dose of utback quirk.

lepabunna and Iga Warta

he area around Mount Serle Station, on the ay into Vulkathunha–Gammon Ranges NP from Copley, is sacred to the Adnyamathanha. It is alive with the tales of the Muda, but it is also where many Adnyamathanha gathered and lived. The area was one of the last true strongholds of their lifestyle and traditions before the European ways crept in.

Later in the 1930s, many Adnyamathanha people were moved to a Lutheran Mission at Nepabunna, which is now a community of around 60 people. Members of the community run the nearby Iga Warta Centre, which offers an insight into the world of the Adnyamathanha today. Aboriginal guides take visitors to hidden rock-art sites and show them the craft of gathering and preparing bush tucker. Camping and cabin accommodation are available, complete with damper and stories around the campfire. See *Contacts*, p. 169.

Vulkathunha–Gammon Ranges National Park

For many visitors, 1280 sq km Vulkathunha–Gammon Ranges NP is the true jewel of the Flinders Ranges – without the crowds of the central ranges, and redder, rockier and gutsier all round. Certain vantage points reveal a landscape

R M Williams – outback legend

R M Williams boots are an Australian legend, like Vegemite and the Hills Hoist. Appropriately, this company had its beginnings in a far-flung corner of the Australian outback, deep within the Gammon Ranges.

Reginald Murray Williams was a classic turn-of-the-century Aussie battler. While he had worked as a camel boy and on the goldfields, when the 1930s Depression hit Williams was digging wells in the northern Flinders Ranges, living with his wife and child in a tent in Italowie Gorge.

It was Dollar Mick, Williams' saddling mate, who came up with the idea of making boots. Together they developed a pattern for a boot with elastic sides, made out of a single piece of leather (making it tougher for stockman working in the saddle). The pattern is today the foundation of a $50 million-a-year business, producing an entire range of bushmen's clothing and gear.

that seems wholly formed of rock, great sculpted mounds of it. Venture down into the crevices, though, and you may find a chasm filled with ferr or a permanently flowing spring.

Access to many sites in the park requires the kind of multi-day, trackless hike that is suitable only for serious bushwalkers. Other sites require more moderate walks, with a handful also accessible by 4WD. For park information, the first stop should be the ranger headquarters at Balcanoona.

Two huts in the park, remnants of old stations, offer an alternative to camping, as does the old Balcanoona Shearers' Quarters (see *Fact File*, p.168). Grindell's Hut in the south comes with its own murder mystery, a tale that dates back to before the accommodation quarters were built, when the sites featured just a one-room stone hut that was the home of pastoralist John Grindell. In 1918, it seemed that the pressures of life in such a lonely, rough and weather-beaten place became too much for Grindell, and he began to suspect his son-in-law of duffing his cattle. Perhaps his suspicions were founded, perhaps not, but in strange circumstances

Opposite *Ridgetop Tours from Arkaroola take visitors over sheer-sided hills to Sillers Lookout.*

Right *High in the sky – the peaks and ravines of Arkaroola Wilderness Sanctuary.*

ne son-in-law went missing. All evidence pointed o Grindell, who was later charged with murder. oday the story adds a certain intrigue to the hut's pectacular, mountain-rimmed location.

Two excellent walking trails start at Grindell's Hut, one to Weetootla Gorge (19 km loop) and nother to Italowie Gorge (16 km one way). Veetootla leads to a permanent spring and series of rock pools that shelter an endangered sh known as the purple-spotted gudgeon. Look ut for yellow-footed rock wallabies on the way. talowie is more rigorous and offers the possibility f a side trip up 1050 m Mt McKinlay.

From nearby Loch Ness Well a 5 km walk vinds along a creek bed to what is arguably the ark's most spectacular sight – Bunyip Chasm. Here, owering walls of rock, their surface like ancient, uckling tiles, narrow into a dark cleft. The scramble hrough the gap to the top is for the brave.

Arkaroola Wilderness Sanctuary

The rugged peaks and ravines that surge across rkaroola Wilderness Sanctuary, a 610 sq km egion immediately north of Vulkathunha–Gammon Ranges NP, speak of a violent geological history, and oday it translates to some of the best adventure in he country.

Paralana Hot Springs in the north is the last emnant of geyser activity in Australia, bubbling with water heated by radioactive minerals. Gold, uranium, and copper ripple through the hills, and Mount Gee, around 10 km north of the village, glints with quartz crystals.

Explorer Sir Douglas Mawson recognised the beauty and importance of the area, but it was his student Reg Sprigg who eventually purchased Arkaroola Station for its preservation. A tourist village in the south, now run by Reg's children, offers incredible hospitality for such a remote outpost. Accommodation ranges from motel rooms to campsites, but it is activities like the famous Ridgetop Tour that most people come for.

The tour traverses an almost impossibly steep and winding 4WD track that goes headlong over the ranges from Arkaroola Village, culminating in a sharp climb to the breathtaking Sillers Lookout. This ridge-top track was built during the mining exploration of the 1960s and 70s; the more manageable lowland track was washed away. Visitors travel with a guide in an open-topped 4WD vehicle, but an additional 100 km of self-guide tracks in the sanctuary cater to the independent explorer.

Stargazing in Arkaroola Observatory is another popular activity with these remote skies thickly studded with stars. Bushwalking trails take in nearby ridges, gorges and waterholes, including Bararrana Gorge, where the walls record ancient rippling tides and pulverising glaciers.

Heysen and Mawson trails

South Australia is home to two of Australia's greatest long-distance trails – the Heysen Trail for bushwalkers and the Mawson Trail for cyclists. The 1200 km Heysen Trail begins on the tip of the Fleurieu Peninsula, ending in Parachilna Gorge. While few people complete the entire length, many complete small sections. Within Flinders Ranges NP the trail heads from Wilpena Pound to Yanyanna Hut, then to Trezona and the Aroona Valley; look out for the red-and-white markers. The 800 km Mawson Trail links Adelaide with Blinman, taking riders over little-used roads, farm-access tracks and national park fire trails, with detours en route. (See *Contacts* p. 169.)

The South-West

sunburnt country

The South-West

The Nullarbor Plain links southern Australia's east and west, and is also a little-known destination for getting back to nature. It merges into the Western Australian Goldfields, full of gutsy towns and evocative gold-rush sites.

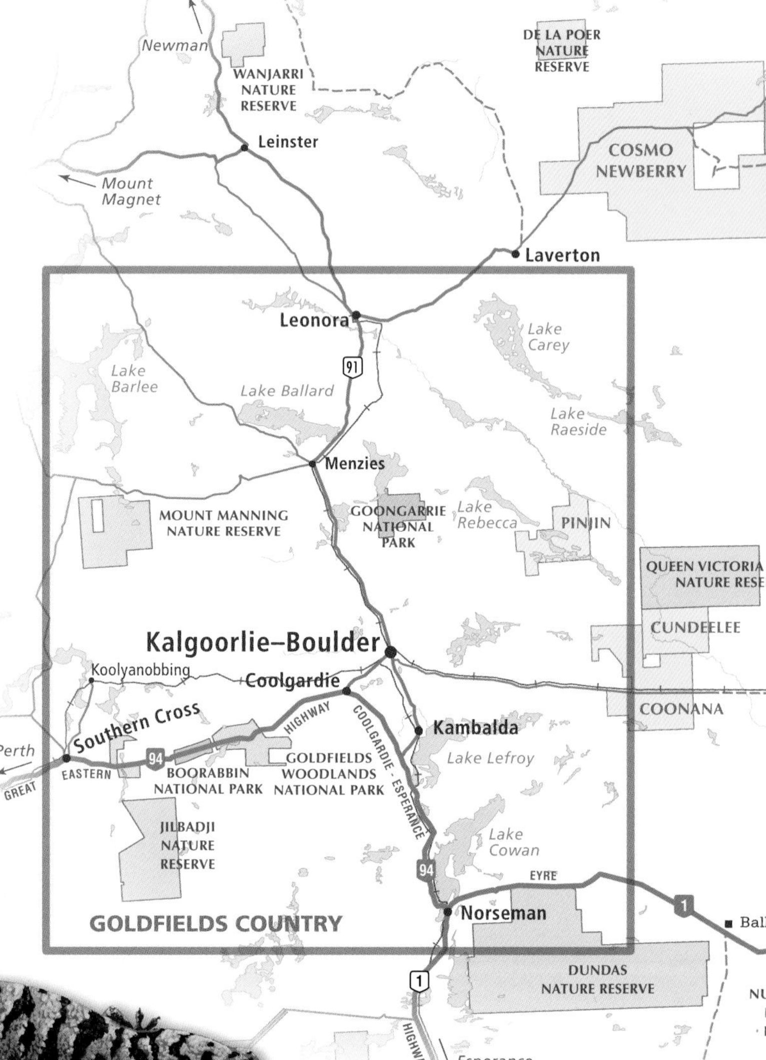

The South-West Regions

Goldfields Country

Kalgoorlie–Boulder is one part stylish, one part brash. A walk down Hannan or Burt Street can leave you marvelling at the sophistication and range of architecture, while a diversion into one of the many hotels will bring you down to earth. Explore the trail of old gold towns that fan out in almost every direction, including deserted sites like Kanowna, and miners' villages like Gwalia, with its original and restored buildings, and a small museum. Granite formations amidst woodlands of she-oak, salmon gum and gimlet make shady sites to set up camp. *See p. 182*

The Nullarbor

The Nullarbor warrants a different approach to travel – one not hinged on bold landmarks or bustling towns, but where travellers are rewarded by the details of the landscape. The lookout at Head of Bight in SA is a great spot for whale sightings and the number of visiting whales in winter rivals the number of human residents. Over the border in WA is Eucla, with the sand-covered ruins of an 1877 telegraph station. Near Cocklebiddy is the Eyre Bird Observatory, a birdwatching outpost among mallee-dotted dunes. *See p. 192*

Bynoe's gecko

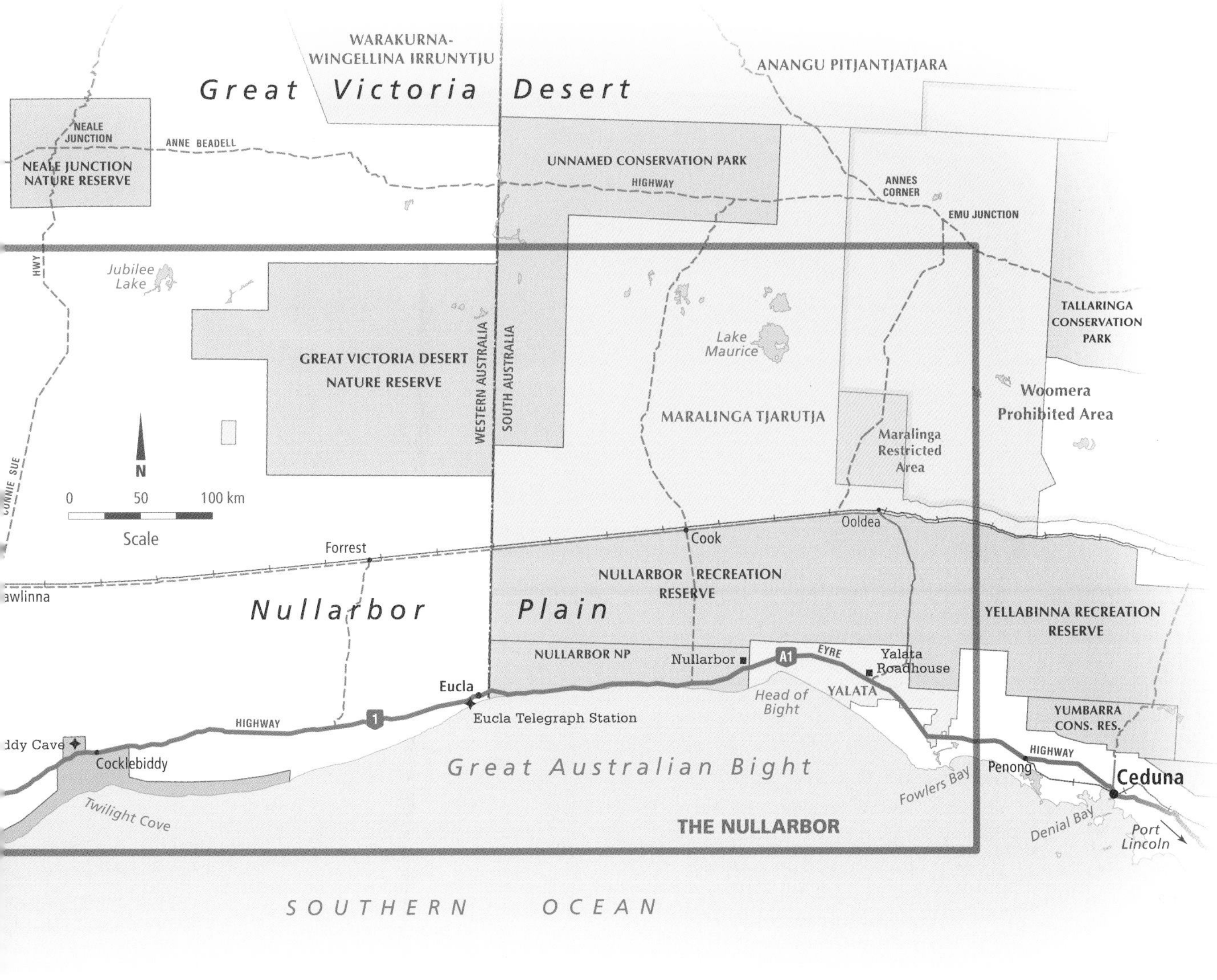

WARAKURNA-
WINGELLINA IRRUNYTJU
ANANGU PITJANTJATJARA
Great Victoria Desert
NEALE JUNCTION
ANNE BEADELL
NEALE JUNCTION NATURE RESERVE
UNNAMED CONSERVATION PARK
HIGHWAY
ANNES CORNER
EMU JUNCTION
HWY
Jubilee Lake
TALLARINGA CONSERVATION PARK
Lake Maurice
GREAT VICTORIA DESERT NATURE RESERVE
WESTERN AUSTRALIA
SOUTH AUSTRALIA
Woomera Prohibited Area
MARALINGA TJARUTJA
Maralinga Restricted Area
N
0 50 100 km
Scale
CONNIE SUE
Ooldea
Cook
Forrest
NULLARBOR RECREATION RESERVE
awlinna
Nullarbor Plain
YELLABINNA RECREATION RESERVE
NULLARBOR NP
Nullarbor
A1
EYRE
Yalata Roadhouse
Eucla
Head of Bight
YALATA
Eucla Telegraph Station
HIGHWAY
1
YUMBARRA CONS. RES.
ddy Cave
Cocklebiddy
HIGHWAY
Great Australian Bight
Penong
Ceduna
Fowlers Bay
Twilight Cove
THE NULLARBOR
Denial Bay
Port Lincoln
SOUTHERN OCEAN

Kalgoorlie–Boulder ☎(08) 9021 1966; www.australiasgoldenoutback.com
The Nullarbor, Eucla Hotel Motel ☎(08) 9039 3468; www.nullarbornet.com.au

Travel Tips

When to go
In the coastal regions of the Nullarbor a sea breeze ensures that both summer and winter are pleasant times to travel; for any detour inland, the cooler months of the year are best. Many people time their trip for June–Oct to catch sight of the southern right whales at Bunda Cliffs. The most pleasant time to visit the Goldfields is April–Nov, when the days are cooler. Spring visits will coincide with blooming wildflowers.

Aboriginal land
Large areas in SA and WA are Aboriginal land and there are also sites of special significance to Aboriginal people. Travellers in the Nullarbor and Great Victoria Desert region should be aware of three areas of Aboriginal land: in SA, Yalata Indigenous Protected Area around the Head of Bight and Maralinga Tjarutja Aboriginal Land above the Trans-Australia Railway; and in WA, Spinifex Aboriginal Land. For information on all, see *Fact File*, p. 194. In the Goldfields region there are no areas of Aboriginal land that require an entry permit. For general information regarding Aboriginal land in WA, contact the WA Department of Indigenous Affairs (DIA): (08) 9235 8000 or 1300 651 077; www.dia.wa.gov.au

Government land
Access to Maralinga Restricted Area is strictly prohibited; however, permits can be arranged for travelling through Woomera Prohibited Area; contact the Defence Support Centre: (08) 8674 3370.

Parks and reserves
South Australia For general information about parks and reserves in SA, contact National Parks and Wildlife SA (NPWSA): (08) 8204 1910;www.environment.sa.gov.au/parks For information on SA's Nullarbor parks contact NPWSA: Ceduna (08) 8625 3144 or SA Tourism: 1300 764 227; www.southaustralia.com

Nullarbor NP, Nullarbor Regional Reserve and the Unnamed Conservation Park are remote and travellers need to be self-sufficient. There is bush camping only. 4WD vehicles are generally required anywhere north of the Eyre Hwy. All fires are banned 1 Nov–30 April; campfires are allowed outside these times though a fuel stove is preferred. Bring firewood and water. For information contact NPWSA Ceduna: (08) 8625 3144.

Western Australia For general information about parks and reserves in WA, contact Department of Environment and Conservation (DEC): (08) 9334 0333; www.dec.wa.gov.au

National parks in the Goldfields region tend to be less developed than the reserves and conservation parks. They generally offer bush camping only, while most reserves have basic facilities. Towards the SA border, Plumridge Lakes and Great Victoria Desert nature reserves have no facilities and are extremely remote. In all areas visitors should observe regional fire restrictions to ascertain whether a campfire is appropriate. BYO firewood and water. For information contact DEC Kalgoorlie: (08) 9080 5555.

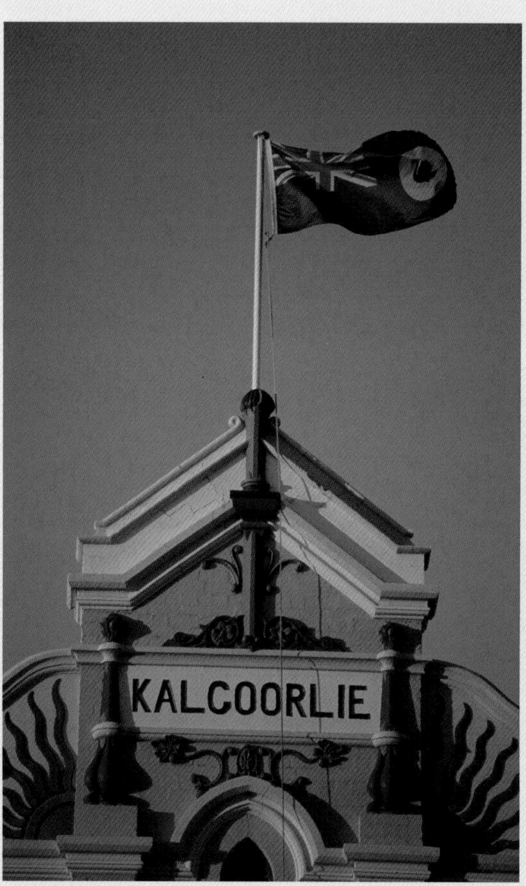

Elaborate detail on Kagloorlie's town hall.

CLIMATE												KALGOORLIE–BOULDER
	J	F	M	A	M	J	J	A	S	O	N	D
Max °C	34	32	30	25	20	18	17	18	22	26	29	32
Min °C	18	18	16	12	8	6	5	5	8	11	14	17
Rain mm	22	28	19	19	28	31	26	20	15	16	18	15
Raindays	3	4	4	5	7	8	9	7	5	4	4	3

CLIMATE												EUCLA
	J	F	M	A	M	J	J	A	S	O	N	D
Max ° C	26	26	25	24	21	19	18	19	21	23	24	25
Min ° C	17	17	16	13	11	8	7	8	9	11	13	15
Rain mm	14	19	22	26	31	30	25	26	21	19	18	18
Raindays	3	4	6	8	10	10	10	10	8	7	6	5

Warnings
Fuel and supplies Those travelling beyond the major highways will need to be well prepared with fuel and water. Within this region there are no roadhouses or serviced towns east of Kalgoorlie, north of the Eyre Hwy.

Road access and closures 4WD vehicles are required north and sometimes south of the Eyre Hwy, and in parts of the Goldfields. All unsealed roads can become impassable after rain. Remote parts of this region are often not covered in road reports by Main Roads WA and Transport SA, but it may still be worthwhile contacting them, particularly in the Goldfields: Main Roads WA,138 138, www.mainroads.wa.gov.au; Transport SA, 1300 361 033, www.transport.sa.gov.au

Remote travel Those venturing into the more remote parts of this region, particularly the northern Nullarbor and the Great Victoria Desert, need to be experienced in outback travel and self-sufficient. It is best to travel in groups and choose travelling times wisely.

Maps Maps in this book are guidelines only. Visitors travelling to remote regions should carry detailed maps and a guide with specific route notes.

See also *On the Road*, p. 246.

The WA Goldfields and the Nullarbor Plain are two vastly different regions – one full to the brim with history, the other a vast natural frontier. Together they offer a huge range of experiences for the traveller; you can be the only person for miles, standing on the edge of some truly fearsome cliffs more than 100 m above the sea, or strolling down the main street of a bustling desert city.

The flat, treeless Nullarbor Plain began its life under water – it is a 250 000 sq km expanse of limestone formed from the skeletons of sea creatures. Sea creatures continue to play a role in the Nullarbor region: southern right whales frequent the coast during winter to mate and calve and can be seen swimming and breaching offshore.

Most travellers head to the Goldfields for a jaunt into the region's rich past and lively present, but leave with an appreciation also of the landscape. In the woodlands salmon gum and gimlet can reach heights of 25 m, an incongruous sight for a part of the world classified as arid.

Kalgoorlie–Boulder is worth a stay of at least several days, and can be used as a base for exploring more far-flung pockets of the Goldfields. It boasts first-class museums and centres that give you an inkling of the bravery, hardship and cameraderie that were present in the early days when Australian, Italian, Cornish and other nationalities were united in their quest for gold. Then, the Goldfields were a world unto themselves, providing for all needs in work, education, news, and even beer.

Goldmining continues in this part of WA, alongside the nickel mines that have existed here since the 1960s.

Above *An arrow-straight stretch of the Trans-Australia Railway trip across the Nullarbor.*

Left *Emus roam the untamed pockets of the WA Goldfields region.*

Goldfields Country

Kalgoorlie–Boulder is at the centre of a region fantastically rich in gold, its lode still far from exhausted. Ghostly old mining sites conjure up life of a century ago – they lie hidden among unexpected thickets of tall trees and shrubs.

Before the 1880s only a handful of Europeans had ventured beyond the agricultural districts around Perth. Inland WA was unknown and unsettling, where the wildlife seemed as strange as the landscape was harsh, and only the best bushmen could find water and food to survive. Out here, Aboriginal tribes were still decades away from having any contact with the new European colony.

It was a wild interior, but spirits were bolstered with the excitement of gold. Gold was found in Southern Cross in 1888, but it was just a whisper of what was to come. A find at Coolgardie in 1892 sparked the greatest rush in Australian history, and the discovery at Kalgoorlie confirmed this as one of the world's great goldfields. Men sprawled out across the ridges like a crazed army, prepared to endure impossible conditions for the slim chance of making a fortune.

Today Kalgoorlie is full of life, and again at its peak with the region's second gold boom. Its prosperity translates to a hearty pride in its pioneering history, its unique architecture and solid, working-class ethic. Old gold towns fan out from here in every direction. Travellers can explore sites that seem little changed since the last miners shut up shop – such as once-thriving Kanowna, now without a building or a soul in sight, and the mining hamlet of Gwalia, whose first mine manager, Herbert Hoover, went on to become president of the USA.

Witness to the heady tales of history is an arid landscape that boasts unusually tall trees – serene salmon gums, gimlets and blackbutts – scattered granite outcrops, and, in true WA style, magnificent wildflowers.

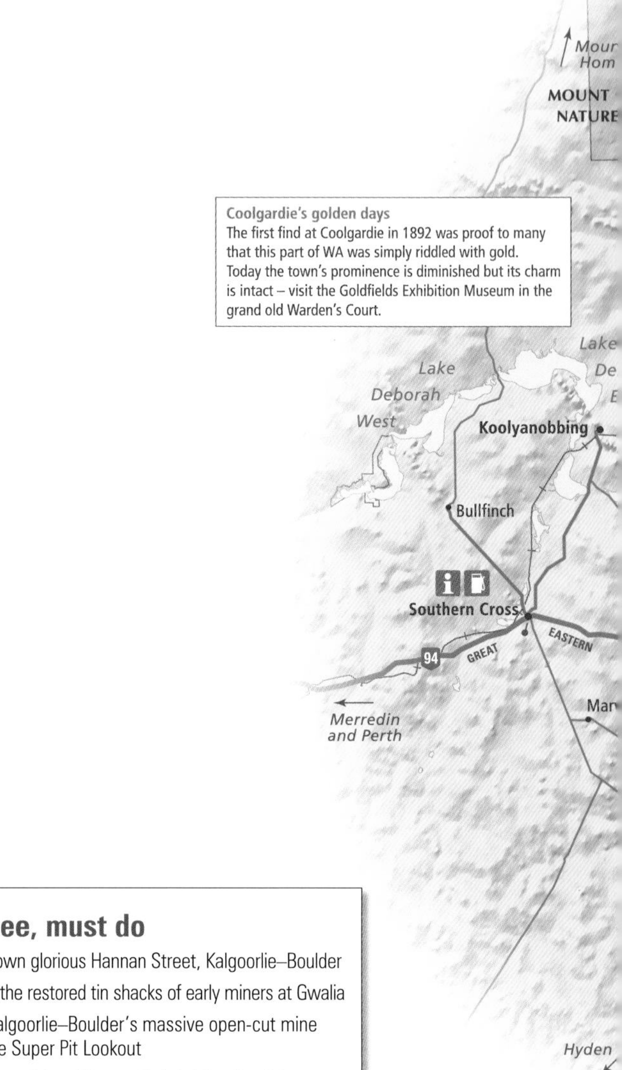

Coolgardie's golden days
The first find at Coolgardie in 1892 was proof to many that this part of WA was simply riddled with gold. Today the town's prominence is diminished but its charm is intact – visit the Goldfields Exhibition Museum in the grand old Warden's Court.

Must see, must do

- Stroll down glorious Hannan Street, Kalgoorlie–Boulder
- Explore the restored tin shacks of early miners at Gwalia
- View Kalgoorlie–Boulder's massive open-cut mine from the Super Pit Lookout
- See the sculptural figures that dot the desolate surface of Lake Ballard
- Camp among the trees at the base of Victoria Rock, south of Coolgardie

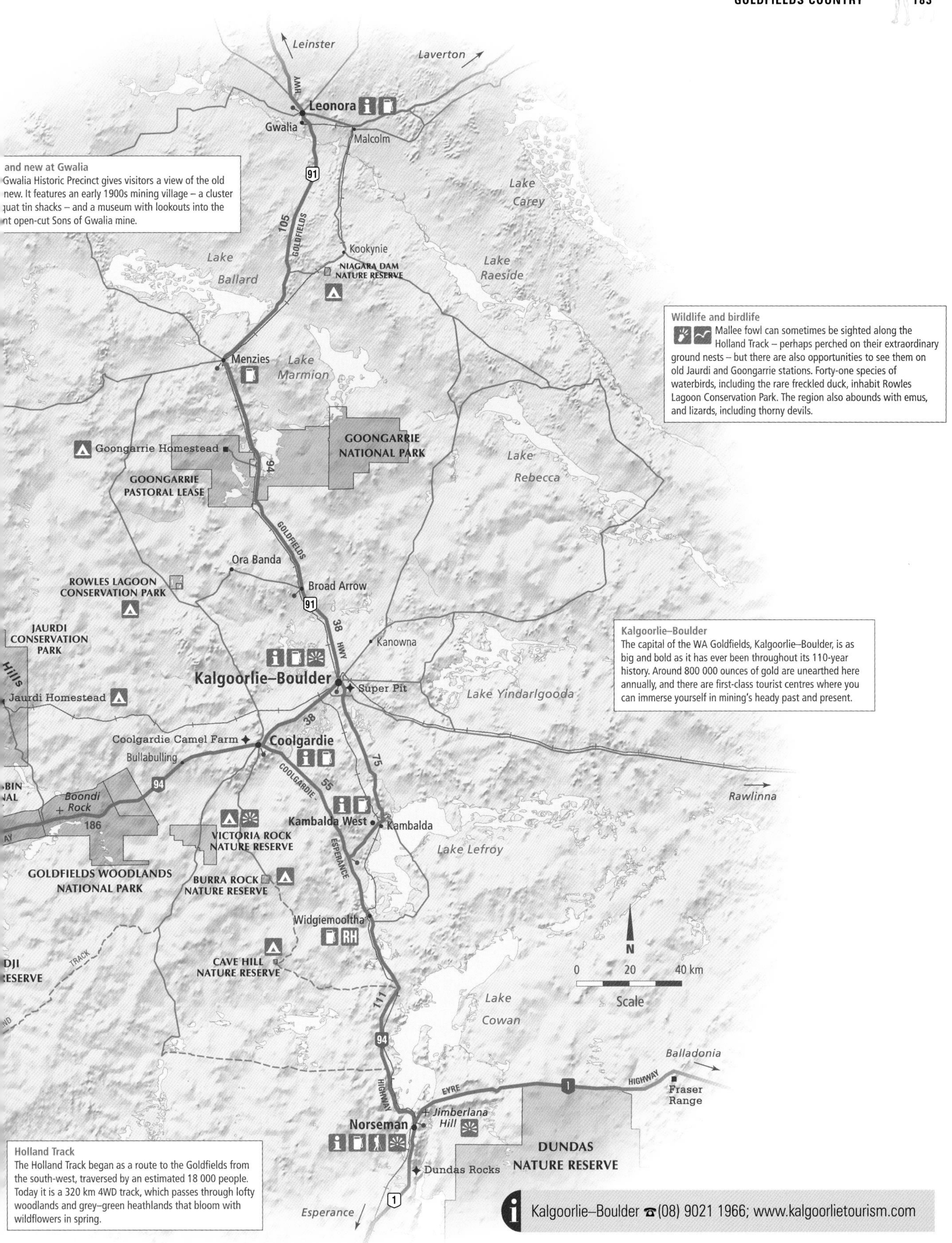

and new at Gwalia

Gwalia Historic Precinct gives visitors a view of the old new. It features an early 1900s mining village – a cluster quat tin shacks – and a museum with lookouts into the nt open-cut Sons of Gwalia mine.

Wildlife and birdlife

Mallee fowl can sometimes be sighted along the Holland Track – perhaps perched on their extraordinary ground nests – but there are also opportunities to see them on old Jaurdi and Goongarrie stations. Forty-one species of waterbirds, including the rare freckled duck, inhabit Rowles Lagoon Conservation Park. The region also abounds with emus, and lizards, including thorny devils.

Kalgoorlie–Boulder

The capital of the WA Goldfields, Kalgoorlie–Boulder, is as big and bold as it has ever been throughout its 110-year history. Around 800 000 ounces of gold are unearthed here annually, and there are first-class tourist centres where you can immerse yourself in mining's heady past and present.

Holland Track

The Holland Track began as a route to the Goldfields from the south-west, traversed by an estimated 18 000 people. Today it is a 320 km 4WD track, which passes through lofty woodlands and grey–green heathlands that bloom with wildflowers in spring.

Kalgoorlie–Boulder ☎ (08) 9021 1966; www.kalgoorlietourism.com

Fact File

Top events

Mar *Norseman Cup*
April *Rhythms in the Outback (music festival, Kalgoorlie–Boulder)*
Kambalda Festival
Aug/Sept *Balzano Barrow Race (Kanowna to Kalgoorlie–Boulder)*
Sept *Kalgoorlie–Boulder Race Round (horseracing)*
Coolgardie Day
Sept/Oct *Western Australian Metal Detecting Championships (Coolgardie)*
Oct *City of Kalgoorlie–Boulder Art Prize*
Leonora Art Prize
Dec *St Barbara's Festival (mining festival, Kalgoorlie–Boulder)*

Parks and reserves

National parks and reserves in WA are administered by the Department of Environment and Conservation (DEC). For general information see *Travel Tips*, p. 180. For general information on parks and reserves in the Goldfields contact DEC Kalgoorlie: (08) 9080 5555. A small newspaper produced by the DEC, *The Goldfields*, gives an overview of the region and has information on camping; it can be picked up at the Kalgoorlie Visitor Centre (see *Contacts*, opposite). Boorabbin and Goongarrie national parks are undeveloped and visitors need to be experienced and self-sufficient if venturing far from the access roads. In other parks and reserves travellers are advised to BYO water. Fires are permitted outside total fire ban days, but BYO wood.

Boorabbin NP No facilities; only access road is the highway; bush camping only.

Goldfields Woodlands NP Camping facilities at Boondi Rock, no booking or payment required; bring drinking water and firewood.

Goongarrie NP No facilities; bush camping only.

Goongarrie, Jaurdi and Mount Elvire homesteads These DEC-managed stations offer basic accommodation and camping; bookings required; ring DEC. Bring drinking water and firewood.

Rowles Lagoon Conservation Park Camping facilities, no booking or payment required; bring drinking water and firewood.

Victoria Rock, Burra Rock and Cave Hill nature reserves Camping facilities, no booking or payment required; bring drinking water and firewood. 4WD access only between Burra Rock and Cave Hill.

Warnings

Fuel and supplies Fuel stops are frequent along the highways, although if venturing into more remote areas, such as the Holland Track between Coolgardie and Hyden (320 km), you may need to carry reserves of fuel. Always carry plenty of water.

Road access and closures All unsealed roads in the region can become impassable after rain. For information on road conditions contact Main Roads WA: 138 138; www.mainroads.wa.gov.au. Some roads, such as the Holland Track, require a 4WD.

See also *On the Road*, p. 246.

The gold booms

Many old names in gold are enjoying a renaissance, such as Davyhurst, Kundana and Kanowna. At these and other locations there are new, mainly open-cut operations, highly mechanised compared with the methods used in the 1890s. These old towns, however, remain defunct, largely because miners can now live in places like Kalgoorlie–Boulder and commute. Although mining has continued sporadically since the early days, the current boom began in the early 1980s after a massive hike in world gold prices.

Kalgoorlie–Boulder

Around 30 000 people live in this city founded on the 'Golden Mile' – two words that have actually delivered on their promise. The approximate square mile of ore holds one of the richest concentrations of gold in the world. Today it is the focus of the 'Super Pit' – an open-cut mine that will eventually reach around 500 m deep, 3.8 km long and 1.35 km wide. In 2003 the Golden Mile-cum-Super Pit mined its 50 millionth ounce, and currently produces around 800 000 ounces a year.

Paddy Hannan, Tom Flanagan and Dan O'Shea found the first Kalgoorlie nuggets in 1893. Over the next few years miners 'specked' most of the alluvial gold, and then mining moved underground. Boulder was originally a satellite town, but today Kalgoorlie and Boulder blur into each other to form a city with two main streets – Hannan and Burt.

Both streets boast magnificent architecture, with stand-out buildings being the two town halls (Boulder Town Hall is home to the elaborate, hand-painted Goatcher Curtain, lowered on a pulle

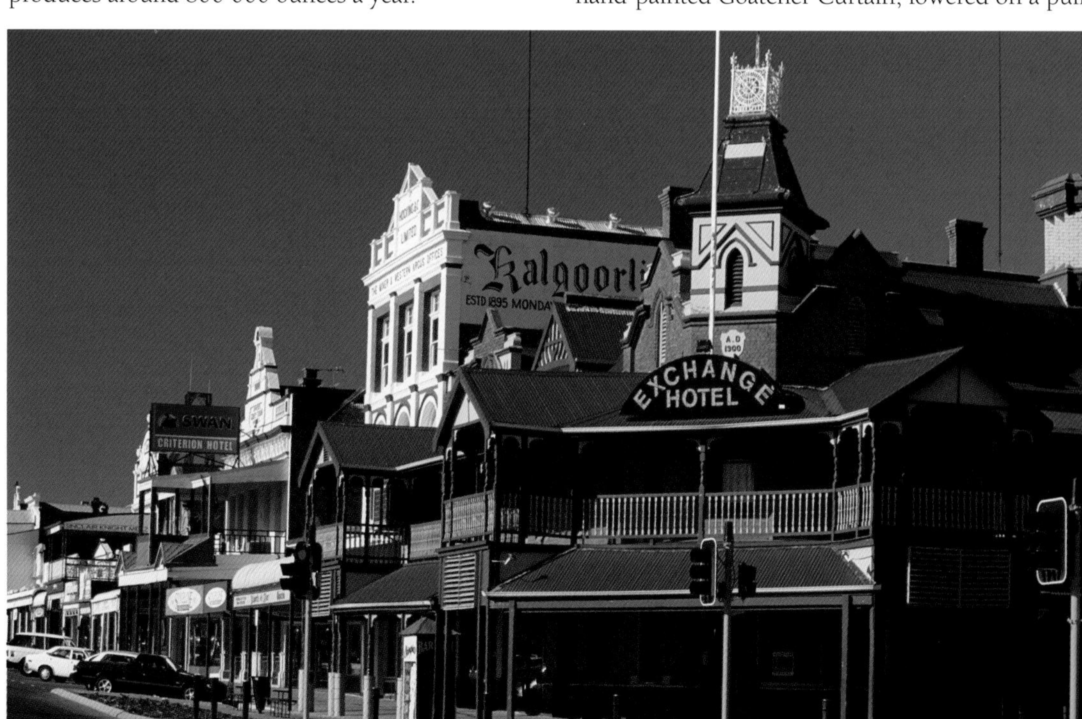

Opposite *A restored miner's cottage in Coolgardie.*

Right *The Exchange Hotel on Hannan Street, Kalgoorlie.*

·ery Tuesday, Wednesday and Thursday) and
annan Street's two flashy, palace-like hotels – the
xchange and the York.

For all its history, Kalgoorlie–Boulder is
so a colourful modern city, even a little unruly.
kimpies' – scantily clad barmaids – serve beer in
me of its livelier hotels, and the 'starting stalls'
ı Hay Street – the rough wooden shacks where
orking women once plied their trade – have
come an attraction.

To the north of town is the Australian
ospectors and Miners Hall of Fame, an impressive
mplex where you can try your hand at gold-
ınning, watch a gold pour and tour the historic
annan's North underground mine. To see real gold
ıggets and delve further into Goldfields history,
sit the Western Australian Museum Kalgoorlie–
oulder in Hannan Street; while to see goldmining
the flesh head to the Super Pit Lookout (east of
e Goldfields Hwy, Boulder), where you can peer
ep into this awesome man-made ravine (you can
so take a scenic flight; see *Contacts*, opposite).

Kalgoorlie Arboretum on Hawkins Street and
arkurla Bushland Park off Riverina Way offer a
ste of the region's indigenous flora, while for art
vers there are a number of galleries featuring
boriginal art. Aboriginal Bush Tours also operates
om town, exploring the region's bush tucker as
ell as sites significant to the Wongutha people (see
ntacts, opposite).

.anowna

hough it no longer has any streets, houses or hotels,
anowna, 18 km north-east of Kalgoorlie–Boulder,
as once one of the Goldfields' biggest towns.
ining centred on ancient alluvial streams, and by
905 there were no fewer than 12 000 people here
ıd an hourly train service from Kalgoorlie. Gold
ver was so heightened that miners had even laid
aim to the cemetery.

Each August/September Kanowna is the starting
oint of the Balzano Barrow Race, which is a throw-
ıck to the early 'barrowmen' – the prospectors
ho could not afford a wagon, horse or camel.
ompetitors race to Kalgoorlie–Boulder wheeling
ırrows loaded with mining tools.

lorth along Goldfields Highway

trail of old gold towns unfurls to the north of
algoorlie–Boulder – many are found along the
oldfields Hwy, or via a short detour. They include

sites with intriguing names like Broad Arrow, Ora Banda and Kookynie (all three of these still have operating hotels), and another still yet to become a ghost – Menzies.

If you tire of ghost towns, there are other gems along this route. From Ora Banda you can head to Rowles Lagoon Conservation Park, where a cluster of four semi-permanent freshwater lakes makes a refreshing sight after so many salt ones. More than 40 waterbird species have been recorded here, and locals come to swim and camp. Another quiet retreat is serene Niagara Dam near Kookynie, a water storage that was in fact never used – an oddity in an area that was always so desperate for water. The dam was completed in 1898 to supply steam trains, but ground water had already been found in the area.

A special site can be found north-west of Menzies at Lake Ballard. Here 51 steel sculptures dot the sparsely covered lake bed, their elongated shapes like an Aboriginal tribe fanning out into the distance.

Contacts

Visitor information

Coolgardie
Goldfields Exhibition Museum
Bayley St
(08) 9026 6090

Kalgoorlie–Boulder
250 Hannan St, Kalgoorlie
(08) 9021 1966
106 Burt St, Boulder
(08) 9093 1083
www.kalgoorlietourism.com

Kambalda
cnr Emu Rocks and
Marianthus rds
Kambalda West
(08) 9027 0192

Leonora
cnr Tower and Trump sts
(08) 9037 7016
www.leonora.wa.gov.au
www.gwalia.org.au

Norseman
Welcome Park, Roberts St
(08) 9039 1071
www.norseman.info/tourism/

Southern Cross
Council offices, Antares St
(08) 9049 1001
www.yilgarn.wa.gov.au

Parks and reserves

See *Fact File*, opposite

Activities

Yamatji Bitja Aboriginal Bush Tours
(08) 9021 5862

Australian Prospectors and Miners Hall of Fame
Goldfields Hwy, Kalgoorlie
(08) 9026 2700
www.mininghall.com

Coolgardie Camel Farm
(08) 9026 6159

Golden Pipeline Heritage Trail
www.goldenpipeline.com.au

Golden Quest Discovery Trail
www.goldenquesttrail.com

Scenic flights
Goldfields Air Services
(08) 9093 2116

Western Australian Museum Kalgoorlie–Boulder
17 Hannan St, Kalgoorlie
(08) 9021 8533
www.museum.wa.gov.au

Station stays

Several old stations are now incorporated in the area's parks and reserves, with their homesteads offering accommodation or a base for camping. DEC harvests sandalwood on old Jaurdi Station, but Jaurdi also protects woodlands, granite outcrops, breakaway country and birdlife, including the mallee fowl; access is from the Great Eastern Hwy between Coolgardie and Southern Cross. Linked with Jaurdi via Mount Manning Nature Reserve is Mount Elvire Station, nestled in a hollow of Lake Barlee (salt); access is from Southern Cross or Menzies. South of Menzies is old Goongarrie Station, with a short circuit walk past an old gnamma hole, sandalwood scrub and mining relics. For information and bookings contact DEC Kalgoorlie (see *Fact File*, p. 184).

Water on the goldfields

Before European settlement, local Aboriginal people were sustained by soaks, called gnamma holes, hidden within the region's many rock formations. The soaks adequately supported a population that was small, nomadic and finely attuned to the environment, but not the rush of hundreds and then thousands of miners that cascaded in after the first discovery at Coolgardie, thinking first of gold and only as an afterthought of survival. The soaks were quickly drained, and Aboriginal people and miners alike faced a decade of severe water shortage and high water costs.

Government Engineer C Y O'Connor's solution to the problem was extremely ambitious – it involved building a weir in the Darling Range outside Perth and piping water to Kalgoorlie, a distance of 557 km – but it worked. Since 1903 this pipeline has supplied water for most urban, agricultural and industrial purposes in the region. Much of the water is stored at Kalgoorlie's Mount Charlotte Reservoir.

If driving to the goldfields from Perth (or vice versa) you could take the Golden Pipeline Heritage Trail through the hills, then the wheat belt, then the semi-arid lands of the Goldfields, a distance of 650 km with plenty of historic sites en route. For information see *Contacts*, p. 185.

These figures were created by British artist Anthony Gormley for the 2003 Perth International Arts Festival, but have remained ever since. The figures were based on body scans of residents from Menzies.

To explore these places and more, you could take all or part of the 965 km Golden Quest Discovery Trail. A comprehensive booklet is available from the Kalgoorlie–Boulder Visitor Centre (see *Contacts*, p. 185).

Gwalia and Leonora

In his search for cheap labour, Gwalia's first mine manager (and later US president) Herbert Hoover employed many newly arrived Italian migrants. The town became the Goldfields' own 'Little Italy', with Italians making up 40 percent o the population in 1936. Instead of damper, beer and cricket, life here featured polenta, grappa and bocce.

Once the second largest gold mine in WA, Gwalia also boasted the state's first tramway (linkec with Leonora); but the death of the mine in 1963 drained the population to almost nothing in the course of a few weeks. Today a handful of shops, homes and shacks have been restored. It is the shacks that hold the most interest, some of them seemingly nothing more than a haphazard stack of tin sheets. In other areas these shacks have been

Looking across the old goldmining town of Gwalia.

regarded as eyesores and demolished, but in Gwalia you can get a glimpse of how miners really lived.

The Gwalia Museum features an old woodline train (see p. 188), an original wooden headframe once used over the top of a mine shaft, and lookouts into the recent open-cut mine.

Leonora, 4 km away, is a town of around 1000 people, and its nickel mining and goldmining operations continue. The town's wide, low-built main street features several historic buildings, including the court house, police station, bank and fire station built in a flurry of civic pride in 1903.

Coolgardie

Coolgardie is now just a sleepy village compared with massive, modern Kalgoorlie–Boulder, but it was the site of the country's greatest gold rush. Arthur Bayley and William Ford's find of 554 ounces (16.6 kg) in 1892 sparked the largest movement of people in Australian history, as if the nation had simply been on hold since the great discoveries at Ballarat and Bendigo in the 1850s, waiting for the next big find.

Within months 'Fly Flat', as it was then known, was a bustling city of tents. By 1898 a city of 15 000 people had come into existence, with 23 hotels, three breweries and six banks.

Many of the miners were ill-prepared for the brutal conditions of the WA goldfields, with blistering summer weather, food and water shortages and disease. Life held its breath each year waiting for the rains, which brought a short-lived abundance of water. To see sepia photographs of this world, visit the Goldfields Exhibition Museum in the old Warden's Court. For a more hands-on experience head to Ben Prior's Open Air Museum, filled with the old wagons, boilers, engines and odds and ends left behind when the smell of gold became stronger somewhere else.

To the west of town, Coolgardie Camel Farm offers short treks and has a small museum dedicated to these gangly beasts, which were used extensively as draft and riding animals in the development of the Goldfields. Bookings are required; see *Contacts*, p. 185.

South of Coolgardie

Two rough bush tracks lead south of Coolgardie – one strikes south-west to Hyden (the historic Holland Track) and the other heads south to Burra Rock and Cave Hill nature reserves through the territory of the old 'woodlines'.

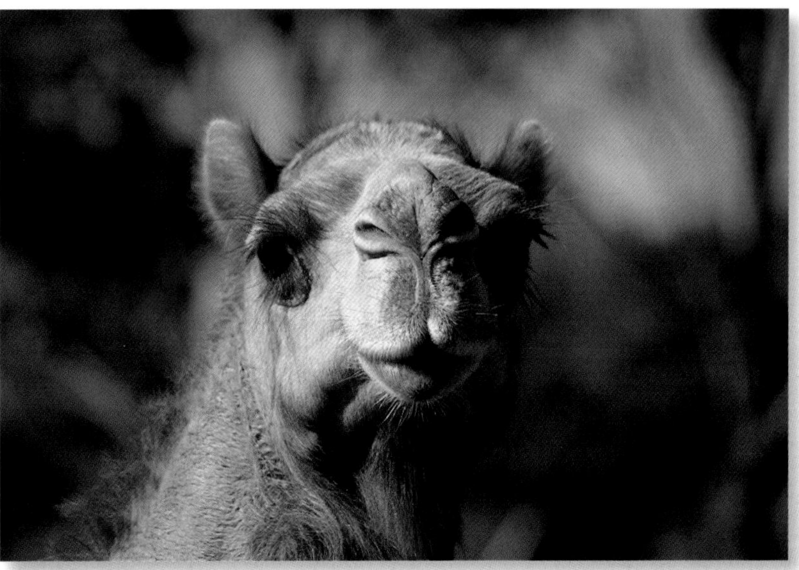

Coolgardie Camel Farm gives a glimpse of the beasts that helped open up the Goldfields.

Holland Track and Victoria Rock

The Holland Track really ends in Broomehill, but most travellers today take it to Hyden. From Coolgardie it meanders through woodlands of salmon gum and gimlet and then across heath-covered sand plains, with very little testament to civilisation in all its 320 km.

It was the work of John Holland, an enterprising farmer and businessman who lived in the Katanning district when the rush to Coolgardie began. At the time there was only one route to the field – from Fremantle through Northam and Southern Cross – and Holland saw the potential for a track from the south-west. In 1893 he and three other men set out to make one, carving the 530 km track in a little over two months.

The track was unused for around 80 years, but was recut for four-wheel drives in 1992.

Coolgardie safe

Coolgardie lends its name to a great Australian invention, the Coolgardie safe. While it is not known exactly who invented it, the food cooler appeared in Coolgardie around the end of the 19th century. It was used across Australia until about the 1950s and had many different permutations – at its roughest, a homemade box on legs with a wooden frame and walls of mesh and hessian. The hessian hung into a tray of water at the top, which kept it wet, and the safe sat outside in the shade to catch a breeze, which evaporated the droplets of water on the hessian and made the air cool inside. Some affluent households had up-market versions made from pressed tin or galvanised iron.

Granite formations are strewn along the route, the biggest of which is Victoria Rock, part of a nature reserve 43 km south of Coolgardie. There are 360 degree views from the summit and a well-equipped campground among the she-oaks at its base. For those travelling only between Coolgardie and Victoria Rock, a conventional vehicle is adequate.

Burra Rock and Cave Hill

A major woodline network came down to Burra Rock and Cave Hill – two prominent granite formations – in the 1920s and 30s. These woodlines were temporary railway lines that began on the edges of towns and eventually spread into the bush. Together, gangs of rail builders and woodcutters harvested and transported the Goldfields' abundant timber that mining and everyday life depended on – to fuel mine boilers and pumping stations, to stabilise underground shafts, and for heating and cooking. By 1965, when the forests were finally left to recover, the woodlines had heaved a total of 30 million tonnes. Even Burra Rock and Cave Hill themselves were drawn in to the woodline operation – both had dams constructed to supply water to the steam trains.

Burra Rock lies 60 km south of Coolgardie and Cave Hill 100 km south. The track between them is 4WD and passes the remnants of old woodcutters' camps. Both reserves offer camping, while Cave Hill, named after the small cave set in its side, is also a popular destination for rock-climbing.

Wood and wildflowers

Sprouting from the red and yellow soils of the southern Goldfields are woodland trees that can reach up to 25 m in height – not much compared with the state's famous karri trees, the 90 m red hardwoods, but staggering considering the region's meagre rainfall of around 300 mm per year. These woodlands are another example of WA's astounding range of flora, all proliferating in poor soils.

Fifty different species of eucalypts can be found in the Kalgoorlie region, with 14 occurring between Coolgardie and Kalgoorlie alone. Beyond Coolgardie towards Southern Cross, are Goldfields Woodlands and Boorabbin national parks. Both are largely undeveloped and set aside to protect a rich flora, including two of the region's best-known species, the delicate salmon gums and red-barked gimlets.

In Boorabbin, the kwongan – an Aboriginal word for the low, heathland vegetation of the state's south-west – meets its westerly limits. Kwongan, which includes many banksias, hakeas and grevilleas, has been compared to tropical rainforests for its species diversity, with no square kilometre quite the same as the next.

Eucalypts merge into mulga around Goongarrie NP (also undeveloped), and the wildflowers change too. While spring in the south and east brings flowers like the orange grevillea, to the north you'll find everlastings, mulla mulla and poached egg daisies, providing there has been decent rain.

Left *Mount Keith nickel mine.*

Opposite top *Woodlands of salmon gum and acacia cloak the low hills around Norseman.*

Opposite below *The golden blooming heath banksia.*

Following page *The Super Pit on the edge of Kalgoorlie–Boulder.*

Southern Cross

outhern Cross is at the crossroads of the wheat elt and the Goldfields, with a history and present ed to both.

It began as the site of the first gold discovery the region, struck in 1888 by Thomas Risely and lick Toomey. The men navigated to the line of hills sing the night sky, and when they struck it rich ey named the goldfields after the Southern Cross onstellation.

For four years Southern Cross boomed, but hen Ford and Bayley rode in with their Coolgardie uggets, the town was soon relegated to a supply op for prospectors heading further east. In the uilding where some of the region's most famous old claims were registered, the Registrar's Office, the Yilgarn History Museum, with memorabilia edicated to both agriculture and gold.

Kambalda

ustralia's first nickel mine began in Kambalda 1966 – it led to a boom that has seen Australia ecome the world's second largest nickel producer, lthough the country's largest operations are now ound at Leinster and Mount Keith, north of eonora.

Kambalda has developed as two separate owns, Kambalda East and Kambalda West, ecause of the rich ore bodies that were found in e middle. At the old goldmining site of Red Hill a trail leads through scrubland up a small hill with views over 510 sq km Lake Lefroy. Sometimes this gleaming salt lake looks to be full of water, although this is usually an illusion. On Sundays local land-yacht enthusiasts often descend on the lake, filling it with their colourful sails.

Norseman

While there have been shaky periods in Norseman's history, this is the only goldfields town, and the only town in the country, that can boast continuous goldmining since it began, in 1894. With little alluvial gold, the find never produced the heady rushes like the discoveries of the north; Norseman simply plodded along, but still produces a respectable 120 000 ounces a year. A century of mining is visible in the towering tailings dump to the east of town.

Nature in the region seems relatively untouched, with gently undulating hills dotted with salmon gums and acacia, and granite outcrops like Dundas Rocks and Jimberlana Hill making fine picnic spots. In town, the Historical Museum and Phoenix Park offer a look at Norseman's mining and pioneer heritage (the quirks of its history include a 'Tin Dog' house, made entirely of bully-beef tins). Beacon Hill Lookout, a short drive north-east, takes in a vista over the town and the surrounding salt lakes, and has a short walking trail through the bush, alive with fairy wrens and honeyeaters.

The Nullarbor

Often thought of as Australia's most monotonous drive, the Nullarbor is in fact a journey worth lingering over, with whale-watching, caves, beaches and cliffs, and landscapes that are almost pure wilderness.

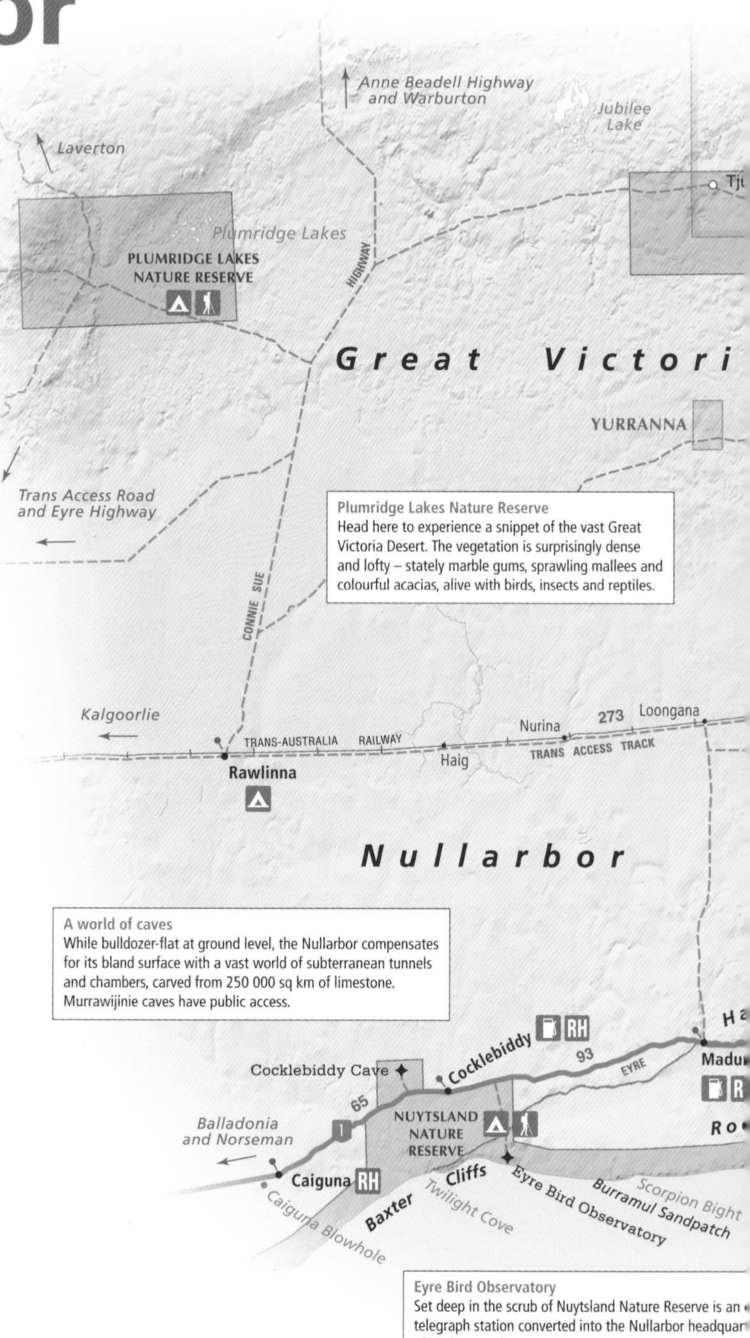

The Nullarbor Plain unravels across the foot of Australia like a giant, speckled carpet, a 250 000 sq km expanse of bluebush that meets the Great Australian Bight in a rough line of cliffs, a tumble of dunes, and more cliffs. Though its size and sameness can be overwhelming, the Nullarbor deserves to be seen as much more than a link between east and west.

This is Australia's largest karst landscape, a vast belt of limestone riddled with caves, tunnels and blowholes. Deep down at the level of the water table are lakes with clear turquoise waters in caves with white limestone ceilings. Fossils of long-extinct animals have been found in these caves, and cave-diving records have been made and broken in one of the longest cave-dive sites on earth, just a few kilometres beyond Cocklebiddy.

In winter a pod of 100 or so southern right whales arrive at Head of Bight to breed and mate, lingering beneath the majestic Bunda Cliffs. Here the one-tonne calves transform into 8-tonne youngsters over the course of a few months, before they begin their journey back to their sub-Antarctic feeding grounds.

Most travellers tackle the Nullarbor on the Eyre Hwy – a smooth, bitumen route, peppered with roadhouses, that measures 1208 km between Ceduna and Norseman. But right at the edge of the highway is the possibility of a 4WD adventure. Tracks head to the lonely, beautiful coast or north to the Trans-Australia railway line and the Great Victoria Desert, gently rustling with mulga, mallee and spinifex.

Must see, must do

- Spot southern right whales at Head of Bight
- Crouch near a blowhole, and witness the earth 'breathe' in and out
- See a piece of a NASA space station at Balladonia Roadhouse
- Walk to the dune-smothered ruins of old Eucla Telegraph Station
- Go birdwatching at the Eyre Bird Observatory

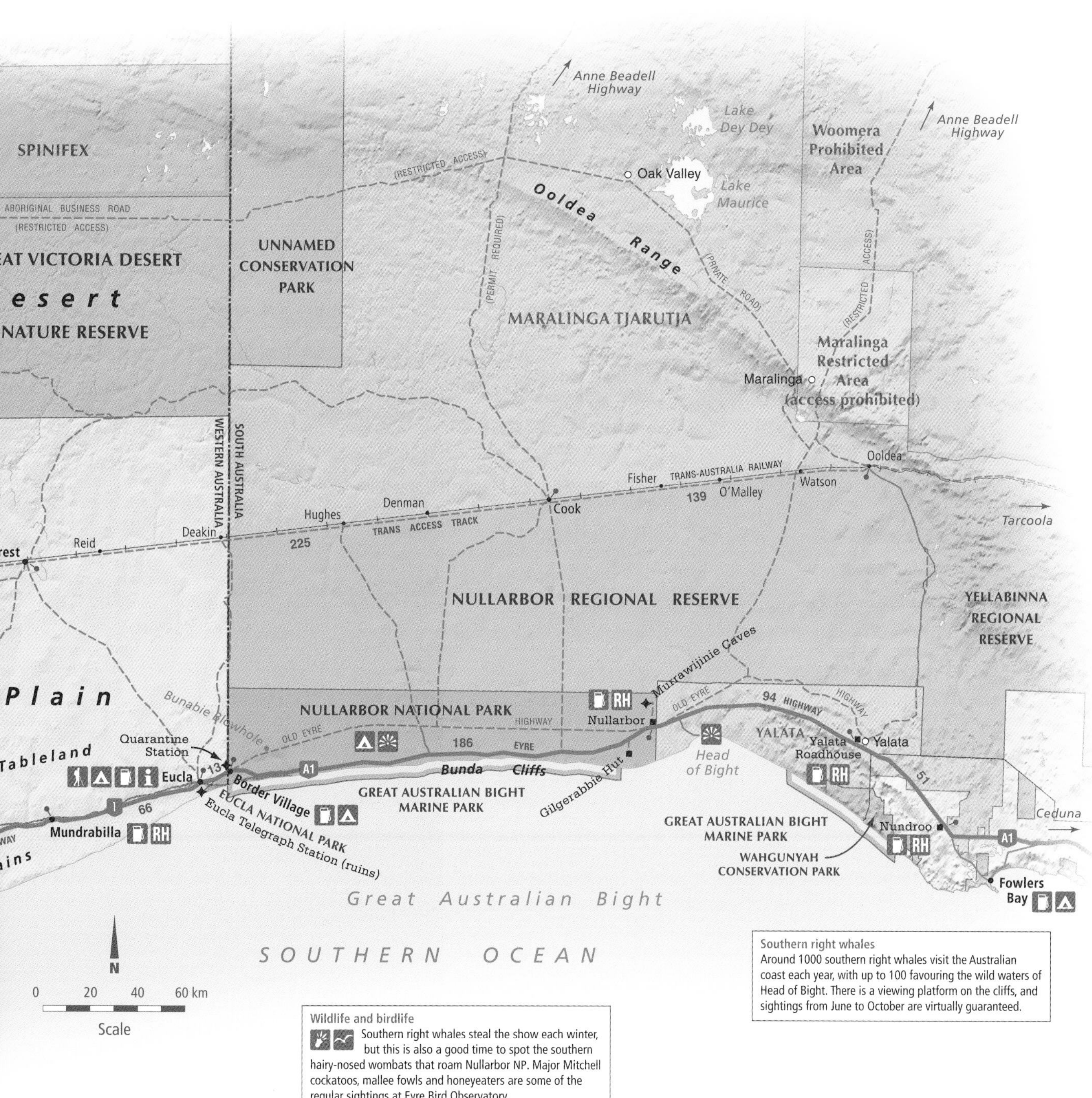

Southern right whales

Around 1000 southern right whales visit the Australian coast each year, with up to 100 favouring the wild waters of Head of Bight. There is a viewing platform on the cliffs, and sightings from June to October are virtually guaranteed.

Wildlife and birdlife

Southern right whales steal the show each winter, but this is also a good time to spot the southern hairy-nosed wombats that roam Nullarbor NP. Major Mitchell cockatoos, mallee fowls and honeyeaters are some of the regular sightings at Eyre Bird Observatory.

The Nullarbor, Eucla Hotel Motel ☎ (08) 9039 3468; www.nullarbornet.com.au

'People of the whale'

The Mirning people once roamed across the coastal margins of the Nullarbor and had a close connection, both real and mythological, with the whales that came to Head of Bight each winter. They believed that in the Dreamtime a white whale came up through a cave and created all the features of the land. When the whales came to the Bight, the Mirning sang to them from the clifftops; the whales often sang back, vocalising with their heads above the water.

Fact File

Top events

April *Nullarbor Muster (gymkhana, Rawlinna)*
Oct *Border Dash (footrace from Eucla to Border Village)*

Permits and regulations

Aboriginal land Head of Bight is located within Yalata Indigenous Protected Area; an entry pass for seeing the whales in season or for visiting the viewing platform in the off-season can be purchased at the visitor centre on site. The Yalata community allows camping at 7 beach sites to the east; camping permits and bookings can be arranged through Yalata Roadhouse; see *Contacts*, opposite. For information see www.yalata.org North of Cook and the Trans-Australia Railway is Maralinga Tjarutja Aboriginal Land. If you intend to travel to the Unnamed Conservation Park and the Anne Beadell Highway you will need a permit. Contact Maralinga Tjarutja Inc. 4–6 weeks in advance: (08) 8625 2946.

For information on Aboriginal lands across the WA border contact the Department of Indigenous Affairs (DIA) Goldfields office: (08) 9021 5666; www.dia.wa.gov.au

Parks and reserves

National Parks and reserves in WA are administered by the Department of Environment and Conservation (DEC). For general information see *Travel Tips*, p. 180.

Eucla NP Camping prohibited (there are several accommodation options in Eucla). For park information contact DEC Esperance: (08) 9083 2100.

Great Victoria Desert Nature Reserve There are no facilities for tourists. The reserve is set aside primarily for nature conservation, and it is easier to visit the Great Victoria Desert on roads such as the Anne Beadell or Connie Sue Hwy. A remote Aboriginal community called Tjuntjuntjarra lies within the reserve. For information contact DEC Kalgoorlie: (08) 9080 5555.

Nullarbor NP Bush camping only, or very basic accommodation in Gilgerabbie Hut (for bookings and information and to pay fees contact NPWSA Ceduna: (08) 8625 3144). Travellers can also camp in roadside parking bays; overnight only; no facilities; free. Fires banned 1 Nov–30 April. In all parts of the park, including Gilgerabbie, visitors need to be entirely self-sufficient with food and water. Take care near cliff edges as they are unstable. Beware of hidden sinkholes. Access to all caves other than Murrawijinie Caves is prohibited. Do not camp in caves.

Nullarbor Regional Reserve Bush camping only; fires banned 1 Nov–30 April. For information contact NPWSA Ceduna: (08) 8625 3144.

Nuytsland Nature Reserve Bush camping at Twilight Cove (4WD required for access); also accommodation at Eyre Bird Observatory (see *Contacts*, opposite). For information contact DEC Esperance: (08) 9083 2100.

Plumridge Lakes Nature Reserve Bush camping only. This reserve is in a remote area and travellers need to be entirely self-sufficient. For information contact DEC Kalgoorlie: (08) 9080 5555.

Unnamed Conservation Park Remote park with bush camping only, within 100 m of public access tracks. Camping permits must be obtained in advance and travellers must fill out a trip intentions form; contact NPWSA Ceduna: (08) 8625 3144. Fires banned 1 Nov–30 April. The two approved access roads to the park pass through Maralinga Tjarutja Aboriginal Land and a permit is required. The route along the Anne Beadell Hwy passes through Woomera Prohibited Area (permit required, contact (08) 8674 3370) and Mabel Creek Station (courtesy call required, contact (08) 8672 5204).

Camping and accommodation

Most roadhouses offer camping and basic accommodation as an alternative to the region's parks and reserves (see above). Ring ahead for information and bookings; see *Contacts*, opposite.

Warnings

Fuel and supplies Travellers on the Eyre Hwy should not rely on roadhouses for water; carry adequate supplies. In the remote regions north of the Eyre Hwy, water is extremely scarce; travellers need to be fully self-sufficient. There is also no fuel available in the northern Nullarbor; travellers planning extended travel in this region must carry reserves. The quarantine station at Border Village prohibits the carrying of fresh fruit and related material east–west. The equivalent SA checkpoint is at Ceduna.

Road access and closures The Eyre Hwy is sealed and well maintained, while almost all roads to the north and south (excluding the road to Head of Bight) are 4WD only. All roads can become impassable after rain. Transport SA does not carry detailed information on road conditions in this area. Main Roads WA has more information: 138 138; www.mainroads.wa.gov.au. Travellers in the northern Nullarbor and the Great Victoria Desert need to be experienced in outback travel, should preferably travel in groups, and should choose travel times wisely.

See also *On the Road*, p. 246.

Opposite *Whale-watching from Head of Bight, on the Nullarbor Plain.*

Below *The Bunda Cliffs meet the Southern Ocean.*

Head of Bight

At Head of Bight, 78 km west of Yalata, travellers from the east get their first real taste of the Nullarbor. Here, a mass of sandhills climbs into the bold Bunda Cliffs. They rise to 80 m, a solid fortress of rock that pushes some 200 km to the WA border.

This is one of Australia's best sites for whale-watching. From June to October up to 100 southern right whales cruise in to the northernmost nook of the Great Australian Bight to give birth and mate, and, it seems, to play up to the crowd of onlookers. A viewing platform can bring visitors as close as 20 m to the action (an entry fee applies, payable at the visitor centre on site). For a different view of the whales and cliffs, Whale Air runs scenic flights in season from Nullarbor Roadhouse (bookings required, see *Contacts*, opposite).

Nullarbor National Park

The Bunda Cliffs form the southern boundary of the 5900 sq km Nullarbor NP. Beyond them any hint of a sea breeze soon runs into the still desert heat of the bluebush plains, a landscape whose supreme lack of features can be unnerving. But for those prepared to settle into the view, these plains boast a few small miracles.

The Nullarbor Plain is composed of thick layers of limestone, the best indication of which are the Bunda Cliffs themselves, with their dull brown upper layers and soft white base. Each layer, stretching north to the beginning of the Great Victoria Desert, represents a period of inundation in times when sea levels were higher. The limestone is formed from the skeletons of marine creatures built up over millions of years.

But limestone can dissolve in water, and in the last 5 million years water has seeped down through the bedrock, hollowing out channels and chambers, some of which reach all the way to the water table, creating underground lakes. It makes the Nullarbor one of the world's largest karst landscapes, and an adventure playground for cavers and cave divers.

The caves within Nullarbor NP include Koonalda Cave, with ancient Aboriginal markings, though Murrawijinie Caves in the east are the only ones accessible to the public. They can be found 10 km north of Nullarbor Roadhouse; cave access is via a clamber down a rocky slope.

The Old Eyre Hwy lies inland from the newer cliff-top route – it is suitable for 4WD vehicles only, but attracts travellers wanting a true taste of the Nullarbor's sparse and lonely extremes. It also leads to Bunabie Blowhole, a smaller version of the one found near Caiguna (see p. 197).

While you're travelling through Nullarbor NP, watch out for southern hairy-nosed wombats – these nuggetty little creatures reside in burrows for most of the day, although they are known to make daylight appearances in winter.

Eucla

Today the township of Eucla is located safely atop the Hampton Tableland, a short distance across the WA border. But in 1877 it began life on the coastal plains to the south as the largest repeater station on the east–west telegraph link. At its centre was a complex of stone buildings where staff relayed a flurry of messages down the line. Messages numbered 24 586 in 1882, and increased with the opening of the WA Goldfields a decade later.

The remains of old Eucla, including the telegraph station, are intermittently covered and uncovered by the advancing Delisser Sandhills. These dunes, protected to the east in the 33 sq km Eucla NP, were overgrazed and set adrift by a rabbit plague in the 1890s. In some places they form

Southern right whales

Once the 'right' whale to hunt because they were slow moving, floated to the surface when killed and yielded plenty of blubber, southern right whales today are a slowly recovering population of up to 7000, around 1000 of which visit Australian shores each year.

The Nullarbor coast is one of their strongholds – it is as they like it, wild and virtually free of development. Female southern rights calve on average once every three years and often do so in the same nursery waters. All southern rights can be identified by their individual pattern of callosities – the white barnacle-like growths around their heads.

Despite its forbidding appearance, the sea beneath the Bunda Cliffs is relatively shallow, which is one of the factors that makes it an ideal calving ground. At some points along the Great Australian Bight the continental shelf only drops away 190 km offshore.

Contacts

Visitor information

Check at roadhouses for information

Roadhouses

Balladonia
(08) 9039 3453

Border Village
(08) 9039 3474

Caiguna
(08) 9039 3459

Cocklebiddy
(08) 9039 3462

Madura
(08) 9039 3464

Mundrabilla
08) 9039 3465

Nullarbor
(08) 8625 6271

Yalata
(08) 8625 6986

Parks and reserves

See *Fact File*, opposite

Activities

Caving information

SA NPWSA Ceduna
(08) 8625 3144

WA DEC Esperance
(08) 9083 2100

Scenic flights

Whale Air
08) 8555 4075
http://warbirdflights.net/whale-air.htm

Other

Eucla Hotel Motel
(08) 9039 3468

Eyre Bird Observatory
(08) 9039 3450

Indian Pacific
13 2147
www.gsr.com.au

Above *Nullarbor NP is a stronghold for southern hairy-nosed wombats.*

Below *The remains of Eucla Telegraph Station.*

smooth hillocks; in others, enormous sweeping ridges and flesh-like flanks.

You can reach the Eucla ruins with a short drive and walk south-west of town. A little further on are the ruins of Eucla Jetty. This was once the principal harbour along the cliff-dominated Nullarbor coast, and today the jetty's weathered grey frame – set off against bright white sand and brilliant aquamarine water, and often topped by a party of cormorants – is a favoured spot for photographers.

To delve into Eucla's telegraph history visit the museum at the Eucla Motel Hotel (see *Contacts*, p. 195).

Cocklebiddy and Nuytsland Nature Reserve

West of Eucla, Mundrabilla and Madura roadhouse are essentially places to refuel and stretch the legs, but Cocklebiddy warrants a little more exploration.

Around 10 km north-west lies Cocklebiddy Cave, which is no longer open to the general publi permits for cave diving associations need to be arranged through DEC Esperance: (08) 9083 2100 Ahead in the darkness, beyond a steep, rough, unmarked scramble, lies a lake – the beginning of an underwater passage that is hallowed ground for cave divers. Currently the cave-diving record at Cocklebiddy stands at 6.25 km, making this one of the longest cave-dive sites on earth.

Along the coast south of Cocklebiddy extends Nuytsland Nature Reserve (6253 sq km), and within the Eyre Bird Observatory. Named after Edward Joh Eyre, who dug for water here on his 1841 expeditio across the Nullarbor and luckily found it, the observatory was created from an abandoned telegrap station in 1977. Set in mallee-covered dunes near th ocean, over 240 bird species have been recorded her with regular sightings of Major Mitchell cockatoos, honeyeaters and, to the north, Naretha bluebonnets a Nullarbor specialty. The observatory is set up for research, but also offers a program of courses for bird enthusiasts as well as basic accommodation (booking required, see *Contacts*, p. 195).

Nullarbor caves

The number of caves and related features found across the Nullarbor is well over 1000. Their depths have yielded the fossilised remains of creatures like the marsupial lion, and rock-art sites up to 20 000 years old, although experts believe there is still plenty more to be discovered. The only caves open to the public are Murrawijinie Caves; access to any others, or to go cave diving, requires a permit or permission and, most often, relevant accreditation. For information see *Contacts*, p. 195.

:aiguna to Balladonia

aiguna and Balladonia are linked by the '90 Mile :raight' – Australia's longest straight stretch of ›ad, and a test of driving endurance that marks the 'estern edge of the Nullarbor.

Out on the straight a short distance beyond aiguna is the Caiguna Blowhole, one of several nall openings in the Nullarbor limestone where ie land appears to breathe in and out according › atmospheric pressure. Crouch near the hole to iscern which way the air is travelling.

Balladonia Roadhouse features a small museum iat covers the Nullarbor's Aboriginal and pastoral istory, and also looks at the region's caves and nattering of meteorites. As well, you can see a ıunk of a NASA space station, which crashed on earby Woorlba Station in 1979 on a return journey om the moon.

Along with Antarctica, the Nullarbor Plain is the te of one of the world's most plentiful collections of ieteorites – not least because the flat and sparsely egetated plains make space debris easy to find. ustralia's largest meteorite, the Mundrabilla Mass, eighing 11.5 tonnes, was found here and many uch smaller tektites have been found. These nall, pebble-like, glassy objects had their origins ; chunks of earth material that were hurled up into rbit by a meteorite impact and fell back to earth nder gravity.

Iorthern Nullarbor

or those without a 4WD, there is only one way to :cess the remote northern Nullarbor – on a train ip from Sydney to Perth (or vice versa) on the *idian Pacific*. This 4352 km journey across Australia .kes three nights and two long, sitting-down days. ıt the desert landscapes it traverses – not least of 'hich are the hundreds of kilometres of Nullarbor .ain – hold a captivating allure.

Between Ooldea in the east and Nurina in the est is a 478 km stretch of railway that does not .clude a single curve. This is the longest straight retch of railway in the world. On the surface it can :em like an engineering fantasy, but in reality it ›mes from the Nullarbor's total lack of obstructions. he Trans-Australia Railway was completed in 1917, ıd its construction was challenged not by hills and ıvines but by the sourcing of building materials, food ıd water, all of which had to be carried in by camel.

The network of roads linking the Eyre Hwy ıd the railway line, once used to access the train sidings, are frequented these days by four-wheel drivers. Today the *Indian Pacific* stops only once on its trip across the Nullarbor, at Cook – a remote ghost town with only a handful of residents. During the short break here, the train changes drivers and takes on water. From Rawlinna (a disused siding that has been partly reinstated with a small lime mine) you can continue north on to the Connie Sue Hwy and Warburton, and from Cook through Maralinga Tjarutja Aboriginal Land to the Unnamed Conservation Park and the Anne Beadell Hwy (permit required, see *Fact File* p. 194). Both routes traverse the Great Victoria Desert, a vast and largely inaccessible tract of sandhills and plains. Plumridge Lakes Nature Reserve offers a taste of this desert.

Western pygmy possums at Plumridge Lakes Nature Reserve.

Plumridge Lakes Nature Reserve

Plumridge Lakes Nature Reserve is for self-sufficient and experienced outback travellers only, but for those with such credentials it offers a rare glimpse of a diverse desert ecosystem.

The Plumridge Lakes lie as saltpans for most of the time, but the surrounding bushland is anything but desolate. Sprouting from the red sand is an understorey of spinifex, bluebush and acacia bushes, and an upper storey of marble gum, black oak and mulga, and mallee and myall trees that burst into red and yellow blooms in spring. The bush quivers with geckos, thorny devils and other lizards, and small mammals – sometimes even a western pygmy possum.

In the south, explore the remnants of an old sandalwood cutters' camp. Various 4WD tracks lead in to the 3090 sq km reserve from the east, south and west. There is bush camping only.

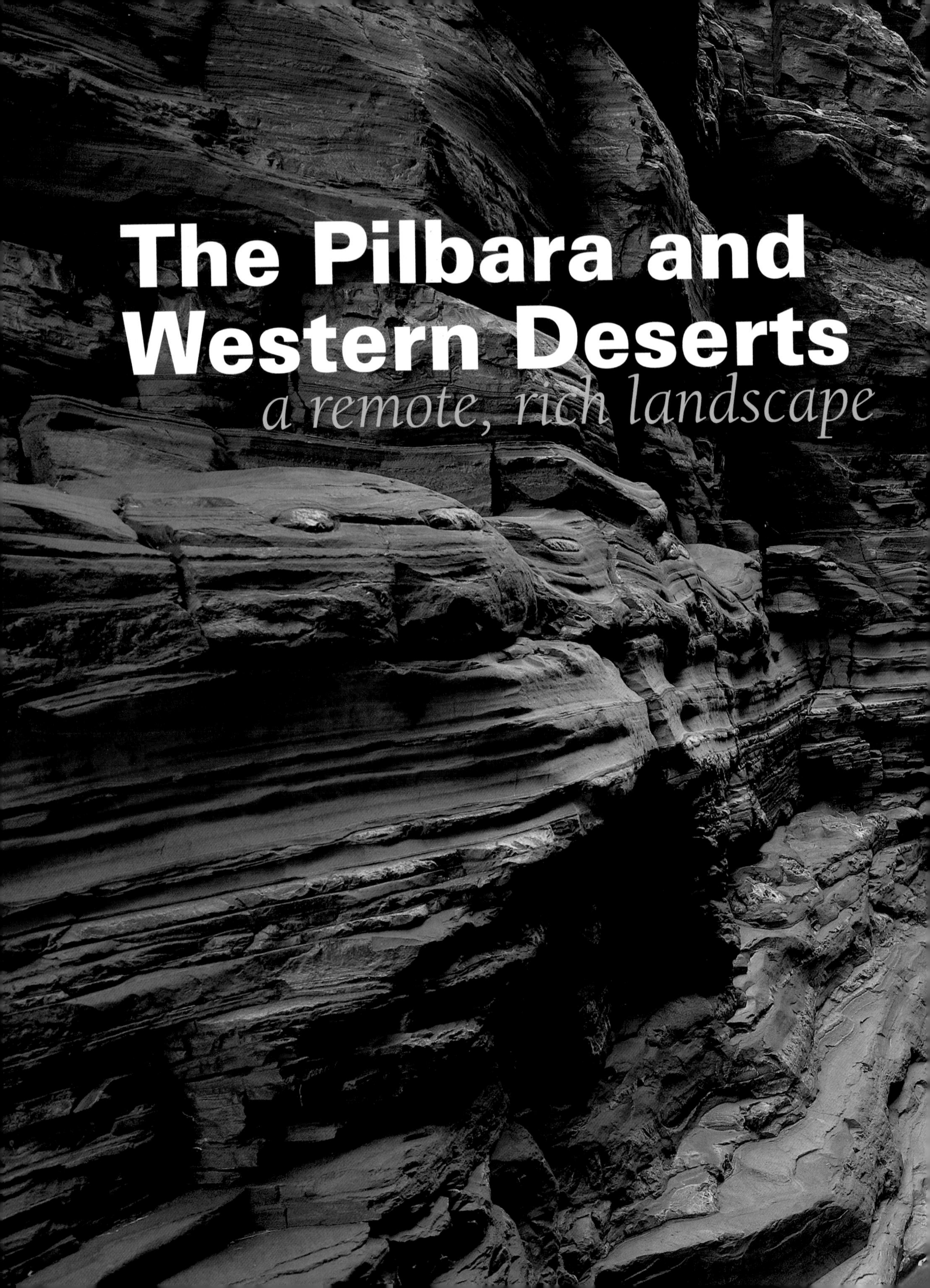

The Pilbara and Western Deserts

a remote, rich landscape

The Pilbara and Western Deserts

Scarcely defined tracks meandering through desert dunes, remarkable coastal scenery, some of the most ancient landforms on earth and industry on an immense scale are features of this vast mid-section of Western Australia.

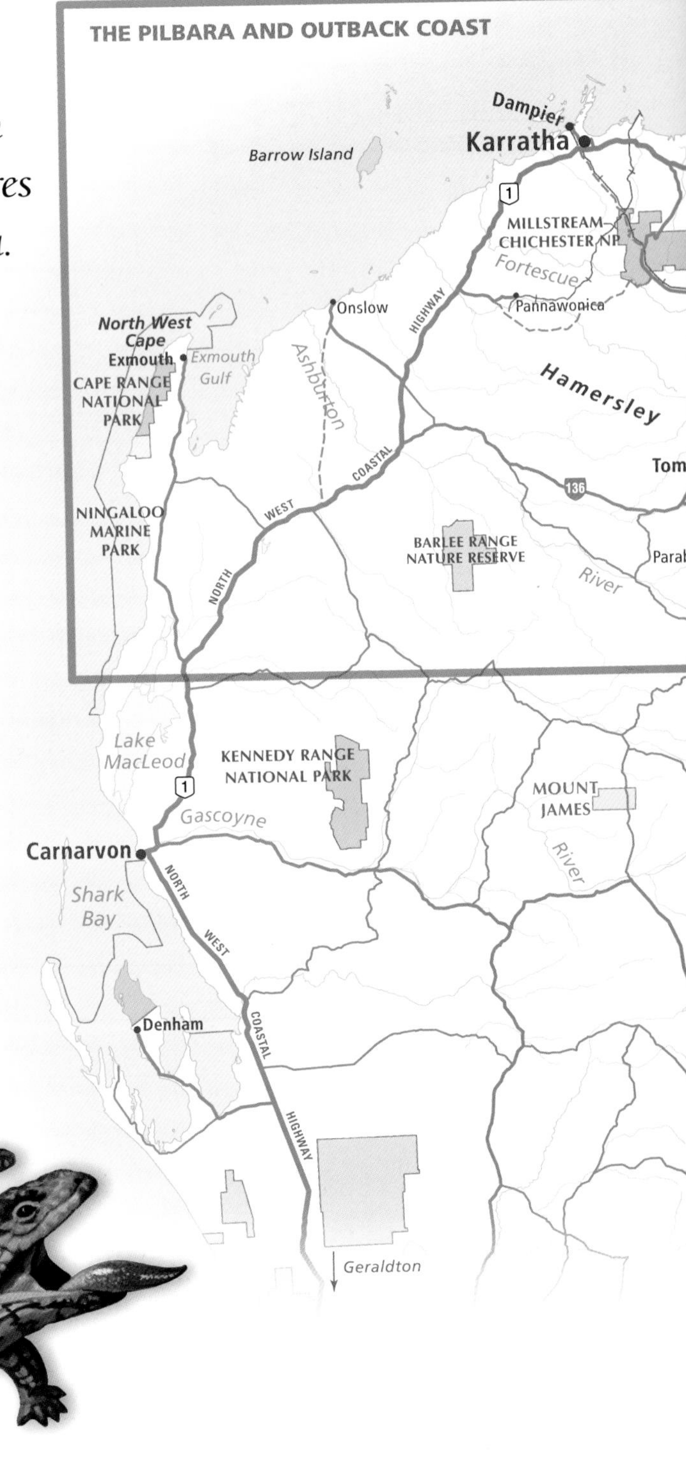

The Pilbara and Western Deserts Regions

The Pilbara and Outback Coast

The Hamersley Range yields not only vast quantities of iron ore, but scenes of enormous beauty. Visit and be amazed by the vastness of the open-cut mines, but leave time to explore the gorges of Karijini NP and the lily-fringed pools of Millstream–Chichester NP. South, the natural wonders of the Coral Coast are too significant to overlook: underground caves, gash-like gorges, cliffs carved of ancient red rock and coral-studded tropical waters mirroring hot, blue desert skies. *See p. 204*

The Western Deserts

The Canning Stock Route and the Gunbarrel Hwy, the work of two of Australia's best-known surveyors, forge routes across Australia's most hostile and least populated area. The usual mainstays of outback travel – roadhouses, stations, Aboriginal communities – are few and far between amid the unceasing roll of the desert plains. Travellers are on their own in terms of facilities and supplies, but freed from the trappings of modern culture, they can enjoy the mythic beauty and immense grandeur of the landscape, a sense of adventure and the roadside camaraderie that is often part of such a journey. *See p. 214*

Blue-tongued lizard

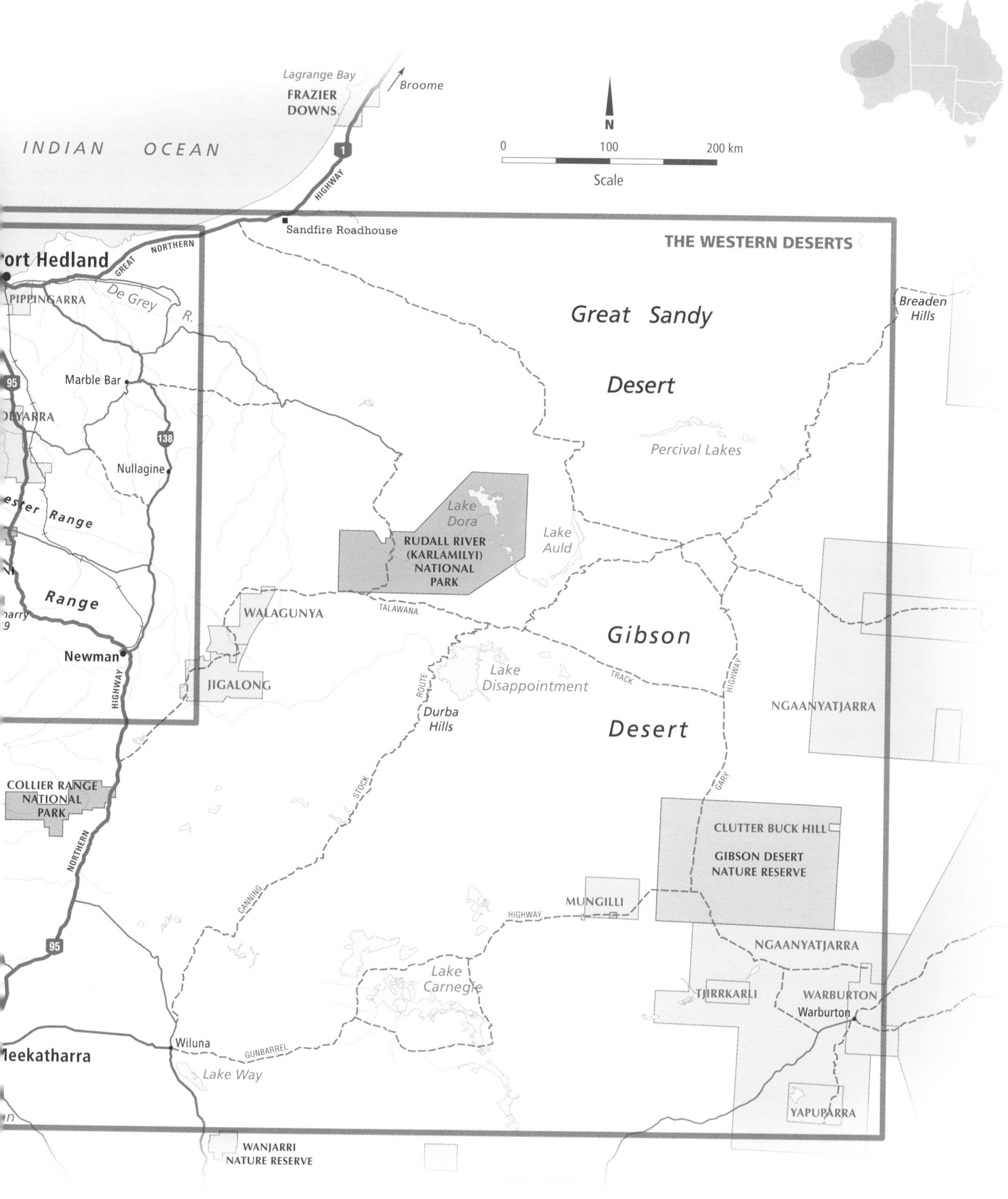

Lagrange Bay
FRAZIER DOWNS
Broome
INDIAN OCEAN
N
0
100
200 km
Scale
HIGHWAY
Sandfire Roadhouse
THE WESTERN DESERTS
ort Hedland
GREAT NORTHERN
PIPPINGARRA
De Grey R.
Great Sandy Desert
Breaden Hills
Marble Bar
95
138
Nullagine
Percival Lakes
Lake Dora
Lake Auld
RUDALL RIVER (KARLAMILYI) NATIONAL PARK
Range
Range
WALAGUNYA
TALAWANA
Gibson Desert
Newman
HIGHWAY
JIGALONG
ROUTE
Lake Disappointment
TRACK
HIGHWAY
Durba Hills
NGAANYATJARRA
COLLIER RANGE NATIONAL PARK
STOCK
GARY
CLUTTER BUCK HILL
GIBSON DESERT NATURE RESERVE
NORTHERN
CANNING
MUNGILLI
HIGHWAY
95
NGAANYATJARRA
Lake Carnegie
TJIRRKARLI
WARBURTON
Warburton
Wiluna
GUNBARREL
eekatharra
Lake Way
YAPUPARRA
WANJARRI NATURE RESERVE

Pilbara ☎(08) 9175 2888; www.australiasnorthwest.com

Travel Tips

When to go

Winter is the high season; spring and autumn are less busy; summer is too hot for comfortable, safe travel in these remote regions. Daily average temperature maximums sit in the 30s in Jan and Feb, and can go much higher. The desert nights can be very cool, even freezing.

Aboriginal land

Aboriginal land areas and communities are found in most parts of remote WA. At present, no specific entry permits are required for the towns, places and routes mentioned in the following regions, but land claims can change requirements, so it is best to check. If you want to visit a community or area not mentioned here, find out about permits by contacting the WA Department of Indigenous Affairs: (08) 9235 8000; www.dia.wa.gov.au Travel on public roads across Aboriginal land is permitted but drivers should not deviate more than 50 m from the main road. Some Aboriginal communities sell fuel and other supplies – permits are not usually required. Phone ahead to check opening times (contact numbers in *Fact File* of each region where applicable). Aboriginal rock art is one of Australia's greatest cultural legacies. Do not touch or disturb sites in any way. Some communities are 'dry', which means that the possession or consumption of alcohol is illegal.

Parks and reserves

National parks and reserves in WA are administered by the Department of Environment and Conservation (DEC). Day pass fees apply to all national parks mentioned in the following sections, except Rudall River (Karlamilyi) NP. Fees can be paid at park visitor centres, at DEC offices in regional centres or at self-registration points. Open fires are not permitted in many parks; use a fuel stove. Carry your own drinking water. Most parks do not accept bookings for campsites; however, this may change so contact individual parks before travelling, particularly in the high season. For general information contact DEC in Perth: (08) 9334 0333; www.dec.wa.gov.au See also contact details for individual parks in the *Fact File* for each region.

Fishing

A recreational licence is required in WA and bag, size and possession limits apply. For further information contact WA Dept of Fisheries: (08) 9949 2755 (Exmouth); www.fish.wa.gov.au

CLIMATE — ROEBOURNE

	J	F	M	A	M	J	J	A	S	O	N	D
Max °C	39	38	38	35	30	27	27	29	32	35	38	39
Min °C	26	26	25	22	18	15	14	15	17	20	23	25
Rain mm	59	67	63	30	29	30	14	5	1	1	1	10
Raindays	3	5	3	1	3	3	2	1	0	0	0	1

CLIMATE — WILUNA

	J	F	M	A	M	J	J	A	S	O	N	D
Max ° C	38	37	34	29	24	20	20	22	26	20	34	37
Min ° C	23	22	20	15	10	7	5	7	10	14	18	21
Rain mm	35	38	36	29	26	25	15	10	4	7	10	20
Raindays	4	4	5	4	4	5	4	3	2	2	3	3

Warnings

Fuel and supplies These areas are remote and long distances separate fuel stops and supplies. Drivers should be well equipped and self-sufficient.

Road access and closures Some roads described in the following regions are 4WD only. Of these, many are not maintained. In these instances, travellers will need a large, high-clearance 4WD vehicle. Watch out for road trains, heavy transport vehicles and, in the Pilbara, rail crossings. Wet weather can close roads; check road conditions before travelling. For further information contact Main Roads WA: 138 138; www.mainroads.wa.gov.au

Remote travel Those venturing away from major centres in this region should consider carrying an emergency communications device (see *On the Road*, p. 246).

Maps Maps in this book are included as a guide only. Visitors travelling to remote regions should carry detailed maps and a guide with specific route notes.

See also *On the Road*, p. 246.

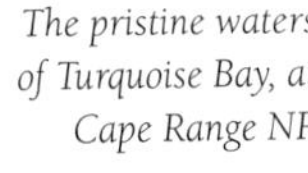

The pristine waters of Turquoise Bay, at Cape Range NP.

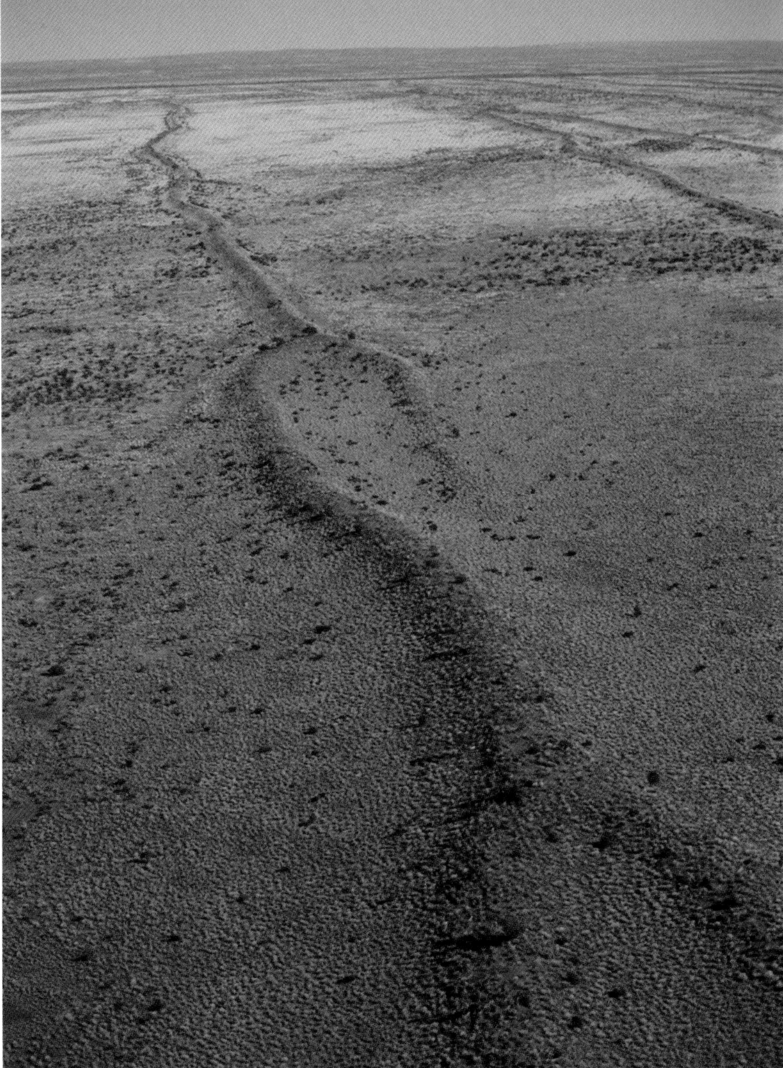

The Pilbara, the wide strip of land that occupies the central third of WA, rolls out from the coast to meet the deserts at the rid heart of the continent. The entire region is a lace of extremes. The temperatures are hotter, the andforms older, the populations smaller, the mines igger, the distances greater and the facilities fewer han in any other place in Australia.

The continent here is made up of sediments hat date back 2.5 billion years and reach 2.5 m below the earth's surface. A profound sense f antiquity registers in every weathered rise and attened plain.

The first inhabitants moved about this country autiously, never overestimating its capacity to rovide. Their exclusive tenure may have lasted 0 000 years. Tribal life continued on longer here han in any other part of Australia, with the people f these deserts the last to make contact with settlers. ven today, the region's scattered communities keep ncient traditions alive.

White settlement has been slow. The first uropean explorers, Francis Gregory and Ernest iles, passed through in the 1860s and 70s, but vere unimpressed by the savage complexion of the andscape. It is telling that the pioneer heroes are ot explorers but surveyors, such as Alfred Canning nd Len Beadell, whose names are immortalised in emote outback routes. They came not to settle the and but to find ways of passing through it.

The fate of the Pilbara in the north has been letermined by the store of iron ore embedded in the ed ochre-hued bulk of the Hamersley Range. With nodern mining technology able to tap the reserves f this isolated region, the Pilbara is now a source f prosperity for the entire country. Since the 1960s, owns have sprung from the red soil, equipped with ools, parks and golf courses, to service massive pen-cut mines.

The entire landscape, although parched and oughened, takes in places of astonishing beauty nd natural wonder. The desert scenery varies onstantly and with exquisite effect: dunes bristle vith spinifex, vast salt lakes radiate with the hot lesert light and rough-hewn cliffs erupt from the latness. Water appears in the most unexpected laces: at the base of the yawning, soundless gorges f Karijini NP; in the sometimes well-vegetated, asis-like springs that line the Canning Stock oute; and in the deep, cold pools of Rudall River Karlamilyi) NP. On the coast, the red-hued shapes of the outback meet the wide, blue stretch of the Indian Ocean, creating contrasts of a sharp and incomparable brilliance.

Although small parts of this region are well serviced with good roads and sizeable towns, nothing can be taken for granted. Travellers are advised to prepare well, ideally travel in the cooler months, be self-sufficient, and always seek local advice on road and weather conditions, which can change suddenly.

Above *The weathered dunes of the Great Sandy Desert, dotted with stunted trees and spinifex.*

Left *One of the Pilbara's many reptiles, a military dragon standing on the Pilbara's red ochre-coloured sand.*

The Pilbara and Outback Coast

The rugged, sun-scorched land that unfurls across Western Australia's most westerly region is home to both giant industrial enterprise and some of the most precious natural environments on the continent.

Around 1300 km north of Perth the ancient, mineral-rich landscape of the Pilbara begins. The centrepiece, scenically and economically, is the red ochre-hued Hamersley Range, which rises 1200 m and stretches over 300 km on an east-south-east course from the coastline south of Karratha. Since the 1960s, iron-ore mining has been carried out here on a massive scale. The sheer magnitude of the operation amazes visitors, and often disturbs those who like their outback relatively unscarred. That said, the various towns, mines, plants, ports and railway lines are mere dots compared with the vastness of the surrounding landscape. Those lucky enough to visit the region's protected areas (Millstream–Chichester and Karijini national parks) will find human endeavour absent or, at the very most, limited to environmentally friendly pursuits such as walking, camping, birdwatching and canoeing.

The outback coast, from the Pilbara south to Coral Bay, takes in industrial centres, historic towns, isolated beaches and the world's longest fringing reef. While the spirit of the outback prevails – the area is isolated, ancient and dusted with the deep, brilliant reds that so characterise the WA interior – it is coastal scenery that dominates. The Indian Ocean, a clear and radiant blue, reaches towards the low, westerly horizon. The beaches are clean, white and often deserted.

Good roads and well-provisioned towns service the area, however, visitors should be aware of the long distances that separate some supply stops.

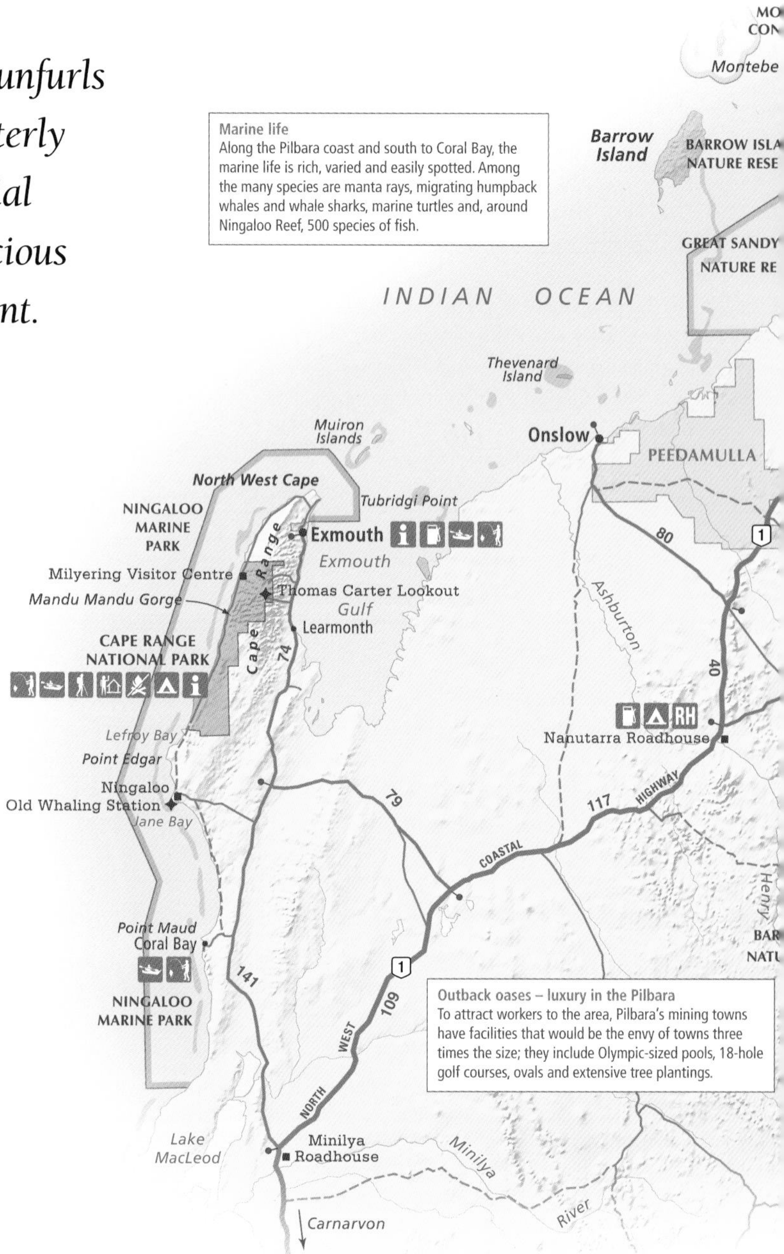

Marine life
Along the Pilbara coast and south to Coral Bay, the marine life is rich, varied and easily spotted. Among the many species are manta rays, migrating humpback whales and whale sharks, marine turtles and, around Ningaloo Reef, 500 species of fish.

Outback oases – luxury in the Pilbara
To attract workers to the area, Pilbara's mining towns have facilities that would be the envy of towns three times the size; they include Olympic-sized pools, 18-hole golf courses, ovals and extensive tree plantings.

Must see, must do

- Visit iron ore mines at Tom Price and Newman
- Swim in the natural pools of Millstream–Chichester NP
- Visit the historic town of Cossack
- Dive or snorkel on Ningaloo Reef
- Walk the gorges of Karijini NP

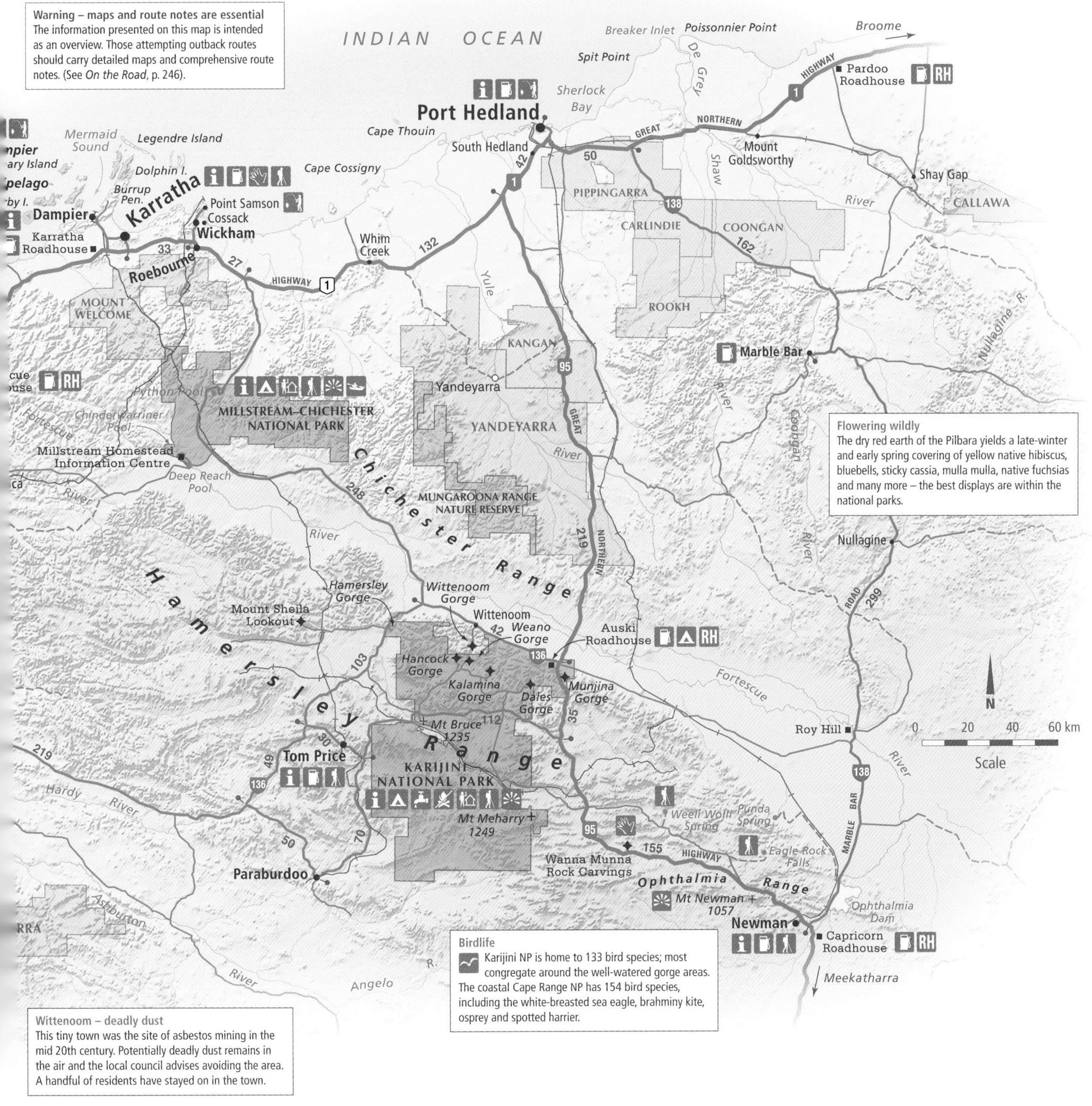

Warning – maps and route notes are essential
The information presented on this map is intended as an overview. Those attempting outback routes should carry detailed maps and comprehensive route notes. (See *On the Road*, p. 246).

Flowering wildly
The dry red earth of the Pilbara yields a late-winter and early spring covering of yellow native hibiscus, bluebells, sticky cassia, mulla mulla, native fuchsias and many more – the best displays are within the national parks.

Birdlife
Karijini NP is home to 133 bird species; most congregate around the well-watered gorge areas. The coastal Cape Range NP has 154 bird species, including the white-breasted sea eagle, brahminy kite, osprey and spotted harrier.

Wittenoom – deadly dust
This tiny town was the site of asbestos mining in the mid 20th century. Potentially deadly dust remains in the air and the local council advises avoiding the area. A handful of residents have stayed on in the town.

Exmouth ☎(08) 9949 1176; www.exmouthwa.com.au
Karratha ☎(08) 9144 4600; www.pilbaracoast.com

Fact File

Top events

Mar *Whale Shark Festival (Exmouth)*
May *Welcome to Hedland Night (Port Hedland)*
June *Black Rock Stakes (wheelbarrow race, Karratha)*
July *Game Fishing Classic (Port Hedland)*
Aug *FeNaCLNG Festival (community festival, Karratha)*
Campdraft and Rodeo (Newman)
Sept *Cultural Festival (Roebourne)*
Pilbara Music Festival (Port Hedland)
Oct *Garnex (gamefishing competition, Exmouth)*
Octoberfest (Newman)

Permits and regulations

Aboriginal land There are pockets of Aboriginal land in this region; do not deviate more than 50 m from the public road if crossing Aboriginal land. Numerous Aboriginal rock-art sites, particularly on the Burrup Peninsula, can be seen – do not disturb in any way.

Parks and reserves

National parks and reserves in WA are administered by the Department of Environment and Conservation (DEC). For general information see *Travel Tips*, p. 202.

Cape Range NP There are numerous campsites in the park; some allow for caravans. At the time of writing, no bookings are required, however, check well ahead of travelling; contact the DEC office in Exmouth on (08) 9947 8000 or Milyering Visitor Centre on (08) 9949 2808. Bring your own drinking water and fuel stove; fires are not permitted. Access roads are unsealed but suitable for 2WD vehicles.

Dampier Archipelago Beach camping is permitted (5-day maximum stay); bring your own water and fuel stove; fires are not permitted. Contact the DEC office in Karratha: (08) 9143 1488.

Karijini NP Check with the visitor information centre regarding the location of campsites: (08) 9189 8121. There is drinking water at the visitor centre, but not elsewhere. Bring your own water and fuel stove; fires are not permitted. Some trails are suitable for experienced walkers only. Most areas are suitable for 2WD vehicles.

Millstream–Chichester NP There are three camping areas; all are suitable for caravans. Bring your own water and fuel stove; fires are permitted only at Snake Creek; BYO wood. For further information contact the visitor centre: (08) 9184 5144; or the DEC office in Karratha: (08) 9143 1488.

Ningaloo Marine Park There are zones specifying permitted activities (such as types of fishing). For information contact the DEC office in Exmouth: (08) 9947 8000.

Fishing

For general information on fishing in this region see *Travel Tips*, p. 202. See also individual park entries.

Warnings

Fuel and supplies In some parts of this region, long distances – up to 200 km – separate fuel stops. Plan your trip accordingly.

Road access and closures Most major roads in this region are sealed and well maintained. Any unsealed roads are generally suitable for conventional vehicles, particularly within national parks. In the Pilbara area, watch out for road trains and heavy transport vehicles (see *On the Road*, p. 246). To check road conditions contact local visitor information centres (see *Contacts*, opposite), or Main Roads WA: 138 138, South Hedland (Port Hedland): (08) 9172 8877, or Carnarvon: (08) 9941 0777.

See also *On the Road*, p. 246.

Opposite *The grand old courthouse at Cossack.*

The Pilbara

Pastoralists settled the Pilbara in the 1860s and prospectors followed in the 1880s, lured by a rich but short-lived gold boom. But it is iron ore that has had the most profound effect on the shape and prosperity of this semi-arid region of red hills and vast plains.

Below *Docking at Port Hedland, one of the busiest industrial ports in the country.*

Geologists guessed at the extent of the region's iron ore deposits as early as the 1930s, but an export embargo imposed in 1938 saw the hills of Hamersley Range slumber undisturbed for another 30 years. The government lifted the embargo in 1960. Major discoveries in the late 1950s and early 1960s opened the way for the establishment of large-scale operations. Since then, Hamersley Iron (a subsidiary of Rio Tinto) and Newman Mining Company (principally owned by BHP Billiton) have operated the region's vast open-cut mines, employing thousands of workers and producing millions of tonnes of product each year.

Coastal Towns

The Pilbara's coastal towns exist primarily as ports and service centres for the mining industry, though other industries – such as salt-harvesting and production of natural gas and other hydrocarbons – have mushroomed in recent times.

The two major ports, separated by around 250 km, are Port Hedland and Dampier, with populations of 15 000 and 2000 respectively. In terms of tonnage shipped, these are two of Australia's biggest ports. Tours of the shipping operations run daily in the visitor season (winter) – check with the relevant

Contacts

Visitor information

Exmouth
Murat Rd
(08) 9949 1176
www.exmouthwa.com.au

Karratha
Karratha Rd
(08) 9144 4600

Newman
cnr Fortescue Ave
and Newman Dr
(08) 9175 2888
www.newman-wa.org

Port Hedland
13 Wedge St
(08) 9173 1711

Tom Price
Central Rd
(08) 9188 1112
www.tompricewa.com.au

Parks and reserves

See *Fact File*, opposite

Mine tours

For information about mine tours ask at the visitor information centres.

sitor information centre. There are also tours of ort Hedland's massive iron ore processing plant, here crushed ore is delivered from the Whaleback ine in Newman aboard 2.6 km long trains.

Both towns are major industrial salt producers, ith Australia's largest evaporative salt fields at ampier (tours are available). Another major local usiness is the North West Shelf Venture, Australia's rgest producer of hydrocarbons, which includes atural gas, liquefied natural gas and petroleum gas, nd crude oil. Operations are scattered throughout e region – there are offshore platforms, and a rocessing plant on the Burrup Peninsula, not far om Dampier (again, tours are available).

Despite the preponderance of industry, the clear fshore waters of these port towns offer excellent shing including barracuda, mackerel and trevally, ith charters available. Dampier boasts some eautiful beaches and is something of a mecca for oaters (the town is said to have more boats per ead than any other Australian town). For those eking nature in its uncompromised state, the lands of Dampier Archipelago lie just 20 minutes way by boat (see *Dampier Archipelago*, p. 208).

The modern town of Karratha (population 1 000), 20 km from Dampier, is the main service entre of the Pilbara. It is a prosperous place with enty of facilities. For visitors, an introduction to the area's Indigenous heritage is the Jaburara Heritage Trail, a three-hour walk featuring Aboriginal rock carvings, a sample of the estimated 10 000 etchings dispersed across the Burrup Peninsula. These carvings, ranging from small engravings of emu tracks to detailed representations of ceremonies, etch the history of Aboriginal occupation over 30 000 years.

After the industry and modernity of the other Pilbara towns, Cossack and Roebourne, north of Karratha, are refreshingly well-worn and rustic in character. Both were established in the 1860s, Cossack as a pearling port and Roebourne as a centre for the fledgling pastoral industry. They share a legacy of handsome stone buildings, built to survive tropical cyclones. Cossack is officially a ghost town – it was abandoned in the 1950s after its harbour silted up – but it manages a steady trade in sightseers and backpackers (a hostel is housed in the old police station). Nearby lie the pretty fishing and swimming beaches of Port Samson. Fishing, sightseeing cruises and swimming are popular in the area.

Millstream–Chichester National Park

This park, approximately 150 km south of Roebourne, occupies the traditional lands of the Yinjibarndi Aboriginal people. Pastoralists arrived in 1865, establishing a large sheep station; the 1919

The vast mining operation of BHP Billiton's Whaleback Mine at Newman.

homestead now serves as the visitor centre for the 2000 sq km park. One of the park's highlights is the mirage-like Chinderwarriner Pool, a body of clear, spring-fed water spread with a blanket of cream-coloured lilies, fringed by a tassel of palms. The pool is located in the south-east, with campsites at Deep Reach Pool and Crossing Pool, nearby. A series of walks lead along the winding banks of the Fortescue River. Swimming and canoeing in the permanent pools are popular.

In the north of the park, the arid-tropical landscape is dominated by the weathered swell of Chichester Range, its slopes bristling with hummocks of spinifex and stands of snappy gums. Visitors camp at Snake Creek, and walk to Python Pool, a permanent, freshwater plunge pool at the base of a cliff in the Chichester Range escarpment. In late winter and early spring a rich tapestry of wildflowers bloom.

Euros and red kangaroos can be spotted, native mice and rats scurry through the dry groundcover, black flying foxes hang in the trees by daylight, and the watercourses and pools attract plentiful birdlife.

Marble Bar

Marble Bar, just over 200 km south-east of Port Hedland, has the dubious honour of being the hottest town in Australia. For 161 days in 1923–24 the temperature stayed above 37.8 degrees Celsius (100 degrees Fahrenheit). The average daily maximum in the summer months sits at 41 degrees Celsius. The town is named after the rich band of jasper – originally believed to be marble – that can be seen in the usually dry Coongan River.

Dampier Archipelago

The 42 islands of the Dampier Archipelago lie just 20 minutes by boat from the port of Dampier. Often craggy and steep-sided, the islands are rimmed by pristine beaches and washed by the Indian Ocean. The archipelago is a haven for wildlife: marine turtles nest in the dunes; dolphins, dugongs and whales cruise the waters; and numerous bird species plait the vivid blue skies. The fishing is legendary (check with locals regarding protected marine zones) and snorkelling, diving and sightseeing tours are popular. Camping is permitted, with a maximum stay of five nights (see *Fact File*, p. 206).

Mining Towns

From the air, the towns of the Pilbara are tiny crosshatched patches of green in the midst of dusty desert plains. The towns have been built from scratch, starting in the 1960s, to house the miners extracting iron ore from the Hamersley Range.

Tom Price sprang into being in the mid-1960s. It is a neat, orderly place, with tree-lined streets. Many visitors use the town as a base to explore the nearby Karijini NP (see below). For a bird's-eye view of the town, mine and surrounding vastness, take a 4WD or walk to Mount Nameless Lookout (1128 m). For an up-close view of the mine, join one of the Hamersley Iron mine site tours – the size, scale and detail of the operation are staggering.

Even more impressive in terms of sheer size is BHP Billiton's Whaleback Mine at Newman, which produces 30 million tonnes of iron ore every year (again, tours are available). The town, with a population of around 3500, is another neat, well-resourced settlement, its arid complexion softened by the 60 000 trees and shrubs planted since the 1970s. Take in the scenery from atop Mt Newman (1057 m), visit the Mining and Pastoral Museum

:lisplays charting the town's short history, or take enic tour on the flying mail run. North of the n is a series of natural pools and Aboriginal :-art sites (see *Newman waterholes*, p. 210).

rijini National Park

ıjini NP – the entrance lies about 50 km west om Price – protects a 6274 sq km slice of the nersley Range, and is the traditional land of the yjima, Kurrama and Innawonga people. In this : of the range, russet-red folds of rock enclose p, gash-like gorges, multicoloured, terraced s and hidden pools and waterfalls, while on plains a brilliant carpet of wildflowers appears ıte winter. Descending to the floor of one of park's gorges is a journey to the beginning of 'ogical time (see *Ancient times, rich iron*, p. 211). s is one of the oldest places on earth, and a sense ıonumental antiquity pervades every aspect of landscape.

Karijini's major drawcard is the network of oreathtaking gorges in the north of the park. king tracks allow visitors to explore many of these areas, however, in some instances the experience is more akin to rockclimbing than it is to walking. Take a 100 m stroll to Oxers Lookout, where there are views of the junction of four gorges. A three-hour walk into Joffre Gorge reveals Karijini's sheltered underworld, a place where native figs cling to the rock walls and butcherbirds and corellas flock to investigate the water supply. Allow two hours to

Above *Emus are just one of 90 bird species at Karijini NP.*

Below *The still waters of Dales Gorge in Karijini NP.*

walk to Circular Pool, which protects a miniature wetland of native conifers, rock figs, kurrajongs, maidenhair ferns and a variety of mosses, sedges and aquatic plants.

The plains are more subtle in their attractions but well worth exploring, their rippled surface a patchwork of acacias, bloodwoods and hardy shrubs. Overall, Karijini is home to 480 plant species. The animal world is represented by 90 species of bird, 90 reptile and amphibian species and 30 mammal species, including red kangaroos and euros.

The park's visitor centre is an attraction in its own right. The award-winning building represents a goanna – an important symbol to the Banyjima people. Within are displays charting the area's natural and Indigenous history. The park has a number of campgrounds and limited facilities; visitors need to be well equipped and self-sufficient (see *Fact File*, p. 206).

Newman waterholes

Between 50 and 100 km north and north-west of Newman, a series of beautiful natural pools, surrounded by gorges, waterfalls and shady river gums, create idyllic settings for bushwalking, swimming and birdwatching. They include Weeli Wolli (with a waterhole and walking track); Eagle Rock Falls (where falls plummet over the ragged gorge walls into a waterhole) and Wanna Munna (Aboriginal art and waterhole). This area is accessible by 4WD only; there are tours from Newman.

The Outback Coast

The Pilbara coastline extends south to Onslow. Further south again lies what is commonly called the Outback or Coral Coast, a narrow ribbon of land where the ancient landforms and vivid red earth of the WA interior meet the electric-blue waters of the Indian Ocean. Exquisite natural features abound – underwater reefs, prolific sea life, wildflowers, rugged gorges and cliffs – providing the perfect antidote to the industrial character of much of the Pilbara.

The clear waters along the coast near Ningaloo Reef.

Exmouth

Some visitors to the area base themselves in this largish centre, which perches on the north-eastern side of North West Cape. It has a population of around 2500 and good facilities for tourists. The town's proximity to the continental shelf, with its abundance of fish, makes Exmouth an ideal choice for anglers. Scenic flights, diving tours and wildlife-watching are all on offer. Those wanting to enjoy the coast's more simple pleasures often choose to stay further south at the tiny town of Coral Bay.

Cape Range National Park

Cape Range NP lies 39 km south of Exmouth and stretches 50 km along North West Cape. The spectacular scenery derives much of its drama from the contrast between the rugged landforms of the cape and the serene, white-sand beaches that rim the coast. The park occupies 505 sq km, spreading out along a rugged limestone range, the highest point of which is 314 m. Heavily incised gorges follow the course of ancient riverbeds. Beneath the range spreads a limestone karst, an intricate system of caves, ranging from tiny air pockets to tunnels several kilometres long. This hidden world is populated by a range of cave-dwelling creatures – many of them species unchanged since ancient times – including invertebrates such as aquatic stygofauna, millipedes, molluscs and spiders.

Milyering, the park's visitor centre, offers an excellent introduction to the region. There are a number of campsites and marked walking trails. The park also provides access to the incomparable Ningaloo Reef (see below). The reddened rock and deep blue waters of Yardie Creek Gorge, where a 2 km return trail follows the course of the creek, is a favourite walk; go in the early morning to watch for black-footed wallabies, listed as a vulnerable species, and for some of the park's 154 bird species. During the winter tourist season boat tours cruise the gorge. At Mandu Mandu Gorge, a 3 km, two-hour return walk leads along the ridge of the rusty-coloured gorge, before snaking down to its base. At Mangrove Bay, a bird hide overlooks a shallow lagoon; visitors can sit in shaded comfort and identify the seabirds and waders that wander past.

Ningaloo Reef

Ningaloo Reef is the longest fringing coral reef in Australia – it extends for 260 km – and is the only

reef in the world found so close to a continental landmass – some coral outcrops lie within 20 m of the shore.

Most visitors reach the reef via the town of Coral Bay (population around 120) south of Cape Range NP. Here visitors can literally step off the beach and swim to reach some wonderful snorkelling spots. A controversial and ultimately failed bid to build a large resort near Coral Bay has led to a boom in tourism in recent times. Book accommodation early to avoid disappointment.

There are numerous ways to explore the wonders of the reef – swim, kayak, dive, or take scenic cruises and flights. The turquoise waters are richly stocked with all manner of marine species: majestic manta rays, migrating humpback whales each autumn, marine turtles and about 500 species of fish, including brightly coloured reef species. The major drawcard, though, is the whale shark, the world's biggest fish. These creatures can reach 18 m in length, but most are between 4 and 7 m. They congregate off the coast from April to June. Diving alongside whale sharks is considered one of Australia's top wildlife experiences, and visitors come from across the country and around the world for the privilege.

The region is well known for its fishing opportunities, both onshore and off. However, visitors should be aware that areas of the reef are off-limits to anglers, and that restrictions will increase in coming years. Check with the local authorities before heading out (see *Fact File*, p. 206).

Above *Yardie Creek, which flows through Cape Range NP, is known for its deep blue waters and red limestone walls.*

Following page *The remarkable red and timeless folds of the Pilbara's Hamersley Range.*

Ancient times, rich iron

Hamersley Range contains some of the world's oldest exposed rock and richest iron ore deposits. The process started 2.5 billion years ago. Rock began forming as sediment on the floor of a vast ocean. The sediments were infused with soluble iron salts, the result of weathering and volcanic activity. Meanwhile, one of the world's first organisms, microscopic cyanobacteria, had formed. The organism perfected photosynthesis and flourished. The process of photosynthesis produced vast amounts of oxygen, resulting in a drop in levels of carbon dioxide (up until this point, the atmosphere, unlike today, contained far less oxygen and much more carbon dioxide). This atmospheric change aided the formation of rich bands of iron in the bedded sediments. Vertical and lateral compression caused the rock to buckle and crack, and then lift and fold; eventually these movements pushed the rock above the surface. Over aeons, weathering and the flow of water sculpted the rock to its present form. The sediments that form the Hamersley Range are estimated to be 2.5 km thick.

The Western Deserts

Roughly defined tracks lead to the largely uninhabited desert heart of Western Australia, an unforgiving land scarcely altered since white settlement.

This desert heartland is an arid place of extreme isolation and harshness. Settlement is confined to one or two towns, small Aboriginal communities and pastoral properties, separated by immense tracts of unsettled territory. Access is via a network of historic outback tracks. The most famous, the Canning Stock Route, snaking through the arid landscape for 1700 km, remains the longest stock route in the world. Travellers need to be extremely well prepared, not only for the brutal nature of the 'roads', but also for the scarcity of facilities, including fuel and other supplies.

For those who plan fully, the rewards are outstanding. Many are surprised at the exquisite and subtle variations of the desert landscape, of the slow unrolling of mulga scrub, spinifex plains, salt flats and drifts of sand dunes. Rock-art sites recall the long tenure of the Western Desert people, the original inhabitants who survived this harsh environment by adapting over thousands of generations. As well, relics of various 19th and 20th century exploration and construction expeditions are scattered across the landscape, their decrepitude a symbol of the area's resistance to settlement.

But it is the experiences that can't be quantified that continue to lure travellers to these challenging environs. For some it is the prospect of waking to a ruby-hued dawn, when the air is still cool and the desert animals are active, or going to sleep beneath a mantle of stars undimmed by city lights. Others take pleasure in testing their mettle as explorers and adventurers on rugged outback roads. Many love the isolation and the long, deep silences of the desert plains, where the noise of modern life gives way to the rustle of spinifex and the creak of the occasional desert oak. Still others enjoy the opportunity to share a campfire with like-minded strangers.

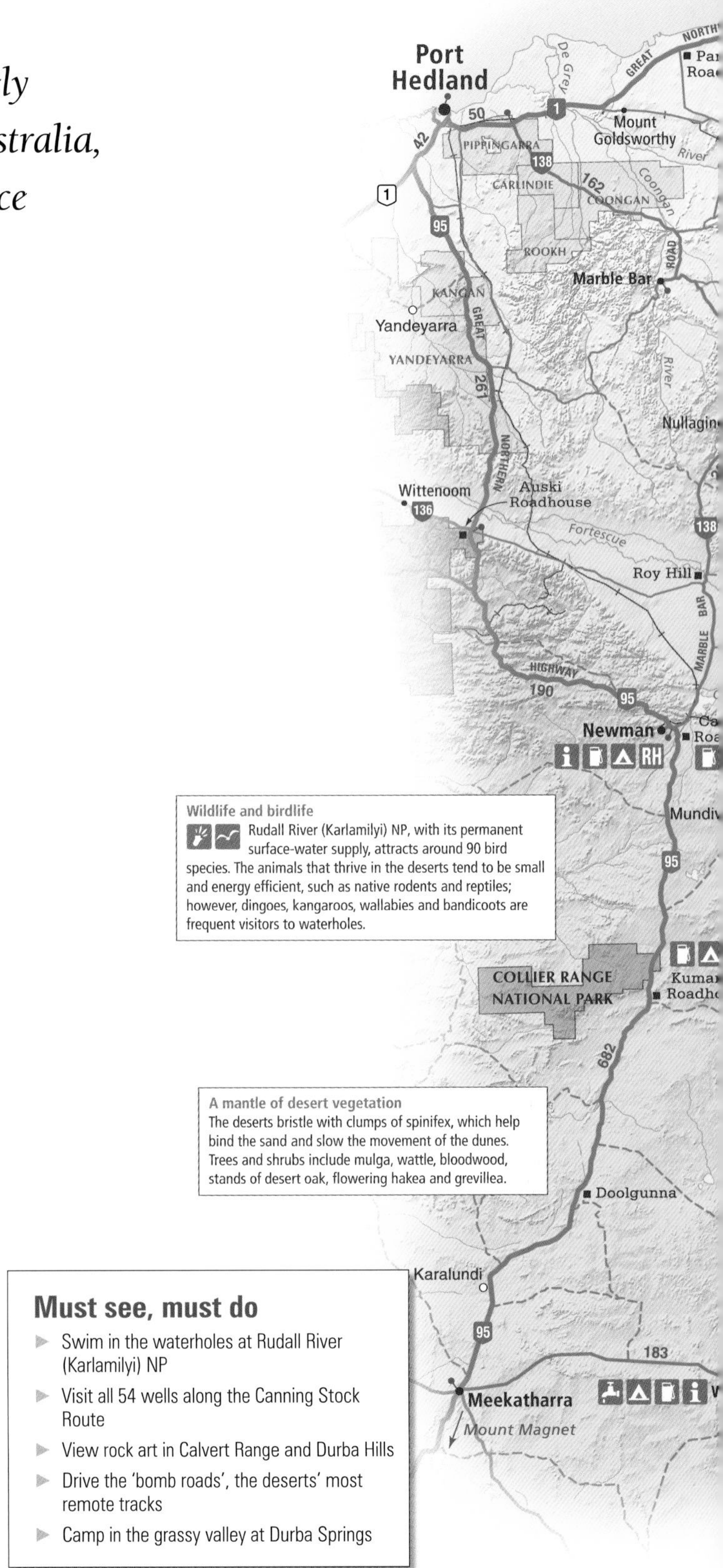

Wildlife and birdlife

Rudall River (Karlamilyi) NP, with its permanent surface-water supply, attracts around 90 bird species. The animals that thrive in the deserts tend to be small and energy efficient, such as native rodents and reptiles; however, dingoes, kangaroos, wallabies and bandicoots are frequent visitors to waterholes.

A mantle of desert vegetation

The deserts bristle with clumps of spinifex, which help bind the sand and slow the movement of the dunes. Trees and shrubs include mulga, wattle, bloodwood, stands of desert oak, flowering hakea and grevillea.

Must see, must do

- Swim in the waterholes at Rudall River (Karlamilyi) NP
- Visit all 54 wells along the Canning Stock Route
- View rock art in Calvert Range and Durba Hills
- Drive the 'bomb roads', the deserts' most remote tracks
- Camp in the grassy valley at Durba Springs

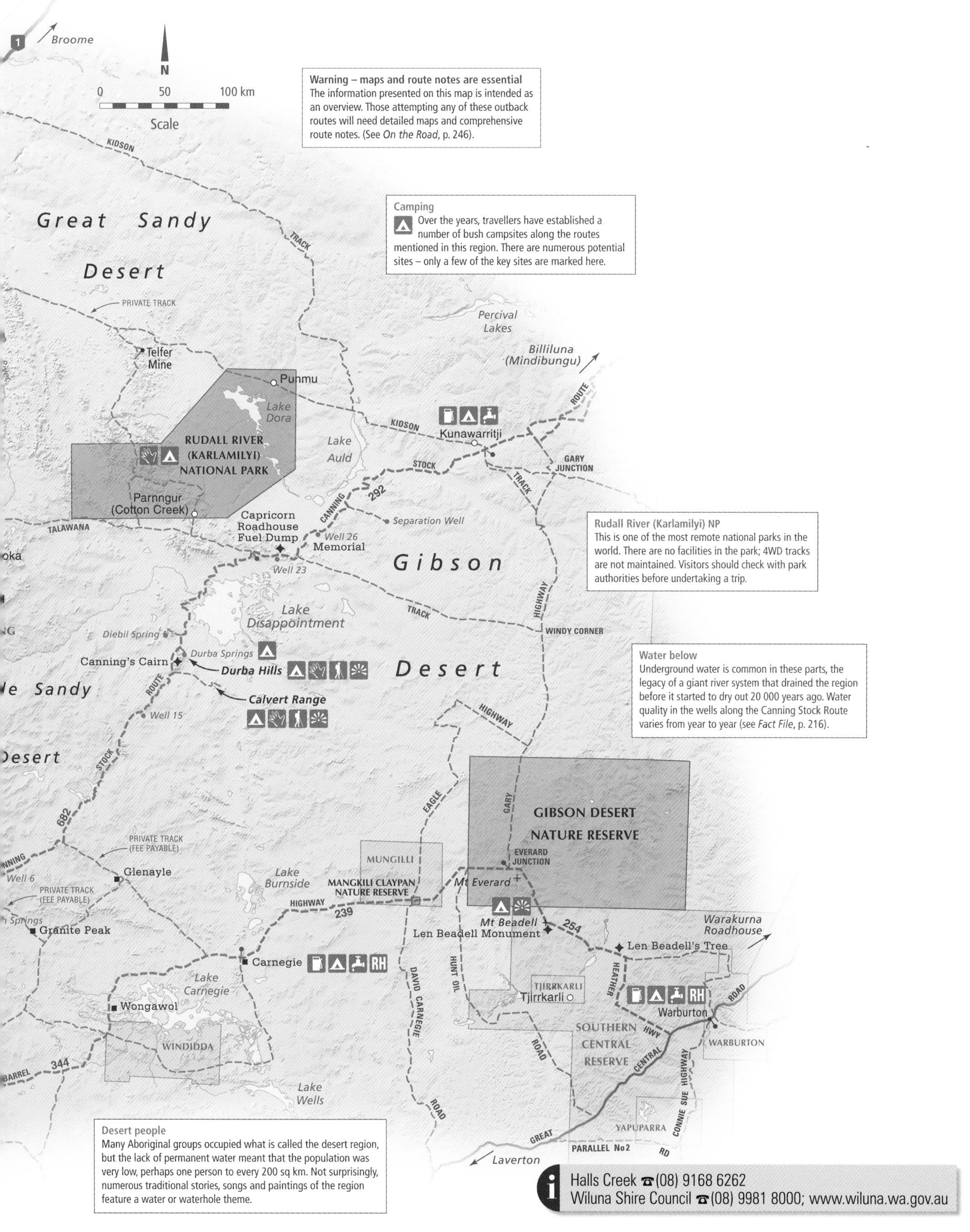

Warning – maps and route notes are essential
The information presented on this map is intended as an overview. Those attempting any of these outback routes will need detailed maps and comprehensive route notes. (See *On the Road*, p. 246).

Camping
Over the years, travellers have established a number of bush campsites along the routes mentioned in this region. There are numerous potential sites – only a few of the key sites are marked here.

Rudall River (Karlamilyi) NP
This is one of the most remote national parks in the world. There are no facilities in the park; 4WD tracks are not maintained. Visitors should check with park authorities before undertaking a trip.

Water below
Underground water is common in these parts, the legacy of a giant river system that drained the region before it started to dry out 20 000 years ago. Water quality in the wells along the Canning Stock Route varies from year to year (see *Fact File*, p. 216).

Desert people
Many Aboriginal groups occupied what is called the desert region, but the lack of permanent water meant that the population was very low, perhaps one person to every 200 sq km. Not surprisingly, numerous traditional stories, songs and paintings of the region feature a water or waterhole theme.

Halls Creek ☎(08) 9168 6262
Wiluna Shire Council ☎(08) 9981 8000; www.wiluna.wa.gov.au

Fact File

Permits and regulations

Aboriginal land Public roads traverse many areas of Aboriginal land. Generally, no special conditions apply, although visitors will need a transit permit to travel the Great Central Road, incorporating parts of the original Gunbarrel Hwy, which links Yulara in the NT and Warburton in WA. For the NT section of the trip contact the Central Land Council: (08) 8951 6320; for the WA section contact Department of Indigenous Affairs: (08) 9235 8000. Travellers following the route described in the following pages will not need permits. Fuel and supplies are available from Aboriginal communities along the Canning Stock Route (CSR) and Gunbarrel Hwy (see below). Two Aboriginal communities are located within Rudall River (Karlamilyi) NP; access is not encouraged. Check with park rangers at Karratha (see *Rudall River NP*, below) before travelling through their lands around Rudall River NP. Many communities in remote WA and NT are 'dry' – do not consume alcohol in these areas.

Parks and reserves

National parks and reserves in WA are administered by the Department of Environment and Conservation (DEC). For general information about parks in WA see *Travel Tips*, p. 202.

Rudall River (Karlamilyi) NP Park authorities recommend that potential travellers undertake a DEC Bushcraft Course; contact (08) 9410 0453 to make a booking. The park is 260 km east of Newman; carry sufficient fuel to get there and back, and to travel around the park. There are no facilities of any kind. Water is generally available but must be boiled before drinking. Contact the Karratha DEC office well ahead of travelling on (08) 9143 1488, to check on road conditions, access and water availability.

Warnings

This region is extremely remote. There are long distances with no fuel or other supplies. Travellers must be completely self-sufficient and should travel as part of a convoy of at least two cars. Travellers will need a large capacity, high-clearance 4WD vehicle for these routes, and will need to carry specialist equipment for emergencies, along with emergency communication equipment (see *On the Road*, p. 246).

Canning Stock Route

Fuel and supplies CSR stretches for well over 2000 km including side trips. The longest distance without fuel is Wiluna to Kunawarritji (around 1300 km including side trips). Check opening times of store at Kunawarritji: (08) 9176 9040. Visitors can arrange to have fuel dumped at Well 23, about 800 km past Wiluna; contact the Capricorn Roadhouse at Newman at least six weeks before travelling: (08) 9175 1535. There is no fuel between Kunawarritji and the Aboriginal community of Billiluna (around 1000 km including side trips); phone ahead: (08) 9168 8988.

Track conditions and access Expect soft sand, compacted earth, heavy corrugations, rocky sections and hundreds of dunes. This route is not suitable for towing trailers, including off-road trailers. Spinifex seeds play havoc with radiators – install a radiator guard. Talk to police before travelling; Wiluna: (08) 9981 7024; Halls Creek: (08) 9168 6000.

Campsites and water There is bush camping only; no facilities. There is no rubbish disposal en route. Carry a bucket and rope to access water from suitable wells (boil water ahead of drinking). Water supply is unreliable; wells can dry up or become polluted with the bodies of dead animals. Carry adequate fresh water.

Gunbarrel Hwy

Fuel and supplies Wiluna to Warburton is 835 km. The longest distance with no fuel is Carnegie Station to Warburton (495 km). Phone before travelling: Carnegie Station: (08) 9981 2991; Warburton Roadhouse: (08) 8956 7656.

Track conditions and access Expect corrugations, ruts, washaways, sand and, depending on the season, mud. The route is not suitable for trailers and definitely not suitable for caravans. The road is irregularly maintained; wet weather may force closures. For information phone Shire of Wiluna: (08) 9981 8000, or Shire of Ngaanyatjarraku (Warburton): (08) 8956 7966. The road passes through pastoral leases and private Aboriginal land; do not deviate from the road.

Campsites and water There are campsites and units at Carnegie Station: (08) 9981 2991. There is bush camping en route; some sites are designated. Bore water is available but must be boiled; carry a bucket and rope to retrieve.

See also *On the Road*, p. 246.

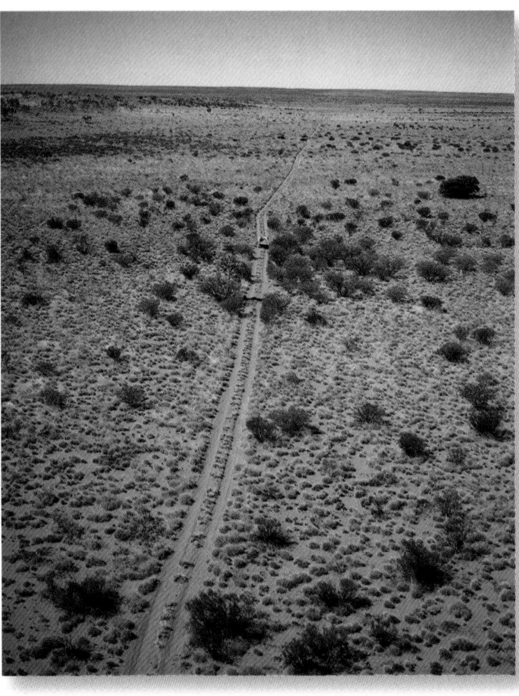

The Canning Stock Route – a tough, 4WD trek of around 1700 km – is not for the faint-hearted.

The Canning Stock Route

The Canning Stock Route is a journey of epic proportions and for many, the ultimate 4WD tour. It runs 1700 km, from Wiluna to Halls Creek on th edge of the Kimberley, crossing four deserts – Little Sandy and Gibson in the south and Great Sandy an Tanami in the north. It takes approximately three weeks to do the drive, and at present only 500 or s vehicles make the trip each year.

The Early Days

Early European reports of these deserts were dispiriting. In 1856, explorer Augustus Gregory skirted the edge of the Great Sandy Desert, but turned back on discovering a wasteland of dry lakes. Others followed during the final decades of the 19th century, but most agreed with explorer John Forrest who, on his 1874 journey to the southern reaches of what is now the Canning Stock Route, declared the landscape 'most wretched'.

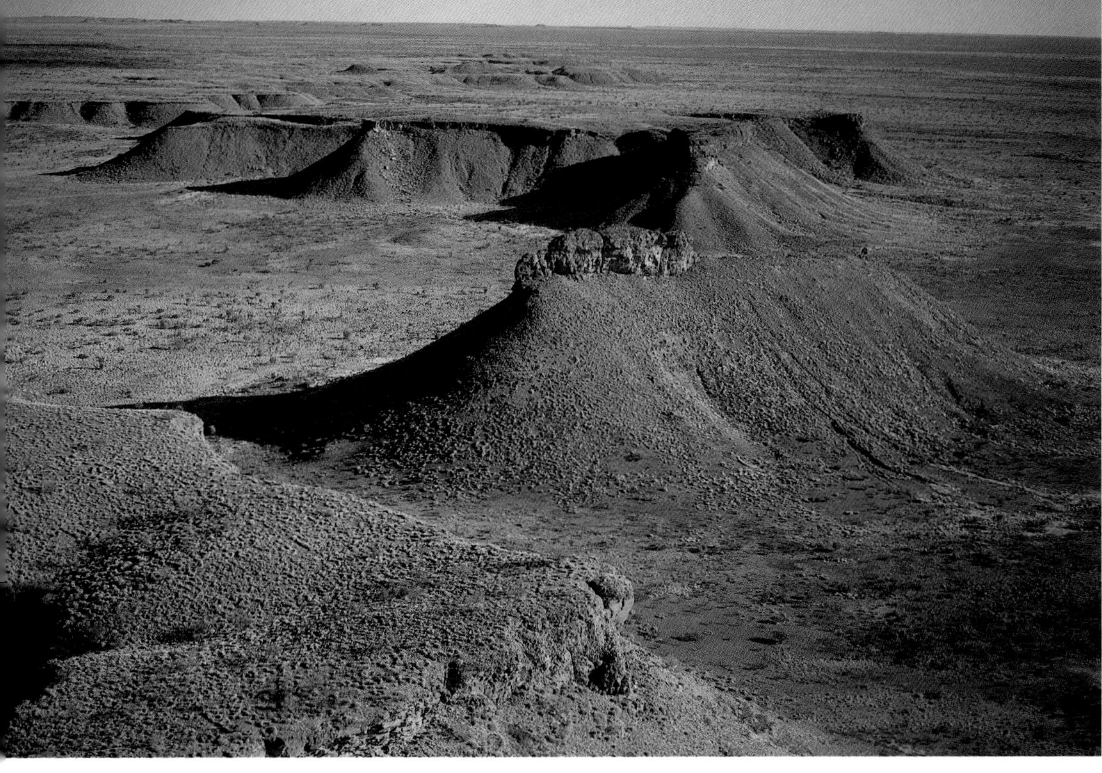

Contacts

Visitor information

Halls Creek
Great Northern Hwy
(08) 9168 6262

Newman
cnr Fortescue Ave
and Newman Dr
(08) 9175 2888
www.newman-wa.org

Wiluna
Scotia St
(08) 9981 8000
www.wiluna.wa.gov.au

Parks and reserves

See *Fact File*, opposite

The ancient landscape of the Breaden Hills, at the northern end of the Canning Stock Route.

Explorers and settlers fared better in the Kimberley to the north. Pastoralists opened up the land, bringing cattle overland from Queensland and NSW. The large cattle properties were soon thriving concerns, but getting stock to the markets of the south-west was a problem. For a while stock was sent by ship, but the cost was prohibitive. In May 1906 surveyor Alfred Canning set off from the southern goldfields towards the Kimberley to explore the feasibility of establishing a stock route across the deserts. His survey took 13 months to complete. He travelled with a team of eight men, 23 camels and two horses. Local Aboriginal people pointed out the sources of water in what, to 'whitefellas', seemed a barren wasteland. Canning decided a route was possible, provided wells were built to draw on the supply of underground water. He returned to the area with a construction party of 20 men. The work, which including the building of 51 wells (a further three were added in 1930), took two years to complete. The first mob of 150 cattle was taken down in 1911; the last of the estimated 31 mobs to use the track was moved in 1959. The first tourists began to arrive in the 1970s, in search of adventure and a brush with history.

A Sea of Sand Dunes

The deserts traversed by the Canning Stock Route receive, on average, less than 250 mm of rainfall a year – this is the measurement used to define an arid environment. Many expect the landscape to be monotonous, but instead discover a place alive with diversity and change.

The most prominent and challenging landscape feature is the 700 or so sand dunes, some as high as 16 m, which run in long rolls across the track. These were formed around 20 000 years ago, sculpted by prevailing winds from the remains of ancient, heavily weathered soils. Spinifex is the dominant vegetation, growing in dense, prickly hummocks on the ridges and plains, helping to stabilise the shifting sands. Salt lakes, like the discouragingly named Lake Disappointment, which occur in several places along the route, are all that remain of the mighty rivers that flowed across these plains more than 20 000 years ago. When the stone country begins to appear, its vibrant outcrops of red sandstone, such as the Durba Hills, provide a welcome relief from the surrounding dune-rippled flatness.

The Journey

Driving the Canning Stock Route is not for the faint-hearted or under-prepared. Tales of foolhardiness and misadventure abound. One tourist reputedly set off with 10 litres of beer, but no water. There are stories of travellers unloading luggage from their clearly inadequate vehicles in order to get over the first sand dune, seemingly unaware that another 699 dunes lay ahead. The *Fact File*, opposite, and *On the Road* section, p. 246, provide some introductory advice on how to negotiate the rigours of this environment, but potential travellers are advised to find out as much as they can about the trip and how to tackle it before heading off.

The southern end of the route begins at the township of Wiluna, 966 km north-east of Perth.

Snappy gums and spinifex in remote Rudall River NP.

Rudall River (Karlamilyi) National Park

Straddling the Great Sandy and Little Sandy deserts, covering 13 000 sq km, Rudall River (Karlamilyi) NP is the second largest national park in Australia. It is also one of the least visited – there are no facilities at all and the roads, where they exist, are unmaintained 4WD tracks (see *Fact File*, p. 216). Most visitors access the park along the Talawana Track, which runs west from Newman to intersect with the Canning Stock Route at Well 23. Visitors come for the chance to experience a pristine environment and true isolation, and are won over by the ragged, rocky hills, clear, cold pools, tinder-dry vegetation and radiant desert skies. Two Aboriginal communities are located within the park; visitor access is not encouraged. You may, however, come across one of the 28 registered rock-art sites, evidence of the long tenure of the Mardu people.

Rudall River, which cuts though the park, flows only when cyclonic weather patterns drive rain inland, which happens approximately twice every three years. Without rain, the river shrinks to a series of pools. The vegetation is surprisingly rich and prolific for an arid area, particularly on the river flats, where a shading fringe of river red gums and coolibahs provides relief from the heat. Elsewhere, thickets of mulga scrub and tussocks of spinifex dominate. Zebra finches, crested pigeons, budgerigars and white peregrine falcons are among the 72 recorded bird species that flock to the park's waterholes.

Bomb roads

The Gunbarrel (see *Gunbarrel Highway*, opposite) could be considered a comfortable, well-provisioned ride compared with the other so-called bomb roads. These tracks, many named after members of Len Beadell's family – Anne Beadell Hwy after his wife, Connie Sue Hwy after one of his daughters – fan across the plains that straddle the WA/SA border, to the immediate north of the Trans-Australia Railway line. This network is still at the frontier of the Australian outback: there are no facilities, the few far-flung settlements are truly remote, and the 'roads' are often little more than a faint parting of the spinifex. Those interested in travelling these routes should contact a 4WD club or consider a commercial tour.

Gazetted in 1898, the town boomed on the back of a gold rush in the 1930s, when its population reached 9000. Around 300 souls now call the desert settlement home. Facilities include a caravan park, hotel-motel, fuel outlet, police station, hospital and post office.

The 54 wells along the Canning Stock Route make excellent route markers, but are also attractions in their own right. Many sit alongside natural springs, such as the picturesque Windich Springs (Well 4A). Some are in a state of disrepair, their waters not suitable for human consumption. Others have been fully restored, such as Well 26, where there is a memorial to the father of the route, Alfred Canning. Some of the wells lie several kilometres off the main track.

Travellers tend to camp at the wells or at natural waterholes, and while there are no facilities, bar a pit toilet at Durba Springs, there is often some shade and a bit of a clearing.

Highlights on this long journey include prolific examples of Aboriginal rock art, particularly in the Calvert Range and Durba Hills; the gum-shaded surrounds of Durba Springs; the shimmering, salty pans of Lake Disappointment; and – at the Kimberley end of the trip – the drovers' graves in the vicinity of Well 37, the natural pools of Breaden Valley, and the awesome Wolfe Creek Crater.

The route ends at Halls Creek (population 1300) in the Kimberley. This is a major rural centre with facilities that include a hotel-motel, hospital, airstrip and the availability of vehicle parts and repairs (see also *The East Kimberley*, p. 238).

Gunbarrel Highway

In the 1950s and early 1960s, 50 years or so after the construction of the Canning Stock Route, army surveyor Len Beadell led a team – which he later named the Gunbarrel Road Construction Party – into Australia's desert wilderness. Their task was to construct a series of roads that would provide infrastructure for the now infamous Woomera rocket tests and Emu A-bomb tests. Beadell has entered the history books as the last of the great Australian explorers, venturing into places that few, if any, Europeans had ever seen. During the construction period, Beadell would leave his men and flog several hundred kilometres in his long-suffering 4WD, assessing the best possible route. In all, the team laid 6000 km of tracks – known as the 'bomb roads' – across 2.5 million sq km of WA and SA desert country.

The Gunbarrel was the first of the major routes, and is probably the most used and best known (see also *Bomb roads*, opposite). Today, much of the original route is out of bounds, traversing the large and inaccessible Aboriginal Land Trust area that straddles the WA, SA and NT borders. Most visitors follow the section of the road that runs for 835 km, east–west between Wiluna and the Aboriginal town of Warburton. Strictly speaking, parts of this route are not on the original Gunbarrel Hwy. But in wild country such as this, a highway is not necessarily a permanent route, rather one subject to the vagaries of weather, land ownership and maintenance.

The journey will take three or four days. Stock-up in Wiluna (see p. 217). The first section, to Carnegie Homestead, is well maintained; after this, there are some challenging corrugations. There is camping at Carnegie and a number of other spots en route. Trip highlights include the Mangkili Claypan Nature Reserve, where the large claypan, which holds water after the rains, supports a range of plant species not normally found in arid regions. Further west, the Gibson Desert Nature Reserve protects a representative area of this 156 000 sq km desert – Australia's fifth largest. The landscape is a sparse embroidery of spinifex plains, sand dunes and stands of hardy mulga. The desert takes its name from a member of Ernest Giles' 1874 expedition, Alfred Gibson, who, like many of his peers, vanished without trace. Look out for Mount Beadell, a hilly rise offering excellent views from the summit; at its base is a memorial honouring Len Beadell. You can camp at Warburton; the roadhouse has limited supplies, and is open only several hours a day on weekends (see *Fact File*, p. 216).

Above *Zebra finches are nomadic, and flock to any source of water in outback regions.*

Below *Red dirt and spinifex define the Gunbarrel Hwy.*

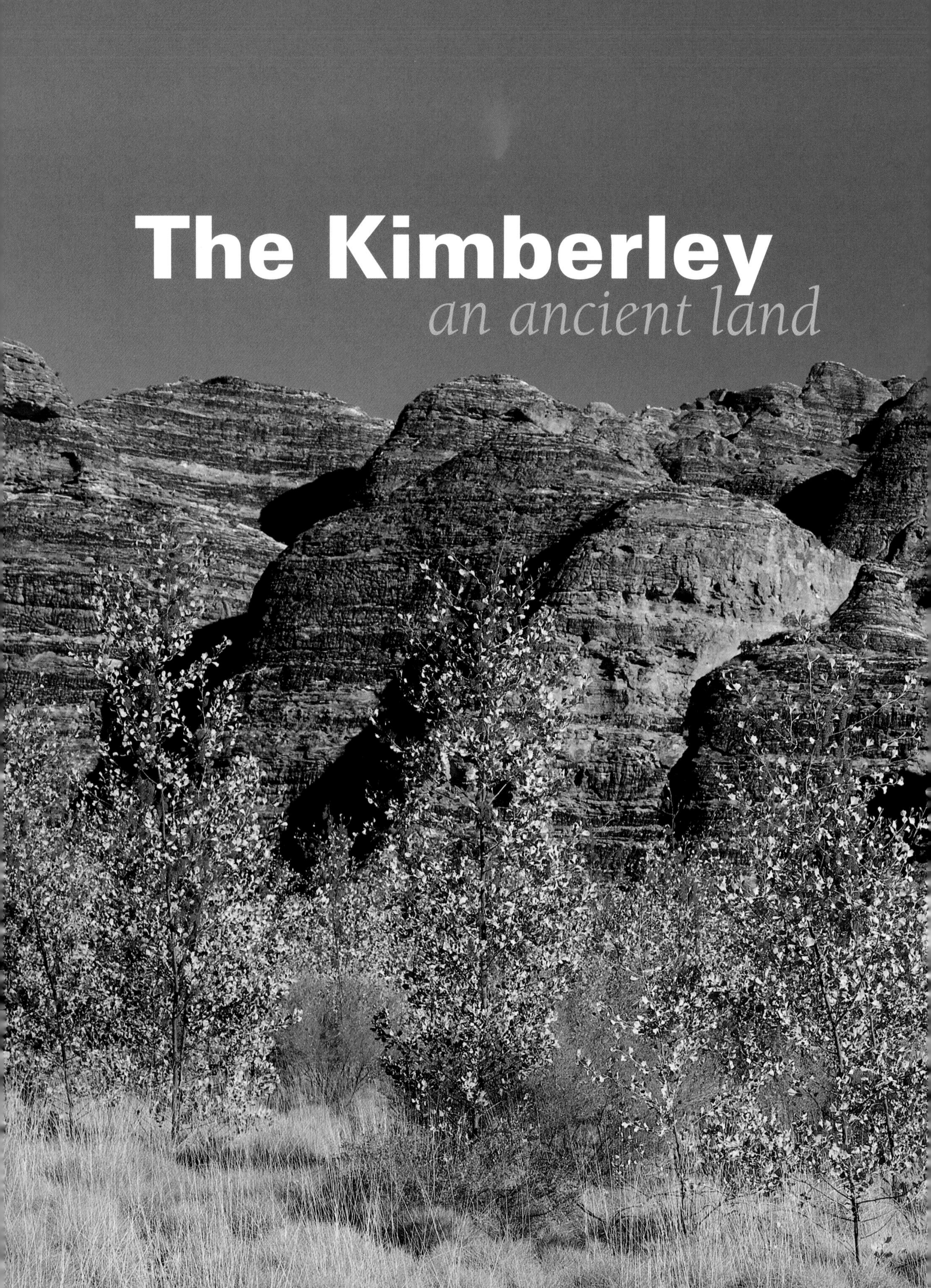
The Kimberley
an ancient land

The Kimberley

A journey to the Kimberley is a step back in time. The far north-west of the continent presents a formidable landscape and, until recently, one that has held European civilisation largely at bay. Signs of Aboriginal occupation, however, reach back over tens of thousands of years.

The Kimberley Regions

Broome and Beyond

Holidaymakers seeking a beach holiday fly in to Broome to relax at resorts, or to cruise the dramatic, deeply fissured coast with its giant tides and great fishing. Some parts of the region still cannot be reached except by boat or aircraft, but visitors are well catered for with a range of tours. Four-wheel drive enthusiasts travel the remote Gibb River Road, detouring into outback stations and isolated gorge country. Others wend their way eastwards and then north on the Great Northern Hwy. The diverse rock art through the region is a reminder that Aboriginal people have occupied this land for millennia. *See p. 226*

The East Kimberley

The sparsely settled East Kimberley is cattle country, but it attracts increasing numbers of tourists. Vast pastoral properties welcome visitors to experience station life, to explore rarely seen rock art and pockets of luxuriant growth flourishing in gorges, to enjoy great birdwatching and good fishing. The northern port of Wyndham, the fascinating Bungle Bungle Range, the Argyle diamond mines and the shimmering inland sea of man-made Lake Argyle are other attractions. *See p. 236*

Flower and seed pod of the kapok tree

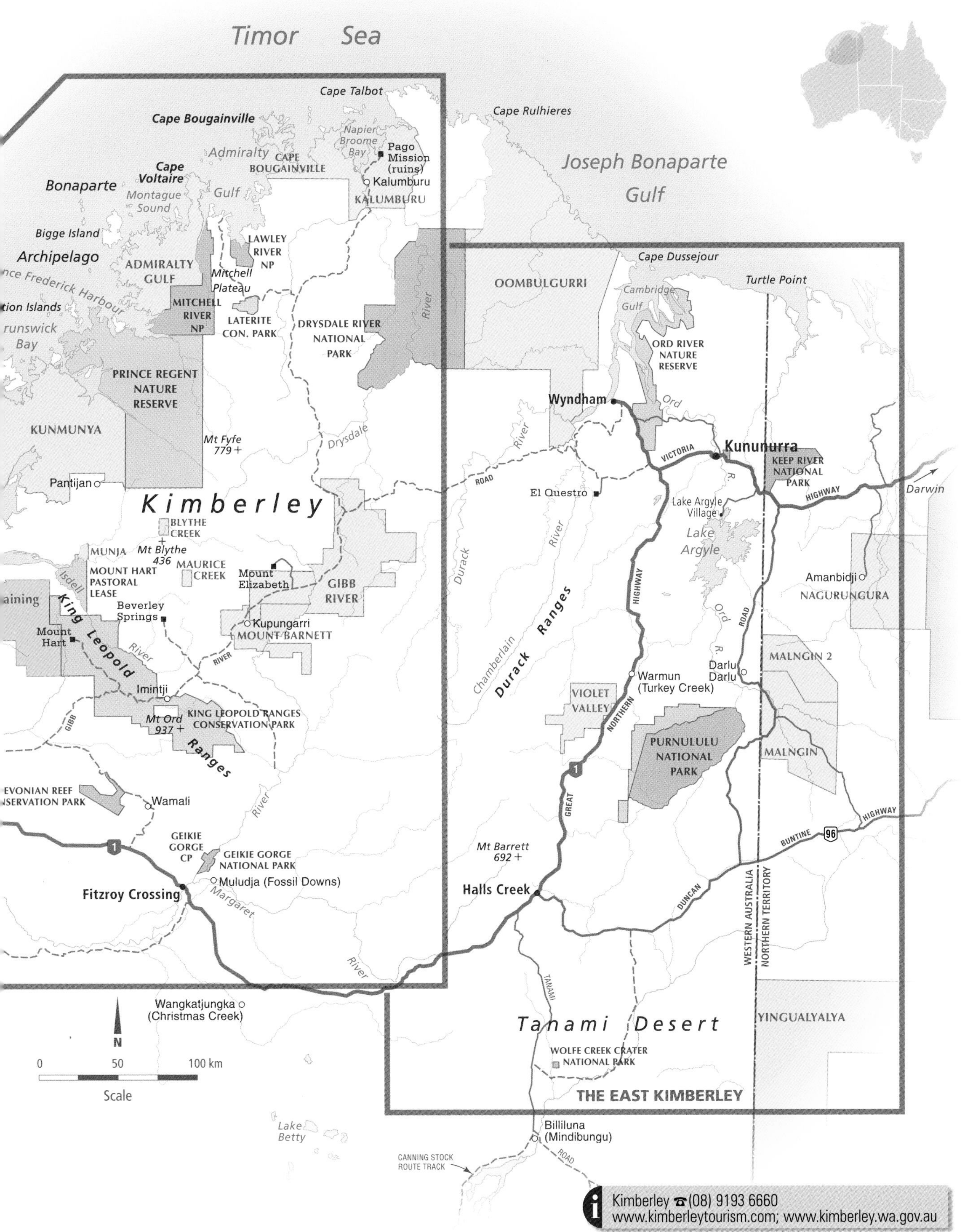

Timor Sea
Joseph Bonaparte Gulf
Kimberley
THE EAST KIMBERLEY
Tanami Desert
Cape Talbot
Cape Bougainville
Cape Rulhieres
Cape Voltaire
Bonaparte Archipelago
Admiralty Gulf
Kalumburu
Pago Mission (ruins)
Wyndham
Kununurra
Halls Creek
Fitzroy Crossing
El Questro
Lake Argyle
Warmun (Turkey Creek)
PURNULULU NATIONAL PARK
DRYSDALE RIVER NATIONAL PARK
PRINCE REGENT NATURE RESERVE
MITCHELL RIVER NP
KEEP RIVER NATIONAL PARK
GEIKIE GORGE NATIONAL PARK
WOLFE CREEK CRATER NATIONAL PARK
Durack Ranges
King Leopold Ranges
GIBB RIVER ROAD
GREAT NORTHERN HIGHWAY
Darwin
Billiluna (Mindibungu)
CANNING STOCK ROUTE TRACK
WESTERN AUSTRALIA
NORTHERN TERRITORY
0 50 100 km
Scale

Kimberley ☎ (08) 9193 6660
www.kimberleytourism.com; www.kimberley.wa.gov.au

Travel Tips

When to go

The Kimberley has two general climate areas. A coastal band extending from the mouth of King Sound to just north of Wyndham experiences a hot, generally moist climate, with a marked dry season during the winter. The remainder of the Kimberley has a dry, hot climate with most rain occurring in the summer. Ninety per cent of the Kimberley's rainfall occurs Dec–Mar. Rainfall within the region varies considerably; the highest rainfall is experienced around the Mitchell Plateau, with the lowest on the edges of the Great Sandy Desert. The wet season can bring cyclones or floods, and large areas can be cut off for weeks, or even months. The winter months are generally considered the best time to travel – safest and most comfortable. For further information, contact the Bureau of Meteorology (BOM): 1900 955 366; www.bom.gov.au

Aboriginal land

There are areas of Aboriginal land in the Kimberley, especially along the coast. Permits are required to pass through Aboriginal land or visit communities on Aboriginal land. Visitors cannot deviate more than 50 m from the road, or camp, without permission. Some Aboriginal communities have shops selling fuel and supplies, and these may be open to the public. If you do enter communities, respect people's privacy. Also be aware that some communities are 'dry' and no alcohol is permitted at all. Visitor information centres in the region can help with up-to-date advice. For further information and to apply for permits, contact the WA Dept of Indigenous Affairs (DIA): (08) 9235 8000 or 1300 651 077; www.dia.wa.gov.au

Private land

Travellers can drive on public roads that cross private property, including pastoral stations, without permission. However, permission must be obtained to drive on private station roads or to camp on private property.

Parks and reserves

National parks and reserves in WA are administered by the Department of Environment and Conservation (DEC). Visitor fees apply at some WA national parks, with annual passes available. Separate fees apply for camping; check before travelling if bookings are needed during the high season. For general information contact DEC in Perth: (08) 9334 0333; www.dec.wa.gov.au See also contact details for individual parks in the *Fact File* for each region.

Fishing

A recreational licence is required for fishing in WA and bag, size and possession limits apply. For further information contact WA Dept of Fisheries: (08) 9193 8600; www.fish.wa.gov.au National parks have their own fishing guidelines; see individual parks in the *Fact File* for each region.

CLIMATE												BROOME
	J	F	M	A	M	J	J	A	S	O	N	D
Max °C	33	33	34	34	31	28	28	30	31	33	34	34
Min °C	26	26	25	22	18	15	14	15	18	22	25	26
Rain mm	158	144	101	30	21	23	4	2	1	1	13	77
Raindays	10	9	7	2	2	2	1	0	0	0	1	5

CLIMATE												HALLS CREEK
	J	F	M	A	M	J	J	A	S	O	N	D
Max °C	37	36	36	34	30	27	27	30	34	37	38	38
Min °C	24	24	23	20	17	14	13	15	19	23	25	25
Rain mm	153	137	74	22	13	5	6	2	4	17	37	77
Raindays	13	13	8	3	2	1	1	1	1	3	6	11

Warnings

Fuel and supplies In some areas long distances separate fuel stops and supplies. Drivers should be well equipped and self-sufficient.

Road access and closures Avoid driving at dawn, dusk and at night, when wildlife and stock can wander onto roads. Many pastoral properties in the Kimberley are unfenced and stock on the road can be a particular hazard. Take special care if approaching or passing road trains. Flooding of both minor and major roads is common in the Wet (Nov–Mar); road conditions can change rapidly. For up-to-date road reports and information on closures contact Main Roads WA: 138 138; recorded service 1800 013 314; www.mainroads.wa.gov.au; or check with visitor information centres, local police or national park rangers.

Remote travel Many areas in the Kimberley are remote and travellers need to be well prepared.

Quarantine restrictions WA is free of many pests, weeds and diseases found elsewhere in Australia. Restrictions apply to the entry of many agricultural products, such as fresh fruit and vegetables and livestock. These must be declared on arrival in WA. Quarantine checkpoints include Kununurra and domestic airports. Random checks also occur on the Laverton–Warburton Road, Tanami Track and Duncan Hwy. Substantial penalties apply. For further information contact WA Quarantine and Inspection Service: (08) 9194 1400. In an effort to eradicate the weed Noogoora Burr, all stations along the Fitzroy River – from Fitzroy Crossing to the river mouth – are quarantined. There is another quarantine area north-east of Wyndham. Entry is prohibited in the quarantine area except for marked public access areas.

Maps Maps in this book are included as a guide only. Visitors travelling to remote regions should carry detailed maps.

Crocodiles Northern Australia has two types of crocodile. Potentially deadly saltwater or estuarine crocodiles (*Crocodylus porosus*) can be found in salt water, brackish and fresh water. They are large, well camouflaged and dangerous. Heed all warning signs. Take care when boating and fishing. Only swim where recommended.

Freshwater crocodiles (*Crocodylus johnstoni*) are smaller and are recognisable by their long narrow snout. They are less dangerous but will still fiercely guard their territory and young if they need to. Stay well away from these crocodiles.

See also *On the Road*, p. 246.

Below *Spotted quolls and other nocturnal marsupials forage for food around the Kimberley's King Leopold Ranges.*

A tracery of boab branches silhouetted against a powdery sky.

The Kimberley, in the continent's far north-west corner, is awe-inspiring, a frontier land that is immense in scale and ruggedly beautiful. Here, he very bones of the land are exposed – ancient, raggy and wind-hewn. Rivers have gouged their vay through rock to create gorges that tower above easonal waterways. Geologically, some of the oldest ocks in the world, formed as much as 2000 million ears ago, shape this sometimes surreal territory. looded mountains, fossil reefs, mighty rivers, eroded ills and grasslands studded with gouty boabs sprawl cross an area of more than 400 000 sq km.

The huge tides of the Indian Ocean that wash hese shores gnaw at the landmass, creating a ramatic and often deeply incised coastline. Sun-leached beaches and muddy mangrove swamps are roken by ragged cliff-faces, while an archipelago of argely uninhabited islands stretches offshore.

As early as 1616, Dutchman Dirk Hartog ighted the coast when he sailed by, en route to Java nd the riches of the Dutch East Indies. Despite his early knowledge of the area by Europeans, he region held little attraction for them, with the irst permanent settlement founded in 1879, and nany areas still sparsely populated today. The now Vorld Heritage-listed Bungle Bungle Range seems to ave been known only to Aboriginal people and a andful of locals and scientists until the 1980s.

Many areas remain scarcely touched – untamed, ntrammelled, and protected by their inaccessibility, he harshness of the terrain and the intense tropical or semi-tropical climate. Towns are small – just three have a population in excess of 2000 – and there are only around 30 000 people scattered across an area three times the size of England.

Aboriginal people have lived in the Kimberley for more than 40 000 years, their long association with the land recorded in the myriad rock paintings and engravings dispersed across the region. As you walk through the high gorges, or chance upon a richly engraved rock-art site, you may well feel that you are the first white person to have stepped on this ground, to have come this way – and you may be right.

More than 40 percent of the population in the Kimberley is Aboriginal. Some live in fairly remote communities; others run or work on cattle properties; some help manage national parks and reserves; others live in towns. Various Indigenous groups have established tourist operations or are involved in music, theatre and art, weaving their traditional skills and culture into the life they lead today.

The Kimberley offers both natural and man-made surprises. Gorges slashed deep through the rusty red rock and fringed with livistona palms, thundering waterfalls, and rare landforms such as the mysterious Bungle Bungle Range are natural treasures. Man has made his mark here in various ways: ancient Aboriginal rock art, huge cattle stations, the deep, still waters of man-made Lake Argyle and diamond mines are among the many other facets of the Kimberley.

Broome and Beyond

Beyond the quirky town of Broome lies the deeply indented and island-strewn Kimberley coastline. Inland, national parks protect precious wilderness, ancient rock art imbues a sense of history, and the iconic Gibb River Road meanders across the heart of one of the world's oldest landscapes.

Crocodile warning
Dangerous saltwater crocodiles inhabit coast waters, freshwater and saltwater inland wate and lagoons. Seek local advice before swimming.

Ocean watch
The warm waters of the Kimberley coast are home to endangered dugongs, several species of marine turtles, giant manta rays and migrating whales in season. More dangerous are the deadly saltwater crocodiles and sharks that cruise these waters.

Broome, once 'the pearling capital of the world', entices national and international visitors with its idiosyncratic blend of resort-type accommodation, easygoing pace ('Broome time'), white-sand beaches and multicultural population.

On Dampier Peninsula, stretching north of Broome, Aboriginal communities are willing to share their traditional skills and knowledge of the region. Along this coast, and in fact all the way north and around to the NT, anglers will find some outstanding fishing. The convoluted coastline, in places ravaged by the power of the tides, offers sandy coves, dramatic cliffs and innumerable tiny islands.

If you don't want to just soak up the sun and gaze at the Indian Ocean's aquamarine waters lapping the sand, the Kimberley reaches in to the interior with some of the country's most startling scenery. Gorges, hidden waterfalls, pandanus-lined waterways, a rich legacy of ancient Aboriginal rock art, and a wealth of wildlife, await those willing to explore just off the beaten track.

Highway 1, the Great Northern Hwy, cuts a serpentine route from Broome in the south-west of the Kimberley to Kununurra in the north-east, and a network of 4WD tracks leads to little-known national parks that guard rarely seen pockets of the landscape. The Gibb River Road traces a path north, through imposing gorge country and sprawling cattle properties. Detours to the magnificent Mitchell Plateau to swim, fish or explore the bush or, with permission, to visit the isolated Aboriginal community of Kalumburu, on the northern coast, are other possibilities.

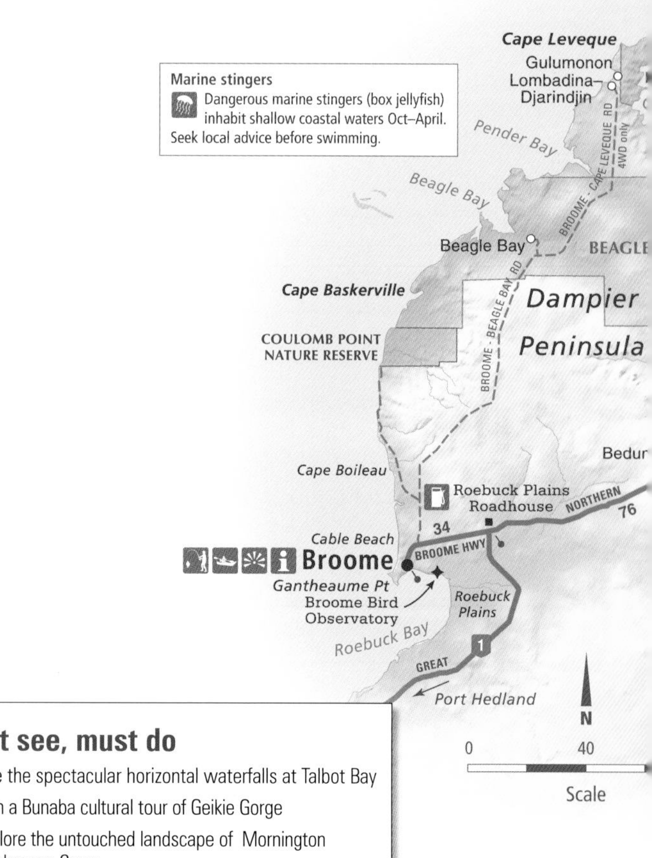

Must see, must do

- See the spectacular horizontal waterfalls at Talbot Bay
- Join a Bunaba cultural tour of Geikie Gorge
- Explore the untouched landscape of Mornington Wilderness Camp
- Travel the Kimberley's famed Gibb River Road
- Watch the thundering waters of the Mitchell Falls (Punamii-Unpuu) in the north of the Kimberley

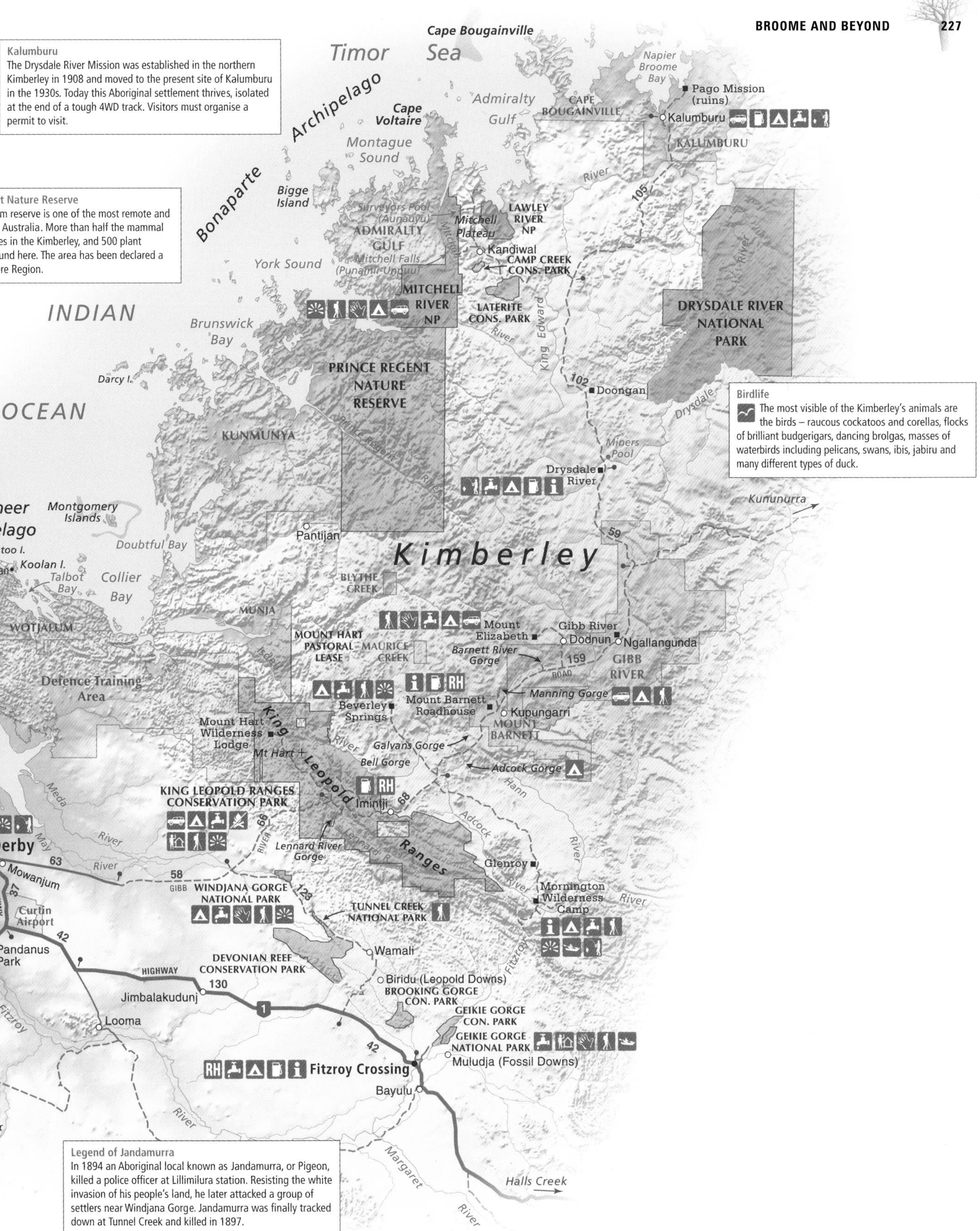

Kalumburu

The Drysdale River Mission was established in the northern Kimberley in 1908 and moved to the present site of Kalumburu in the 1930s. Today this Aboriginal settlement thrives, isolated at the end of a tough 4WD track. Visitors must organise a permit to visit.

…t Nature Reserve

…m reserve is one of the most remote and … Australia. More than half the mammal …es in the Kimberley, and 500 plant …und here. The area has been declared a …ere Region.

Birdlife

The most visible of the Kimberley's animals are the birds – raucous cockatoos and corellas, flocks of brilliant budgerigars, dancing brolgas, masses of waterbirds including pelicans, swans, ibis, jabiru and many different types of duck.

Legend of Jandamurra

In 1894 an Aboriginal local known as Jandamurra, or Pigeon, killed a police officer at Lillimilura station. Resisting the white invasion of his people's land, he later attacked a group of settlers near Windjana Gorge. Jandamurra was finally tracked down at Tunnel Creek and killed in 1897.

Kimberley ☎(08) 9193 6660; www.kimberleytourism.com
Broome ☎(08) 9192 2222; www.broomevisitorcentre.com.au

Opposite *Camels trek along Broome's renowned Cable Beach.*

Fact File

Top events

Easter *Dragon Boat Regatta (Broome)*
May *King Tide Day (Derby)*
June *Mowanjun Festival (Indigenous art and culture, Derby)*
June/ July *Race Round (horseracing week, Broome)*
Fitzroy Crossing Rodeo
Boab Festival, Derby
Aug/ Sept *Shinju Matsuri Festival (pearl festival, Broome)*
Opera Under the Stars, Broome
Nov *Mango Festival (Broome)*

Permits and regulations

Aboriginal land There are areas of Aboriginal land in this region and within some national parks and conservation areas. There are a number of communities on the Dampier Peninsula. Visitors should check with visitor information in Broome for up-to-date advice on access. A permit to enter the Aboriginal town of Kalumburu is required from the WA Department of Indigenous Affairs (DIA): (08) 9235 8000 or 1300 651 077. On entry, a permit fee is payable to the Kalumburu Aboriginal Corporation; accommodation must be booked before arriving. For further information contact the Kalumburu Aboriginal Corporation: (08) 9161 4300. See also *Travel Tips*, p. 224.

Parks and reserves

National parks and reserves in WA are administered by the Department of Environment and Conservation (DEC). For general information about parks in WA see *Travel Tips*, p. 224. During the wet season most of the parks in this region have restricted access or are inaccessible.

Geikie Gorge NP Park open for day visits only. No camping permitted. Boat trips and Aboriginal cultural tours available April–Oct (see *Contacts*, opposite). There are on-site rangers April–Nov. Contact DEC at Broome: (08) 9195 5500.

King Leopold Ranges Conservation Park Camping at Silent Grove (near Bell Gorge). BYO everything, including adequate water. No campfires. Sites available on a first-come, first-served basis. Contact DEC at Broome: (08) 9195 5500.

Mitchell River NP Visitors must be totally self-sufficient. Camping with limited facilities near the start of the Mitchell Falls Track. The traditional owners have requested that, for spiritual reasons, visitors do not swim below the falls or in the Surveyors Pool (Aunauyu). Contact DEC at Kununurra: (08) 9168 4200.

Prince Regent Nature Reserve A permit is required to enter the area. No road access; scenic flights and boat tours can be organised in Derby (see *Contacts*, opposite).

Tunnel Creek NP Park open for day use only. No camping permitted. Contact DEC at Broome: (08) 9195 5500.

Windjana Gorge NP There are two campsites (one allows generators), with on-site rangers during the dry season. Beware of crocodiles. Contact DEC at Broome: (08) 9195 5500.

Fishing

For general information on fishing in this region see *Travel Tips*, p. 224.

Warnings

Fuel and supplies Long distances separate fuel and supply stops on many routes in this region. Travellers need to be well equipped and self-sufficient. April–Sept can be very busy; accommodation bookings are advised. Note that some pastoral stations that offer accommodation do not sell fuel. Always carry adequate water supplies.

Road access and closures The Broome to Cape Leveque road is 4WD only. Travellers must be completely self-sufficient. The road is usually closed Dec–April, due to seasonal rains. High-clearance 4WD vehicles with long-range fuel tanks are recommended for the Gibb River Road. Camp only at designated sites. Caravans and trailers are not suitable for the Gibb River Road, Dampier Peninsula and most 4WD routes in this region. For further information contact Main Roads WA: 138 138 or 1800 013 314; www.mainroads.wa.gov.au

Crocodiles Freshwater and dangerous saltwater crocodiles are widespread along coastal and tidal river areas in this region. Be crocodile-wise; heed warning signs; swim only where recommended. Take care when fishing and boating. Do not allow children to play near the edge of waterways. See also *Travel Tips*, p. 224.

See also *On the Road*, p. 246.

Ibis Aerial Highway

The Ibis Aerial Highway, a network of airstrips located at remote communities, homesteads, national parks and various places of interest, has been introduced as a way of making air travel through the region more readily accessible. It is not necessarily cheap, but it's an excellent way to appreciate the extraordinary scale of the Kimberley and to see parts that you might not otherwise reach.

Broome

Broome is the unofficial capital of the Kimberley – at least, the tourist capital. Around 2200 km north of Perth and 1800 km south-west of Darwin, the small coastal town has a distinctive quality all its own.

Port of Pearls

In the late 19th century, when pearl shell was highly prized, Broome was a thriving port with more than 400 luggers working Roebuck Bay. The first divers were local Aboriginal people who free-dived in the shallow coastal waters. As deeper diving and heavier equipment came into use, Japanese, Malays and Koepangers made up the crews. Chinese merchants and shopkeepers also came and soon a Chinatown was thriving. By all accounts it was an exotic hub, with foreign divers along with wealthy pearlers in white suits and pith helmets treading the piers. But pearling, and the tropical climate of cyclones and storms, was dangerous and, for many, carried out a long way from home. More than 900 Japanese are buried in the cemetery, the carved headstones a lonely echo of their Japanese origins.

Broome's multicultural heritage permeates the town's architecture, but has also influenced its cuisine and culture – dragon boat festivals, Indigenous art and classical opera (performed under the stars) all have their place in the 'what's on' calendar.

Broome is a town of around 14 000, but it offers many distractions for visitors. The Historical Society's museum is excellent (the fascinating photos more telling than many stories), restored pearl luggers can be inspected, or guests can sink into a deckchair on a balmy evening and catch one of the latest movies at the historic outdoor picture gardens. Cultured-pearl farming has replaced the pearl shell industry and boutiques display elegantly set pearls. A weekly market is held in front of the handsome courthouse, built in colonial style in 1889 as the original Cable House, when a telegraph cable first linked Broome with Java. Bush tucker tours, a visit to the Broome Crocodile Park (home to more than 4000 crocodiles) and air tours are a few of the other activities on offer.

Contacts

Visitor information

Broome
cnr Broome Hwy and Bagot St
(08) 9192 2222
www.broomevisitorcentre.com.au

Derby
2 Clarendon St
(08) 9191 1426
www.derbytourism.com.au

Fitzroy Crossing
(08) 9191 5355
(see also *Station stays*, below)

Parks and reserves

See *Fact File*, opposite

Station stays, lodges

Drysdale River Station
(08) 9161 4326
www.drysdaleriver.com.au

Mount Elizabeth Station
(08) 9191 4644

Mount Hart Wilderness Lodge
PO Box 653, Derby,
(08) 9191 4645
www.mthart.com.au

Mornington Wilderness Camp
(08) 9191 7406 or
1800 631 946
www.australianwildlife.org

Activities

Broome Bird Observatory
(08) 9193 5600

Broome Crocodile Park
(08) 9192 1489

Geikie Gorge Tours
Boat tours (08) 9191 5121

Darngku Cultural Tours
contact Fitzroy Crossing
Visitor Information (see above)

One of Broome's key claims to fame is the bone-white Cable Beach, a 22 km ribbon of sand named in honour of the telegraph cable. Many visitors opt for the rolling gait of a camel ride to explore the Indian Ocean shoreline. Surfing and kayaking are also popular. During the cooler, drier months, a flotilla of boats leave from here to explore the Kimberley coast, or on fishing safaris.

At Gantheaume Point, 6.5 km from town, at very low tide the water ebbs away to reveal a tangible reminder of the Kimberley's ancient origins: the 120 million-year-old footprints of a warm-climate dinosaur. More recent wildlife is visible on the shores of Roebuck Bay, where the Broome Bird Observatory, about 18 km from Broome, is ideally located for spotting some of the more than 300 species of waders and shorebirds, including migratory species from as far north as Siberia (see *Contacts*, opposite).

Dampier Peninsula

Broome is at the base of the Dampier Peninsula, a jutting fist of land with an unspoiled coastline of scrubby red cliffs, occasionally indented by pale sand beaches. A 4WD-only, red-dirt road stretches 200 km north from Broome to the lighthouse at Cape Leveque.

The peninsula is home to several Aboriginal language groups including the Jawi, Bardi and Ngumbarl people. Visitors willing to make the effort to reach these isolated communities – often a spine-jarring journey on corrugated roads – have the opportunity to learn about traditional survival skills and Indigenous culture. Visitors must make arrangements with Aboriginal communities before arriving. Contact Broome visitor information (see *Contacts*, opposite).

At Beagle Bay, 118 km north of Broome, French Trappist monks started a mission in 1890, later taken over by the Pallotine order. Both the monks and Aboriginal residents worked tirelessly to build the small Sacred Heart Church, with its richly embellished mother-of-pearl interior.

The road traverses open eucalypt country, past the Aboriginal community at Lombadina–Djarindjin to the white beacon of Cape Leveque lighthouse, emerging from the greenery and paprika-red soil. From here you can look out across the Indian Ocean and see fish and, in season, whales swimming in the crystalline waters.

Despite the intense beauty of some beaches along this coast, swimming is rarely an option – sharks, sea snakes, saltwater crocodiles, and stingers (box jellyfish) in season make these waters very dangerous.

The Buccaneer Archipelago

Along a spectacular coast, the Buccaneer Archipelago still manages to impress with its network of 800 to 1000 small, steep, rocky islands, often rimmed by mangroves. Some of the islands have been mined for iron ore (the deposits were among the world's richest), but others are pristine. Aboriginal rock art and abundant bird and marine life are among the islands' treasures.

At Talbot Bay, twice a day the giant tides sluice through the narrow openings; then, as the tide rapidly falls, the water thunders back into the ocean,

The Gibb River Road, a former stock route, cuts across the heart of the region.

creating whirlpools and 'horizontal waterfalls'. Boat cruises and flights to see the spectacle leave from Broome and Derby.

Heading Inland

From Broome, the Great Northern Hwy heads inland, east then north-east, 1060 km to Kununurra. Roughly 164 km from Broome, soon after you cross the Fitzroy River you reach Willare Bridge Roadhouse. Here, you can turn north to Derby on the coast, or continue east towards Fitzroy Crossing (see p. 231).

Derby

Perched on the edge of King Sound, the town of Derby is renowned for its massive tides and steamy summer climate. The bizarrely contorted limbs of Kimberley's iconic boab trees twist above the wide, quiet streets.

The Fitzroy, May and Meda rivers flow into King Sound where, twice a day, giant tides up to 11 m high leave a sludge of mudflats, heaving with mudskippers, mudcrabs, shellfish and waterbirds foraging for a seafood meal.

Established in the 1880s as a port for wool shipments, Derby was the first town settled in the Kimberley. When gold was discovered in 1885 at Halls Creek (see *The East Kimberley*, p. 236) many prospectors landed here. Today Derby is a supply point for outback stations and mining communities, but it is also a jumping-off point for those heading to the Buccaneer Archipelago, or inland on the Gibb River Road. Camping and fishing safaris (the fishing is superlative) can be organised from here.

The Gibb River Road

Although more people are tackling the Gibb River Road each year, it is still comparatively isolated and the drive retains a sense of adventure. The 660 km, 4WD-only former cattle route wends its way across the heart of the Kimberley, providing access to some of the region's most spectacular gorges, rugged ranges and vast working cattle stations, some of them offering accommodation.

The road varies from short stretches of bitumen to rocky earth, with clouds of bulldust later in the Dry. All or parts of the road may be closed during the rainy season, from November/December to April. Many places along the route close even before the rains, in early November, when the daytime temperature can be a scorching 43°C or so.

Windjana Gorge

Around 125 km east of Derby, a 20 km detour from the Gibb River Road leads to Windjana Gorge, protected within Windjana Gorge NP. The gorge walls soar up to 100 m above the flood plains of the ephemeral Lennard River, creating a 3.5 km gash through the Napier Range. The deeply fissured cliffs are part of a 350 million-year-old fossil reef, from the era when this landscape was below water.

Freshwater crocodiles – smaller and less threatening than their saltwater cousins, but still not to be approached – can often be seen sunning themselves along the riverbanks or in the dry-season pools. Majestic river red gums, spindly native figs and glossy-leaved Leichhardt trees fringe the riverbanks, providing shade for the many waterbirds and raucous corellas that flock to the gorge's cool, deep pools of water.

A 7 km return walk along the eastern wall of the gorge is popular, but there are other walks. Wandjina paintings – strange, mouthless spirit figures said to control the rain and lightning (see *Kimberley rock art*, p. 233) – recall the district's long occupation by Indigenous people.

Tunnel Creek National Park

About 30 km south-east of Windjana, the relentless flow of water has eroded the fossilised sandstone of the Napier Range over millennia to create a cave system. The creek here flows through a tunnel in the cave system during the Wet, though it often shrinks to waterholes in the Dry. In the gloomy tunnel water trickles into still pools, shafts of light break through where the roof has collapsed and fig tree roots trail, seeking a precarious toehold. Those willing to wet their feet and wade past bat colonies and beneath dripping stalactites can follow the tunnel for 750 m or so. Freshwater crocodiles enjoy the cool pools, so make sure to carry a reliable torch to light the way. The tunnel is within Tunnel Creek NP.

Fitzroy Crossing and Geikie Gorge

Almost 400 km east of Broome, along the Great Northern Hwy, is the small township of Fitzroy Crossing, a good base for exploring Geikie Gorge. The town, with a population of around 430, services the surrounding cattle country.

The floodwaters of the Fitzroy River have gouged their way through the limestone of the Oscar and Geikie ranges, carving the 30 m high walls of Geikie Gorge. Each year, swollen by monsoon rains, the Fitzroy is transformed from a peaceful stream to a raging torrent, often flooding the park with up to 7 m of water. But in the Dry, you can enjoy the weeping paperbarks, spiky pandanus and the wild passionfruit vines that edge the river. Freshwater crocodiles, sawfish, and sometimes even stingrays cruise these waters. The park is also a haven for birdlife.

The traditional custodians, the Bunaba, call the gorge Darngku. With park rangers they arrange boat trips and cultural tours, sharing their immense knowledge of the local environment and their ancient heritage. The tours are usually available from April to October (see *Fact File*, p. 228).

King Leopold Ranges Conservation Park

Returning to the Gibb River Road, the trail leads north-east past sudden jump-ups or escarpments and then cuts across the King Leopold Ranges as it crosses King Leopold Ranges Conservation Park.

Covering 3920 sq km, the park straddles almost the entire length of the King Leopold Ranges, and takes in the former Mount Hart Station homestead, the scenic Bell Gorge with its tiered waterholes, and Lennard River Gorge. This is the Kimberley's highest mountain range, a remote and rugged terrain of startling dimensions.

An impressive array of wildlife calls this region home. During the day you may see lizards, knob-tailed geckos or water monitors sunning themselves on rocky outcrops. In the evening, nocturnal marsupials such as spotted quolls, bandicoots and occasionally wallabies will be out foraging for food.

Mount Hart Station, first taken up as a pastoral lease in 1914 and run as a cattle station for many years, now offers homestead accommodation. Visitors are welcome to explore the isolated landscape with its rich flora, and diverse bird and animal life, to bushwalk or simply to enjoy the environs of the historic homestead.

In Australia, gouty boab trees usually are found only in the Kimberley.

The multi-hued walls of Geikie Gorge, reflected in the Fitzroy River.

Prince Regent Nature Reserve

Flanked by high cliffs for much of the way, the Prince Regent River flows as straight as an arrow for more than 100 km along a fracture line in the sandstone bedding. The river is within a nature reserve, a wilderness area covering 6300 sq km, and declared a UNESCO World Biosphere Reserve in 1978. This is the Kimberley's highest rainfall pocket, dense with rainforest, waterfalls and prolific flora and fauna. There are no roads in, but it is possible to cruise up the river by tour boat or take a scenic flight.

There is camping elsewhere in the park, with around 10 sites at Silent Grove near Bell Gorge (make sure to arrive early during the tourist season – it can be very busy). Boabs line Bell Creek, which cascades through a series of gorges into a wonderful swimming hole, a cool oasis in the summer heat, and one of the prettiest spots in the Kimberley.

Once back on the road, the roadhouse at the Aboriginal community of Imintji is the only chance between Derby and Mount Barnett to fuel up and collect supplies.

Mornington Wilderness Camp

A 4WD track south-east off the Gibb River Road leads to another exceptional Kimberley property, the 3120 sq km Mornington Station, where guests are accommodated at the Mornington Wilderness Camp. There is a choice of luxury safari tents or more basic camping. The Australian Wildlife Conservancy – a national, independent, non-profit organisation committed to helping save Australia's native wildlife – owns and runs this property. It is a vast, isolated tract of land in a near-pristine state, crossed by four major river systems. The still waters of lovely Dimond Gorge are ideal for kayaking and swimming; more than 180 bird species, including the endangered Gouldian finch (see *Gouldian finch*, p. 90) enjoy the peaceful bush and the pandanus-lined creeks.

Gorge Country

North-east of the King Leopold Ranges Conservation Park lies some of the Kimberley's finest pastoral country. There are also some wonderful gorges, such as Adcock Gorge, known for its many cockatoos, Galvans Gorge with its rock art, tranquil Manning Gorge, and the paperbark- and palm-shaded Barnett River Gorge. Always seek local advice before camping at any of these gorges.

There is camping at Manning Gorge (check at Mount Barnett Roadhouse for permits) and bush camping at Barnett River Gorge. Mount Elizabeth Station, north of Barnett River Gorge, offers homestead accommodation and camping. If you can, arrange a tour of the property to view ancient rock art with some of the traditional custodians. For those keen to take it easy, there is good fishing to be had in the waterholes.

From the turn-off to Mount Elizabeth Station it's about 69 km to the junction of the Gibb River and Kalumburu roads (see *The East Kimberley*, p. 236). The Kalumburu Road is 267 km of often corrugated, red-dirt road as it meanders north through open woodland country, with numerous river and creek crossings, to the Aboriginal community at Kalumburu.

Drysdale River Station, roughly 60 km from the junction, is another working cattle property where you can arrange accommodation, camp, buy fuel and supplies or arrange scenic flights.

Mitchell River National Park

Approximately 101 km north of Drysdale River Station on Kalumburu Road is the turn-off west to the Mitchell Plateau and Mitchell River NP. Not far from the turn-off is the King Edward River crossing, a welcome place to relax after

the spine-jarring drive. The plateau is known as Ngauwudu to the Wunambal people who have lived here for thousands of years. Mitchell River NP sprawls across 1150 sq km, a rugged landscape of distinctive livistona palms, scattered fragments of rainforest, woodlands and paperbark-fringed watercourses. There are spectacular gorges, cool swimming holes, exceptional rock art, the wonderful tiered Mitchell Falls (Punamii-Unpuu) and Surveyors Pool (Aunauyu). During the season a helicopter is often based near the carpark, to take people on a flight over the falls – it's a fantastic trip if you get the chance to do it.

The best time to travel is early in the dry season – to see the falls flowing with a vengeance, before the grass becomes parched and heat shimmers off the rocks, and before there are too many others sharing the outback with you.

Kalumburu

Back on the Kalumburu Road, another 105 km north takes you to the historic town and Aboriginal community of Kalumburu. You must have permission and accommodation arranged before arriving at the settlement (see *Fact File*, p. 228). The town was established as a mission, but today the thriving community runs a cattle property. Kalumburu is just a few kilometres from the mouth of the King Edward River – there is good reef fishing off the coast or the chance to haul in a barramundi from the river.

Kimberley rock art

For thousands of years, Aboriginal people in the Kimberley painted and engraved rock as part of their religious, cultural and daily lives. The legacy is a history played out on stone, a record that reaches down across the ages. The two key styles are the titanic Creator beings known as Wandjinas and the graceful, elongated figures referred to as Bradshaw paintings or, to use the Ngarinyin term, Gwion-Gwion.

The Wandjinas are otherwordly in appearance: monumental in scale, staring from large, mouthless faces. As well, there are serpents, kangaroos, goannas and other creatures painted and sometimes engraved on rock. They are said to have been painted by the great Creator ancestors who maintain the natural cycle of the cosmos, bringing rain and sometimes torrential storms or flood. Wandjina art is believed to be comparatively recent, perhaps only several thousands of years old.

In complete contrast are the dynamic and highly decorative Gwion-Gwion figures – they sway and dance, a jangle of bracelets, elaborate headpieces and spears. For many years they were called Bradshaw paintings after pastoralist Joseph Bradshaw, who recorded them in the 1890s, but their age and meaning is still clouded in mystery.

Rock art is widely scattered across the Kimberley region. In some areas it is dense – as you walk, you find more and more art on rock overhangs and in shelters. The best way to view the art is with a guide, who can offer an insight into its meaning and explain the techniques and history.

Following page *Cape Leveque lighthouse at the northern tip of Dampier Peninsula.*

Left *Monumental Wandjina figures stare from rock walls and cave shelters.*

The East Kimberley

Everything here seems larger than life – roads that appear to go on for ever, yawning gorges, mighty rivers and pastoral stations that sprawl to the horizon. Two of the region's special treasures are the World Heritage-listed Bungle Bungle Range and the immense, island-studded waters of man-made Lake Argyle.

By any standards the Kimberley is remote – certainly from Australia's southern and eastern states, but even from the state's capital city. Kununurra, the largest town in the East Kimberley, lies more than 3200 km north of Perth.

It's surprisingly easy to travel across the Kimberley – the sealed Great Northern Hwy winds from 45 km east of Kununurra, south past Halls Creek and west past Fitzroy Crossing, to the well-known town of Broome. But the region is really 4WD territory. It's the buckled-road diversions and detours off the main track that reveal the region's true heart.

In an area of breathtaking landforms, two great natural features still stand out. Wolfe Creek Crater, a vast, lunar-like scar just off the red-dirt Tanami Track, bakes in the fierce northern sun, as it has for over 300 000 years. Even more astonishing is the Bungle Bungle Range. The crumpled range of domes, towers and chiselled gorges was scarcely known outside the region until the 1980s. Now, protected within Purnululu NP, it has a World Heritage listing, and visitors travel to this remote corner to marvel at its shapes, rich colours and hidden gorges.

The climate dictates much of life in the Kimberley as it does elsewhere in northern Australia. Well into the tropics, most of the region is pounded by monsoonal rains over the summer months, when swollen rivers slice through the sandstone plateau as they have done for thousands of years, carving deep gorges. From May to October is generally the safest, easiest time to explore this unique corner of Australia.

Must see, must do

- Marvel at the scale of Wolfe Creek Crater, on the edge of the Tanami Track
- Float in the cool, freshwater springs of Palm Springs, near Halls Creek
- Watch waterbirds wheeling overhead at Parry Lagoons Nature Reserve
- Explore the tiger-striped towers and secluded gorges of the Bungle Bungle Range
- Cruise amongst the bays and islands of man-made Lake Argyle

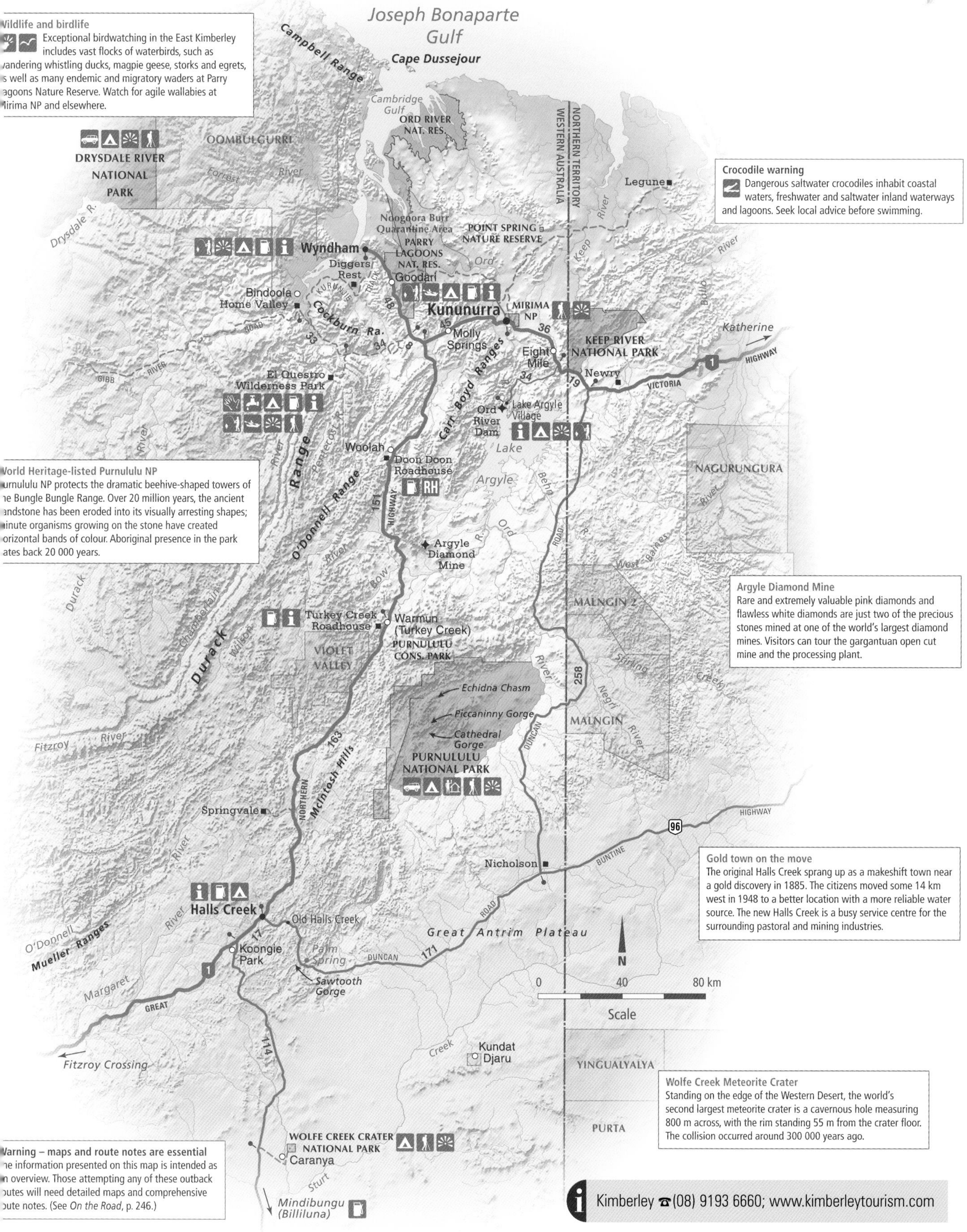

Vildlife and birdlife

Exceptional birdwatching in the East Kimberley includes vast flocks of waterbirds, such as vandering whistling ducks, magpie geese, storks and egrets, s well as many endemic and migratory waders at Parry agoons Nature Reserve. Watch for agile wallabies at Mirima NP and elsewhere.

Crocodile warning

Dangerous saltwater crocodiles inhabit coastal waters, freshwater and saltwater inland waterways and lagoons. Seek local advice before swimming.

Vorld Heritage-listed Purnululu NP

urnululu NP protects the dramatic beehive-shaped towers of he Bungle Bungle Range. Over 20 million years, the ancient andstone has been eroded into its visually arresting shapes; ninute organisms growing on the stone have created orizontal bands of colour. Aboriginal presence in the park ates back 20 000 years.

Argyle Diamond Mine

Rare and extremely valuable pink diamonds and flawless white diamonds are just two of the precious stones mined at one of the world's largest diamond mines. Visitors can tour the gargantuan open cut mine and the processing plant.

Gold town on the move

The original Halls Creek sprang up as a makeshift town near a gold discovery in 1885. The citizens moved some 14 km west in 1948 to a better location with a more reliable water source. The new Halls Creek is a busy service centre for the surrounding pastoral and mining industries.

Wolfe Creek Meteorite Crater

Standing on the edge of the Western Desert, the world's second largest meteorite crater is a cavernous hole measuring 800 m across, with the rim standing 55 m from the crater floor. The collision occurred around 300 000 years ago.

Varning – maps and route notes are essential

he information presented on this map is intended as n overview. Those attempting any of these outback outes will need detailed maps and comprehensive oute notes. (See *On the Road*, p. 246.)

Kimberley ☎(08) 9193 6660; www.kimberleytourism.com

Opposite top *Wolfe Creek Crater scars the landscape on the edge of the Great Sandy Desert.*

Opposite below *Cattle farming is still big business in the Kimberley.*

Fact File

Top events

April *Battle of the Barra (Wyndham)*
May *Kimberley Moon Experience (Kununurra)*
Ord Valley Muster (Kununurra)
July *Kununurra Agricultural Show*
Munumbara Music Festival (Wyndham)
Aug *Halls Creek Cup*
Wyndham Races
Kununurra Races

Permits and regulations

Aboriginal land There are areas of Aboriginal land in the eastern Kimberley. At present, no specific permits are required for the towns, places and routes mentioned in this region. For further information about Aboriginal land, see *Travel Tips*, p. 224.

Parks and reserves

National parks in WA are administered by the Department of Environment and Conservation (DEC). For general information about parks in WA see *Travel Tips*, p. 224.

Mirima NP Day-use park only, no camping. For further information contact DEC at Kununurra: (08) 9168 4200.

Parry Lagoons Nature Reserve The Parry Creek Road may be closed in the wet season. No camping, but there are campsites and cabins at nearby Parry Creek Farm (see *Contacts*, opposite).

Purnululu NP The park is open April–31 Dec (weather permitting). It is accessible to 4WD vehicles only. There are campsites with facilities (toilets and water) at Walardi and Kurrajong Camp. Visitors must be self-sufficient. A fuel stove is recommended and all rubbish must be carried out. Advise a ranger (there are rangers on site) before undertaking any long or overnight walks. For further information contact DEC at Kununurra: (08) 9168 4200.

Wolfe Creek Crater NP Camping, toilets; no water available. Gravel road only accessible to 2WD vehicles in dry season (May–Oct). For further information contact DEC at Kununurra: (08) 9168 4200.

Fishing

For general information on fishing in this region see *Travel Tips*, p. 224.

Warnings

Fuel and supplies On the highway north of Fitzroy Crossing, there are fuel and supply stops at Halls Creek, Warmun (Turkey Creek), Doon Doon Roadhouse, Wyndham and Kununurra.

Road access and closures Many roads in this region are impassable or cut off in the west season. The Great Northern Hwy is sealed, but may be closed at times during the wet season. Those planning to visit stations or national parks should book ahead, and are advised to check road conditions; some properties have 4WD access only. For further information contact the Shire of Wyndham–East Kimberley on (08) 9168 4100; or Main Roads WA: 138 138 or 1800 013 314; www.mainroads.wa.gov.au

Crocodiles Dangerous saltwater crocodiles inhabit coastal waterways and tidal estuaries in this region. Be crocodile-wise; heed warning signs; swim only where recommended; take care when fishing and boating.

See also *On the Road*, p. 246.

Wolfe Creek Crater

From Fitzroy Crossing (see *Broome and Beyond*, p. 226) it's 259 km west east on the bitumen, and then 137 km south, down the dusty Tanami Track to Wolfe Creek Crater. The walls of the crater rise abruptly from the desert floor, on the fringe of the Great Sandy Desert's barren plains. To the Djaru people this was Kandimalal, where a serpent Creation being emerged from the ground. Scientists believe that 300 000 years ago a meteorite, plummeting through space at a million kilometres an hour, gouged a crater almost a kilometre across and 150 m deep on impact. Over time, the shifting desert sands have partially filled the hole, but its scale is still awesome. Wattles, paperbarks and various shrubs have taken root on the crater floor, providing a scrubby home for birds and wildlife that can survive the arid environment.

The best view is from the air (flights leave from Halls Creek and Kununurra), where the scale and symmetry of the crater come into sharp focus. There is camping at Wolfe Creek Crater NP, but no water.

Once you've bumped your way back along the Tanami Track to the Great Northern Hwy, it's 17 km of sealed road to Halls Creek.

Halls Creek

Charles Halls and Jack Slattery are said to have made WA's first payable gold strike just south-east of present-day Halls Creek, in 1885. The prospect of instant riches quickly lured 15 000 diggers to the north's parched interior. A jumble of shanties and stone buildings sprang up, but as the gold dwindled so too did the population. In 1955 the townsfolk relocated to a position better sited for water and an airport, on the Great Northern Hwy.

Halls Creek, with a predominantly Aboriginal population of about 1600, is a busy centre for surrounding communities and the pastoral and mining industries. It is also the first supply stop after Fitzroy Crossing (see *Broome and Beyond*, p. 226), 289 km to the west, and the last major town before the trip south on the legendary Canning Stock Route (see *The Western Deserts*, p. 214). Like the Kimberley as a whole, Halls Creek holds a number of surprises. Within an hour's drive of the desert township you can be soaking in the cool, freshwater springs of Palm Springs, or fishing in the tranquil environs of Sawtooth Gorge, another of the secluded swimming spots around town.

The area is known for its Aboriginal art; check at the visitor information centre for details. History buffs and fossickers detour to the old township, though there is little more to explore than crumbling walls, pale stone against a stark blue desert sky.

North-east of Halls Creek stands one of Australia's most intriguing geological formations, the Bungle Bungle Range.

Contacts

Visitor information

Halls Creek
Hall St
(08) 9168 6262

Kununurra
Coolibah Dr
(08) 9168 1177
www.kununurratourism.com

Lake Argyle Tourist Village
(08) 9168 7777

Wyndham
Kimberley Motors
(08) 9161 1281

Parks and reserves

See *Fact File*, opposite

Farms, station stays

Diggers Rest Station
(08) 9161 1029
http://diggersreststation.com.au

El Questro
(08) 9169 1777
www.elquestro.com.au

Home Valley Station
(08) 9161 4322
www.homevalley.com.au

Parry Creek Farm
(08) 9161 1139

Activities

Check with visitor information regarding scenic flights (from Halls Creek and Kununurra) and cruises (from Kununurra).

Access to diamond mines is restricted; tours must be booked.

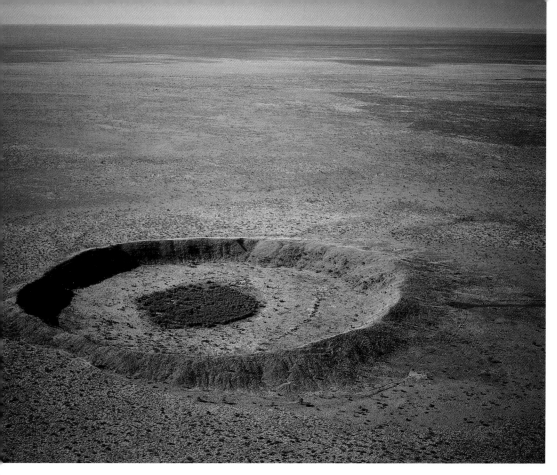

ᴾurnululu National Park

:he domed shapes of the Bungle Bungle Range ise like striped beehives, a startling and intricate naze of towers cleft by serpentine, sheer-sided ;orges. Remarkably, this range appears to have been known only to Aboriginal people and a handful of local pastoralists and scientists until the 1980s, when it was filmed for a documentary and gained worldwide exposure. It has become a symbol of the Kimberley, and is a declared World Heritage Area for ts outstanding scientific importance and exceptional natural beauty.

From the southern side, the dramatic sandstone orms of the range emerge from a sea of bleached and and spinifex plains. They stand 200 to 300 m ibove the plains, with steep cliffs guarding the vestern face. The sandstone and conglomerates rocks mixed with pebbles, boulders and finer naterial) have been eroded into these shapes over ?0 million years. Layers of rock either coated by lgal growth or stained by minerals create the regular horizontal bands of orange and black or grey that give the domes their distinctive appearance and add o their intrigue.

Cloistered within the towers of the range lies hidden world of dry creek beds, cool pools and hadowy gorges, where fan palms take root in the ractured rock and crevices, casting long shadows n the golden late-day light.

Cattle kings

The Kimberley is cattle country. Numbers may have dropped, and other industries (notably tourism) now play a major part in the region's economy, but the pastoral families and the properties they pioneered are now embedded in Australian history.

In the 1880s, families such as the Duracks and the Buchanans overlanded cattle from the eastern states in epic journeys that, literally, took years. Today, cattle properties account for more than half of the Kimberley's 421 000 sq km, and the average station area covers more than 2000 sq km. Some of these properties now supplement their incomes by taking in paying guests, who can experience life on a working station.

Like the Kimberley as a whole, the Bungle Bungle Range has a rich cultural heritage. Indigenous people traditionally spent time in the area during the wet season, when plant and animal life flourished, providing a plentiful supply of bush tucker, and shelter was easily accessible. Scattered rock-art and burial sites are tangible reminders of that long history.

The range is protected within Purnululu NP, 2397 sq km of Kimberley country that provides a buffer region. The Bungle Bungle is fragile and at present recreational activities are restricted to the western and southern sides of the range. The track in from the Great Northern Hwy is 4WD only (it is only 55 km, but prepare yourself for a bumpy three-hour driving stint).

Most walkers head for Cathedral Gorge, a half-hour walk to see the gorge widen into a huge amphitheatre. Those wanting to explore Piccaninny Creek and Gorge will need to devote a day or two and camp overnight, but will be rewarded with tranquil, palm-rimmed waterholes, polished-pebble creek beds, wildflowers and the chance to spot wildlife, including some of the park's 130 or more bird species. At sunset, the light burnishes the towers in fiery reds and golds.

One of the best ways to appreciate Purnululu NP is to take a scenic flight from Halls Creek or Kununurra. As the park is closed during the Wet, an eagle's-eye view is the only way to witness the transformation monsoonal rains bring – lush green grass, and waterfalls cascading into gullies and fast-flowing creeks.

Warmun (Turkey Creek) and Beyond

Warmun, formerly Turkey Creek, is the next town north of Halls Creek. Again, it's a mainly Aboriginal community, with a population of around 1000, where you can top up your supplies, including fuel, at the local roadhouse. Then the highway heads north, through range and granite country, with thousands of giant granite boulders interspersed with rubbly escarpments. To the east, the profile of the rugged Carr Boyd Ranges is silhouetted against the sky.

Strangely rippled, ruched and rounded forms within Purnululu NP.

Just over 150 km from Warmun, the road forks: travellers can head north-west to Wyndham or continue on Highway 1, east to Kununurra.

Kununurra

Kununurra – the name is said to be Aboriginal for 'meeting of big waters' – was established in the 1960s to service the Ord River Irrigation Scheme. Located on part of the original Ivanhoe Station (established by the pioneering Durack family), the town of 5000 people is a busy modern centre, a green oasis on the fringe of the Kimberley. It is less than 40 km from the WA/NT border.

Kelly's Knob, the town's best lookout, provides a panorama of the town, the Ord Irrigation Area and Lake Kununurra. Keen anglers may want to test the waters at Ivanhoe Crossing, the concrete causeway over the Lower Ord River, about 15 km from Kununurra, and a well-known fishing haunt. Barramundi is the favourite catch, but take care where you stand as saltwater crocodiles are present. Swimming is definitely not recommended.

For those interested in the results of the Ord Irrigation Scheme (see *Lake Argyle – inland sea*, p. 242), a drive around the irrigation areas north and south of Kununurra reveals a patchwork of crops – sugarcane, sunflowers, melons, mangoes, bananas and pumpkins all flourishing. Although the scheme has had serious problems, and for many years was considered a white elephant, the visionaries and those with persistence have been rewarded, with economic benefits at last being reaped.

Argyle Diamond Mine

Broome is well known for its creamy, opalescent pearls, which are transformed into fine jewellery. But the East Kimberley has its gems too. Buried deep within the chiselled red rock of the region, diamond-bearing ore has yielded over 600 million carats of diamonds. The Argyle Diamond Mine, the world's only source of the rare pink diamond, is also the world's most productive diamond mine. Public access is limited to one-day flying tours from Kununurra (check with visitor information, see *Contacts*, p. 239).

Mirima National Park

For those unable to make the trip to Purnululu NP to see the Bungle Bungle Range, or to travel even deeper into the region, Mirima NP, just 2 km from Kununurra, is worth visiting. Although small – the park covers just 21 sq km – its timeworn rock formations, stretches of spinifex grassland and tropical species, such as the gnarled boabs and brilliant yellow-flowering kapok trees, provide a tantalising glimpse of the Kimberley.

Sunflowers bloom in the irrigated Ord River valley.

There are two short walking trails. If you have time, do the steep, 1 km return Didbgirring Trail, for fine views of Kununurra and the park. While walking, watch for agile wallabies – which will dart for cover if disturbed – and the more stealthy dingoes. Reptiles are common here as elsewhere in the Kimberley – goannas, snakes and tiny geckos frequently warm themselves near water. Finches also flock to water, and can frequently be heard chirping noisily; while a flash of red through the vegetation is often the sign of the vivid male crimson finch.

Mirima is a day-use park only, but there are tables for picnics and plenty to explore.

Wyndham

Wyndham, WA's most northerly town, faces the tidal waters of Cambridge Gulf and the meeting of the King, Pentecost, Durack, Forrest and Ord rivers. Supplies for the Kimberley's earliest pastoralists, including the pioneering Durack family, were unloaded here in the 1880s and prospectors landed on their way to the goldfields at Halls Creek.

Today, with a mainly Aboriginal population of 800, the town is a strategic port for the pastoral industry, with live cattle exports to Asia and the Middle East, and raw sugar from the Ord Valley shipped to Indonesia.

Past and present

On the edge of Lake Argyle are symbols of the past and the present. Historic Argyle Downs Homestead (see *Lake Argyle – inland sea*, p. 242), which was owned by the pastoralist Durack family, was moved block by block before the property was flooded. Today it is a museum. Also at the northern end of the lake is the Ord River Hydro-electric Power Station, opened in the 1990s, which supplies some of the power needs of the Argyle Diamond Mine and Kununurra.

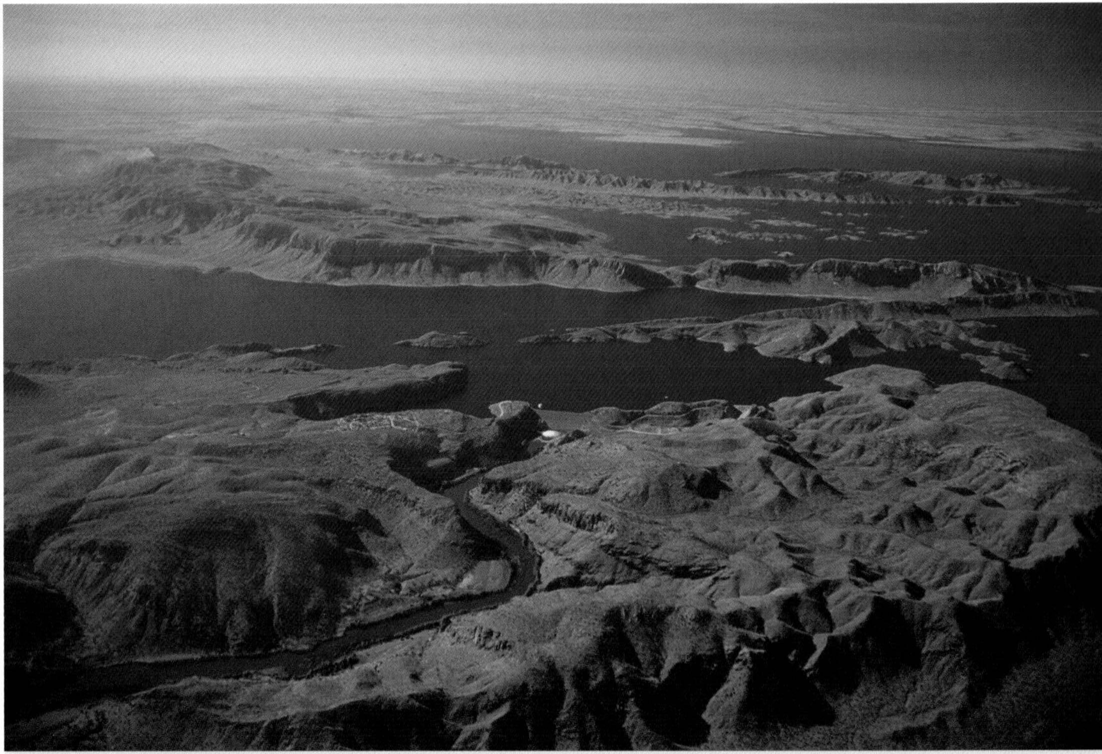

A bird's-eye view of the immense Lake Argyle.

Lake Argyle – inland sea

It's hard not to be impressed by the Kimberley's natural features – the fascinating tiger-striped towers of the Bungle Bungle Range, the tiered waterfalls and secluded gorges, the giant tides that pummel the coast, and much more. But also impressive is one of the region's man-made features – Lake Argyle.

The lake was formed by damming the Ord River to create a storage reservoir to supply the Ord River Irrigation Area. The scheme began in the 1960s. When Argyle Downs, a former cattle station in the Carr Boyd Ranges, was inundated, it formed not just a lake, but a vast inland sea. At normal levels, the lake covers almost 1000 sq km and holds 20 times the volume of Sydney Harbour; during a major flood, it may hold three times that amount of water. The drowned mountain peaks now form islands and there are bays, narrow inlets, and even waterfalls in season. So vast is its water surface that it affects the weather, causing storm winds and thunderstorms to blow-up.

The lake has also developed an ecology of its own, with the waterway and environs sustaining a wealth of flora and fauna. Watch for some of the hundreds of species of birds, including osprey, jabiru and pelicans, as well as turtles and freshwater crocs.

The usually placid waters have become a venue for sailing, waterskiing, fishing, swimming, windsurfing and kayaking. There are also cruises along the Ord River to the diversionary dam (110 km return), cruises on Lake Argyle and scenic flights.

Noogoora burr

The introduced noxious weed noogoora burr can poison and injure stock, tangle in fleece affecting the value of the wool, and spread as a dense growth that can prevent animals from reaching water. The weed can also infest agricultural crops, reducing production. To stop the spread of the weed in the Kimberley there are two quarantine areas – all pastoral leases from Fitzroy Crossing to the Fitzroy River mouth, and an area north-east of Wyndham near the Ord River. There is no public access in these areas.

Five Rivers Lookout, on the bulky Bastion Range (a short but steep drive from town), offers sweeping views of the countryside and the rivers as they edge their way into the gulf. Many visitors to Wyndham come for the fishing, but birdwatching, horseriding in the ranges, scenic flights or a visit to the crocodile park, are other options.

For those in a 4WD, the Kurunjie Track winding 80 km south-west, from Wyndham to the Gibb River Road, offers a worthwhile diversion. The track passes the northern face of Cockburn Range's rippled sandstone escarpment and the broad flood plains of the mighty Pentecost River. The Cockburn Range stands 600 m above the plains; over time, the rivers have gouged steep-sided gorges through the sandstone.

Parry Lagoons Nature Reserve

Fifteen kilometres from Wyndham along the Parry Creek Road, the wetlands of Parry Lagoons Nature Reserve are the ideal site for some exceptional birdwatching. On the Marglu Billabong as many as 20 000 birds congregate even in the dry season – great flocks of whistling ducks, magpie geese,

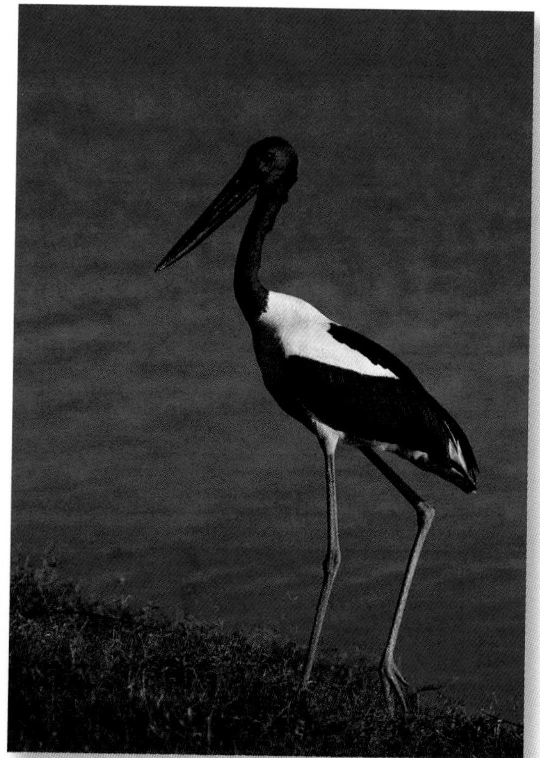

brolgas, jabirus, egrets, herons and more. The wetlands are a feeding and breeding ground for migratory shorebirds, some from as far afield as Siberia. As well, you may spot raptors hovering in search of an easy meal. Don't focus only on the sky, however – these waterways attract dangerous saltwater crocodiles, so take care. The Parry Creek Road may be closed in the wet season.

East Kimberley – station stays

El Questro, perhaps the best known of the Kimberley stations that accommodate visitors, is the most expansive. It ranges across 1 million acres, or 4000 sq km, a 'wilderness park' that embraces towering gorges and thermal springs, mountains, river frontage and Aboriginal rock-art sites. Located 100 km west of Kununurra by road, off the Gibb River Road, El Questro offers basic campsites, tented cabins, or the ultimate five-star luxury of the homestead. Visitors cruise the rivers, ride horses, take helicopter flights, fish, join bush tucker and rock-art tours, swim in waterholes and watch the wildlife. Travellers can purchase a week-long pass and explore the park at their own pace (4WD is recommended).

Just two minutes off the Gibb River Road, 125 km from Kununurra, Home Valley Station – another immense pastoral lease – invites visitors to explore its imposing gorge country, rock pools, riverscapes and inspiring views. It offers B&B or camping, and a range of activities, such as fishing in the Pentecost and Durack rivers, birdwatching, or the chance to just soak up the Kimberley atmosphere.

Diggers Rest, 7 km from Wyndham, on the banks of the King River, is a working cattle station with a rustic homestead, and facilities for visitors. There are different levels of accommodation, including bush camping, a warm outback welcome and the opportunity to catch a barra, ride a horse, or just listen to some of the locals yarning about the Kimberley, past and present. (See *Contacts*, p. 239 for station phone numbers.)

Above *River arteries on the plains near Wyndham.*

Above left *A jabiru or black-necked stork, on the banks of Lake Argyle.*

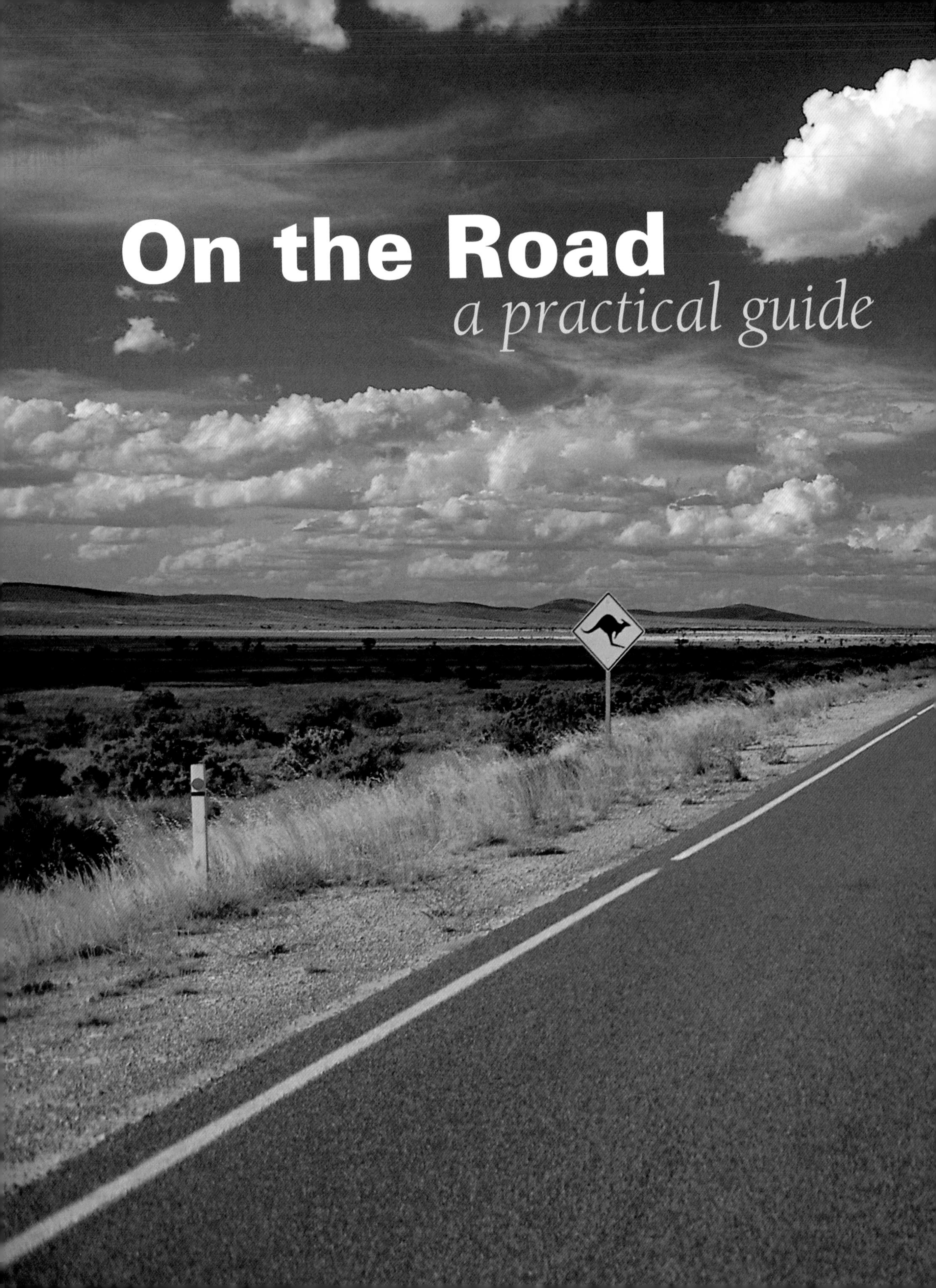
On the Road
a practical guide

On the Road

The Australian outback is a place of great adventure, but it can be dangerous; its landscapes are scenically extraordinary, but environmentally fragile. Some thoughtful planning will help ensure that travellers enjoy a safe trip and minimise the impact of their activities on their surroundings.

Contents

Planning Your Trip

Planning is the key to successful outback travel. The distances are too great and the conditions too harsh to leave things to chance. Heading off to, say, the Simpson Desert during the summer months will not simply be uncomfortable, it could be life-threatening. For safety, as well as to make the trip more enjoyable, research the best time of year to travel, what route to take and what to expect in terms of facilities en route and at your destination.

When to Go

Most outback travellers take advantage of Australia's milder climate from autumn through to late spring (approximately April to October). During summer, temperatures in the centre of the continent are very high (high 30s to 40 degrees celsius plus), while the coastal areas of the remote north experience extreme humidity and high temperatures, as well as torrential downpours and cyclone-strength winds in what is known as the Wet (approximately November to March). Discomfort aside, this can result in sudden road closures, regardless of whether or not a road is sealed or even a major highway. The Wet is also the season of the venomous marine stinger, which inhabits coastal waters (see *Dangerous Creatures*, p. 262). For weather information on long-range forecasts, warnings or tomorrow's temperature, contact the relevant Bureau of Meteorology service (see *Useful Numbers*, p. 265).

The increasing popularity of outback travel means that the peak season can be busy, even in remote places – particularly during school holidays and over Easter. Make inquiries about campsites and other accommodation ahead of travelling, particularly for high-volume tourist areas such as the Red Centre. The *Fact File* at the beginning of each subregion provides details of places where bookings may be required, particularly national parks.

Many outback towns stage festivals during the winter, or dry season, providing great fun and a way of experiencing the outback spirit and meeting the locals. Rodeos are popular, particularly in outback Queensland and the NT. As well, look out for Aboriginal cultural festivals, country race meetings, agricultural shows, and festivals celebrating historic events. Refer to the events list in the *Fact File* at the beginning of each subregion. Contact visitor information centres ahead of travelling as accommodation is often booked out well in advance.

Above *To get the most from your trip, plan the time of year to travel and make sure you are well equipped. These campers prepare for an evening in the Simpson Desert.*

Opposite *The ability to read a map is still essential for remote travel.*

Visitor Information

Visitor information bureaus and centres are the essential first call when planning a trip. Centres are no longer confined to big cities and major towns. Many small rural centres have an outlet, be it self-contained or part of another business. Many centres make accommodation and tour bookings.

Before travelling, contact the state-based bureaus (see *Useful Numbers*, p. 265) for relevant brochures, maps and other trip-planning information. Town-based and regional visitor information centres are listed under *Contacts* in each subregion in this book. In many cases, tourist organisations have excellent websites detailing the attractions as well as activities and accommodation – relevant sites are listed throughout this book.

Finding Your Way

Detailed maps are required for travel to remote areas. The maps in this book are intended to provide a general sense of location, but are not sufficient for navigational purposes. Recommended are the topographic maps produced and published by the government organisation Geoscience Australia. The maps are drawn to three scales: 1:100 000; 1: 250 000; 1: 1 million. Geoscience also distributes highly detailed Department of Defence maps of northern Australia, which are drawn to a scale of 1: 50 000. You can purchase maps direct (contact Geoscience on 1800 800 173; www.ga.gov.au) or at good map shops.

Tracks appear and disappear in the outback and maps can date quickly. For remote areas, other navigational equipment will be required. A good compass will always be a necessity. In addition, travellers should consider investing in Global Positioning System (GPS) technology (see *Global Positioning System*, p. 252).

Suggested Reading

Four-wheel-drive touring
The Complete 4WD Guide (Explore Australia Publishing, 2008)

Camping, caravanning
Camping in Australia, Cathy Savage and Craig Lewis (Explore Australia Publishing, 2007)

Explore Australia by Caravan and Motorhome, John and Jan Tait (Explore Australia Publishing, 2008)

Safety
Australia's Most Dangerous (Australian Geographic, 2003)

Don't Die in the Bush, Sven Klinge and Adrian Hart (New Holland Publishers, 2000)

Outdoor Survival, Garth Hattingh (New Holland Publishers, 2004)

Plant identification
Bush Tucker Field Guide, Les Hiddins (Explore Australia Publishing, 2003)

Wildlife-watching and conservation
Australian Mammals, Leonard Cronin (Envirobook, 2000)

Australian Reptiles and Amphibians, Leonard Cronin (Envirobook, 2001)

Care of Australian Wildlife, Erna Walraven (New Holland Publishers, 2004)

Caring for Australian Wildlife, Sharon White (Australian Geographic, 1997)

Field Guide to Australian Birds, Michael Morecombe (Steve Parish, 2000)

General interest
The Canning Stock Route, E. and R. Gard, D. Hewitt and M. Bamford (Australian Geographic, 2002)

Central Australia, Charles Rawlings-Way et al (Lonely Planet, 2009)

The Corner Country, Mitch Reardon (Australian Geographic, 2002)

Discover Australia: National Parks, Ron and Viv Moon (Hema, 2002)

The Kimberley, David McGonigal (Australian Geographic, 2003)

The Red Centre, Jenny Stanton and Barry Skipsey (Australian Geographic, 2001)

The Top End, David Hancock (Australian Geographic, 2001)

Choosing a Route

Many travellers will be pleased to know that most roads in major tourist areas are sealed and maintained (although true outback adventurers may well be looking for the challenge offered by unsealed and even poorly maintained roads). When planning an outback trip, travellers should ask themselves the following questions about the route they intend to travel.

- Are all the roads sealed? If not, will a 4WD vehicle be required?
- Do long distances separate places where supplies, including petrol, are available?
- Will it be necessary to carry extra fuel and water?
- Are roads likely to close? If this is a possibility, what information is available?
- Is there accommodation available en route? If not, are there places to camp? Will bookings be necessary?
- Will a communications device be needed?

A high-clearance 4WD is needed to tackle many sand dunes and rugged roads.

Nearly all of the routes outlined in this book are along public roads, however, there are occasional diversions across private land – usually pastoral land or Aboriginal land. In some cases, particularly with Aboriginal land in the NT, you must apply for a permit well ahead of travelling. (See the *Fact File* at the beginning of each sub-region; see also *Private Land*, p. 258 and *Useful Numbers*, p. 265.)

Numerous national parks and conservation reserves are scattered throughout remote Australia. Before travelling, visitors should check national park websites or with offices for information on camping (bookings may be necessary), walking trails, road conditions and any special warnings (see *Parks and Reserves*, p. 258).

Tours, Clubs, Organisations

For travel to very remote places, joining a tour makes good sense. Those who like to keep a degree of autonomy should consider a tag-along tour; that is, one where you drive your own vehicle as part of a convoy, with an experienced guide at the head. These operators provide various degrees of assistance, including carrying extra equipment and supplies. Start your research by contacting the state and territory visitor information bureaus (see *Useful Numbers*, p. 265).

There are numerous 4WD clubs around Australia. These organisations, small and large, offer members a range of benefits, from

A convoy of 4WDs heads into Bunyeroo Valley in the Flinders Ranges.

competitively priced insurance to driver training, advice networks and equipment trade opportunities. Many clubs organise regular 4WD trips for their members – a safe and rewarding way to travel. Good clubs will be affiliated with peak state or territory associations, which in turn come under the umbrella of the Australian National Four Wheel Drive Council (see *Useful Numbers*, p. 265).

Most people turn to their state-based motoring organisation for emergency roadside repairs (although this service is only available for a price in remote locations – see *Vehicle Insurance and Roadside Assistance*, p. 250). These organisations also make travel bookings, offer insurance, provide motoring advice and sell a range of travel products, from maps to car accessories. All state and territory motoring organisations offer reciprocal rights to members from other states (see *Useful Numbers*, p. 265).

Travel Insurance

Although travellers often insure themselves when travelling overseas, many underestimate – or forget altogether – how costly it can be if you have an accident in Australia. Your vehicle may be insured, but are you? For example, if you are injured in a remote area and need to be rescued by air ambulance, such as the Royal Flying Doctor Service (RFDS), there is a very substantial cost involved. Make sure that you are covered, as well as your vehicle.

Getting Equipped

Being well equipped is essential for a safe and enjoyable outback trip. Set aside plenty of time for this task – choosing a vehicle, the right camping gear, even the containers for carrying extra fuel requires research.

What Type of Vehicle

Contrary to expectation, many of Australia's remote outback regions have sealed and maintained roads. In these places a conventional 2WD vehicle should be adequate. The vehicle should be in good working order because of the long distances that separate service centres in many areas. Airconditioning is often regarded as a necessity not a luxury when travelling in the outback.

Many areas have reasonably well-maintained gravel and dirt roads. Again, conventional vehicles may be all right in some cases, although, to be safe, you should contact the local shire office, tourist information centre or roadhouse ahead of travelling to check road conditions.

The extreme outback is for large, high-clearance 4WD vehicles. Places such as the Canning Stock Route, a remote stretch of cattle track with around 700 dunes, are impossible in smaller vehicles. You will need not only the power, but also the capacity to transport extra supplies, including fuel. Many travellers to such places opt for vehicles that are light-coloured (to deflect heat).

Drivers should watch for wildlife and livestock on the road, especially at dawn and at dusk.

Vehicle Insurance and Roadside Assistance

Make sure your car insurance covers the activities you have planned in the areas you intend to visit. This is particularly the case if off-road travel is involved. Many companies offer extra cover at extra cost, including such items as free or cheap car hire in the event of an accident. Shop around for the best package. Carry copies of your policies with you.

Most new motor vehicles are sold with a manufacturer's warranty that includes roadside assistance in the event of breakdown. The warranty varies from one to three years depending on the make and model of the vehicle. Check your policy carefully before you go. Make sure it covers you for the kind of travel you want to do and the places you want to go. Motorists without a new vehicle warranty, or who do not believe that the warranty is adequate, should become members of their state-based motoring organisation (see *Useful Numbers*, p. 265). Different levels of membership are offered. Those travelling to remote areas should opt for top-level cover, which generally provides for unlimited service calls and free towing (towing can be extremely expensive). That said, organisations will charge members a fee for a service call to remote locations. This is calculated on the distance your car is from the nearest depot (the first 30 to 100 km is free – depending on your level of cover). This means that cost for a service call along, say, a remote desert track could be prohibitive. Those planning outback travel need to equip themselves with some basic automotive skills and consider travelling with a good supply of spares and tools (see *Spares, Tools, Repairs* p. 251).

Hiring a 4WD

This is a good option for those who go off-road only occasionally, or who want to fly into a particular area, such as Alice Springs, and then set off under their own steam.

It is more expensive to hire a 4WD vehicle than a conventional car, and the standard insurance excess is very high – around $5000. However, for an extra $30 or $40 a day you can often reduce the excess to around $1000.

When hiring a vehicle, if you explain exactly where you intend to go the operator will let you know whether the vehicle you have in mind is suitable. For example, in Alice Springs, a small 4WD will get you around the popular Mereenie Loop but not into the rugged Palm Valley. Taking a rental vehicle on inappropriate tracks could result in problems with insurance claims, should damage occur.

Book your vehicle well ahead of travelling, particularly for the peak winter months.

Extras for the Car

Many travellers fit their vehicles with a few extras to help make things safer and a little more comfortable. Any extra equipment you need will depend on where you intend to go. Some items to consider are listed below.

- *Fire extinguisher* Check with your local fire brigade what model is most suitable for travel in a 4WD.
- *Tie-points* Great for preventing luggage from moving around on bumpy roads.
- *Cargo barriers* These separate the luggage from the passengers, preventing passengers from being hit by flying luggage in the event of an accident.
- *Dual-battery system* A good idea if you are going to run electrical equipment off the car battery – winches, fridges, entertainment equipment and the like.
- *Aftermarket suspension* This is heavy-duty suspension for regular travel on very rough roads – ask your vehicle dealer.
- *Snorkel* This attachment helps keep the air clean in dusty conditions, and helps avoid water seeping into the motor during water crossings.
- *Tow bar* Essential for towing trailers or vans, and for recovering bogged vehicles.
- *Bullbar* Practical for protecting the vehicle from accidents with animals along outback roads, but dangerous in cities and built-up areas.

- *Roof-racks* Good for additional equipment.
- *Trailer* Excellent for carrying extras for long-haul trips; heavy-duty, off-road trailers are available, but on some routes (for example, the Canning Stock Route) even these will not be suitable.

Spares, Tools, Repairs

Distances of 1000 km or more separate towns in some outback areas, which means it can be a long way to the mechanic. If you intend to travel to very remote places, consider taking a basic course in car mechanics, and carry a range of tools and spares. What you take will depend on your vehicle and where you are going, but basics would include globes, tyre-changing equipment, fuses, plugs, spare tyres, engine oil and jumper leads.

Vehicle Recovery Equipment

Travellers going off-road will need to carry equipment for the recovery of bogged vehicles. A basic list includes an axe; a long-handled shovel; a pair of thick gloves; a jack and jacking plate; a snatch strap, which runs between the towing vehicle and a bogged vehicle; and a basic winch – hand-powered or electric – which can be attached to any stable object, such as a tree. Those unfamiliar with recovery techniques should consider a course offered by one of the 4WD clubs.

Provision for Carrying Fuel

Fuel is readily available across Australia but in some areas long distances separate fuel stops. Travellers to these areas will need to carry extra fuel. The ideal is a dedicated long-range tank. Otherwise, fuel must be carried in approved containers such as metal or plastic jerry cans; these containers must be stored in racks. Fuel should never be carried inside the passenger compartment.

To calculate the amount of fuel you will need, load your vehicle up and take it off-road for a trial run. Remember, your vehicle will use a lot more fuel when towing and over very rough terrain, such as sand dunes. (See also *Fuel Availability*, p. 257.)

Communication Equipment

A communication device is a sensible investment when travelling to remote areas. Such devices can save lives. Every year, search and rescue authorities spend thousands of man-hours looking for adventurers who could have been found very quickly had they been carrying the right device. Do not rely on your mobile phone. At present, coverage of regional areas still rarely extends far beyond population centres, which leaves most of the continent out of range. The main options are as follows.

In many outback regions there can be long distances between fuel stops.

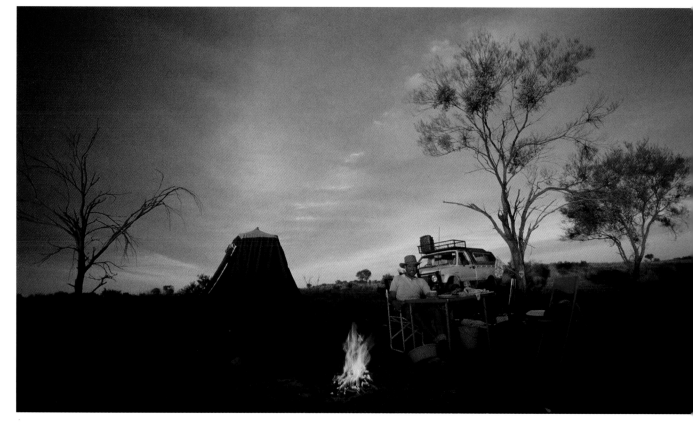

Settling down for the evening in a one-man tent on Curtin Springs Station in the NT.

HF radio This is a reliable form of communication, although quite expensive – new units range from $3000 to $4500. Most outback travellers use the VKS-737 radio network – this has twice-daily schedules, position reporting, message service, plus a host of additional services. Direct-dial phone calls are made through HF service providers such as Radtel (they also offer a basic emergency service but also recommend membership of VKS-737). Most HF radio sets have an emergency button to directly raise the RFDS. Despite the proliferation of satellite phones in recent years (see below), many individuals and companies still rely heavily on this long-established technology.

Satellite phone The signal from these devices is relayed by satellite. This means that, unlike mobile phones, their coverage is virtually universal and reliable except in certain circumstances, such as very poor weather or heavily forested surrounds. Units are now well below $1000 purchase price – cheap when compared with HF radio. Call costs are $1 to $2 per minute depending on the plan. Increasing numbers of outback travellers now hire satellite phones – the cost is approximately $17 to $20 per day.

Emergency Position Indicating Radio Beacon Basic EPIRBs cost a few hundred dollars and are readily available for sale or for hire. Their portability makes them an excellent device for walkers. Unlike the other devices, they are not for voice communication; in case of distress, the individual activates an emergency call signal that is picked up by Australian Search and Rescue, which then notifies local authorities. It is important to avoid activating this device for anything other than a life-threatening emergency.

CB radio Citizen Band (CB) radio is useful for people travelling in convoys of two or more vehicles. CB radios should not be relied upon for life-saving communications as interference regularly causes problems with transmission. Sets start at around $100

Global Positioning System (GPS)

In addition to good maps and a compass (see *Finding Your Way*, p. 247), travellers should consider investing in GPS technology, a satellite-based navigation system developed by the US military. A GPS receiver determines the user's position, accurate to within 100 m, by collecting distance and time measurements from satellites. GPS can also be used to determine speed of travel, altitude, distance to a proposed destination and estimated time of arrival.

Most GPS receivers have the capacity to remember at least several routes. The preloaded data includes information on road networks and major geographical features. GPS receivers and antennae range in price from several hundred dollars to a couple of thousand.

A laptop computer, loaded with interactive mapping software downloaded from a CD-ROM and connected to a GPS receiver, offers a hi-tech visual navigational aid.

A GPS ground receiver can pinpoint a geographic location to within 20 to 100 m. Hand-held devices retail for upwards of $200. Map software can be loaded onto hand-held devices or laptop computers. The initial set-up costs may be quite high (software, laptop, receiver), but the benefits for travellers to remote locations are enormous.

Camping Gear

If you are going into fairly remote areas, it's a good idea to keep your camp simple. You'll want to save the space for fuel, water and food, which will enable you to travel longer distances with greater safety. Many people choose to travel the outback with a camper trailer or caravan (although these are not suitable for very challenging terrain, particularly dune-bound routes). Many service stations and roadhouses have areas for caravans, and some national parks allow them as well – just don't expect powered sites in parks; they are the exception rather than the rule (see *Where to Camp*, p. 258).

Tents Most importantly, a tent should be easy to put up. Those planning overnight treks will need something that is light and easily transportable. Look for quality material and stitching; insect screening, ventilation and sewn-in floors are also important.

Sleeping bags and swags The nights can be very cold in the outback; invest in a good-quality bag, making sure to check the temperature rating before you buy. Blow-up mattresses or self-inflating mattresses are more space-efficient than foam rolls or stretchers. Swags (a bed roll with a tough, waterproof outer covering) are popular with those who want true portability. In coastal and northern areas a mosquito net is a wise investment.

Cooking gear A barbecue plate, saucepan, frying pan and billy are the basics. A fuel stove is essential – many national parks do not permit the lighting of fires. Think about what you use at home (good knives, chopping board, can-opener) and shop accordingly. Camping stores have a wide range of equipment and are often staffed by people with hands-on experience who can offer helpful advice.

Lighting Few campsites in remote areas have electricity. Many national park sites do not permit the use of generators. Portable 12-volt fluorescent lights draw power from a car's battery and provide good light, although gas lanterns are probably a little more atmospheric. Pack at least two torches and, of course, matches.

Refrigeration A means of refrigeration is a good idea when travelling to places without supplies. There is a wide range available, from an icebox to an expensive multivoltage, compressor-driven refrigerator–freezer combination. If you are planning to run a unit from the car battery (the most common method) you will need to fit a dual-battery system to avoid flattening the main battery.

Water supply

Ensuring an adequate supply of water is one of the most important aspects of preparing for a trip to the outback. Many remote camping areas, including national park sites, do not have a supply of fresh drinking water. In some cases there is a creek, dam or well (water from these sources should always be boiled before drinking).

The standard recommendation is that you make provision to carry 5 to 10 litres of water per person per day in areas where the supply is limited, unreliable or not available. In addition, carry a spare 20 litres per person in case you get lost or bogged, or break down. This may seem like a lot, but in very hot weather you may need to drink a litre an hour. It is worth noting that when you first arrive in a hot climate, you may not feel as thirsty as you should – you may already be dehydrated by the time you start to feel thirsty.

Ideally store water in several containers, so that if one bursts you will not lose your entire supply. An alternative is to fit your vehicle with a stainless steel water tank, complete with tap.

Food

For an extended trip, a supply of non-perishable staples such as pasta, rice, nuts, dried fruit and tinned food will be a good back-up to fresh food. Buy before you travel into remote places. Even if there are shops, prices increase the further you are from a major centre. This is particularly the case for fresh fruit and vegetables. Carry vegetables that will last such as potatoes and pumpkin. Store food in large plastic containers with sealable lids. Remember that there are restrictions on the movement across state borders of fruit, vegetables and some foodstuffs, such as honey. Carry extra, sealable plastic containers for rubbish.

Clothing

Travellers to the outback need to prepare for the extremes: hot and cold; wet and dry.

For cold, wet weather, clothing made from artificial fibres designed to keep out the wind, keep in the warmth and dry out quickly are ideal. (Remember that temperatures in the outback can plummet during the night.) Numerous retail outlets cater for outdoor enthusiasts and staff may offer knowledgeable advice.

For hot weather, natural – cotton – is still best. Choose light-coloured clothing that covers as much of your body as possible to protect against sunburn. A wide-brimmed hat is essential, along with a good pair of sunglasses.

Footwear is important. You will need sturdy boots to support your feet, and to protect you from potential dangers such as sharp rocks, ant nests and venomous snakes.

Medical Items and First Aid

A good-quality first-aid kit is a high priority. These can be bought from camping stores and St John Ambulance outlets. St John has a range of kits, which have been designed to suit different environments and situations. See *First-aid kit*, right, for a list of common first-aid items. St John is also the major provider of first-aid courses across Australia. Such training is a sensible idea generally but is probably a necessity for those heading into very remote areas. Contact the organisation direct.

Other health items and issues to consider include the following.

- *Sunscreen and insect repellent* Both essential items in the outback. Test a few brands to rule out allergies and irritation.
- *Pharmaceuticals* Get your doctor to provide you with a sufficient number of repeats on prescribed medicine. If that's not possible, carry a letter from your doctor, or a copy of your medical records.
- *Other medicines* Alternative treatments or other, more unusual non-prescription medicine may not be available in remote areas – carry sufficient supplies.
- *Ambulance cover* If you have private insurance, check that you are covered in all circumstances. If not, take out direct membership. Medical transportation from remote areas is extremely expensive.

Royal Flying Doctor Service

The RFDS HF radio network, set up to give residents of the outback access to medical services and advice, has been used as a safety net by travellers venturing into remote corners of the country. Many HF radio sets are fitted with an RFDS emergency call button, which can transmit a distress signal to the nearest staffed base. Many sick and stranded travellers have relied on the organisation's famous medical service, which comprises 20 bases in remote areas and a fleet of aircraft for the transportation of medical staff and patients. The organisation offers excellent advice for travellers to outback regions, based on over 50 years of experience. For contact details see *Useful Numbers*, p. 265.

First-aid kit

A practical first-aid kit for on-the-road travel could contain:

- first-aid handbook
- tweezers to remove splinters, prickles and ticks
- scissors to cut dressings, tape and so on
- gauze bandages to hold dressings in place and protect wounds
- cottonwool and cotton buds to clean and dress wounds
- elastic bandages to support joint injuries and treat spider bites and snake bites
- pins or clips to hold elastic bandages in place
- triangular bandages to use as a sling, to secure a splint, and to cover head wounds
- bandaids (various shapes and sizes)
- non-adhesive dressings to cover wounds and abrasions
- anti-itch cream to treat bites, stings and some rashes
- antiseptic to treat open cuts and wounds
- alcohol swabs to clean around wounds (not suitable for some stings)
- cold pack to treat sprains, swellings and some bites
- latex gloves to prevent the spread of infection
- diarrhoea tablets
- anti-nausea tablets
- motion-sickness tablets
- aspirin and/or paracetamol
- throat lozenges
- eye soother
- lip balm
- antihistamines to treat allergenic reactions.

Heading Out

While the outback can be fun, relaxing and rewarding, travellers should take care to ensure their own safety, and to make certain that their activities don't impact unnecessarily on the environment.

Remote Travel

Travellers to outback regions must be self-sufficient. In order to stay safe, they should consider some or all of the following.

- Travel with a companion vehicle.
- Carry a reliable communication device (see *Communication Equipment*, p. 251).
- Make sure one member of the party has first-aid knowledge.
- Before heading off, leave a detailed itinerary with a reliable family member or friend. Call every few days or whenever you can. Let the person know if your itinerary changes.
- If heading into a particularly remote area, let local authorities know (police, national park staff). This also applies to walkers (see *Walking*, p. 260). In some cases, such as remote national parks in NT and WA, this is a requirement not a request. When you have completed your journey, advise the relevant authority.
- Keep emergency numbers close at hand (see *Useful Numbers*, p. 265).

Outback Driving Hazards

Outback driving is very different from city and town driving, and it is worth taking a specialist driving course or at least becoming familiar with the type of terrain and conditions you might encounter. Specialist 4WD instruction is also recommended.

Road trains A road train will have a primemover with up to three trailers attached, a total length of over 50 m. You need at least a kilometre of clear road to pass. Make sure the driver can see you in their rear-view mirror, and then wait for a signal to pass. The safest way to negotiate an oncoming road train is to pull over until it passes. Never expect a road train to give way to you.

Wildlife and livestock Watch for wildlife and stock on the roads, especially early in the morning at dusk and at night when animals may be feeding. Ideally avoid driving at these times; observe speed limits and warning signs. Many outback drivers fit bullbars to protect their vehicles. These do the job, but remember, these fittings can be dangerous to pedestrians and other vehicles – drive responsibly.

Drivers should be especially cautious when driving towards or passing semi-trailers and road trains.

Sand and mud Soft sand and mud should be negotiated in a 4WD at reasonable speed and in a high gear. Examine the road surface first. Do not enter deep mud without establishing the depth. Deep sand requires low tyre pressure – about 15 to 18 psi.

Creeks Never drive straight across a creek or river. Stop, get out of the car and try to gauge the depth. In some cases this may mean wading across (although this is not recommended in crocodile territory). Drive in slowly; if it looks as if the water might rise above the wheels, consider another route. If you must cross, wrap the front of the radiator area with a groundsheet to avoid water flowing in and drowning the engine. Drive through in low-range first gear or high-range second gear. Attaching a snorkel to your car will help avoid damage to the vehicle during water crossings (see *Extras for the Car*, p. 250).

Bulldust This occurs in areas where the surface of the road breaks into a very fine dust. Drive at a slow, steady pace to avoid stirring up large plumes of dust that can choke your air filter – check your filter daily, and clean it if necessary. Wind up your windows and turn up your airconditioning – this will keep the inside pressure greater than the outside pressure, which will tend to hold the dust out. Keep a good distance from other cars.

Some outback stations are not fenced – drivers should be wary of livestock wandering onto the road.

Corrugations Slow down and take it easy with corrugations, particularly around corners. Lowering the tyre pressure will help.

Getting bogged This is a common outback experience. The fastest and easiest way out is to use a snatch strap: one end is attached to the towing vehicle, the other to the bogged vehicle. If this does not work, you will need a winch – hand-powered and electric models are available. These methods can require some expertise. Drivers should consider taking a vehicle-recovery course ahead of travelling (available through 4WD clubs – see *Useful Numbers*, p. 265).

Dune driving Routes such as the French Line through the Simpson Desert and the Canning Stock Route are heavily dune-bound, making them a challenge for drivers and vehicles. Towing trailers is not recommended, and it is a good idea to affix a tall, bright flag to your 4WD so you can be detected earlier by oncoming vehicles and avoid collision. Low tyre pressure is essential. Crossing the Simpson Desert from west to east is recommended for first-time travellers, as the dunes have a gentler upsweep.

Grassy country A major hazard when travelling through grassy country is the possibility of getting spinifex seeds caught in the exhaust system; the heat generated can cause the highly combustible resin in the spinifex to ignite. Spinifex seeds clog radiators; this reduces airflow and causes the vehicle to overheat. Travellers to such grassy areas should get a cover for their radiators, and clean the radiator regularly.

Safe Driving

Outback driving conditions can be very demanding. There's the heat, the glare, the long stretches of straight road, heavily corrugated tracks, creek crossings or billowing clouds of bulldust. Drivers need to take the following basic precautions to help keep themselves, and others, safe.

- Be attentive.
- Swap drivers regularly.
- Drive within the speed limit and within the capacity of your vehicle.
- Take extra care when towing, as your vehicle becomes more difficult to control.
- Do not travel when tired or after consuming alcohol.
- Be wary of the effect of prescription drugs and even non-prescription drugs such as painkillers; talk to your doctor ahead of travelling.
- Be mindful of wildlife and wandering stock.
- Slow down when oncoming vehicles appear on gravel and dirt roads.

Road Closures

Road closures are a fact of life in remote Australia, particularly at the height of the Wet when sudden rains can cause flash floods. Bushfires and roadwork can also close roads. In Aboriginal Arnhem Land, roads may close for special ceremonies, such as funerals.

The easiest way to check for road closures is to listen to local radio. Most government road authorities also offer regularly updated recorded information – see *Useful Numbers*, p. 265. Police, national park staff and roadhouses are other good sources of information. In many cases a road may remain open, but conditions may be difficult (a swollen creek, extensive roadwork). Check before travelling so that you can plan accordingly.

Fuel Availability

Fuel is consistently more expensive in remote areas so budget accordingly. Long distances separate fuel stops in some places. If there is only one fuel outlet in the next town, ring ahead to check availability and opening times. This is particularly the case in remote Aboriginal communities where the local store may shut early on weekends or for a particular ceremony or event. Contact numbers for remote roadhouses and communities are provided in the *Fact File* of relevant subregions. Travellers to particularly remote areas may have to carry a supply of fuel.

Leaded petrol is being phased out across Australia as of January 2005 and so is no longer a reliable option.

Diesel is widely used in the outback, so is usually available. While the availability of Liquefied Petroleum Gas (LPG) has increased steadily over the last decade, it may not be available everywhere. The website for the Australian Liquefied Petroleum Gas Association has information on where to find LPG outlets in all parts of Australia; check their website at www.lpgautogas.com.au

Certain Aboriginal sites of cultural and religious significance are protected by law.

Aboriginal Land

Aboriginal communities own or hold leases over large areas of land in regions such as Central Australia, Arnhem Land, the Kimberley and Cape York. In some areas traditional owners request that visitors obtain a permit to enter or stay before travelling. This helps the owners protect the privacy of the communities, and allows them to regulate visitor activities such as fishing and viewing Aboriginal art sites.

The number of visitors to western Arnhem Land is restricted; note that permits to drive across Arnhem Land to reach and enter Garig Gunak Barlu NP, north-east of Darwin, can take about three or four weeks to process from the time of application.

Public roads traverse many areas of Aboriginal land. Generally, no special conditions apply, but there are a few exceptions. For example, visitors need two permits to travel the Great Central Road that links Yulara in the NT and Warburton in WA (contact Central Land Council and WA Department of Indigenous Affairs – see *Useful Numbers*, p. 265). The Meerenie Loop, linking Yulara and Watarrka in NT, also requires a permit, though this can be purchased readily on the day at several outlets. Even with a permit, visitors should keep to the road and not venture more than 50 m from the roadside. Aboriginal community shops may be the only source of fuel and supplies in a remote area and, again, visitors are usually welcome provided they make their purchases and move on.

Further information can be found in the *Travel Tips* box at the beginning of each major region in this book. Regulations do change, so always check ahead. Contact details for the various Aboriginal organisations that provide information on access and permits are listed under *Useful Numbers*, p. 265.

Many visitors find it easier to simply join a tour so that arrangements are made on their behalf. This is particularly the case for travel into remote regions such as Arnhem Land and the Kimberley.

Note that a number of Aboriginal communities in Australia are 'dry', or alcohol-free. Do not drink or distribute alcohol within these communities; it is an offence and fines apply. In some cases, you may be permitted to pass through the community with unopened alcohol in your car (out of view); if in doubt contact the nearest police station.

Road trains consist of a primemover with up to three trailers attached – on outback roads they have right of way.

Parks and Reserves

Australia has hundreds of national parks and many more designated conservation areas, including marine reserves.

Each state and territory administers its own parks. The federal body, Parks Australia, oversees the management of a small number of parks, including World Heritage-listed Kakadu NP and Uluṟu–Kata Tjuṯa NP, and Booderee NP at Jervis Bay.

Ranger offices are located in many rural centres, and often within parks as well. A few parks, particularly the more popular, have a dedicated information centre on site. These are listed throughout the book. Regulations to do with the lighting of fires and fishing vary from park to park, as does the availability of drinking water and firewood.

In some states, entry passes are required to visit national parks. These can be purchased by contacting the central authority before travelling, and at ranger/information stations within the park. Many parks also have self-registration sites. No forward planning is required unless you intend to camp. If this is the case, contact the relevant authority to make sure camping is permitted and, if necessary, book a site. In some parks, sites are heavily booked well in advance, particularly during peak periods – these places are highlighted in the *Fact File* at the beginning of each subregion.

Listed below are common guidelines that apply to all national parks around Australia; these have been developed to help protect the natural and, in some cases, cultural heritage of some of the country's most spectacular environments.

- Firearms and pets are not allowed.
- All flora, fauna and cultural and heritage sites are protected; items are not to be disturbed or removed.
- Visitors must stay on walking and vehicle tracks.
- Fires should only be lit as directed, most often in fireplaces provided. In some cases open fires are not permitted at all. Bring your own firewood, or use firewood provided by rangers. Do not collect dead timber for fires in national parks.
- Take all rubbish with you.
- Do not feed animals.

With other reserves, regulations vary from state to state. Anglers should check restrictions that apply in protected coastal areas, such as Ningaloo Reef in WA, and possession limits and closures in inland areas, particularly as applies to barramundi fishing in northern Australia.

Private Land

There are tracts of private land, particularly in the remote northern half of Australia, where owners allow travellers to camp and sometimes fish. Most of these places are rural stations located off the beaten track, and are sometimes discovered through word of mouth. Always obtain permission to camp on private land. The nearest visitor information centre can, in some instances, provide you with contact details for the landholder. Failing that, it may be a matter of stopping in at the homestead. Don't forget to leave gates as you find them and to clean up your campsite or fishing spot (see *Code of the Outback*, p. 263). Some working stations offer accommodation tours, and an insight into life on an outback station (see the *Contacts* box in relevant subregions).

Where to Camp

Wherever you decide to pitch your tent – be it within a national park or alongside a little-used bush track – observe basic environmental guidelines (see *Caring for the Environment*, p. 259).

National parks National parks are the first choice for many travelling campers. Even remote parks will often have dedicated campsites; others often permit bush camping (a small number of parks do not allow camping at all). Facilities range from comprehensive to virtually non-existent. Always try to ring ahead for up-to-date information about the availability of drinking water and firewood, regulations relating to the lighting of fires and the use of generators, and any closures or fishing guidelines. Information on individual parks is outlined in the *Fact File* of each subregion. National parks across Australia have a particular set of conservation guidelines that visitors must observe. Some parks are extremely popular and a campsite booking system may be in place – check ahead of travelling (see also *Parks and Reserves*, p. 258).

Private campgrounds Caravan parks usually have tent camping areas. In high-volume tourist areas, these book up quickly. Most outback roadhouses have camping areas, along with facilities such as showers and toilets. Although bookings are generally not required, it's a good idea to ring ahead and check availability and facilities. The *Fact File* and/or *Contacts* box in each subregion list roadhouses, particularly in more remote areas.

Beach/bush/roadside Wherever possible, check with local authorities before setting up camp on public land. In many areas, travellers have established sites in protected locations, close to water – particularly in remote areas such as along the Canning Stock Route. Camp in places where others have camped before to minimise damage to the area; if this is not possible, choose the site that will least disturb the surrounding vegetation and area.

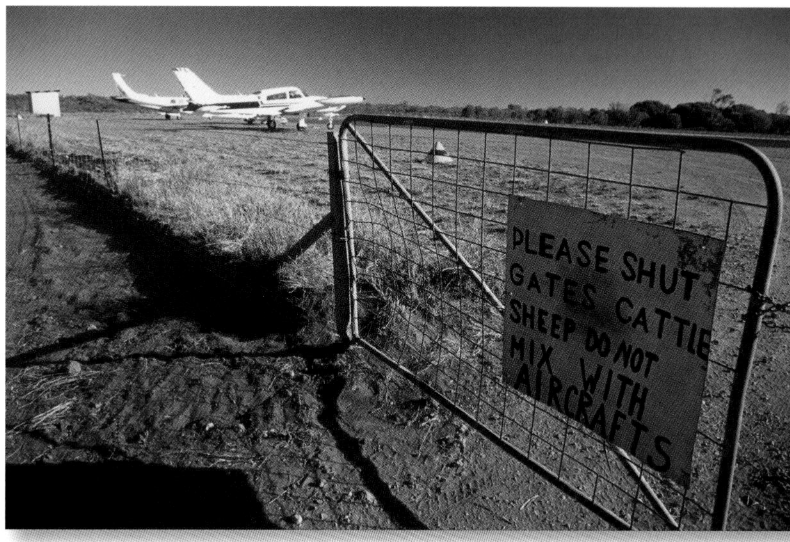

In the outback, the rule is always to leave gates as you find them.

Private land/Aboriginal land Always seek permission ahead of camping on any area of private land (see *Private Land*, p. 258 and *Useful Numbers*, p. 265). Remember, laws protect landowners from trespass.

Camping Tips

When camping, it is important to respect the rights of others and to take measures to ensure your safety.

- Get to the place where you intend to camp well ahead of nightfall – trying to erect a tent and establish a campsite in an unfamiliar place when it's dark is not an experience you'll want to repeat too often.
- Keep your site clean.

Caring for the environment

- Wherever possible, drive and walk on already established tracks.
- Don't drive or walk across dunes unless they form part of the designated route (as with Canning Stock Route).
- Avoid driving through creeks and rivers if there is another choice.
- Make sure your vehicle is well maintained: fix oil leaks, check your muffler (excessive noise can severely frighten and even damage the hearing of native animals).
- Wash down the tyres and undercarriage of your vehicle if going into areas at risk of being affected by dieback (a disease caused by an introduced fungus).
- Avoid tracks when they are wet and muddy to prevent erosion of the terrain.
- If camping in the bush, use sites established by other travellers, or choose a site where your presence will have minimal impact.
- Use toilets where they are available. Otherwise, bury waste at least 100 m from tracks, campsites and waterways.
- Be aware of fire restrictions – fires are banned in many national parks.
- Never chop down a living tree for firewood. Use dead timber minimally – it is an important part of the ecosystem. In some areas collecting or burning timber is banned.
- Do not use a fire as an incinerator for rubbish.
- Do not use soap, shampoo, detergent or cleaning products of any kind in waterways. Wash at least 50 m from the water's edge.
- Do not remove or damage wildlife or plants.
- Take all rubbish with you – do not bury it. There are dumpster bins on the outskirts of towns and, in some cases, national parks.

For more information go to the website of Tread Lightly!, a recreation organisation with a strong environmental focus: www.treadlightly.org

- Don't play loud music.
- Stick to previously established campsites if bush camping.
- Observe fire restrictions.
- Observe crocodile warnings and camp at least 50 m from the water's edge.
- Avoid camping under trees that might drop branches.
- Choose a place with some shade.

Walking

There are sensational opportunities for walkers throughout remote and outback Australia. In many of the national parks discussed in this book there are networks of signed walking tracks, ranging from a half a kilometre stroll to rugged treks that can take days. In some parks and in many other remote areas there are no tracks. In all cases, walkers must take all necessary precautions to ensure their personal safety and that of their companions. Bushwalkers of all levels of experience should consider joining a club. Clubs offer courses in bushcraft and access to a network of experts, and run guided bushwalking tours. They are located around Australia; most are affiliated with reputable state-based peak bodies. Contact the Bushwalking Australia website for links to clubs; go to www.bushwalkingaustralia.org

When planning a walking trip, consider the following tips (see also *Outback Survival*, p. 264).

- Do a basic bushcraft course. These are offered by national park authorities and bushwalking clubs.
- Walk as part of a group. If possible, walk with someone who is familiar with the area; at the very least, ensure that a member of the group has basic bushcraft skills and first-aid training.
- Plan a route that suits the least fit member of the group.
- Carry a compass and good maps.

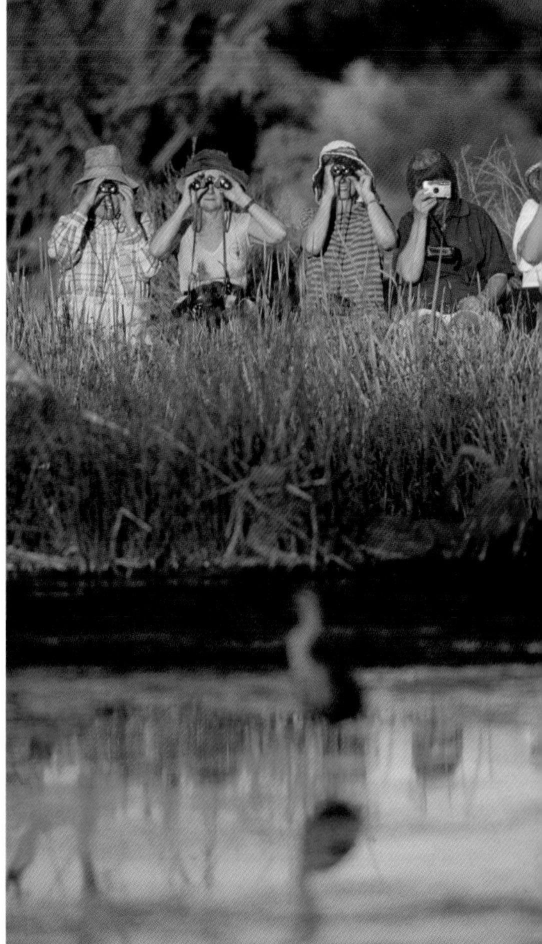

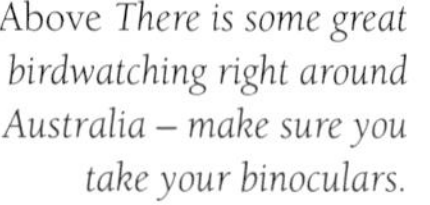

Above *There is some great birdwatching right around Australia – make sure you take your binoculars.*

Right *Bushwalkers talk with a park ranger near Simpsons Gap in the Red Centre.*

- Check weather conditions before heading out.
- Check for possible bushfire risk before heading out.
- Carry an EPIRB – an electronic device that pinpoints your position – in case of an emergency (see *Communication Equipment*, p. 251).
- Leave a clear record of your trip intentions with a responsible friend or relative or with national park staff and police. In some parks, you must contact staff before tackling some of the more difficult walks (see the *Fact File* in each subregion).

Birdwatching and Wildlife-watching

Many of the areas covered in this book give travellers extraordinary opportunities to observe birds and wildlife in their natural habitat. Those with a special interest should consider carrying a field guide to help with species identification (see *Suggested Reading*, p. 248). For bird enthusiasts, Birds Australia (www.birdsaustralia.com.au) offers general information on where to go and what to look out for – and don't forget the binoculars.

A few basic birdwatching and wildlife-watching tips include the following.

- Do not disturb creatures or their habitats.
- Try and hide or use available cover.

- Do not offer food to animals, even around townships.
- Try to avoid travelling in outback areas with domestic pets.
- Remember that some creatures are potentially dangerous (see *Dangerous Creatures*, p. 262), including some that many think of as benign, such as kangaroos and emus.

Whenever possible, travellers should report injured wildlife to authorities. If you are in a national park, contact park rangers. The website of the NSW organisation WIRES has excellent information on caring for injured wildlife and abandoned baby wildlife (www.wires.org.au).

Fishing

Fishing is a big part of many adventure holidays in Australia's remote north, where barramundi cruise the rivers and coastline waters, and big-game fish proliferate further offshore. As with any activity, common sense is your best guard against potential danger. In out-of-the-way places, fish with a friend. Let people know where you are going. If using a boat, make sure it's equipped with all the required safety gear. Anglers going offshore should have a communication device (see *Communication Equipment*, p. 251). Those fishing in rivers, estuaries and along the shorelines of the tropical north need to be aware of the dangers posed by potentially deadly saltwater crocodiles. Fishing regulations, important for protecting the environment and preserving healthy stock of vulnerable species, vary from state to state; for details, see the *Travel Tips* box at the start of each region. Remember, national parks often have their own regulations – always check with park staff.

Dealing with the Elements

The Australian environment is harsh and unpredictable and travellers should be prepared for climatic extremes.

Sun and heat The sun and high temperatures are among the biggest dangers for travellers in outback Australia. Even in the cooler months, daytime temperatures hover in the thirties, while in summer, maximums in the mid-forties are not uncommon. To avoid sunburn, dehydration and heat exposure, take the following precautions.

A close-up of a goanna, or lace monitor. These reptiles are well suited to arid conditions.

- Confine activities to the cooler part of the day – morning or evening.
- Look out for the early symptoms of heat exposure and dehydration: muscle cramp, headache, faintness and nausea.
- Limit and regulate activity; this applies particularly to those who are very fit and likely to drive themselves harder.
- Seek shade, and rest as often as possible.
- Drink plenty of water – 4 litres a day in hot weather (carry extra water in case of emergency).
- Wear a hat, sunglasses and protective clothing.
- Apply sunscreen regularly.

Extreme cold Yes, it does get cold in the Australian outback, particularly in the interior desert zones. In the winter months, night-time temperatures can drop below freezing. Keep safe and warm by observing the following tips.

- Carry and wear suitable clothing; include some wet-weather gear, particularly if walking.
- Eat high-calorie food and have plenty of warm drinks; avoid alcohol.
- Make sure you carry a sleeping bag with an appropriate temperature rating.
- Keep active but avoid physical exhaustion.
- Look out for early warnings of hypothermia: shivering, tiredness, falling body temperature, decline of mental faculties (poor judgement, lack of coordination).

Above *The orange-red glow of a bush grassfire.*

Below *Saltwater crocodiles, or salties, are found right across northern Australia and can be extremely dangerous.*

Bushfire If entering a high-risk zone for bushfires, check with local authorities and, if possible, listen to local radio as you travel. Help prevent fires by checking your exhaust system regularly when travelling in dry, grassy country. Bushfires travel fast. If you are caught in your vehicle in the path of an approaching fire:

- Find the clearest possible area (no trees or high grass).
- Turn on hazard lights.
- Close all windows, wrap yourself in a blanket and lie on the floor of the vehicle.
- Wait until the fire passes.
- If equipped with a fire extinguisher, use it to put out spot fires.

Flood Flash flooding may be a problem if you are driving in a steep-sided valley or along a creek and it has been raining heavily. Check with local authorities and avoid places that may pose a risk in bad weather. Never camp in dry creek beds when there is a risk of rain.

Dangerous Creatures

Some of Australia's creatures can cause discomfort and inconvenience, typically with small bites and stings; some are potentially dangerous, and a few are deadly. Avoidance is the best tactic. Basic medical knowledge of how to cope with stings and bites is a useful skill when in a remote area (see also *Suggested Reading*, p. 248). Consider taking a first-aid course designed specifically for outback travellers, and make sure your first-aid kit is adequate (see *Medical Items and First Aid*, p. 254). The National Poisons Information Centre provides helpful information on bites and stings (see *Useful Numbers*, p. 265).

Crocodiles Two varieties are found in northern Australia: potentially deadly saltwater or estuarine crocodiles and the less dangerous freshwater species. Saltwater crocodiles are found in tidal estuaries and waterholes, but can travel to freshwater areas, sometimes as far as 300 km upstream, as well as up to 100 km out to sea. Freshwater crocodiles are much smaller, and are recognisable by their long narrow snout, but they can be vicious, especially during the mating season or if protecting their young. They are found in tropical rivers. Both varieties are well camouflaged. Be crocodile-wise. Take the following precautions.

- Heed local warning signs.
- Take special care in tidal estuaries.
- Do not swim, paddle or walk near water in crocodile-infested areas.
- Some swimming holes are managed for crocodiles (such as in Litchfield NP in the NT), but always check first with park staff.
- Anglers should avoid wading into rivers or leaning out of boats in crocodile-infested areas.
- Do not clean fish by the water's edge.
- Keep children and pets well away from the water's edge.
- It is recommended that you camp at least 50 m from the water's edge, although a greater distance may be necessary – check with park staff and locals.

Snakes Australia is home to some of the world's most venomous species. Around 10 percent of the country's 140 snake species are regarded as

highly dangerous, including taipans, copperheads, death adders, red-bellied black snakes, tiger snakes and brown snakes. Snakes are not aggressive: if left alone, they won't bother you; the overwhelming majority of bites occur when the victim has provoked the creature in some way. To prevent being bitten, wear sturdy boots (and even gaiters if you are doing a lot of walking); never handle snakes, including injured snakes; do not put hands or feet in log hollows or rock crevices; avoid walking in long grass. Snakes don't necessarily inject venom when they bite, nevertheless, all snake bites should be treated as a medical emergency (antivenenes are available). Recommended first-aid procedures are aimed at immobilising the bitten area, so as to prevent the spread of venom while awaiting medical assistance; the procedure is as follows.

- Apply a firm bandage or strip of clothing to the bitten limb. Start at the bottom of the limb (above fingers and toes) and move upwards, covering as much of the limb as possible.
- Ensure that the bitten limb/area is kept motionless by applying a splint.
- Keep the patient calm and still.
- Do not wash the wound, use a tourniquet, suck the wound or give the patient food or alcohol.

Dingoes In rare instances, these native dogs have attacked and killed children. Although individual dogs may seem tame – even domesticated – the species is wild and unpredictable. Observe the following safety tips:

- Stay close to your children (even teenagers).
- Walk in small groups.
- Never offer food.
- Keep your campsite clean and free of scraps of food and rubbish.
- If a dingo approaches you, stand at full height, cross your arms, maintain eye contact and back away slowly.

Marine stingers (box jellyfish) There are two species of dangerous jellyfish, or marine stingers, found in Australia's tropical waters north from Agnes Waters in Queensland to Exmouth in WA. The highly venomous chironex box jellyfish and the less common irukandji are present from October to May. Many popular beaches in northern Queensland have a stinger-resistant enclosure for swimmers. It is not safe to swim at other places. Observe signs and heed local warnings. In case of a sting, seek immediate medical aid. Douse the sting in vinegar (never alcohol). Ice packs can be applied to relieve pain, but do not rub. Immobilisation procedures (see *Snakes*, opposite) may help. CPR may be required – a severe attack can slow down or stop breathing, or cause heart failure. Antivenene is available.

Other marine creatures Travellers to outback coastal regions should be aware of the range of dangerous creatures that inhabit the coastal waters and shores.

- Sharks are present around Australia's coastline. Many species will attack without killing, but the larger, faster species, notably tiger sharks and white sharks, are proven killers. Shark attack can be avoided by swimming in patrolled areas, swimming with others, avoiding discoloured and/or churned up water, and leaving the water before sunset.
- Sea snakes – there are some 21 species – swim in Australia's tropical waters; some are potentially venomous for humans. Antivenene is available. Seek medical advice immediately if bitten.
- Stonefish are found in the tropics, usually near shallow coral reefs, near rocks or camouflaged in mud or sand. The brownish-green fish has 13 venomous dorsal spines, which can cause a painful sting when pressure is applied. Avoid contact by wearing sturdy sandshoes around the water. Seek medical advice immediately if stung.

Code of the outback

- Leave gates as you find them.
- Do not interfere with windmills, water bores, tanks or wells.
- Never camp near stock watering holes as animals will avoid coming in to drink.
- Don't travel on unsealed roads when they are wet – it can damage the road surface causing inconvenience for the locals.
- Don't light a fire on private property without permission.
- When crossing private property, pastoral leases or Aboriginal land, seek permission if you want to leave the road corridor.

See also *Caring for the Environment*, p. 259.

- Blue-ringed octopus are small creatures, common on shallow coral reefs and in rock pools around Australia. They are pale brown to yellow in colour, but electric blue rings light up when the octopus is threatened. Definitely do not touch – their bite can cause paralysis; there is no antivenene available; immobilisation procedures (see *Snakes*, p. 262) may help.

Spiders and insects Australia has thousands of species of spiders and insects; of these, three have bites capable of causing death – the funnel-web spider (and related atrax species), the red-back spider and the paralysis tick. Ticks and funnel-webs are found along the east coast; red-backs are common across Australia. Ticks should be levered out using tweezers or curved scissors – it is important that the whole body is removed. For spider bites, apply an icepack and seek medical attention. The immobilisation procedure (see *Snakes*, p. 262) may be useful for the treatment of tick and funnel-web spider bites, but not for red-back spider bites. In the case of red-back spider bite, apply an icepack, but do not freeze the skin. Seek immediate medical aid.

Mosquitoes These insects, which proliferate in hot and humid conditions, are not only annoying, but, in the north, can be carriers of Ross River virus (a debilitating illness with glandular fever-type symptoms) and encephalitis (a virus causing the brain to swell). To avoid being bitten, wear long-sleeved shirts and trousers in the morning and around sunset, and use insect repellent. Use mosquito nets when camping.

Above *Travellers should carry a well-equipped first-aid kit in case of spider or insect bites.*

Pages 266–7 *Sheep are mustered into pens on an outback station near Broken Hill, NSW.*

Outback Survival

Even the best prepared traveller can miss a turn and lose sight of the track. Getting bogged is common, as is mechanical failure. Walkers can wander off the track, or suffer illness or injury. In these circumstances, stay calm, take stock of the situation and employ the following safety procedures.

Stay with your vehicle This is the key to your survival. A vehicle is easier to spot than someone walking across the dunes; your vehicle will also provide shelter and access to your supplies. Walkers are also advised to stay in the one spot.

Getting attention If you have communication equipment on board, use it to alert authorities. Try to provide clear directions. Remember that an EPIRB should only be activated in a life-threatening situation. If you hear another vehicle or a plane, use your car mirrors, or any large shiny object that reflects the sun, to attract attention. Burning rubber or plastic will create a smoky beacon; fan the smoke with a blanket to indicate human activity.

Waiting for help If the weather is cold (it can be freezing at night in some outback regions), rug up in the warmest, driest clothes you have and use materials such as newspaper and plastic bags for insulation. Huddle alongside others in the group. Protect yourself from sun and heat by rigging up a shelter next to the vehicle. Avoiding drinking coffee and alcohol as both speed up the process of dehydration. Conserve your energy but stay alert.

Finding water Adults can survive a couple of weeks without food, but water is essential, especially in hot conditions. If you have prepared well, you should have a reasonable supply. Here are a few useful water-gathering techniques.

- If you have a fridge, turn it off and collect the water that gathers.
- Place a plastic bag over fleshy plants or the green leaves of a tree to gather condensation.
- In the cooler part of the day, look for watercourses; if they are dry, dig down (sometimes as far as a metre) and you may find water (ground water should be boiled).

Food Consume your perishables first; leave tinned and preserved food until last. Be wary of eating unidentified plants; many native plants are toxic.

Useful Numbers

Emergency

Police, ambulance and fire Dial 000

National Poisons Information Centre
Advice on treatment of bites and stings
13 1126

St John Ambulance
First-aid kits, training
1300 360 455; www.stjohn.org.au

Royal Flying Doctor Service (RFDS)
Outback communication, medical emergency
National office: (02) 8259 8100
www.flyingdoctor.org.au

Roadside assistance (service)
13 1111 (Australia-wide)

Bureau of Meteorology Information Services
www.bom.gov.au

AUS 1900 926 113
NSW 1900 955 361
NT 1900 955 367
QLD 1900 955 360
SA 1900 955 365
WA 1900 955 366

State Tourism Associations

NSW Tourism NSW: (02) 9240 8788; www.visitnsw.com.au

NT Tourism Top End: (08) 8980 6000; www.tourismtopend.com.au; Central Australian Tourism Industry Association (CATIA): (08) 8952 5800; www.centralaustraliantourism.com

QLD Tourism Queensland: 13 8833; www.queenslandholidays.com.au

SA South Australian Tourism Commission: 1300 655 276; www.southaustralia.com

WA Tourism Western Australia: 1300 361 351; www.westernaustralia.com

State Motoring Associations

Roadside assistance anywhere in Australia: 13 1111

ACT/NSW National Roads & Motorists Association (NRMA): 13 1122; www.nrma.com.au

NT Automobile Association of NT (AANT): (08) 8925 5901; www.aant.com.au

QLD Royal Automobile Club of Queensland (RACQ): 13 1905; www.racq.com.au

SA Royal Automobile Association of SA (RAA): (08) 8202 4600; www.raa.net

TAS Royal Automobile Club of Tasmania (RACT): 13 2722; www.ract.com.au

VIC Royal Automobile Club of Victoria (RACV): 13 7228; www.racv.com.au

WA Royal Automobile Club of Western Australia (RAC): 13 1703; www.rac.com.au

Four-Wheel-Drive Associations

AUS Australia National Four Wheel Drive Council: www.anfwdc.asn.au

NSW Recreational Four Wheel Drive Clubs Association of NSW and ACT: 1800 646 630; www.4wdnsw-act.asn.au

NT Northern Territory Association of Four Wheel Driving Clubs Inc: PO Box 37476, Winnellie, NT 0821

QLD Queensland Association of Four Wheel Drive Clubs Inc: www.qafwdc.com.au

SA South Australian Association of Four Wheel Drive Clubs: (08) 8359 0627; www.saafwdc.asn.au

TAS Tasmanian Recreational Vehicle Association: www.4wdtasmania.org

VIC Victoria Association of Four Wheel Drive Clubs Inc: (03) 9857 5209; www.vafwdc.org.au

WA Western Australian Association of Four Wheel Drive Clubs: 08) 9390 7895; www.wa4wda.com.au

Road Conditions

NSW Roads and Traffic Authority: 13 2701; www.rta.nsw.gov.au

NT Department of Planning and Infrastructure (DPI): 1800 246 199; www.ntlis.nt.gov.au/roadreport

QLD RACQ road reporting service: 13 1905; www.racq.com.au

SA Transport SA: 1300 361 033; www.transport.sa.gov.au

WA Main Roads Western Australia: 1800 013 314; www.mainroads.wa.gov.au

Aboriginal Land Authorities

NT Central Land Council: (08) 8951 6211; www.clc.org.au
Northern Land Council: (08) 8920 5100; www.nlc.org.au

QLD Aboriginal & Torres Strait Islander Peoples: www.atsip.qld.gov.au (links and phone numbers for individual communities)

SA Maralinga Tjarutja Inc (land north of the Trans-Australia rail line): (08) 8625 2946

WA Department of Indigenous Affairs: (08) 9235 8000; www.dia.wa.gov.au

National Park Authorities

NSW New South Wales Parks and Wildlife Service (NPWS): 1300 361 967; www.environment.nsw.gov.au/nationalparks

NT Department of Natural Resources, Environment, the Arts and Sport: (08) 8999 4555; www.nt.gov.au/nreta/parks

QLD Queensland Parks and Wildlife Service (QPWS): 1300 130 372; www.derm.qld.gov.au

SA National Parks and Wildlife South Australia (NPWSA): (08) 8204 1910; www.environment.sa.gov.au/parks

WA Department of Environment and Conservation (DEC): (08) 6467 5000; www.dec.wa.gov.au

Index

The first section of this index (see below) is a listing of places; it includes towns, visitor attractions, water features and landforms, and national parks and other reserves. The second index (see p. 274) lists activities and sights, such as Aboriginal rock-art sites, walking trails, station stays and more. The third index (see p. 279) is a listing of practical information and advice on outback travel covered in On the Road, *pp. 244–65.*

The following abbreviations and contractions are used in the index:
NSW – New South Wales
NT – Northern Territory
Qld – Queensland
SA – South Australia
Tas – Tasmania
Vic – Victoria
WA – Western Australia

Places

D

E

F

O

P

Q

R

S

T

U

V

W

Y

Activities and attractions

Activities and outback sites and attractions – such as Aboriginal art, crocodiles, geological wonders, old gold-mining towns, and great fishing spots – appear in **bold** *in the index below. For a summary of Australia's best outback features, activities and not-to-be-missed attractions, go to* Best of the Outback, *pp. 1–25.*

Practical advice

This index is a guide to the practical advice and information as well as useful contact details in On the Road, *pp. 244–65. Practical advice about travelling in the outback also occurs throughout this book.*

Acknowledgements

EXECUTIVE EDITORS
Astrid Browne, Explore Australia Publishing
Averil Moffat, Australian Geographic

SERIES EDITORS
Margaret Barca
Ingrid Ohlsson

PROJECT EDITOR
Margaret Barca

AUTHORS
Margaret Barca
Ingrid Ohlsson
Rachel Pitts

DESIGN
Sandy Coventry and Peter Dyson, PAGE Pty Ltd

LAYOUT
Sandy Coventry, PAGE Pty Ltd

CARTOGRAPHY
Will Pringle, Australian Geographic

ADDITIONAL CARTOGRAPHY
John Cleasby, Australian Geographic;
Laurie Whiddon, Map Illustrations

ADDITIONAL WRITING
Jacinta Le Plastrier Aboukhater

PICTURE RESEARCH
Margaret Barca
Chrissie Goldrick, Australian Geographic

COPY EDITOR
Kate Daniel

PROOFREADER
Bettina Stevenson

INDEX
Fay Donlevy

PRE-PRESS
Print + Publish, Melbourne

SPECIAL THANKS
The publisher would like to thank the following for assistance with information and/or generous assistance with photographs. Assistance from National Parks, and on-site rangers is also greatly appreciated.
Bureau of Meteorology
Craig Lewis and Cathy Savage
Dept of Conservation and Land Management (CALM), WA
El Questro, The Kimberley, WA
Northern Territory Tourist Commission
South Australian Tourism Commission
Tourism New South Wales
Tourism Queensland
National Parks and Wildlife SA
National Parks and Wildlife Service NT
NSW National Parks and Wildlife
Queensland Parks and Wildlife Service

PHOTOGRAPHY CREDITS

COVER
Boab tree in Kununurra, Western Australia, Julie Fletcher

BACK COVER
Desert sand dunes in Cordillo Downs, South Australia, The Right Image ©/Willdlight

HALF-TITLE AND TITLE PAGE
A brown falcon clutches a lizard, JL/AG
Kata Tjuta, The Red Centre, Peter Harrison

CONTENTS
iv Touring in the Red Centre, BS/AG
v (top to bottom) Twelve Mile Lagoon, Gulf Country, MS/AG
Lawn Hill Creek, Gulf Country, MS/AG
Pandanus, MS/AG
vi Ivanhoe Crossing, The Kimberley, Robbi Newman/AG
Sea eagle, Arnhem Land, DH/AG
Camels at Silverton, The Arid South-East, JLR/Aus
vii Anangu cultural tour at Uluru, BB/AG
Mungo Woolshed, The Arid South-East, JM
Camooweal Rodeo, Gulf Country, MS/AG
Goanna – traditional bushtucker, BS/AG

THE LAND BEYOND
xi Red rock in the Kimberley, Robbi Newman/AG

DOUBLE-PAGE OPENINGS
1 Best of the Outback: Windjana Gorge NP, The Pilbara, AusSc
26 The Red Centre: Uluru, BB
62 The Top End: East Alligator River, Kakadu NP, JPF/Aus
94 Tropical Outback: Upper Lawn Hill Gorge, Wayne Lawler/Aus
128 Corner Country: Strzelecki Desert, Ted Mead
150 The Arid South-East: Flinders Ranges, Ted Mead
176 The South-West: Nullarbor NP, Jeff Drewitz
198 The Pilbara and Western Deserts: Karijini NP, AGr
220 The Kimberley: The Bungle Bungle Range, JPF/Aus
244 On the Road: Wonoka Plains, The Arid South-East, ML/AG

BEST OF THE OUTBACK
Page 2 J. Kleczkowski/LT; 3 DH/AG; 4 Tom Till/Aus; 5 NTTC; 6 ML/AG; 7 DS/AG; 8 NTTC; 9 TQ; 10 ML/AG; 11 NTTC; 12 ML/AG; 13 BS/AG; 14 SATC; 15 NTTC; 16 NTTC; 17 DH/AG; 18 NTTC; 19 NTTC; 20 NTTC; 21 El Questro; 22 DH/AG; 23 NTTC; 24 TQ; 25 SATC.

THE RED CENTRE
Page 30 SW/AG; 31 BS/AG; 34 NTTC; 35 AusSc; 36 AusSc; 37 (top) NTTC, (bottom) ES/AG; 38 (top) ES/AG, (bottom) NTTC; 39 DS/AG; 42 BS/AG; 43 BS/AG; 44 BS/AG; 45 NTTC; 46 (top) JLR/Aus, (bottom) JL/AG; 47 JM; 48–9 AusSc; 52 MR/AG; 53 (top) BS/AG, (bottom) JLR/Aus; 54 NTTC; 55 NTTC; 58 BS/AG; 59 (top) DH/SkyS, (bottom) SW/AG; 60 NTTC; 61 (top) NTTC, (bottom) Daniel Zupanc/Aus.

THE TOP END
Page 66 DH/SkyS; 67 (left) DH/AG, (right) Thomas Wielecki/AG; 70 BB/AG; 71, NTTC; 72 DH/AG; 73 DH/AG; 74 DH/SkyS; 75 DH/SkyS; 78 DH/SkyS; 79 JPF/Aus; 80 (top) DH/SkyS, (bottom) MR/AG; 81 DH/SkyS; AusSc ; 82–3 AusSc; 86 DH/AG; 87 DH/AG; 88 BS/AG; 89–91 DH/AG; 92 DH/SkyS; 93 (top) DH/AG, (bottom) DH/AG.

TROPICAL OUTBACK
Page 98 ML/AG; 99 (top) JPF/Aus, (bottom) Ian Brown/AG; 102 Ferrero-Labat/Aus; 103 TQ; 104 TQ; 105 (top) TQ, (bottom) Barry Ashenhurst/Aus; 108 Barry Ashenhurst/Aus; 109 Tim Elliott/AG; 110 TQ; 111 TQ;112–13 ML/Aus; 116 FK/Aus; 117 (top) MS/AG, (bottom) TQ; 118 MS/AG; 119 BB/AG; 120 MS/AG; 121 (top) MS/AG, (bottom) MS/AG; 124–6 TQ; 127 JLR/Aus.

CORNER COUNTRY
Page 132 DS/AG; 133 (top) NR/AG, (bottom) ES/AG; 136 Colin Beard/AG; 137 FK/Aus; 138 DS/AG; 139 (top) AG, (bottom) JLR/Aus; 140–1 JPF/Aus; 144 ES/AG; 145 ES/AG; 146 (top) DS/AG, (bottom) Tim Webster/AG; 147 NR/AG.

THE ARID SOUTH-EAST
Page 154 ML/AG; 155 (top) JM, (bottom) BS/AG; 158 BS/AG; 159 BS/AG; 160 JPF/Aus; 161 (top and bottom) TNSW;162 JLR/Aus; 163 MR/AG; 164–5 AusSc; 168 ML/Aus; 169 ML/AG; 170 ML/AG; 171 Esther Beaton/AG; 172–5 ML/AG.

THE SOUTH-WEST
Page 180 BB/AG; 181 (top) DS/AG, (bottom) MR/AG; 184 BB/AG; 185 J. Kleczkowski/LT; 186 Dennis Sarson/LT; 187 MR/AG, 188 (top) MR/AG, (bottom) Esther Beaton/AG; 189 DDP/AG; 190–1 BB/AG; 194 MR/AG; 195 SATC; 196 (top) MR/AG, (bottom) DS/AG; 197 JL/AG

THE PILBARA AND WESTERN DESERTS
Page 202 AusSc; 203 (top) JL/AG, (bottom) JL/AG; 206 FK /Aus; 207 JL/LT; 208 FK/Aus; 209 (top and bottom) DDP/AG; 210 AGr; 211 DDP/AG; 212–13 AusSc; 216 DS/AG; 217 DS/AG; 218 JL/AG; 219 (top) NR/AG, (bottom) DS/AG.

THE KIMBERLEY
Page 224 MR/AG; 225 ML/AG; 229 Brett Dennis/LT; 230 FK/Aus; 231 MR/AG; 232 AGr; 233 D. Parer & E.Cook/Aus; 234–5 DS/AG; 239 (top) Pip Smith/AG, (bottom) ML/AG; 240 Robbi Newman/AG; 241 ML/AG; 242 ML/AG; 243 (left) ML/AG, (right) Rory McGuinness/AG; 244–5 Tim Webster/AG.

ON THE ROAD
Page 246 ML/AG; 247 ES/AG; 248 Peta Hill/AG; 249 Peter Mc Neill/AG; 250 ES/AG; 251 NR/AG; 252 MR/AG; 255 Frances Mocnik/AG; 256 MS/AG; 257 ML/AG; 258–9 Thomas Wielecki/AG; 260 (top) NR/AG, (bottom) BS/AG; 261 Esther Beaton/AG; 262 (top) BB/AG, (bottom) DH/AG; 264 Peter McNeill/AG; 267–8 DS/AG.

ABBREVIATIONS

AG	Australian Geographic
AGr	Andrew Gregory
Aus	Auscape
AusSc	Australian Scenics
BB	Bill Bachman
BS	Barry Skipsey
DDP	David Dare Parker
DH	David Hancock
DS	Dick Smith
ES	Edward Stokes
FK	Fred Kamphues
JL	Jiri Lochman
JLR	Jean-Marc La Roque
JM	John Meier
JPF	Jean-Paul Ferrero
LT	Lochman Transparencies
ML	Mike Langford
MR	Mitch Reardon
MS	Murray Spence
NR	Nick Rains
NTTC	Northern Territory Tourist Commission
SATC	South Australian Tourism Commission
SkyS	Skyscans
SW	Steve Wilson
TNSW	Tourism New South Wales
TQ	Tourism Queensland

Explore Australia Publishing Pty Ltd
85 High Street
Prahran Victoria 3181, Australia

Published by Explore Australia Publishing Pty Ltd in association with Australian Geographic Pty Ltd, 2010

ISBN 978 1 74117 339 0

Printed and bound in China by C & C Offset Printing Co. Ltd

Publisher's Note: Every effort has been made to ensure that the information in this book is accurate at the time of going to press. The publisher welcomes information and suggestions for correction or improvement. Write to the Publications Manager, Explore Australia Publishing, 85 High Street, Prahran 3181, Australia, or email info@exploreaustralia.net.au

Disclaimers: The publisher cannot accept responsibility for any errors or omissions. The representation on the maps of any road or track is not necessarily evidence of public right of way. The publisher cannot be held responsible for any injury, loss or damage incurred during outback travel. Travellers should be aware that conditions in remote areas change; it is vital to research any proposed trip thoroughly and seek the advice of relevant state and travel organisations before you leave.

Maps incorporate Data which is Copyright Commonwealth of Australia 2005. The Commonwealth has not evaluated the Data as altered and therefore gives no warranty regarding its accuracy, completeness, currency or suitability for any particular purpose.